Alfred P. Sloan, Jr.

MY YEARS WITH GENERAL MOTORS

Edited by
JOHN McDONALD
with
CATHARINE STEVENS

With a New Introduction by
PETER F. DRUCKER

CURRENCY

DOUBLEDAY

New York   London   Toronto   Sydney   Auckland

A CURRENCY BOOK
PUBLISHED BY DOUBLEDAY
a division of Bantam Doubleday Dell Publishing Group, Inc.
1540 Broadway, New York, New York 10036

CURRENCY and DOUBLEDAY
are trademarks of Doubleday, a division of
Bantam Doubleday Dell Publishing Group, Inc.
Library of Congress Cataloging-in-Publication Data applied for

ISBN 0–385–04235–3
Copyright © 1963 by Alfred P. Sloan, Jr.
Introduction © 1990 by Peter F. Drucker
All Rights Reserved
Printed in the United States of America
November 1990

5 7 6 4

Contents

Part Two

Why My Years with General Motors *Is Must Reading*

PETER F. DRUCKER

Alfred P. Sloan's *My Years with General Motors* was an instant bestseller when it appeared in 1964—two years before Sloan's death in 1966, at age ninety. It has remained a favorite among managers and management students. Everyone to whom I have recommended it—and I have been recommending it for twenty-five years to friends, clients, and students—has found it fascinating and enjoyable reading. But Sloan himself would have been dismayed by this response. The only time he was really angry at me in our twenty-year relationship—it began in 1943 and ended only a few months before his death in 1966—was when I praised the book as enjoyable in my review of it in the *New York Times*. I had, Sloan scolded, knowingly misled the reader. The book was not meant to be "enjoyable." It was meant to establish a new profession, that of the professional manager, and to spell out the professional manager's role as leader and decision maker.

My Years with General Motors was written primarily to rebut—or at least to counterbalance—a book Sloan thought to be pernicious: *my* book on General Motors, *Concept of the Corporation*, published in 1946. *Concept of the Corporation* was the first study of management as a discipline, the first study of a big corporation from within, of its constitutional principles, of its structure, its basic relationships, its strategies and policies. It was the result of two years of research undertaken in 1943–45 with the full cooperation of GM management and at GM's invitation. But when the book came out, GM's senior executives were so greatly offended by it that it became unmentionable in GM for many years and was, in effect, "verboten" for GM managers. For it asked whether some GM policies—e.g., labor and employee relations, the use and role of central-office staffs, and dealer relations—had not become obsolescent. This was *lèse-majesté* for GM executives, and I have never been completely forgiven. But Sloan was cut from a different cloth. When his associates

attacked me in a meeting called to discuss the book, Sloan immediately rose to my defense. "I fully agree with you," he said to his
colleagues. "Mr. Drucker is dead wrong. But he did precisely what
he told us he would do when we asked him in. And he is as entitled
to his opinions, wrong though they are, as you or I." Indeed, that
meeting marked the beginning of my personal relationship with
Alfred Sloan. While I had been working on the book I had seen
Sloan quite often but usually in a fairly big meeting and at a GM
office. For the next twenty years he would, however, ask me once
or twice a year to have lunch alone with him in his New York apartment. There he would discuss the plans for his philanthropies, especially the Sloan-Kettering Institute for Cancer Research and the
Sloan School of Management at MIT. Above all, he wanted to talk
about *My Years with General Motors,* on which he was working for
many years. He asked for my opinions and carefully listened—and
he never once took my advice.

Sloan was the first to realize—well before I myself did—that my
book *Concept of the Corporation* was going to establish management
as a discipline, as it has indeed done. But that was exactly what was
wrong in Sloan's eyes. He was proud, and deservedly so, to have
been the first to work out systematic organization in a big company,
planning and strategy, measurements, the principle of decentralization—in short, basic concepts of a discipline of management. Indeed—to digress—Sloan's work as the designer and architect of
management was a major element in America's performance in
World War II. It enabled American industry to mobilize itself for
record production and to do so practically overnight, from total
unpreparedness and deep, demoralizing depression. And it surely
was a foundation for America's economic leadership in the forty
years following World War II, and for the major lesson the Japanese
learned from us and used to become a great economic power themselves. But to Sloan the *discipline of management* came second—
and a very distant second—to the *profession of the manager.*

Going back all the way to Plato and Aristotle, there have been two
parallel but separate approaches to governance. One is the constitutionalist approach: government in politics or organizations has to
be based on a clear structure that, above all, provides for orderly
succession and safeguards against tyranny. The other approach is
what in the history of political thought has been called "the education of the prince"—what matters is the character and the moral

principles of rulers. We have long known that both are needed. Indeed my own books fall into both categories (with my 1954 *Practice of Management* primarily constitutionalist, and the 1966 *The Effective Executive*—published only a few months after Alfred Sloan's death—squarely in the tradition of "the education of the prince"). Sloan, who was an amazingly well-read man, knew both traditions. He more than once told me how he had gone back again and again to the American Constitution to develop management organization and management concepts for General Motors and for the large corporation altogether. But it was axiomatic to him that the core had to be the ruler, that is, the professional manager, as a practitioner, as a leader, and as exemplar. He immediately saw that *Concept of the Corporation* was important—and that was why he thought it so pernicious. It would, he told me, misdirect and lead far astray both practicing managers and academicians. Expressed in today's language, Sloan criticized me for putting *management* before *leadership*. He felt it his duty to produce the antidote.

Sloan had originally planned to retire as CEO in 1943 at age sixty-seven after thirty-five years of running GM—first for ten years as chief operating officer and then for twenty-three years as chief executive officer. In preparation for this he had begun in the late thirties to gather material for an autobiographical sketch—not even meant for publication but as a kind of farewell address to his colleagues. But when 1943 came America was at war. The three or four men whom Sloan had been grooming for GM's top management were all working for the war effort and too old to take over by the time they would become available again. Sloan therefore decided, reluctantly, to stay on for the duration of the war and for the transition period following it. During this time he would then be grooming another and younger team to succeed him and the colleagues of his generation. Then, when he decided that he had to write a book to establish the persona of the professional manager, he went back to the notes he had made almost ten years earlier and for an entirely different purpose.

The result is an extraordinary achievement. Ostensibly it is an autobiography, and it reads like one. Actually, it is far more a succession of "case studies." Yet despite its didactic purpose, it is lively, enjoyable, readable, and about a person. Only the person is not really Alfred P. Sloan as he was. It is Alfred P. Sloan as a model and exemplar for the professional manager.

The Sloan of *My Years with General Motors* is often criticized as "impersonal" and "cold." This is, in truth, how he portrays himself in the book. He strongly believed that a chief executive must not have friends on the job. He pointed out to me that neither Abraham Lincoln nor Franklin D. Roosevelt, the most effective Presidents in American history, had friends among their colleagues and associates. And the Presidents who did—Grant, Truman (of whom Sloan thought highly), and Eisenhower (whom he distrusted)—had promptly been betrayed by their friends. "A friend only too easily becomes a favorite," Sloan argued, "and a CEO has to be impartial and judge only by performance." But until deafness isolated him in old age, Sloan had been a man of strong friendships. And not all of them were "off the job." His closest friend, for many years, was Walter P. Chrysler, who had been the head of GM's Buick Division until Sloan persuaded him to strike out on his own. Chrysler started the automobile company that bears his name in large part because Sloan pointed out to him the opportunity created by the decline of the Ford Motor Company in the mid-twenties, but also because Sloan clearly saw that with Ford rapidly going downhill, GM, in its own interest, needed a strong competitor. And Chrysler remained a close friend until he died in 1940, at age sixty-five.

Above all, Sloan had tremendous personal warmth and was unbelievably generous—with his time as well as with his money. Wherever I went in GM in the course of my study, I was told, often by fairly junior people, how Sloan had come to their rescue, usually unasked—how, for instance, he had given up an entire Christmas vacation to find the hospital where the badly burnt child of a plant manager could get the best medical care, and he had never even met the plant manager. I always asked, "To whom would you go if you were in a serious jam?" Most people immediately answered, "Alfred Sloan, of course." Sloan built GM as much through inspiring personal admiration and trust in his integrity as he did through policy and strategy. The strong chieftains who were running GM's large divisions—Chevrolet, Buick, Cadillac—through the twenties, and in some cases much longer, had been the founders and had built successful large companies before selling out to GM. Each was older than Sloan and infinitely richer. For the accessory business that Sloan sold to GM in 1916, as a result of which he moved into GM management, was still quite small. Each of these men was a very large GM shareholder. Each was intensely jealous of his autonomy and resented any "interference" from headquarters. But within a few years, each became a Sloan admirer and a faithful team member.

Indeed, Sloan was "people-focused" to the point of being quixotic. *My Years with General Motors* was substantially finished in 1954, yet not published until ten years later. For Sloan refused to publish as long as any of the GM people mentioned in the book was still alive. "A manager does not criticize subordinates in public," he said. "And some of the things I say in the book may be interpreted as criticism." Sloan was then already eighty years old and beginning to be frail, and some of the still-living GM people mentioned in the book were a good fifteen years younger. Sloan's editor at Doubleday pleaded, "Mr. Sloan, you risk not living long enough for the book to be published." And the editor actually went to those people, all of whom, without exception, said that they did not feel "criticized" in the least and urged Sloan to publish. But Sloan did not budge. "If I don't live long enough," he said, "you'll have to publish posthumously; people come before publishing schedules." He did outlive every one, and on the day of the death of the last living person mentioned in the book, Sloan released it for publication. To be sure, Sloan was not "touchy-feely." But he was extraordinarily concerned about people, focused on them, and above all, respectful of them.

Yet there are no people in Sloan's *My Years with General Motors*—for the "professional manager," Sloan believed, manages through the force of facts and not through the force of personality. "Bedside manners," I once heard him say in a speech to GM managers, "is no substitute for the right diagnosis."

Sloan also rigorously censored out of *My Years with General Motors* every one of his personal concerns and interests. He was deeply involved with politics—always on the losing side—and took an active part in the Landon campaign of 1937 and the Dewey campaign of 1948. He had a twelve-year love-hate relationship with Franklin D. Roosevelt. He admired Roosevelt's effectiveness. But he detested Roosevelt the man, and opposed the New Deal. "Al Smith was a much better man but Roosevelt was surely a much better President," he once said to me, to my great surprise. Yet the only mention of Roosevelt in Sloan's book is of someone in remote Washington who refused to stop Michigan's Governor Frank Murphy from supporting the union in the 1937 sitdown strike at GM. Of the New Deal there is no mention at all! "These were very important events for me and for GM, but they were historical accidents and have nothing to do with the job of the professional manager," he said when I argued that a history of the thirties without the New Deal and Roosevelt is like *Hamlet* without the Prince.

Similarly, there is no mention whatever in the book of the two causes to which Sloan devoted long, loving hours: automotive safety and the General Motors Institute in Flint (now GMI Tech). There is only the briefest mention of his half-brother, Raymond, who, eighteen years younger, was Sloan's "only child"—his death, while only in his fifties, "was the greatest personal tragedy in my life," Sloan once said. There is no mention at all that through Raymond, who was a pioneer in the field, Alfred Sloan became deeply interested in hospital management and worked hard on the organization of the Sloan-Kettering Institute and the planning and direction of its cancer research. "These are self-indulgences," he said. "They no more belong in a book on the professional manager than that my wife collects antiques or that a chief financial officer wears loud ties."

Far more important, however, than that *My Years with General Motors* presents Sloan the mentor, rather than Sloan the man, is that the book does not, for most readers, make clear the lessons for the sake of which Sloan wrote the book. It is, I still maintain, the best management book—and whether one agrees with everything Sloan proposes is quite irrelevant. But it has had remarkably little impact on the practice of management despite its wide readership and popular appeal. That it presents itself as an "autobiography" explains in large measure why it is not being read as the Guide to Action Sloan intended it. When he told me of his plans, I was enthusiastic. A book on the profession of management and on the professional manager was, I thought, a first-rate idea, and I still think so. But to cast it into the form of an autobiography would, I was afraid, diffuse the focus. Why not write a book on the topic itself and use GM only to give examples? No, Sloan came back, he wasn't competent to do that. "But, Mr. Sloan," I argued, "why not call it something like *The Professional Manager*, with a subtitle such as 'Lessons from Forty Years with GM'?" Sloan thought that far too pretentious. "At least," I proposed, "put a short section at the end of each chapter to point out the lesson." "Mr. Drucker," Mr. Sloan said sternly, "I am not writing for morons; I am writing for experienced managers. They have no need for me to point out the obvious." But as every editor soon learns, the obvious is precisely what needs to be pointed out—otherwise it will be overlooked.

What, then, are the main lessons in *My Years with General Motors*, at least as I read Alfred Sloan's intentions? This is how I would paraphrase them:

• The first is that management is a profession and that the manager is—or should be—a professional. This may sound trite in 1990— it was far from obvious thirty years ago. But frankly, while most managers by now preach it, not too many yet practice it.

• Like any other professional, a physician, for instance, or a lawyer, the professional manager has a "client": the enterprise. He is bound to subordinate his own interests to those of the client. It is duty to the client that characterizes the "professional."

• Professionals do not make decisions by opinions nor according to their preferences. They make them according to the facts. This, I believe, is the meaning of the one section in *My Years with General Motors* that many readers, myself included, find overly long: the chapter on Charles F. Kettering's copper-cooled engine. Sloan had the greatest admiration for Kettering and considered him America's outstanding twentieth-century inventor. But even so great a man, Sloan says in this chapter in so many words, can only damage and defeat himself when he clings to his preferences and predilections against the facts.

• The job of a professional manager is not to like people. It is not to change people. It is to put their strengths to work. And whether one approves of people or of the way they do their work, their performance is the only thing that counts, and indeed the only thing that the professional manager is permitted to pay attention to. I once said to Sloan that I had rarely seen more different people than the two men who during my study had run the most profitable divisions of GM, Chevrolet and Cadillac. "You are quite mistaken," he said. "These two men were very much alike—both performed."

• But performance is more than the "bottom line." It is also setting an example. And this requires integrity. Limited only to these twin boundaries, business performance and performance as example and mentor, there should be absolute tolerance and indeed the greatest diversity.

• Dissent, even conflict, are necessary, are indeed desirable. Without dissent and conflict there is no understanding. And without understanding, there are only wrong decisions. To me the most fascinating parts of Sloan's book are the memoranda in which he first elicits dissent and then synthesizes dissenting views into an understanding, and, in the end, into consensus and commitment.

Leadership is not "charisma." It is not "Public Relations." It is not showmanship. It is performance, consistent behavior, trustworthiness.

• Finally—and perhaps the most important lesson—the professional manager is a servant. Rank does not confer privilege. It does not give power. It imposes responsibility.

One can argue with Sloan's postulates—indeed Sloan very much wanted the reader to argue with them: "Otherwise they won't take them seriously," he once said when I raised the question. But they are why Alfred Sloan wrote the book and why *My Years with General Motors* is "must" reading.

Preface

THAT this book tells the story of General Motors in good part from my point of view is reasonably justified, I trust, by the circumstance that, as chief executive officer of the corporation for twenty-three years, and as a member of the board and a participant in its committees for forty-five years, I have been situated at the focal point of major policy making and administration. I trust, too, that the use made of materials from the past, which I either wrote or was responsible for, is justified for a similar reason. They either made or influenced policy and thereby bear a relation to the events of history. This approach to the book made it necessary to do a substantial amount of research, and it should not be surprising therefore that considerable collaboration was required.

I am indebted first of all to John McDonald of *Fortune* magazine, who worked closely with me in conceiving the book and in helping me to set down on paper what I know about General Motors—including, I might say, many things that I did not know, or had forgotten, when we began this project a number of years ago. I asked Mr. McDonald to work with me, and the editors of *Fortune* kindly granted him a leave of absence. Our first intention was to write a series of essays on American business with special reference to General Motors. As we got into a study of the facts, the project grew far beyond our original concept. We felt compelled, stage by stage, to stay with it to the end. The designation of Mr. McDonald as editor, which he chose, is broadly defined as I have indicated. Mr. McDonald's scholarship, craftsmanship, imagination, professional standards, and understanding of business strategy made possible the creation of this book.

I am indebted equally to Catharine Stevens, who has served as close associate to me and Mr. McDonald from the beginning. We were fortunate to receive the benefit of her spirit and intelligence and her versatile capabilities in organizing and managing a project of such magnitude and complexity. She was, you might say, as well, our editor. John, Catharine, and myself were the motivating force that kept the work in motion to completion. And we had help from other quarters.

To our editorial and technical assistants Felice Faust, Barbara Mullen, and Mary Ross, I give my admiration and thanks for their loyalty and high performance over the long period of their service on the project. I also wish to thank Doris Foster, Lynne Goree, and Margaret Breckenridge for their fine contributions.

To Alfred D. Chandler, associate professor of history, Massachusetts Institute of Technology, I am indebted for his assistance as our consulting historian and research associate. One of our major studies of the evolution of General Motors was most creatively carried out by him, and he has given his good mind to reviewing successive drafts of the manuscript.

From time to time in one place or another I have called upon a number of professional talents. Among those whose contributions are importantly reflected in the book are Daniel Seligman of *Fortune*, whose editorial skill and judgment helped to solve a number of thorny problems; and William Whipple, who gave fine editorial assistance throughout the book.

I want to record my thanks for the substantial aid of Sanford S. Parker of *Fortune*, who applied his powers of economic analysis and editorial organization to several areas of study, notably the automobile market and its history.

I am also grateful for the special assistance of Charles E. Silberman of *Fortune;* Franc M. Ricciardi, formerly of the American Management Association, now of Monroe Calculating Machine Company (Litton); Nathan Glazer, the sociologist; Louis Banks of *Fortune;* Ruth Miller, formerly of *Fortune;* Francis Wilson of John Wiley & Sons; and Sidney S. Alexander of the Massachusetts Institute of Technology; and for the interest of Jason Epstein. Mary Grace of *Fortune* gave her meticulous eye to reviewing the manuscript, and Ralph Stein, author of *Sports Cars of the World*, kindly advised us with his special knowledge of early automobiles. The distinguished photographer Walker Evans was our picture editor.

Although this book represents my own personal views and is not a corporation matter, I am indebted to all the divisions and the general offices of General Motors for their co-operation. The number of individuals is so large that I can only salute them here as a group and send each of them my warm appreciation of their valued personal contributions to my effort. Among many old friends and associates whom I consulted are Donaldson Brown, the late Harlow H. Curtice, Harley J. Earl, Paul Garrett, the late Richard H. Grant, Ormond E. Hunt, Charles Stewart Mott, the late James D. Mooney, John L. Pratt, Meyer L. Prentis, John J. Schumann, Jr., the late Edgar W. Smith, the late Charles E. Wilson, Walter S. Carpenter, Jr., the late George Whitney, and Henry C. Alexander.

Quite a number of people in different walks of life corresponded with me or came to see me to assist with one matter or another that came up in the book. I wish especially to thank Win Murphy, formerly secretary to W. C. Durant, for a number of recollections going back before 1920; Frank A. Howard for helpful talks on the evolution of concepts of research; William Zeckendorf for a conversation in which he gave me some inspiring thoughts on Mr. Durant; Eddie Rickenbacker for his recollection of the sale to him of Eastern Air Lines; the late James H. Kindelberger for kindly reviewing a portion of the text dealing with our interest in North American Aviation; Dr. Arnold J. Zurcher for valued comments; Hedley Donovan for wise observations on our earliest manuscript; and my brother Raymond for reading and commenting on the entire book.

With all that we have done in research and checking, in our effort to cover the subject accurately, we recognize, as everyone who researches and writes must recognize, the limits of human visibility. I can only say we have done the best we could to present an accurate picture. Although the number of persons who assisted me is large and many of their contributions are directly reflected in the book, I am of course personally responsible for the conclusions and opinions expressed here and for the book as a whole.

ALFRED P. SLOAN, JR.

New York City
October 1963

Introduction

I HAVE undertaken in this book to give an account of the progress of General Motors. There is much to say about the world's largest private industrial enterprise. Its history covers the present century and many parts of the earth, wherever there is a road to travel. It involves a good deal of the modern development of the engineering arts. Tangibly, the corporation is represented in the market by Chevrolet, Pontiac, Oldsmobile, Buick, Cadillac, and GMC Truck & Coach, jointly the producers of about half the passenger cars and trucks manufactured in the United States and Canada today. Our overseas operations—Vauxhall in England, Adam Opel in Germany, General Motors-Holden's in Australia, and our manufacturing plants in Argentina and Brazil—produced in 1962 about one tenth of the passenger cars and trucks made outside the United States and Canada in the free world. The corporation also produces a substantial quantity of the world's locomotives, diesel and gas-turbine engines, and household appliances. Since General Motors is mainly a producer of automotive products—about 90 per cent of current civilian business—I have stayed for the most part in that area. I have, however, given separate chapters to the non-automotive area and to General Motors' role in war and defense.

My impressions of all this after more than sixty-five years in and around the automobile industry—forty-five of them in General Motors proper—are the basis of this book. However, the long period covered in the story, the scale of the subject itself, and the limitations of human memory led me to base the story on the record as well as on my impressions of the past. I have also turned often to the memories of my associates. To bring all this into focus I have centered my thoughts on certain elements which seem to me to have influenced most importantly the evolution of the enterprise —broadly speaking, the origin and development of General Motors' scheme of decentralized organization, its financial controls, and its concept of the business as expressed in its approach to the intensely competitive automobile market. These three elements, as I see it, form the foundation of General Motors' way of doing business.

As to history, I have sketched the full span of General Motors' life, from its founding by the industrial genius W. C. Durant in 1908—and earlier events—to the present. But I have concerned myself mainly with the period after 1920, or what I have called the modern corporation, and more particularly the period from 1923 to 1946, when, as president and then chairman, I was chief executive officer of the corporation. In this period the corporation developed some of the basic characteristics which it has today. I have described the old, pre-1921 corporation to show what we began with when we set out to build the modern corporation.

As to autobiography, I have sketched my early history in the industry and the way I happened to come into the corporation in 1918. General Motors and the Hyatt Roller Bearing Company, an enterprise of which I was the head and part-owner before it became a part of United Motors Corporation and later of General Motors, have been almost the sole interests of my business life. Since joining the corporation I have been a substantial shareholder in it. For a long time I was one of its largest individual shareholders, with about 1 per cent of the common stock. Almost all of the fortune that this represents has gone and is going into the charitable foundation which bears my name, and from there into education and scientific research in medical and other fields.

Thus the shareholder's point of view is natural to me. I have always taken a strong stand for the shareholder, especially in such matters as representation on the board of directors and its committees, and the payment of dividends. Yet I have also considered myself as one of the breed that we now call the "executive." Management has been my specialization. On many occasions when I was chief executive officer I had individual responsibility for initiating policy. However, it is doctrine in General Motors that, while policy may originate anywhere, it must be appraised and approved by committees before being administered by individuals. In other words, General Motors has been a group management comprised of very competent individuals. And so I shall often say "we" instead of "I," and sometimes when I say "I," I may mean "we."

In accounting for the progress of General Motors a number of diverse elements must be recognized in the background. General Motors could hardly be imagined to exist anywhere but in this country, with its very active and enterprising people; its resources, including its science and technology and its business and industrial know-how; its vast spaces, roads, and rich markets; its characteristics of change, mobility, and mass production; its great industrial expansion in this century, and its system of freedom in general and free competitive enterprise in particular. Adapting to the distinctive character of the American automobile market has been a critical and rather complex element in General Motors' progress. If in turn we have contributed to the style of the United States as expressed in the automobile, this has been by interaction.

Consider, for example, that survival in the automobile industry in the United States has depended upon winning the favor of buyers of new cars each year. Part and parcel of this is the annual model, the spur to which the organization must respond or die. The urge to satisfy this requirement is the dynamism of General Motors. Many things regarding the progress of the enterprise and the industry fall into place through an understanding of the annual model—its origin and evolution, and the associated concept of upgrading cars, in which General Motors played a prominent role in contrast to the early Ford organization.

I cannot fail to note, too, that the automobile presented one of the greatest industrial opportunities in modern times. General Motors was fortunate to be in on the ground floor. From this thought has come the concept of the first two chapters dealing with the early period of General Motors. Furthermore, the automobile, by giving General Motors an intimate association with the development of the internal-combustion engine, enabled us logically to participate in the application of this type of prime mover to a variety of power needs, notably the airplane and the locomotive. Our growth has been almost exclusively in the mass production of vehicles powered by the internal-combustion engine. It will not come as a surprise to anyone that I am enthusiastic about General Motors and its performance. But I think I am objective in saying that General Motors has capitalized its historic opportunity to the satisfaction of the interests in and around the enterprise, from the shareholder and employees at one end to the consumer at the other.

However, being the largest of private industrial enterprises—with over one million shareholders, some 600,000 employees, $9.2 billion in assets, $14.6 billion in sales, and $1.46 billion in profits in 1962—is a distinction that sometimes makes the corporation a political target. I am glad to meet the issue of size, for to my mind the size of a competitive enterprise is the outcome of its competitive performance; and when it comes to making things like automobiles and locomotives in large numbers for a large home country and the world market, a large size is fitting. It should not be forgotten that the dollar value of these products is relatively high; even a "small" automobile producer may rank among the first hundred largest industrial corporations in the United States.

Growth, or striving for it, is, I believe, essential to the good health of an enterprise. Deliberately to stop growing is to suffocate. We have had examples of that in American industry. In the automobile industry, and in a number of others, the process of growth has given us large-scale enterprise, which is now characteristic of our society. We do things in a big way in the United States. I have always believed in planning big, and I have always discovered after the fact that, if anything, we didn't plan big enough. But I did not foresee the size of General Motors or have size in mind as an objective. I simply took the view that we should go at the job vigorously and without hampering restrictions. I put no ceiling on progress.

Growth and progress are related, for there is no resting place for an enterprise in a competitive economy. Obstacles, conflicts, new problems in various shapes, and new horizons arise to stir the imagination and continue the progress of industry. Success, however, may bring self-satisfaction. In that event, the urge for competitive survival, the strongest of all economic incentives, is dulled. The spirit of venture is lost in the inertia of the mind against change. When such influences develop, growth may be arrested or a decline may set in, caused by the failure to recognize advancing technology or altered consumer needs, or perhaps by competition that is more virile and aggressive. The perpetuation of an unusual success or the maintenance of an unusually high standard of leadership in any industry is sometimes more difficult than the attainment of that success or leadership in the first place. This is the greatest challenge to be met by the leader of an industry. It is a challenge to be met by the General Motors of the future.

It should be clear from this that I do not regard size as a barrier. To me it is only a problem of management. My thoughts on that have always revolved around one concept which contains considerable complexity in theory and in reality—the concept that goes by the oversimplified name of decentralization. The General Motors type of organization—co-ordinated in policy and decentralized in administration—not only has worked well for us, but also has become standard practice in a large part of American industry. Combined with the proper financial incentive, this concept is the cornerstone of General Motors' organizational policy.

An essential aspect of our management philosophy is the factual approach to business judgment. The final act of business judgment is of course intuitive. Perhaps there are formal ways of improving the logic of business strategy, or policy making. But the big work behind business judgment is in finding and acknowledging the facts and circumstances concerning technology, the market, and the like in their continuously changing forms. The rapidity of modern technological change makes the search for facts a permanently necessary feature of the industry. That seems obvious, but some of the biggest changes of position in the industry came about in part because someone got an idea he thought was eternal.

It takes more than the structural design of an organization, however, to ensure sound management. No organization is sounder than the men who run it and delegate others to run it. They are in a position to tip the balance in a decentralized organization toward centralization and even one-man rule. General Motors' long-term survival depends upon its being operated in both the spirit and the substance of decentralization.

It seems appropriate in this connection to speak of General Motors as an institution. In the corporation there is an atmosphere of objectivity and enjoyment of the enterprise. One of the corporation's great strengths is that it was designed to be an objective organization, as distinguished from the type that gets lost in the subjectivity of personalities.

Let me say, however, that my experience tells me that there is no simple formula in this matter of organization. The role of personality can be so important that sometimes it is necessary to build an organization, or rather perhaps a section of it, around one or more individuals rather than to fit individuals into the organization. This will be seen in rather dramatic form in my account of the development of our early engineering staff work. Great constraint, however, is required when any part of a corporation has to be adapted to an individual, because there are limits to this process as well as to the other. And as I have said above; it is imperative for the health of the organization that it always tends to rise above subjectivity.

If I have expressed or implied in this book a so-called ideology, it is, I suppose, that I believe in competition as an article of faith, a means of progress, and a way of life. It should be recognized that competition takes various forms: General Motors, for example, has competed with other enterprises as a type of organization (decentralized) and in its long-range way of doing business (upgrading the product), as well as in the usual day-to-day business activities. The elder Henry Ford, on the other hand, believed more in centralized organization and in a static car model. Such competition in basic policy has at times been decisive. We proceeded, too, with a belief in progress, which is evident in our forward investment planning. We set out to produce not for the chosen few but for the whole consumer public on the assumption of a continuously rising standard of living. Our interpretations of the significance of the rising standard of living marked an important difference between us and others in the formative years of the modern market.

The area in General Motors that I have staked out for this book is one that is not usually visible. It extends from the board of directors to the producing divisions, and consists of the general administration, the executive officers, the policy committees, the line and staff organization, and the interactions between the producing divisions; in other words, the area in which the part contributes to the whole and the whole to the part. Not the interior of the producing divisions, therefore, but the interior of the constellation we call General Motors is my subject.

The book is divided into two parts. Part One is an integrated, continuous story of the main lines of General Motors' progress, involving the origin and development of the corporation's basic management concepts in the areas of organization, finance, and product. Part Two consists of individually distinct sections dealing in some detail with engineering, distribution, overseas operations, war and defense products, incentive compensation, and other aspects and branches of the enterprise. I have not, however, attempted to be comprehensive. It would have been an impossible undertaking for me to try to tell the whole story of General Motors, covering more than a half century. I have selected—as all authors must—largely from my own experience, and I am prepared to be judged accordingly.

The approach of this book is to deal with business from the logical point of view, and to combine ideas and history. The structure of the book, particularly the sequence of chapters in Part One, resulted from a consideration of the logic of management in relation to the events of the automotive industry. There were, of course, other possible approaches, psychological, sociological, subjective, and so forth. The logical approach was chosen because it made possible the presentation of a large amount of complex material in a limited space. It also made it possible to give a clear view of the business as a business. Such an approach was appropriate to the subject of General Motors, since one aspect of the corporation's business strategy has been a conscious effort to be objective in the pursuit of business aims.

Necessarily, I have emphasized work done in times past, when many long-term, basic policies were first laid down. I recognize, however, that in the operation of the corporation year in and year out, new creative efforts have to be continuously made which result in refining and modifying the early policies. Furthermore, new policies have to be formulated to meet new conditions. Change, as I have often said, means challenge, and the ability to meet challenge is the sign of good management. Far-reaching changes in product, demand, and outside pressures have had to be met to maintain General Motors' growth and prosperity. Indeed, the present management of General Motors is meeting and taking care of entirely new problems unique in its generation.

Part One

Chapter 1

THE GREAT OPPORTUNITY—I

Two events occurred in 1908 that were to be of lasting significance in the progress of the automobile industry: William C. Durant, working from his base in the Buick Motor Company, formed the General Motors Company—predecessor of the present General Motors Corporation—and Henry Ford announced the Model T. Each of these things represented more than a company and its car. They represented different points of view and different philosophies. History was to assign these philosophies to leading roles in the automobile industry in successive periods. Mr. Ford's was to come first, to last nineteen years—the life of the Model T— and to bring him immortal fame. Mr. Durant's pioneer work has yet to receive the recognition it deserves. His philosophy was an emerging one in the Model T era and was afterward to be realized not by him but by others, including myself.

No two men better understood the opportunity presented by the automobile in its early days than Mr. Durant and Mr. Ford. The automobile was then widely regarded, especially among bankers, as a sport; it was priced out of the mass market, it was mechanically unreliable, and good roads were scarce. Yet in 1908, when the industry produced only 65,000 "machines" in the United States, Mr. Durant looked forward to a one-million-car year to come—for which he was regarded as a promoter of wildcat ideas—and Mr. Ford had already found in the Model T the means to be the first to make that prediction come true. The industry produced more than a half-million cars in the United States in 1914. In 1916 Mr. Ford alone produced more than a half-million Model T's and at his high point in the early 1920s he produced more than two million in one year. The downfall of that great car in later years, after it had served its historic purpose, is one of the pivotal facts of this story.

Both Mr. Durant and Mr. Ford had unusual vision, courage, daring, imagination, and foresight. Both gambled everything on the future of the automobile at a time when fewer were made in a year than are now made in a couple of days. Both created great and lasting lines of products whose names have been assimilated into the American language. Both created great and lasting institutions. They were of a generation of what I might call personal types of industrialists; that is, they injected their personalities, their "genius," so to speak, as a subjective factor into their operations without the discipline of management by method and objective facts. Their organizational methods, however, were at opposite poles, Mr. Ford being an extreme centralizer, Mr. Durant an extreme decentralizer. And they differed as to products and approach to the market.

Mr. Ford's assembly-line automobile production, high minimum wage, and low-priced car were revolutionary and stand among the greatest contributions to our industrial culture. His basic conception of one car in one utility model at an ever lower price was what the market, especially the farm market, mainly needed at the time. Yet Mr. Durant's feeling for variety in automobiles, however undefined it was then, came closer to the trend of the industry as it evolved in later years. Today each major American producer makes a variety of cars.

Mr. Durant was a great man with a great weakness—he could create but not administer—and he had, first in carriages and then in automobiles, more than a quarter century of the glory of creation before he fell. That he should have conceived a General Motors and been unable himself in the long run to bring it off or to sustain his personal, once dominating position in it is a tragedy of American industrial history.

It may not be generally known that at the turn of the century Mr. Durant—who had started from scratch—was the leading wagon and carriage producer in the United States; that he entered and reorganized the failing Buick Motor Company in 1904 and by 1908 was the leading motorcar producer in the country. He built 8487 Buicks in 1908, as compared with a production in that year of 6181 Fords and 2380 Cadillacs.

Mr. Durant incorporated the General Motors Company on September 16, 1908. Into it he brought first Buick, on October 1, 1908; then Olds, on the following November 12, and then, in 1909, Oakland and Cadillac. The old companies retained their corporate and independent operating identities in the new one, which was a holding company—that is, a central office surrounded by autonomously operating satellites. By various means, mainly exchanges of stock, Mr. Durant between 1908 and 1910 brought into General Motors about twenty-five companies. Eleven were automobile companies; two were electrical-lamp companies, and the remainder were auto-parts and accessory manufacturers. Of the automobile companies, only four, Buick, Olds (now Oldsmobile), Oakland (now Pontiac), and Cadillac, were to have a permanent place—first as companies, later as divisions—in the evolution of the corporation. The other seven early automobile companies were only shadow enterprises; they had principally engineering designs and little plant or production.

Putting together organizations in that period often involved "stock watering" and other manipulations, and this financial alchemy sometimes changed water into gold. I doubt whether that can be said to be the case when the General Motors Company was formed, for Buick was a very profitable enterprise before it became the cornerstone of General Motors. It earned about $400,000 on about $2 million in sales in 1906; about $1.1 million on $4.2 million in sales in 1907, a year of national economic "panic"; and an estimated $1.7 million on $7.5 million in sales in 1908—clearly a nice growth and profitability.

But Mr. Durant was interested in consolidation, through the extension of his product lines and through integration. He was advanced for his time in his general methods of production. Unlike most early motorcar producers, who merely assembled components made by the parts manufacturers, Mr. Durant already had Buick making many of its own parts, and he expected to bring about increasing economies in this direction. A prospectus of his for an unrealized consolidation of Buick with Maxwell-Briscoe Motor Company in 1908 specifies economies expected in purchasing, sales, and integrated production. It notes that one of Buick's plants in Flint "is situated in the midst of a group of 10 independent factories which manufacture bodies, axles, springs, wheels and castings" and reports that options were held on some of them. Mr. Durant thus showed a considerable sophistication in economic matters, very different from the popular image of him as a mere stock-market plunger. I cannot say that he was precise in the application of his economic philosophy; but he emerged prominently from a period that saw the birth and death of a great many automobile companies.

I see three simultaneous patterns in the way Mr. Durant set up General Motors. The first was variety in cars for a variety of tastes and economic levels in the market. That is evident in Buick, Olds, Oakland, Cadillac, and, later, Chevrolet.

The second pattern was diversification, calculated, it seems, to cover the many possibilities in the engineering future of the automobile, in search of a high average result instead of an all-or-none proposition. Among the nonsurvivors in General Motors, there was, for example, the Cartercar, which had a "friction drive" that was then considered a potential rival of the sliding-gear transmission; and also the Elmore Manufacturing Company, an outgrowth of a bicycle-manufacturing enterprise, which had a two-cycle motor that looked as if it might have a chance for a demand of some kind. There were a number of other random gambles which I shall only name: the Marquette Motor Company, the Ewing Automobile Company, the Randolph Motor Car Company, the Welch Motor Car Company, the Rapid Motor Vehicle Company, and the Reliance Motor Truck Company. The last two were combined and named Rapid Truck, which was absorbed by the General Motors Truck Company, organized on July 22, 1911.

The third pattern in Mr. Durant's arrangements was his effort, mentioned in connection with Buick, to increase integration through the manufacture of the parts and accessories that make up the anatomy of the motorcar. Mr. Durant brought into the original company a number of component manufacturers: the Northway Motor and Manufacturing Company, an enterprise producing motors and parts for passenger cars and trucks; the Champion Ignition Company of Flint, Michigan, a manufacturer of spark plugs, later renamed the AC Spark Plug Company; the Jackson-Church-Wilcox Company, a manufacturer of parts for Buick; the Weston-Mott Company of Utica and later of Flint, a producer of wheels and axles; and others. He also brought in the McLaughlin Motor Car Company, Ltd., of Canada, which had been a fine-carriage maker. This company bought Buick parts and manufactured the McLaughlin-Buick car in Canada. This move brought into association with General Motors the talents of R. Samuel McLaughlin, who was to be largely responsible for the development of General Motors in Canada.

Not all of these additions were companies acquired by Mr. Durant. He created Champion Ignition, for example, by putting up all the money, and gave Albert Champion 25 per cent for his know-how. It remained a partially owned subsidiary until 1929, when General Motors purchased the minority interest from Mr. Champion's widow.

Altogether, from the standpoint of potential integration, Mr. Durant brought into General Motors in the beginning an important group of component enterprises. On the other hand, he also paid more for a property called the Heany Lamp Companies, which became worthless, than he did for Buick and Olds combined. The Heany shares were purchased at a cost of about $7 million, paid for principally in General Motors securities. Heany's main asset consisted of an application for a patent for tungsten lamps, which the Patent Office later threw out.

Mr. Durant's approach, whatever its validity might have been in the long run, was in the short run his undoing. For Buick and Cadillac, especially Buick with its combination of quality and volume, were about all the substance there was to the original General Motors. They accounted for most of its car production, which in 1910 represented about 20 per cent of the automobile output in the United States. The rest of the company's cars were of little consequence. And so, as it turned out, General Motors was soon overextended and in financial difficulties. In September 1910, just two years after he created the General Motors Company, Mr. Durant lost control of it.

An investment banking group, headed by James J. Storrow of Lee Higginson and Company of Boston and Albert Strauss of J. and W. Seligman and Company of New York, came in to refinance General Motors and in this connection took over its operation through a voting trust. A loan was obtained on stiff terms, through a $15-million five-year note issue, from which the proceeds to General Motors were $12,750,000. The note issue carried a "bonus" to the lenders in the form of common stock which would eventually be vastly more valuable than the notes. Mr. Durant, a large shareholder in General Motors, was still a vice president and member of the board of directors, but he was forced to step aside in matters of management.

For five years thereafter, from 1910 to 1915, the banking group ran the General Motors Company efficiently though conservatively. They liquidated the unprofitable units, writing off about $12.5 million—a huge amount at that time—in the value of inventories and other assets. They organized the General Motors Export Company, on June 19, 1911, to sell General Motors products overseas. The automobile industry as a whole expanded rapidly during this period, from about 210,000 units in 1911 to about 1.6 million units in 1916, due mainly to Ford's operations in the low-price field. General Motors increased its sales from about 40,000 units in 1910 to about 100,000 in 1915 but lost in relative position—down from 20 per cent to 10 per cent of the market in units—owing to Ford's rise. General Motors was not then represented in the low-price field. The company, however, was in good shape financially. Its efficiency in operations was due largely to its then president, Charles W. Nash.

Mr. Nash came to General Motors in this way. He had been with Mr. Durant in the Durant-Dort Carriage Company for about twenty years and had stayed on as manager there when Mr. Durant first went into the automobile business. He was as steady and careful as Mr. Durant was brilliant and daring—or reckless, as you may choose to call it. In 1910 Mr. Nash had had little experience in automobiles, but he had demonstrated talent in the art of manufacturing and administration. It was, I understand, at Mr. Durant's suggestion that the banker, Mr. Storrow, engaged Mr. Nash to take over the management of Buick. In any event, Mr. Nash became president of the Buick subsidiary in 1910 and did so well there that he went on to become president of the General Motors Company in 1912.[1]

It was no accident that Buick remained the mainstay of General

[1] Mr. Nash, although the first president of General Motors to play a large role in that office, was in fact the fifth person to hold the title. Mr. Durant, in founding the company, chose the position of vice president for himself. The first person with the title of president was George E. Daniels; his term lasted less than a month, from September 22 to October 20, 1908. The second was William M. Eaton, who was in office about two years, from October 20, 1908, to November 23, 1910. James J. Storrow was an interim president for two months, from November 23, 1910, to January 26, 1911. The fourth was Thomas Neal. His term ran from January 26, 1911, to November 19, 1912.

Motors throughout its early years. It had a management of stars. Mr. Storrow, a director of American Locomotive, discovered Walter P. Chrysler in one of that company's shops and recommended him to Mr. Nash. Mr. Nash hired Mr. Chrysler in 1911, I believe, as works manager of Buick. In 1912, when Mr. Nash moved up to be president of General Motors, Mr. Chrysler remained at Buick, where he was later to be president and general manager. Between 1910 and 1915, the period of banking control, Buick together with Cadillac continued to make just about all the profits of the General Motors Company.

General Motors at that time needed the prestige which the banking group gave it. The proceeds of the $15-million five-year note issue enabled the company to liquidate its past-due obligations, but working capital still was needed. This made necessary large borrowings from banks, which at one period rose to about $9 million. By 1915, however, General Motors was in such good financial condition that the directors, at a meeting on September 16 of that year, declared a cash dividend of fifty dollars a share on the common stock, the first cash dividend since the founding of the company seven years earlier. This action involved a distribution of over $8 million divided among the then 165,000 shares, and it amazed the financial community, for it was the largest cash dividend per share ever declared on a stock listed on the New York Stock Exchange up to that time. The minutes of the board meeting say that the motion to declare this dividend was made by Mr. Nash and supported by Mr. Durant. However, the period of the voting trust was running out and a momentous conflict between Mr. Durant on the one hand, and the banking group and the Nash management on the other, was brewing as Mr. Durant sought to regain control of the company.

After being forced to step aside from the management of General Motors in 1910, Mr. Durant once again showed his enterprising spirit in the automobile industry. He backed Louis Chevrolet in experiments with a light car. In 1911 Mr. Durant and Mr. Chevrolet together started the Chevrolet Motor Company. Within four years Mr. Durant had built it into a nationwide organization, with several assembly plants and wholesale offices across the country and in Canada. At some time or other in this period he also began increasing the amount of stock of the Chevrolet Company and offering it in exchange for General Motors stock. He hoped thus through Chevrolet to regain a controlling interest in General Motors.

It was about this time that the du Ponts came into the picture and began their significant role in the story of General Motors.

The man chiefly responsible for bringing the du Ponts into General Motors was John J. Raskob, then treasurer of the du Pont Company and personal financial adviser to Pierre S. du Pont, then president of that company. Mr. du Pont, testifying in 1953 in a suit brought by the government attacking the relationship between the du Pont Company and General Motors, said that he had bought about 2000 shares of General Motors around 1914 as a personal investment. One day in 1915, he said, Louis G. Kaufman, president of the Chatham and Phenix National Bank, of which Mr. du Pont was a director, explained to him the situation in General Motors. Mr. Kaufman described the history of the company and the forthcoming expiration of the bankers' voting trust. There was to be a meeting in September 1915 to propose a new directorate for election in November. Mr. du Pont said that he was informed that Mr. Durant and the Boston bankers were in harmony. Mr. du Pont and Mr. Raskob accepted an invitation to attend the meeting. This was the first time that Mr. du Pont remembered meeting Mr. Durant.

Mr. du Pont also said:

Instead of a harmonious meeting as Kaufman had expected to find, the two factions were at loggerheads; the Boston bankers on one side, Durant on the other. They failed to come to an agreement as to what the new directorate slate would be.

. . . After much conversation, Mr. Kaufman drew me aside. Then we returned to the meeting and it was announced that if I would name three neutral directors for the company, they would make up the slate from that, each faction having seven directors and I would name three.

In the meantime, they had appointed me chairman of the meeting . . .

The slate was agreed upon and elected by the shareholders at the annual meeting on November 16, 1915. At the organization meeting of the board on the same day, Pierre S. du Pont was elected chairman of the General Motors Company and Mr. Nash was reelected president. The Boston bankers and Mr. Durant, however, continued to be in deadlock over control of the company, and it was widely rumored then that Mr. Durant held the upper hand. He asserted a claim to control and a proxy contest loomed up, but did not materialize. The bankers chose not to fight and abdicated in 1916. Through his control of Chevrolet, Mr. Durant had control of General Motors.[2]

After Mr. Durant's victory, inducements were offered to Mr. Nash to stay with General Motors. But on April 18, 1916, he resigned from the presidency of the company, and, with the backing of Mr. Storrow of the Boston banking group, started the Nash Motors Company. In July 1916 he bought the Thomas B. Jeffery Company of Kenosha, Wisconsin, a former bicycle manufacturer which was producing an automobile called the Rambler. I bought some of the Nash Motors stock at the time. It was very profitable. When Mr. Nash died some years ago he was reputed to have left an estate of between $40 million and $50 million, an impressive record for a conservative businessman.

On the day Mr. Nash's resignation was formally accepted by the board, June 1, 1916, Mr. Durant took over the presidency of General Motors and the big show was on again. He soon transformed the General Motors Company—a New Jersey corporation—into the General Motors Corporation—a Delaware corporation—and increased its capitalization from $60 million to $100 million.[3] The car-manufacturing subsidiary companies—Buick, Cadillac, and the others—were made operating divisions, so that the General Motors Corporation became an operating company, as distinguished from the old holding company. In August 1917 the new corporation and its operating divisions were formally joined.

Mr. Durant, it appears, then sought a substantial financial part-

[2] The fact that the Chevrolet Motor Company held a controlling interest in General Motors was proved in 1917. Of the 825,589 shares of General Motors Corporation common stock outstanding (after the exchange of five shares of General Motors Corporation common stock for each share of General Motors Company common stock), 450,000 shares were owned by the Chevrolet Motor Company; thus Mr. Durant clinched his earlier claim.

This odd knot, in which Chevrolet controlled General Motors, was not undone until some years later. General Motors, in May 1918, bought the operating assets of Chevrolet and paid for them in General Motors common stock. Still later the General Motors stock owned by the Chevrolet Motor Company was distributed to the latter's shareholders upon the dissolution of the Chevrolet Motor Company. The Chevrolet Motor Company became the Chevrolet Division of the General Motors Corporation.

[3] The General Motors Corporation was incorporated on October 13, 1916, under the laws of the state of Delaware. The New Jersey company was dissolved and its assets taken over by the corporation as of August 1, 1917, and the latter became the active operating corporation on that date.

ner and looked to the du Pont group. The question arose in the du Pont Company whether they should come in. Mr. du Pont outlined the events as follows:

He [Raskob] believed it [General Motors] was a very good investment for du Pont, and gave the reason that the du Pont Company needed an investment of good earning power and good dividend power in order to supplement its current dividend. Du Pont had lost the military business, or we knew it would be lost very shortly, and in the interim between the earnings of the military business and what might come after that, we needed something to support the dividends of the du Pont Company. . . . General Motors was already in full swing. They had established a good line of cars, and they were very popular, and there was every promise that their dividends would continue at the then rate which was good, or maybe would be higher. That was the attractive point to Raskob and it also became my idea that it was a very good investment, and one that could not be duplicated, so far as we knew, anywhere else.

Mr. du Pont stated further:

The General Motors Corporation and the industry itself had not advanced to a general acceptance. It was regarded as being something very risky, and consequently the stock was selling at about par at that time, which was a very good investment apparently from the actual earnings, but the public hadn't learned to believe that, so that the investment that was possible to make was extremely interesting, and that was the starting of the proposition to the du Pont Company . . .

We had been through a great many financial arrangements in relation to the military business of the du Pont Company, and Durant needed financing or financial management in his corporation. He acknowledged that he wanted that, and he was very glad to take on du Pont interest to run that part of his business . . .

In a memorandum to the Finance Committee of the du Pont Company dated December 19, 1917, Mr. Raskob, with extraordinary insight into the future of the automobile industry, argued for du Pont Company participation in General Motors. Mr. Raskob wrote:

The growth of the motor business, particularly the General Motors Company, has been phenomenal as indicated by its net earnings and by the fact that the gross receipts of the General Motors-Chevrolet Motor Companies [sic] for the coming year will amount to between $350,000,-000.00 and $400,000,000.00. The General Motors Company today occupies a unique position in the automobile industry and in the opinion of the writer with proper management will show results in the future second to none in any American industry. Mr. Durant perhaps realizes this more fully than anyone else and is very desirous of having an organization as perfect as possible to handle this wonderful business . . . Mr. Durant's association with . . . [the du Pont group] has been such as to result in the expression of the desire on his part to have us more substantially interested with him, thus enabling us to assist him, particularly in an executive and financial way, in the direction of this huge business. The evolution of the discussion of this problem is that an attractive investment is afforded in what I consider the most promising industry in the United States, a country which in my opinion holds greater possibilities for development in the immediate future than any country in the world; that rather than have a coterie of our directors taking advantage of this in a personal way, thus diverting their time and attention (to some degree at least) from our affairs, it would be far preferable for the Company to accept the opportunity afforded, thus giving our directors the interest so desired through their stock ownership in the du Pont Company.[4]

Mr. Raskob summarized his views in favor of the investment in five points, as follows: The first was that with Mr. Durant the du Pont Company would have joint control. The second was that the du Pont people would "assume charge and be responsible for the financial operation of the Company." The third was a forecast of expected return. The fourth was that the purchase would be made on better than an asset basis. The fifth I quote: "Our interest in the General Motors Company will undoubtedly secure for us the entire Fabrikoid, Pyralin, paint and varnish business of those companies, which is a substantial factor."[5]

[4] In quoting, I have followed original materials as closely as possible. This results in some variation in spelling, punctuation, and the like.

[5] The entry of the du Pont interests into General Motors became the basis of a suit by the government against du Pont and General Motors—filed in 1949, or more than thirty years after the fact. The basic charge was that the acquisition violated the antitrust laws and had enabled du Pont to secure for its own benefit the business of General Motors in products produced by du Pont. This charge was denied by General Motors and du Pont. The district court, after hearing testimony over a period of several months of a broad cross-section of the active participants in the matter and the examination of many hundreds of documents, found there was no evidence to support the contentions of the government and dismissed the case. The Supreme Court on review held that the acquisition by the du Pont interests, some thirty years earlier, was illegal because there was a reasonable probability that the acquisition was likely to result in a restraint of trade. The Supreme Court

On December 21, 1917, the du Pont board, on the recommendation of Pierre S. du Pont and Mr. Raskob, authorized the purchase of $25 million worth of the common stock of General Motors and Chevrolet. Whereupon, at the beginning of 1918, the du Pont Company took a position in General Motors amounting to 23.8 per cent of General Motors common stock, which was purchased in the open market and from individuals. The du Pont Company investment in General Motors was increased to $43 million, or 26.4 per cent, at the end of 1918.

The period of co-operation between the du Pont Company and Mr. Durant began when the first investment was made. Du Pont representatives took over the responsibility of the General Motors Finance Committee, John J. Raskob becoming its chairman. Mr. Durant was the only member of the Finance Committee not from the du Pont Company. Financial affairs were assigned exclusively to this committee; it also set compensation for top executives. The Executive Committee, on the other hand, took complete charge of all operations, except matters assigned to the Finance Committee. Its chairman was Mr. Durant, and J. A. Haskell, who served as liaison man for du Pont in operations, was a member. Mr. Haskell, like Mr. Durant, sat on both the Executive Committee and the Finance Committee.

By the end of 1919, with the further expansion of General Motors, the du Pont Company increased its investment in the corporation to about $49 million, giving it ownership of 28.7 per cent of the General Motors common. Then, Pierre S. du Pont has said, "they made a declaration that that would be the end of their investment, and they would take no more." But events dictated otherwise.

In the period 1918 through 1920 Mr. Durant took General Motors through a large expansion of operations, in which he was enthusi-

---

agreed, however, with the finding of the trial court, stating that "considerations of price, quality and service were not overlooked by either du Pont or General Motors" and that "all concerned in high executive posts in both companies acted honorably and fairly, each in the honest conviction that his actions were in the best interests of his own company and without any design to overreach anyone, including du Pont's competitors." The trial court's judgment of dismissal was reversed and the case remanded for relief. On remand, and after further litigation and appeal, the district court decreed that the du Pont interests divest themselves of their General Motors stock over a period of years. It appears to me, as a layman, that the reasoning of the Supreme Court in the case is almost purely academic and is not supported by the realities of the situation as found by the district court.

astically supported by Mr. Raskob and the Finance Committee, which obtained the capital for the expansion.

The acquisition of Chevrolet in 1918 gave the corporation a car that was potentially competitive with Ford in the low-price class, although it could not compete with Ford at that time in quality and was priced above it. Along with Chevrolet came Scripps-Booth, a small car company owned by Chevrolet.

The important association with Fisher Body was begun in 1919 with the acquisition of a 60 per cent interest in that company and a contract for the manufacture of bodies.

The Sheridan car, made by a small outfit, was purchased in 1920, giving the corporation for a time a line of seven cars. The Cadillac, the Buick, the Olds, the Oakland, and the Chevrolet, along with the General Motors Truck, were already established, although the Cadillac and the Buick were still the only worthwhile cars in the line.

Two special projects, one in tractors and the other in refrigeration, were brought into the corporation on the personal initiative of Mr. Durant. On occasion, when out in the field, he would make informal deals to get something started, and this sometimes caused uneasy moments in the general office. But in the end his intuitive and impulsive moves were supported.

So it was that in February 1917 he caused General Motors to buy into a small enterprise called the Samson Sieve Grip Tractor Company of Stockton, California, which had an invention for driving a tractor like a horse—"the Iron Horse" it came to be called. And to this he later added the Janesville Machine Company of Janesville, Wisconsin, and the Doylestown Agricultural Company of Doylestown, Pennsylvania, to form in General Motors the Samson Tractor Division—a very unprofitable venture, as it turned out. In June 1918, on the other hand, Mr. Durant bought a small company in Detroit, called the Guardian Frigerator Company, and made out his own check for it in the amount of $56,366.50, for which he was repaid by General Motors on May 31, 1919. This embryo enterprise took on importance later as the Frigidaire Division.

A number of other enterprises were started or taken into the corporation in the period 1918–20: General Motors of Canada, Ltd.; the General Motors Acceptance Corporation, which was organized to finance the sale of General Motors cars and trucks; a group of Dayton companies in which Charles F. Kettering was interested; a number of manufacturing divisions which were set up to supply axles, gears, crankshafts, and the like for General Motors' automobile divisions, and a group of parts and accessory companies called United Motors, of which I was president.

Thanks mainly to Mr. Durant, General Motors had then the makings of a great enterprise. But it was in good part physically unintegrated and in management unco-ordinated; the expenditures for new companies, plants and equipment, and inventories were terrific —some of them not to bring a return for a long time, if ever—and as they went up, the cash went down. General Motors was heading for the crisis from which the modern General Motors Corporation would emerge.

Chapter 2

THE GREAT OPPORTUNITY—II

To tell how I came into General Motors it is necessary to begin with smaller matters than those I have described. I was born in New Haven, Connecticut, on May 23, 1875, a time when, to say the least, the style of the United States was quite different from what it is today. My father was in the wholesale tea, coffee, and cigar business, with a firm called Bennett-Sloan and Company. In 1885 he moved the business to New York City, on West Broadway, and from the age of ten I grew up in Brooklyn. I am told I still have the accent. My father's father was a schoolteacher. My mother's father was a Methodist minister. My parents had five children, of whom I am the oldest. There is my sister, Mrs. Katharine Sloan Pratt, now a widow. There are my three brothers—Clifford, who was in the advertising business; Harold, a college professor; and Raymond, the youngest, who is a professor, writer, and expert on hospital administration. I think we have all had in common a capability for being dedicated to our respective interests.

I came of age at almost exactly the time when the automobile business in the United States came into being. In 1895 the Duryeas, who had been experimenting with motor cars, started what I believe was the first gasoline-automobile manufacturing company in the United States. In the same year I left the Massachusetts Institute of Technology with a B.S. in electrical engineering, and went to work for the Hyatt Roller Bearing Company of Newark, later of Harrison, New Jersey. The Hyatt antifriction bearing was later to become a component of the automobile, and it was through this component that I came into the automotive industry. Except for one early and brief departure from it, I have spent my life in the industry.

Hyatt then was a tiny enterprise, employing about twenty-five people. A ten-horsepower motor drove all of its plant machinery. Its product was a special kind of antifriction bearing, invented by John Wesley Hyatt, who also invented celluloid, the first of the modern plastic materials, intended but never realized as a substitute for ivory in billiard balls. At that time antifriction bearings were not well developed or well known. But the Hyatt bearing was no cruder than other mechanical parts made in those days; and we were able to put some of our bearings on traveling cranes, paper-mill equipment, mine cars, and other machinery. We were doing a business, when I went with the company, of under $2000 a month. I was a kind of office boy, draftsman, salesman, and general assistant to the enterprise at a salary of $50 a month.

I did not then see much future in Hyatt and soon left it to become associated with a household electric-refrigerator enterprise which seemed to offer better prospects. It was making one of the early efforts to supply centrally located electric refrigeration in apartment houses. After about two years I came to believe that its particular product could not develop because of its complicated mechanism and high cost.

Meanwhile, affairs of the Hyatt Roller Bearing Company had not progressed very well—the company had never been on a profit-making basis—and it came to the point where the individual who was promoting it, John E. Searles, was not willing to put up any more money to cover the losses. In 1898 it appeared that the company would have to liquidate. But my father and an associate of his combined to put $5000 into Hyatt with the understanding that I would go back for six months and see what I could do with it. I accepted the proposition and teamed up with a young man, Peter Steenstrup, who was then the bookkeeper, later the sales manager. At the end of six months we had made some advances in volume and economy, and a $12,000 profit, and that put the business in a position where we recognized that it might be made successful. I assumed the high title of general manager. I could not know then that through Hyatt I had entered one of the headwaters of General Motors.

For the next four or five years at Hyatt we had growing pains. It was difficult to get business, and when we got it and expanded, we needed working capital that we could not get outside the company. It was easier at that time, however, to build a business from scratch, because the government did not tax away the profits as it does now. In five years we made progress. Our profits got up to about $60,000 a year, and the prospects improved as the young automobile industry opened up a new market.

It was around the turn of the century that the automobile business began to break out in numerous small enterprises. Antifriction bearings came into the picture then and we began to get a few orders from those who were experimenting with automobiles. A letter I wrote to Henry Ford on May 19, 1899, asking for his business, is said by Allan Nevins in his biography of Ford to be on file in the Ford archives. Mr. Ford at that time was experimenting with automobiles, and was about to go into the business. But in the first decade of this century the application of our bearings in the mechanical arts expanded slowly. Most of the hundreds of automobile companies organized in that period made only sample cars and then expired. My partner, Mr. Steenstrup, did a great deal of traveling to make sales contacts with these embryo producers. When he saw or heard of someone who was going to make a new car, I would get in touch with the person and go into the problems from the engineering point of view. I would design Hyatt bearings into the axle or perhaps some other part, and in doing so facilitate the sale of our roller bearings in any subsequent production.

As our work became better known, I succeeded in getting myself into a position where I was a kind of consulting sales-engineer to a good many of those companies and their suppliers on bearing problems to which our particular product was applicable. I would be called in when any change of design or new design was contemplated and this gave me the opportunity to get our bearings incorporated into the rear axle or the transmission, or both.

This sales-engineering of ours continued at an increasing pace, especially from 1905 to 1915 when some of the manufacturers, such as Ford, Cadillac, Buick, Olds, Hudson, Reo, Willys, and others, began to develop important volume. Hyatt's business flowed logically wherever we had customers like these that stayed in business and grew. Our business became so good that it got to be a question of how rapidly we could expand our production, with new buildings, new machinery, new methods, and the like, to keep up with the rapidly expanding automobile business.

My first personal experience with automobiles was much like that of others at the time. I wanted one but couldn't afford it. Only about 4000 cars were made in the year 1900, and they were expensive. My father bought one of the early Wintons as a family car. Around 1903 I bought for the Hyatt Company a car called the Conrad, which we got for company purposes, and incidentally used to go from the plant in Harrison into Newark for lunch and errands. It had a two-cycle engine with four cylinders, and was a good-looking car, painted red. But it was a lemon. The Conrad was manufactured from 1900 to 1903, and then passed out of the picture. We got another car, called the Autocar. This one worked better and I used it to some extent on business trips, and sometimes went to Atlantic City in it. Like the Winton and the Conrad, it was discontinued, but an Autocar truck was developed and became a factor in the automotive industry; Autocar was consolidated with the White Motor Company in 1953. The first car I bought for myself was a Cadillac, about 1910. As was the custom then, I got a Cadillac chassis and had the body made to order.

Early Cadillac engineering had an important influence on the industry and upon my operations in Hyatt. This was largely due to Henry Leland, who, I believe, was one of those mainly responsible for bringing the technique of interchangeable parts into automobile manufacturing. His first work in the industry was for Olds, around 1900. He was at the head of Cadillac when it went into General Motors in 1909, and he remained at the head of it until 1917, when he retired. Afterward he created the Lincoln car, which he sold to the Ford Motor Company.

Mr. Leland was one of my early acquaintances in the industry. He was a generation older than I and I looked upon him as an elder not only in age but in engineering wisdom. He was a fine, creative, intelligent person. Quality was his god. I had trouble at first, in the early 1900s, in selling Mr. Leland our roller bearings. He then taught me the need for greater accuracy in our products to meet the exacting standards of interchangeable parts. Mr. Leland came to the industry with a mature experience in general engineering and in gasoline engines, which he had long made for boats. One of his specialties was precision metalwork, which went back to his experience in toolmaking for a federal arsenal during the Civil War, and which he afterward developed in the Brown and Sharpe Company, machine-tool makers of Providence, Rhode Island. It has been called to my attention that Eli Whitney, long before, had started the development of interchangeable parts in connection with the manufacture of guns, a fact which suggests a line of descent from Whitney to Leland to the automobile industry.

The cluster of men who made the industry in the beginning was not large. As a supplier of an important component of the automobile, I came to know most of them over the period of the first twenty years of the business, and I learned a great deal from them as business associates and friends. In the early days I sometimes sold direct to automobile producers—Cadillac, Ford, and others— but more often I sold to a supplier, who, in turn, sold a component of the automobile to the assembler. One of the most important of these suppliers for me was the Weston-Mott Company of Utica, maker of axles; a rear axle would take six bearings, some of which were Hyatt types. After Charles Stewart Mott moved his company from Utica to Flint in 1906 to be close to the area where the automobile industry was developing, I made it a practice to visit him there once a month. I recall that both sides of Saginaw Street, the main street of Flint, were lined with hitching posts, and on Saturday night the street was crowded with the horses, wagons, and carriages that brought the farmers into town for their weekly shopping and night out. In that setting a small society of automobile and parts producers met socially and on business for several years: Mr. Mott, Charles Nash, Walter Chrysler, Harry Bassett, myself, and others, all of whom, except myself, were then in General Motors. I must have seen Mr. Durant there, too, but I can only recall seeing him on the train between New York and Detroit, and our saying "Good evening" and "Good morning." My real connection with General Motors then was through Mr. Mott, who had taken his company into General Motors in 1909, and was a supplier of axles to Buick, Oakland, and Olds. To be exact, General Motors acquired 49 per cent of his company's stock in 1909 and the balance in 1912. Through Weston-Mott I succeeded in getting Hyatt roller bearings into General Motors cars.

I first knew Walter Chrysler in Flint. As works manager and then head of Buick, he would pass judgment on my product when the axle designs came in from Weston-Mott. We saw a lot of each other in the course of time, in General Motors and out of it, and were personal friends throughout his life. In later years, when we were rival heads of our respective enterprises, Chrysler and General Motors, we sometimes took a vacation trip together, with business taboo on those occasions. Mr. Chrysler was a man of high ambition and imagination. He was a practical man with broad capabilities; his genius I think was in the organization of automobile production. Like Mr. Nash, he recognized the opportunity offered by the young and promising automobile business. They both were true leaders of its early development and became heads of great enterprises.

Over at the Ford Motor Company in Detroit, I—as a Hyatt salesman—used to see Mr. Ford and occasionally have lunch with him, but I conducted my business there mainly through C. Harold Wills, his chief engineer, and later the creator of the fine but short-lived Wills-Sainte Claire automobile. Mr. Ford owed much to Mr. Wills' talent in engineering, especially metallurgy. Because of our ability at Hyatt to produce and deliver reliably, we were eventually favored with 100 per cent of the Ford business to the extent that our bearings were applicable to the Ford design. As Mr. Ford's company grew, he became our best customer, with General Motors second. The development of Hyatt's volume caused me to open a sales office in Detroit on West Grand Boulevard. In later years, through an unpredictable chain of events, this office was to become the nucleus of the site of the General Motors Building in Detroit.

One day in the spring of 1916 I received a call from Mr. Durant, asking me to come in to see him. As the founder of General Motors and Chevrolet, Mr. Durant was a celebrated figure in the automobile and financial worlds. I have described how he had been out of General Motors for a number of years and was about to return at that time as president. I found Mr. Durant a very persuasive man, soft-spoken and ingratiating. He was short, conservatively and immaculately dressed, and had an air of being permanently calm—though he was continuously involved in big and complicated financial deals—and he inspired confidence in his character and ability. He asked me if the Hyatt Roller Bearing Company was for sale.

After all those years of building up the Hyatt business the idea of selling it was a shock to me, but it opened up a new vista in my thinking and caused me to analyze the situation at Hyatt. Mr. Durant's offer brought forcibly to my mind a combination of three factors that were developing in the business.

The first of these was that, because of the way Hyatt's business had evolved, it had come to depend upon a limited number of customers. Ford alone represented about half of the sales. This business if lost could not be replaced because no new customer of such magnitude existed: a complete reorganization would have to be undertaken.

Second, I recognized that the kind of roller bearing we made at that time was destined through the evolution of automobile design to be supplemented and perhaps superseded by other types. And what then? Another reorganization, a different product, in effect a new business. I have always been interested in improving a product; but this was a special-product business and the choice was whether to proceed independently or within an integrated enterprise. I may say that in the past forty-five years what I thought would happen to the product has happened. Hyatt's old type of antifriction bearing has gone out of automobile design along with other types of then existing antifriction bearings.

Third, I had spent my working life—I was forty years old then—developing a property and I had a large plant with a great deal of responsibility, but I never got much yield out of it in dividends. Mr. Durant's offer presented an opportunity to convert Hyatt's profits into readily salable assets.

Of the three factors, I think the second, the potential changes in the old Hyatt roller bearing, was decisive in my mind. Thus, the way I added it up was that, while Hyatt's short-term profit position was good, the long-term position would benefit from the proposed association; and Mr. Durant's offer promised a conversion of assets. I decided to take the offer, got my four directors together, and recommended that we tell Mr. Durant that we were prepared to sell at a price of $15 million. A couple of the directors thought the price was high, but I did not think so considering our strength and the growth potential of the automobile industry. I entered negotiations with two of Mr. Durant's associates, John Thomas Smith, his lawyer, and Louis G. Kaufman, the banker, and after a lot of dickering back and forth settled on a proposition to sell the property for $13.5 million.

When the question of payment came up, I agreed to take half in cash and half in the stock of a new enterprise that Mr. Durant proposed to organize, called United Motors Corporation. But when it came to closing the deal, I found that some of my Hyatt associates were unwilling to take stock in the new company. This led to my having to take more than my share of the stock and give up the equivalent in cash. Since my father and I owned a substantial part of Hyatt, I finished with an important position in the stock of United Motors Corporation.

Mr. Durant set up United Motors in 1916 to buy Hyatt and four other parts and accessory manufacturers. These properties were, besides Hyatt, the New Departure Manufacturing Company of Bristol, Connecticut, a producer of ball bearings; the Remy Electric Company of Anderson, Indiana, a producer of electrical starting, lighting, and ignition equipment; Dayton Engineering Laboratories Company of Dayton, known as Delco, a producer of electrical equipment using a system different from Remy's, and the Perlman Rim Corporation of Jackson, Michigan.

For the first time my business horizon widened beyond a single component of the automobile. I became president and chief operating officer of United Motors with a board of directors made up of the people who put their properties into the enterprise. Mr. Durant did not come on the board and did not concern himself with the affairs of this corporation, but left the management entirely up to me. On my own initiative, and with the approval of my board, I afterward brought into United Motors the Harrison Radiator Corporation and the Klaxon Company, then a well-known producer of horns; I organized the United Motors Service, Inc., which sold and serviced throughout the United States the parts made by the various United Motors companies. The combined group had net sales of $33,638,956 in its first year. Hyatt was the best earner.

For many years the United Motors group sold to manufacturers outside General Motors; but the leaders of General Motors foresaw that as a car producer it would eventually require most of the output of United Motors. Hence, in 1918, by mutual agreement, and largely through negotiations between John J. Raskob, then chairman of the Finance Committee of General Motors, and myself, United Motors' assets were acquired by General Motors.

The space I have given here to the Hyatt story is not a measure of its relative position in the General Motors scheme of things. It just gets me into the story in a logical way. I joined General Motors as vice president in charge of the same accessory companies that I had operated in United Motors. I also became a director of

General Motors and a member of its Executive Committee, of which Mr. Durant was then chairman.

In General Motors from 1918 through 1920 my operating responsibility continued to be with the accessory group, but as a member of the Executive Committee of the corporation, my horizon again widened. Also, I had proprietary as well as professional reasons for taking an interest in the corporation as a whole, since most of my personal assets had been converted into General Motors shares. It was not long therefore before I began to take a close look at Mr. Durant's general policies.

I was of two minds about Mr. Durant. I admired his automotive genius, his imagination, his generous human qualities, and his integrity. His loyalty to the enterprise was absolute. I recognized, as Mr. Raskob and Pierre S. du Pont had, that he had created and inspired the dynamic growth of General Motors. But I thought he was too casual in his ways for an administrator, and he overloaded himself. Important decisions had to wait until he was free, and were often made impulsively. Two examples from my personal experience:

My office was next door to his in the old General Motors Building on New York's Fifty-seventh Street. I would sometimes go in to see him. One day in 1919 I went in and told him that I thought that, in view of the large public interest in the corporation's shares, we should have an independent audit by a certified public accountant. Our books were not then being so audited, though they had been earlier under the bankers' regime. Mr. Durant did not have a sound concept of accounting as such and did not realize its great significance in administration. However, when I spoke to him about it, he said at once that he agreed with me and told me to go and get one. That was the way he worked. He had a financial department to handle affairs of that kind, but since I had made the suggestion I got the assignment. I brought in the firm of Haskins & Sells, which had audited the accounts at United Motors. This firm still audits General Motors' accounts.

Another time I found Mr. Durant in his office with some people talking about the new office building that was to be put up in Detroit. It was to be called the Durant Building, but is now known as the General Motors Building. They were inspecting a map of Detroit. Mr. Durant, as usual, invited me to come into the discussion. They were considering a location in the Grand Circus Park area downtown. The United Motors sales office on West Grand

Boulevard was uptown, north a couple of miles. I knew the location well and it was natural that I should think of it. There were good reasons for considering it for the new building: it was closer for everyone who lived on the north side of the city, and at that time the traffic there was lighter than downtown. I mentioned these things to Mr. Durant, whereupon he turned to me and said that the next time we went to Detroit we would all go up and take a look at it, and we did. I can see Mr. Durant now. He started at the corner of Cass Avenue, paced a certain distance west on West Grand Boulevard past the old Hyatt Building, which had become the United Motors Building. Then he stopped, for no apparent reason, at some apartment houses on the other side of the building. He said that this was about the ground we wanted, and turned to me and said, as well as I can remember, "Alfred, will you go and buy these properties for us and Mr. Prentis will pay whatever you decide to pay for them." I wasn't in the real-estate business. I didn't even live in Detroit. But I went ahead and organized the assembly of the properties and if I do say so myself, I think we did a good job. I assigned Ralph S. Lane, president of the United Motors Service Corporation, to handle the purchases of property. It is an interesting piece of business to buy up a block of small parcels of real estate. If you disclose your intention you influence the price. When we got the half block that Mr. Durant wanted, he said we ought to buy the rest of it. So we went back to work and bought the whole block. I don't know that he intended to use all of it immediately, but it was soon used. The General Motors Building which was built there started a new business district in Detroit.

Mr. Durant's informal ways of doing business were often effective in that formative period, and for the confidence he placed in me on these and other occasions I had reason to feel well disposed toward him. The criticisms I make of him are purely from the viewpoint of basic business administration. I was particularly concerned that he had expanded General Motors between 1918 and 1920 without an explicit policy of management with which to control the various parts of the organization.

A distinction should be made between the expansion itself and the need for organization which grew out of it. There may have been disagreement at the time over the soundness of the expansion program, responsibility for which was shared by Mr. Durant and Mr. Raskob. But time in the long run has shown that the major part of the program, at least so far as the automobile developments were concerned, was sound and desirable. Since the automobile is a high-value product made for a mass market, the industry needed an extensive capital structure. Mr. Durant and Mr. Raskob anticipated this need.

As to organization, we did not have adequate knowledge or control of the individual operating divisions. It was a management by crony, with the divisions operating on a horse-trading basis. When Walter Chrysler, one of the best men in General Motors, became a general executive of the corporation, he collided with Mr. Durant over their respective jurisdictions, I believe. Mr. Chrysler was a man of strong will and feeling. When he could not get the arrangement he wanted, he left the corporation. I remember the day. He banged the door on the way out, and out of that bang came eventually the Chrysler Corporation.

The significance of the weakness in General Motors' organization was not clearly visible during World War I and for a time during the postwar inflation. It first took critical form in late 1919 and 1920. At this time large sums were being allotted upon request to all divisions for plant-expansion programs, and, at the same time, rising material and labor costs ate up these funds before the projected expansions could be completed. There were overruns on appropriations—that is, expenditures beyond the established limits—by almost every division.

It was a case of competition among the divisions for available capital and of different preferences at the top. For example, Mr. Durant was strong on tractors. The Finance Committee on October 17, 1919, turned back his request for tractor appropriations with a request for further information on the expected return on investment. At the same meeting the Finance Committee supported a request of mine for about $7.1 million for the New Departure Division. Then Mr. Durant at an Executive Committee meeting on October 31, 1919, opposed the appropriation request for New Departure. Later in the same meeting the committee agreed to finance New Departure to the extent of one third of the request, the other two thirds to come from a preferred-stock issue. At the same meeting Mr. Durant opposed a request for $7.3 million for additional costs on the Durant (General Motors) Building in Detroit. According to the memory of Meyer L. Prentis, then treasurer of General Motors, Mr. Durant opposed the supplementary appropriations for

the Durant Building because—in opposition to Mr. Raskob—he preferred to allocate funds to plant and working capital rather than to
real estate. John L. Pratt, who had left du Pont to assist Mr. Durant,
also remembers this difference in investment preference. The incident is recalled to my mind by the memory of Mr. Durant leaving
the chairman's seat to take another one at the table and make the
motions not to grant the requests. The Executive Committee supported him. There was in fact, as he saw, a shortage of funds to
meet all these demands. Attention thereupon was given not to the
question of how to divide scarce investment funds but how to raise
more money.

The Finance Committee, meeting in New York on November 5,
1919, heard a report from Mr. Durant showing estimated receipts
and expenditures for the fifteen months ending December 31, 1920,
"and after discussion, it was moved and unanimously carried that
the expenditures proposed in said report should go forward and
immediate steps be taken to arrange for the sale of $50,000,000. par
value debenture stock, and, if possible, an additional $50,000,000.,
making a total of $100,000,000."

That afternoon the Executive Committee met in New York and
took up the same matter. The minutes say: "Mr. J. J. Raskob, Chairman of the Finance Committee, came before the meeting and made
a brief report as to future financing. He recommended that the
Company sell an additional amount of its debenture stock, and
that it proceed to take action upon the several appropriation requests which were 'not granted' at the last meeting." The Executive Committee then unanimously passed the appropriations for the
Durant Building, New Departure, the tractors, and the rest, and
the Finance Committee approved them.

Later, in a study of our appropriations procedure, I reflected on
this situation as follows: "The practical result [of the lack of a
proper appropriations procedure], therefore, was that the approval
of any member of the Executive Committee of an Appropriation
Request by a Division over which he had supervision, necessarily
carried with it the support of the other members of the Executive
Committee. In other words, from the practical standpoint, the
supervision supposed to be exercised by the Executive Committee
was more theoretical than practical."

Accordingly, everyone who had an appropriation request to make
was to be satisfied; but fortune was not entirely in accord. The

debenture-stock sale was not successful. An effort was made to raise $85 million, but only $11 million was realized. This was the first signal from the outside financial environment that the corporation was in conflict with realities, despite its growth in sales from $270 million in 1918 to $510 million in 1919, which would become $567 million in 1920.

The competition for capital appropriations brought to the fore the whole question of financial organization. On December 5, 1919, Mr. Durant stated in the Executive Committee that the prevailing method of handling appropriation requests was unsatisfactory, a proposition on which all could agree. He outlined a procedure for investigating these requests and reporting them to the president. I embodied this in a motion for a special committee, of which Mr. Pratt was made chairman. At the same time I moved that another committee be appointed to work out regular rules of procedure to govern such requests. I was made chairman of this "Committee on Appropriation Request Rules." The aim of the committee was properly to place responsibility for authorizing expenditures. This was one of three projects in the field of organization which I undertook in this period.

The main thing to note here is that neither the Executive Committee nor the Finance Committee had the needed information or the needed control over the divisions. The divisions continued to spend lavishly and their requests for additional funds were met. The minutes of the Executive and Finance committees in late 1919 and early 1920 show continued massive overruns on appropriations. In one meeting the Executive Committee approved $10,339,554 in overruns on current appropriations, of which Buick, Chevrolet, and Samson Tractor took the largest share. The meeting was not unusual. Overruns on capital investment had become the rule.

The question of the corporation's ability to meet an economic slump came up at the end of 1919. On December 27 of that year I moved and the Executive Committee unanimously passed the following resolution:

RESOLVED, that a committee be appointed to study and recommend a policy for the Finance Committee to follow in the matter of providing cash surplus to meet increased capital requirements, should a serious recessing in business occur, or should plants be suddenly shut down due to serious strikes extending over a period of several months.

The imminence of a slump, however, was still unsuspected by us, as it was by most people in the United States. For this reason, I presume, the leading committees did not then appreciate how critical would be the significance of the lack of control over the actions of the divisions. Late in February 1920, however, Mr. Haskell informed the general managers, with the approval of the Executive Committee, of the "necessity of again presenting to the Executive Committee all appropriation requests which may be affected by change in conditions, before proceeding with the work thereby authorized." It was a mild warning, with no teeth of enforcement in it.

Inventories followed the same runaway course as the overruns on capital expenditure. In November 1919 production schedules for the coming fiscal year were set 36 per cent higher than for the closing year. These production schedules were made by rule of thumb, or the division manager's ambition. To meet the schedules, the divisions began immediately to make heavy purchases of inventory. Late in March 1920 the Executive Committee approved for the corporation as a whole an optimistic production schedule of 876,000 cars, trucks, and tractors for the year beginning in August 1920. In March and April, Mr. Raskob, as chairman of the Finance Committee, began making arrangements for the sale of $64 million worth of common stock to provide money for continuing capital expenditures aggregating about $100 million. The du Ponts, J. P. Morgan and Company, and some British interests participated in this effort, and representatives of the new interests came on the board.

In May 1920 the minutes of the Executive Committee show that Mr. Raskob took pause, and expressed apprehension over unplanned expenditures for plant and equipment and rising inventories. Failure to remain within limits for inventory—then set at $150 million—he cautioned, could endanger the corporation's financial position.

A week later a special Inventory Allotment Committee consisting of Mr. Durant, Mr. Haskell, Mr. Prentis, and myself approved a detailed list of maximum permissible expenditures for each division. Even with reduced production schedules, however, the division managers failed to stay within their authorized limits on inventory or capital expenditures, and nothing was done effectively to control them. This was decentralization with a vengeance.

While the expenditures continued upward, the automobile market, after a brief rise in demand in June 1920, went down. In August both the Finance and Executive committees sharply warned the division managers to stay within the expenditure limits set in May. Early in October the Finance Committee appointed an inventory committee headed by Mr. Pratt to try to get control over the situation. But the damage was done. Total corporation inventories in January 1920 had stood at $137 million; in April at $168 million; in June at $185 million; in October at $209 million, exceeding by $59 million the limit set in May. And the worst was yet to come.

In September the bottom dropped out of the automobile market. To meet the situation Mr. Ford cut his prices on September 21 by 20 to 30 per cent. Mr. Durant, supported by the division sales managers, attempted for a time to maintain prices and to guarantee dealers and customers against any reduction. By October the situation had become so serious for General Motors that many managers were having difficulty in locating cash to pay invoices and payrolls. In that month we borrowed about $83 million from banks on short-term notes. In November all the major car-producing divisions, except Buick and Cadillac, had virtually shut down their plants, and those two were operating at reduced rates. The whole economy of the United States fell into a slump.

Before these events took place I had become increasingly disturbed by the trend of affairs inside General Motors. In late 1919 and early 1920 I developed a plan of organization intended to correct deficiencies in the operating organization, and presented it to Mr. Durant. He appeared to accept it favorably, though he did nothing about it. I think this was due in part to the fact that he was not prepared then to take up organizational matters; he was overburdened with all manner of immediate operating and personal financial problems which made it extremely difficult for him to consider a broad plan of this kind.

My anxiety about the management of the corporation and the direction it was taking became such that in the early summer of 1920 I asked for a thirty-day vacation to get away and decide what I should do. Everything I owned was tied up in the stock of the corporation. At first I thought that, like Mr. Chrysler, I should retire from General Motors. I had a potential offer of a partnership in the banking firm Lee Higginson and Company, with the prospect of working on industrial analysis. The offer came from Mr. Storrow, who, as I have described, had directed the financial affairs of General Motors in the 1910–15 period, and who had since become the principal backer of Nash Motors. I hesitated about making this change, and went to Europe to think it over. My hesitation was due to the fact that I did not feel that I should protect my financial position by selling my shareholdings while Mr. Durant, rightly or wrongly, was trying, with every resource at his command, to maintain the market value of General Motors stock in the crisis. In England I ordered a Rolls-Royce with the intention of going on a tour with my wife, but I never took delivery of the Rolls or made the tour. I returned to the United States in August, and finding that a considerable change had taken place and that the situation was coming to a head, I decided to wait.

The business slump of 1920 was accompanied, as is often the case, by a break in stock-market prices. This, together with the near closing of most of the General Motors plants, brought to an end an era in the corporation's history. A record of the events leading to Mr. Durant's resignation from General Motors was written down by Pierre S. du Pont in a letter to his brother Irénée du Pont, then president of E. I. du Pont de Nemours & Company. The letter was dated November 26, 1920.

Dear Sir:

Recent developments in General Motors Corporation's affairs make it necessary to record developments of the past two weeks, which I do from notes made by me and from circumstances that are still clearly in mind. Before dealing with this part of the history I should like to record a few words in regard to my previous understanding of Mr. Durant's personal affairs.

Since my first acquaintance with Mr. Durant some years ago he had never up to Thursday, November 11th, 1920, said anything to me concerning his personal affairs. When the du Pont interests bought into the General Motors Company and acquired an investment of $25,000,000. worth of stock at slightly above par, it was understood from Mr. Durant that he, possibly together with his immediate family, held a similar amount of stock (including his holdings in the Chevrolet Company, which was then, as now, a holding company of General Motors Common stock). It was known to us at that time that the larger part of Mr. Durant's stock stood in the name of brokers, but this was supposed to be a matter of convenience. I am quite sure that if Mr. Durant was a borrower on this stock at the time, nothing was said about it. During the months that followed our acquisition of stock up to last spring I knew at times that

Mr. Durant had permitted his stock to be lent in the street. I also knew that he was at times purchaser of stock, both directly and through advising people to buy. I had never supposed that he purchased other than by payment outright or in amount within his ability to carry, in view of his seemingly large fortune. I do not remember his mentioning any case in which he was a seller of stock, nor does it appear now that he has ever been other than a purchaser. I have never abetted Mr. Durant in any thoughts of stock and market control which he mentioned to me; in fact, what little has been said would tend to discourage market operations rather than to encourage them; but, as I said before, Mr. Durant has never spoken to me about personal affairs and it has never appeared that the stock operations were anything but personal. I have a strong impression, which Mr. Raskob confirms, that Mr. Durant was entirely out of the stock market in the spring of 1920. I have supposed that he owed no money, particularly on brokers' accounts. When syndicates were formed in recent months by Morgan & Company, it was my understanding that Mr. Durant would not operate in the stock market in any way, as it is impossible for two parties to act independently in a satisfactory way. I have been disappointed during recent weeks to hear Mr. Durant mention supporting the market, in view of the fact that the Morgan syndicate was not doing so properly. My judgment has been against this independent action, but I am not sure that the subject has been discussed in a way that has indicated to Mr. Durant any clearcut ideas on my part; in fact, I have pictured his purchases to sustain the market as being limited to a number of shares well within his supposed purchasing power and that of his immediate friends who might be helping him in placing the stock. I have felt quite certain up to November 11th that Mr. Durant was not operating in the stock market and was not a borrower of money.

Notwithstanding the above opinions that were quite firmly fixed in my mind, there have been rumors of Durant's speculations. Both Mr. Raskob and I have felt that Morgan & Company have been ignorant of the extent of Mr. Durant's operations since they became purchasers of General Motors Common stock. Morgan & Company have had every opportunity to question Mr. Durant on the subject and I have not felt it my duty to pry into Durant's affairs. Some time within the past six weeks Mr. [Dwight W.] Morrow of Morgan & Company asked Mr. Raskob and me some questions regarding Mr. Durant's personal affairs, particularly as to his possible stock market operations. To this we replied that we knew nothing of his personal affairs and that he had never confided in us. I advised Mr. Morrow that he question Mr. Durant personally, as we felt sure that he would be candid in his answers. This led to a meeting in Mr. Morrow's office in November, 1920 at which he, Mr. Durant, Mr.

Raskob and I were present. During that meeting I stated that it was fair that the partners in ownership of General Motors stock should know each others position and informed the meeting on the part of the du Pont interests that all of our stock, both General Motors and Chevrolet, was held by the company, unpledged, and that we were not buyers or sellers of stock in any amount. I also stated that I, personally, was not a borrower of money on the stock; that my shares were held by me, and that I had not bought or sold stock recently. I stated that so far as I knew, none of the individuals in the du Pont group were borrowers on General Motors stock or operating in any way. Mr. Morrow stated that the shares purchased by Morgan & Company and their friends were still held and that there was no intention to sell. I do not remember that Mr. Durant made as positive a statement on his part, but he did not give any intimation that he was a borrower on the stock or operating in the market in any way. Mr. Morrow asked him the direct question whether he knew of any weak accounts in the market, to which Durant replied "no." He left us with the impression that his holdings were as clear as our own. Knowing Mr. Durant and the peculiarities of his makeup, I do not think that he intended to deceive us in any way; but Mr. Morrow, who was not inclined to be as generous, I think censures Mr. Durant severely for his failure to be frank with us.

We now come to Thursday, November 11th, 1920. Without any idea in the heads of Mr. Raskob or the writer that Mr. Durant was involved in any way, on the date above mentioned Mr. Durant asked us to lunch with him. At the meeting he stated that he had been informed that "the bankers" had demanded his resignation as President of the General Motors Company, to which demand he was ready to accede, as he was determined to "play the game," for the reason that the company as well as he, personally, "was in the hands of the bankers" and must act accordingly. I immediately took exception to his statement about the company, explaining that our borrowings were not greater than could be prudently carried in view of our large working capital and other assets and in view of the cash balance carried by the company and the forecasts of our financial affairs. I explained that our banking partners concurred in this opinion and saw no difficulty in carrying our loans until liquidation through the operations of the business could be accomplished. Mr. Durant stated that he was worried about his personal accounts but made no definite explanation, and no opportunity was presented for an inquiry, which did not seem necessary at the time. However, after leaving this meeting, Mr. Raskob speculated on the probable meaning of Mr. Durant's words. In answer to Mr. Raskob's question the next day as to the condition of Mr. Durant's affairs and particular[ly] as to whether his indebtedness amounted to "six or twenty-six million dollars," Mr. Durant replied that he would have to look up the matter. Mr. Raskob and I left New York on Friday (12th) and did not return until the following Tuesday, November 16th, at which time we went to Mr. Durant's office in the morning, with the determination to endeavor to find out his true position, as we had agreed in conversation that Durant's personal affairs, if seriously involved, might indirectly affect the credit of General Motors Company. Mr. Durant was very busy that day, seeing people, rushing to the telephone, and in and out of his room, so that, although we waited patiently for several hours, interrupted only by lunch time, it was not until four o'clock that afternoon that Mr. Durant began to give us figures indicating his situation. He had pencil memoranda of the number of loans at banks. The total memoranda, as written down by us from what he said, showed an indebtedness of twenty million dollars, all presumably on brokers' accounts and supported by 1,300,000 shares of stock owned by others and by an unknown amount of collateral belonging to Durant; also, $14,190,000 which Durant estimated he owed personally to banks and brokers, against which he held three million shares of General Motors stock, this, of course, exclusive of the 1,300,000 shares owned by others. Mr. Durant stated that he had no personal books or accounts and was wholly unable to give definite statements as to the total indebtedness; what part of it was his personal and what part was the indebtedness of others on which he had lent collateral without other commitment. Apparently, he had no summary of brokers' accounts in hand. However, the whole situation, besides being very involved, seemed very serious. Mr. Durant promised to ask his brokers for accounts in order to make some positive statement.

On Tuesday evening (Nov. 16th) Mr. Durant had a call from McClure, Jones & Reed, brokers, for $150,000, to support his account. This amount was fixed up in some way.

On Wednesday (Nov. 17th) we inquired for the brokers' accounts and found that directions had been given to make the statement as of the close of business Wednesday, November 17th, so that nothing could be done that day. Meantime, the statements already given appeared so indefinite that Mr. Raskob and I were loath to believe the accounts in any way accurate. However, the situation seemed serious enough to warrant speculating on a plan for relief. We decided that, in order to avert a crisis, it might be possible to organize a company to take over Mr. Durant's holdings, issuing $20,000,000. of notes, which would be offered as collateral to the holder of obligations, and that the du Pont interests might invest $7,000,000., or even $10,000,000. in securities of the company in order to furnish cash to liquidate pressing accounts and make payments, in part, of others.

On Thursday, November 18th, the broker accounts started to come in, and it required all of that day to get the statement in shape that was agreed upon by Mr. Durant as correct. The statement, however, was not capable of accurate checking, excepting from the broker accounts presented. There was nothing to show that these covered all the broker accounts, and there was nothing very definite in regard to bank loans, nor to the syndicate accounts in which Mr. Durant was involved as lender of collateral. However, a summary sheet was made up from the data and given to the typist for copying late Thursday afternoon. About that time Mr. Durant called Mr. Raskob and me to his office, stating that some of the Morgan partners were to call upon him shortly and asked us to be present at the meeting. We told him that his position differed so entirely from that represented to us and to Morgan & Co. that it was impossible for us to sit in a meeting with him and the Morgan partners, unless he agreed to make a complete statement to them. He did not agree to this point and we left the room. About 6:30 P.M. we started to leave for the hotel and met Messrs. Morrow, [Thomas] Cochran and [George] Whitney, who had met Mr. Durant, with a promise on the part of Mr. Whitney to return at nine o'clock that evening. Mr. Morrow called me aside and stated that they wanted to get in touch with me for a few minutes' interview. He and his associates and I then repaired to Mr. Raskob's room and, after a few preliminaries, I asked whether Mr. Durant had made a complete statement to them. To this Mr. Morrow replied "yes," and produced a copy of the typed summary which I had prepared but which I had not yet myself seen in finished form. Then ensued a discussion of the whole subject, in which the Morgan partners outlined their opinion of the extreme seriousness of the situation and the panic that might result, in the event of Mr. Durant's failure, which might possibly involve the failure of several brokers and some of the banks, particularly as there were two large and critically weak accounts in the street. Mr. Morrow stated that he would give up an engagement and return at nine o'clock and I agreed to break an engagement and do likewise. Our conversation occupied not much more than a half hour. I returned to the hotel and, together with Mr. Raskob, went to the office at the appointed time, where three Morgan partners had assembled. Mr. Raskob outlined to Mr. Morrow our rough plan of giving assistance, in which it appeared that, we representing the du Pont interest, were willing to help materially in this very desperate situation. Mr. Morrow stated that he thought the plan impossible of execution because of the very critical condition in the market and recommended that we endeavor to place a loan of $20,000,000. among the banks, in order that an offer of cash for all Mr. Durant's indebtedness might be made. Mr. Raskob and I agreed on part of the du Pont interests that we could furnish $7,000,000.00, and sufficient additional collateral toward the project.

The Morgan partners were very complimentary as to the willingness of du Pont to help in the situation, Mr. Cochran using the expression that "there are two firms in this country who are real sports, viz., du Pont and Morgan."

Discussion ensued as to the treatment of Mr. Durant, Mr. Morrow making the suggestion that one-fourth of the equity in the shares should remain with Durant and that some portion of this equity might have to be used in order to help place the notes. He stated in the beginning that Morgan & Company would ask no commission or payment of any kind for their services in the deal. This division of the equity was discussed with careful consideration of justice to Mr. Durant and those carrying the load. After this preliminary discussion, the Morgan partners stated that they must go as carefully as possible into Mr. Durant's accounts before any attempt was made to float a loan. This investigation they proposed to start upon immediately and, therefore, went to Mr. Durant's room, and checking of the accounts was carried forward and the proposition of relief presented to Mr. Durant by Mr. Morrow. Mr. Durant thought that one-fourth of the equity returned to him was harsh. Mr. Morrow then moved to one-third. Mr. Durant suggested to me that 40% to him and 60% to the du Pont interests would be more nearly fair. This part of the negotiations was all in good spirit and with apparent endeavor on all sides to be just in a difficult situation. Checking of accounts and discussion of the subject continued without interruption until about 5:30 o'clock Friday morning, about which time Mr. Durant and I signed a memorandum, agreeing to the general proposition of a $20,000,000 note issue and issue of stock to support the $7,000,000 furnished by the du Pont interests; also, the loan of additional collateral, estimated at 1,300,000 shares. Memorandum also agreed that the equity in the stock representing the selling price above $9.50 per share, plus costs and interest, should be divided one-third to Durant and two-thirds to du Pont. Even at this date the total indebtedness was uncertain and the syndicate accounts still involved.

After a hurried breakfast we all retired for a couple hours' sleep and returned to business at 9:30 o'clock that morning. Messrs. Morgan & Co. arranged a loan of $20,000,000. with the principal banks in New York before five o'clock that evening (Nov. 19th). In the meantime, the plan was suggested that the du Pont interests take 8% Preferred stock for their cash, and for the loan of collateral, 80% of the Common stock, the latter representing the equity in the selling price of the stock above $9.50, plus costs and interest. Twenty per cent. of this common stock was set aside for the bank interests furnishing the loan of $20,000,000. On that day the du Pont Finance Committee met and agreed to divide the 80% Common stock equally with Mr. Durant, leaving the proportions 40% Durant, 40%

du Pont and 20% bankers. This is the plan that has been finally consummated. While rumors of the deal were active on Saturday (Nov. 20th), announcement was not made until Monday (Nov. 22nd), when Morgan & Company started to gather in the stock. Throughout the whole transaction the Morgan partners have appeared to greatest advantage. They threw themselves into the situation wholeheartedly, stating at the start that they asked no compensation. They have acted with remarkable speed and success, the whole deal involving $60,000,000. or more, having been planned and practically completed in less than four days, in which are included a Saturday and Sunday.

On November 30, 1920, Mr. Durant resigned as president of General Motors.

With all I have said in appraising Mr. Durant's methods, he was no more responsible than was Mr. Raskob for the collision between General Motors' expansion and the business cycle. Mr. Raskob went ahead pushing the expansion and paying the bills. Mr. Durant's management methods let things get out of control. I have heard that Mr. Durant became pessimistic about the national economy in late 1919, but I can find no record of it. On the record, both Mr. Durant and Mr. Raskob were strong, optimistic expansionists. They seemed to disagree on occasion only on what to put the money into.

I think that Mr. Durant's personal stock-market operations were motivated essentially by his great pride in General Motors and everything relating to it, and by his unbounded confidence in its future, a judgment that has been well vindicated over the years. I think also that the arrangement the Morgans and du Ponts made with him to take over his stock obligations in such a critical period was a generous one.

Consider the following: Mr. Durant in 1921 sold back to the du Ponts his interest in the company formed to bail him out. He received for his interest 230,000 shares of General Motors stock, whose market value at the time of acquisition was $2,990,000. Mr. Durant's disposition of those shares is not part of this story. However, their market value if he had held them to the time of his death, March 19, 1947, would have been $25,713,281, on which he would have received an aggregate of $27,033,625 in dividends and from the sale of rights.

To return to the events of 1920, the slump in the national economy and its impact on the corporation, the lack of control of operations, and Mr. Durant's resignation shook the enterprise to its foundation and started an entirely new period in its history—which is where the main part of my story begins.

INDUSTRIAL & AUTOMOBILE PRODUCTION AND METAL PRICES
DURING FOUR YEAR PERIOD INCLUDING 1920-1921 ECONOMIC SLUMP

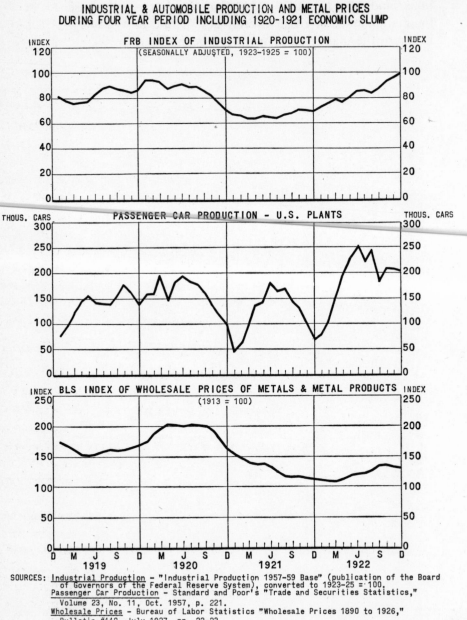

SOURCES: <u>Industrial Production</u> – "Industrial Production 1957-59 Base" (publication of the Board
    of Governors of the Federal Reserve System), converted to 1923-25 = 100.
    <u>Passenger Car Production</u> – Standard and Poor's "Trade and Securities Statistics,"
    Volume 23, No. 11, Oct. 1957, p. 221.
    <u>Wholesale Prices</u> – Bureau of Labor Statistics "Wholesale Prices 1890 to 1926,"
    Bulletin #440, July 1927, pp. 22-23.

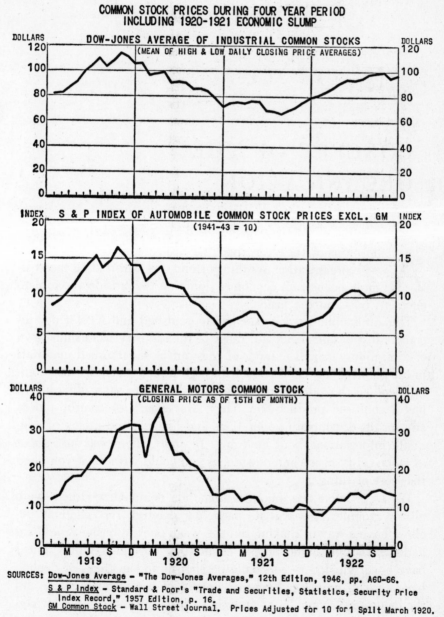

COMMON STOCK PRICES DURING FOUR YEAR PERIOD
INCLUDING 1920-1921 ECONOMIC SLUMP

DOW-JONES AVERAGE OF INDUSTRIAL COMMON STOCKS
(MEAN OF HIGH & LOW DAILY CLOSING PRICE AVERAGES)

S & P INDEX OF AUTOMOBILE COMMON STOCK PRICES EXCL. GM
(1941-43 = 10)

GENERAL MOTORS COMMON STOCK
(CLOSING PRICE AS OF 15TH OF MONTH)

1919   1920   1921   1922

SOURCES: Dow-Jones Average – "The Dow-Jones Averages," 12th Edition, 1946, pp. A60-66.
S & P Index – Standard & Poor's "Trade and Securities, Statistics, Security Price Index Record," 1957 Edition, p. 16.
GM Common Stock – Wall Street Journal. Prices Adjusted for 10 for 1 Split March 1920.

Chapter 3

CONCEPT OF THE ORGANIZATION

AT the close of the year 1920 the task before General Motors was reorganization. As things stood, the corporation faced simultaneously an economic slump on the outside and a management crisis on the inside.

The automobile market had nearly vanished and with it our income. Most of our plants and those of the industry were shut down or assembling a small number of cars out of semifinished materials in the plants. We were loaded with high-priced inventory and commitments at the old inflated price level. We were short of cash. We had a confused product line. There was a lack of control and of any means of control in operations and finance, and a lack of adequate information about anything. In short, there was just about as much crisis, inside and outside, as you could wish for if you liked that sort of thing.

We were not alone among automobile companies. Others were also in trouble. That was no particular comfort, for economic declines have a way of shaking out the weak ones in business, and we had weaknesses. Some people cannot see beyond a slump, but I have never yielded to economic pessimism and in times of decline have kept in mind the eventual upturn of the business cycle and the long-range dynamics of growth. Confidence and caution formed my attitude in 1920. We could not control the environment, or predict its changes precisely, but we could seek the flexibility to survive fluctuations in business.

The immediate future of the automobile market was, to say the least, uncertain. However, we believed in the future of the product as well as of the economy. I mention this because confidence is an important element in business; it may on occasion make the difference between one man's success and another's failure. It was our settled belief that the automobile was then in the course of creating a new transportation system in the United States, and that the market for it therefore was bound in time to return with strength. We stated this in the annual report for 1920, along with a review of the progress of the automobile industry up to that time; and gave our attention to the problems at hand.

Before anything else, we had to have a new president to take the place of Mr. Durant. I did not have to think twice to decide who I thought should be the new president. I knew Pierre S. du Pont in a personal way only slightly. But it was apparent that he was the one individual in General Motors who had the prestige and respect that could give confidence to the organization, to the public, and to the banks, and whose presence could arrest the demoralization that was taking place. He was chairman of the corporation, and he represented the largest shareholder interest. He had shown his capability for business leadership in the du Pont Company and in his financial association with General Motors. The only other man in the corporation who might have been considered for president was John J. Raskob, Mr. du Pont's close and influential adviser, and chairman of General Motors' Finance Committee.

Mr. Raskob's Alger-boy career has been told many times. I do not personally know his early years, but the story is that he went to work as a typist and secretary to Pierre S. du Pont around the turn of the century. Mr. du Pont was impressed with his lively imagination and financial capabilities. As Mr. du Pont moved up to be treasurer of the du Pont Company, Mr. Raskob moved with him as his assistant and adviser, succeeding him as treasurer of the du Pont Company. Mr. du Pont and Mr. Raskob were very close business associates for many years. But they did not at all have the same kind of temperaments.

Mr. Raskob was brilliant and imaginative where Mr. du Pont was steady and conservative. Mr. du Pont was tall, well built, and reticent. He would not put himself forward. Mr. Raskob was short and not reticent. He was very friendly, a fine fellow to talk with, and a man of big ideas. I remember his often coming into my office with an idea and wanting to get it into action by waving a magic wand; he would want the whole organization to come to a meeting right off. His faults, if they should be called that, were those that go with an aggressive, impatient intelligence—the very thing that made him good. Not many men foresaw the future of the automobile industry as well as he did.

Both Mr. Raskob and Mr. du Pont thus had their strong points, but on balance it seemed to all of us who were concerned that Mr. du Pont was the man we needed. No one else at the time could qualify in so many particulars.

There was only one drawback. Mr. du Pont had no intimate knowledge of the automobile business. I happen to be one of the old school who thinks that a knowledge of the business is essential to a successful administration. But in the situation that existed then, the immediate needs for a general constructive leadership in administration and a re-establishment of confidence in the future were more important than intimate knowledge of the business. Other men were available or could be obtained who had that knowledge. Hence I urged in the informal discussions that took place that Mr. du Pont was the logical choice.

Not that my urging had much or anything to do with the decision. Other persons were more influential, and Mr. du Pont had reasons of his own for allowing himself to be persuaded to accept management as well as financial responsibility in General Motors. The du Pont Company had taken over the Durant stock in the crisis, and by 1921 would increase its ownership to about 36 per cent of the total common stock of the General Motors Corporation. Mr. du Pont had an obvious responsibility in the situation. He later said: "I was very loath to accept the position [of president]. I had recently retired from business, but I said that I would do whatever they thought best, and I was put in as president with the distinct understanding that I was only to stay there until a better posted man could be found to take the job."

When Pierre S. du Pont accepted the presidency, Mr. Raskob continued as chairman of the Finance Committee and for several years served as the public spokesman of the corporation. J. Amory Haskell and I became Mr. du Pont's right- and left-hand men, so to speak. In a letter distributed at the board meeting of December 30, 1920, Mr. du Pont stated that Mr. Haskell and I were "competent to settle executive questions, acting for the Executive Committee between meetings, and for the President in his absence." The Executive Committee was re-formed and reduced temporarily to four men: Mr. du Pont, Mr. Raskob, Mr. Haskell, and myself. This new committee took charge of operating policy and of a certain amount of administration as well. The old Executive Committee, made up in large part of division managers, was made an advisory operations committee.

These changes, though of an emergency nature, coincided with a sweeping reorganization of General Motors, going to the roots of industrial philosophy. The language of corporation minutes is laconic, but the consequences can be far reaching, as they were in this instance. The first business of the new administration, taken up at the last meeting of the old Executive Committee on December 30, 1920, is recorded as follows:

The President submitted for the consideration of the Executive Committee a new Organization Chart of our Corporation together with an explanatory letter, and same was discussed at length.[1]

This was unanimously approved and ordered sent to the board of directors, who also approved it. It was made effective on January 3, 1921.

The plan thus adopted was with modifications the one I had drafted about a year earlier under the title "Organization Study" and submitted to Mr. Durant for his consideration.[2] Since this plan has become the foundation of management policy in the modern

[1] A copy of this chart is at the end of the chapter.

[2] It is only in recent years that I have had occasion to recall the surrounding circumstances and now for the first time I am able to place the approximate time when I drafted the study. It was at the end of 1919—some time after December 5 and before January 19, 1920—instead of in the spring of 1920 as I had long thought. I reach this conclusion from the fact that the study refers to the Appropriations Committee, which was created by the Executive Committee on December 5, 1919, and from a letter to me from H. H. Bassett, then general manager of Buick, dated January 19, 1920, in which he expresses his enthusiasm for the study. "I have read over every word of the attached report and I firmly believe it is a wonderfully thought out scheme of organization and certainly has my unqualified endorsement," said Mr. Bassett, very kindly. I replied to him on January 21 as follows:

"My dear Harry:—I have your letter of January 19th and am pleased to note that the plan in general meets with your approval and support.

"I do not know what action, if any, is going to be taken, but I hope that something will be worked out that will be satisfactory to all because I really believe that it would be desireable to have things a little more definitely arranged."

General Motors—an expression of the basic principles of "decentralization" that govern its organization—and is said thereby to have had some influence on large-scale industrial enterprise in the United States, I shall say something here about its origin and substance.

First as to its origin. It has been supposed by some students that General Motors took its decentralized type of organization from the du Pont Company, as a result of the relationship of the two companies. Both managements at that time were in fact independently concerned with problems of organization, and both eventually adopted principles of decentralization. But they proceeded from opposite poles. The du Pont Company then was evolving from a centralized type of organization, common in the early days of American industry, while General Motors was emerging from almost total decentralization. General Motors needed to find a principle of co-ordination without losing the advantages of decentralization. These different backgrounds of the General Motors Corporation and the du Pont Company, together with the differences in nature and marketing of the products of the two enterprises, made it impractical for the same model of organization to serve properly for both of them.

Du Pont executives had been working on their own reorganization problem for a couple of years; but it was not until nine months after General Motors adopted its plan of organization that the du Pont Company also adopted a decentralized scheme. The two plans did not share their particulars, but only the management philosophy of decentralization.

The two types of operating problems, one arising from too much centralization (du Pont) and the other from too much decentralization (General Motors), were soon to be met by many large American manufacturing enterprises. One reason, perhaps, why General Motors and du Pont met and answered their organization problems early was that in 1920 and 1921 their operating problems were larger and more complex than those of most contemporary American industrial enterprises. I believe it is also true that we recognized the problems and thought more in terms of organizational principles and philosophies than did most businessmen of that time. The principles of organization got more attention among us than they did then in the universities. If what follows seems academic, I assure you that we did not think it so.

I wrote the "Organization Study" for General Motors as a possible solution for the specific problems created by the expansion of the corporation after World War I. I cannot, of course, say for sure how much of my thought on management came from contacts with my associates. Ideas, I imagine, are seldom, if ever, wholly original, but so far as I am aware, this study came out of my experience in Hyatt, United Motors, and General Motors. I had not been much of a book reader, and if I had been, I understand that I would not have found much in that line in those days to help; and I had no military experience. In the course of my twenty years or so at Hyatt I learned to operate a single industrial unit, relatively small in size and with one basic product. This unit contained the elementary functions of a manufacturing business: engineering, production, sales, and finance. But I had only a small board of directors, no executive committee, and no organization problems of the General Motors type.

In United Motors I met for the first time the problems of operating a multiple-unit organization with different products made by separate divisions. All that held United Motors together in its beginning was the concept of automotive parts and accessories. We made horns, radiators, bearings, rims, and the like, and we sold them to both automobile producers and the public. Certain limited areas of possible co-ordination presented themselves; for example, the servicing of the numerous small products made by the different divisions. Separate service agencies for such small items were uneconomic. I therefore set up a single, nationwide organization called United Motors Service, Inc., on October 14, 1916, to represent the divisions, with stations in twenty-odd large cities and several hundred dealers at other points. The divisions naturally resisted this move for a while, but I persuaded them of the need for it, and for the first time learned something about getting decentralized management to yield some of its functions for the common good. The service organization is still operating in General Motors and has grown along with the business as a whole. I considered setting up a common laboratory for research, and most likely would have done so if we had not entered General Motors. I did establish in United Motors a unity of business purpose through the principle of return on investment. By placing each division on its own profit-making basis, I gave the general office a common measure of efficiency with which to judge the contribution of each division to the whole. In this connection I devised a system of standard accounting which Albert Bradley, long-time chief financial officer of General Motors, later was kind enough to say was pretty good for a layman.

In the great expansion in General Motors between 1918 and 1920, I had been struck by the disparity between substance and form: plenty of substance and little form. I became convinced that the corporation could not continue to grow and survive unless it was better organized, and it was apparent that no one was giving that subject the attention it needed.

An example, close to home for me: When the United Motors group was brought into the General Motors Corporation in late 1918, I found that if I followed the prevailing practice of inter-corporate relations I would no longer be able to determine the rate of return on investment for these accessory divisions individually or as a group. This would necessarily mean that I would lose some degree of managerial control over my area of operations. At that time, material within General Motors was passing from one operating division to another at cost, or at cost plus some predetermined percentage. My divisions in the United Motors Corporation had sold both to outside customers and to their allied divisions at the market price. I knew that I operated a profit-making group, and I wished to continue to be able to demonstrate this performance to the general management, rather than to have my operating results on interdivisional business swallowed up in the extra bookkeeping profits of some other division. It was a case of keeping the information clear.

It was not, however, a matter of interest to me only with respect to my divisions, since as a member of the Executive Committee, I was a kind of general executive and so had begun to think from the corporate viewpoint. The important thing was that no one knew how much was being contributed—plus or minus—by each division to the common good of the corporation. And since, therefore, no one knew, or could prove, where the efficiencies and inefficiencies lay, there was no objective basis for the allocation of new investment. This was one of the difficulties with the expansion program of that time. It was natural for the divisions to compete for investment funds, but it was irrational for the general officers of the corporation not to know where to place the money to best advantage. In the absence of objectivity it was not surprising that there was a lack of real agreement among the general officers. Furthermore, some of them had no broad outlook, and used their membership on the Executive Committee mainly to advance the interests of their respective divisions.

I had taken up the question of interdivisional relations with Mr. Durant before I entered General Motors and my views on it were well enough known for me to be appointed chairman of a committee "to formulate rules and regulations pertaining to interdivisional business" on December 31, 1918. I completed the report by the following summer and presented it to the Executive Committee on December 6, 1919. I select here a few of its first principles, which, though they are an accepted part of management doctrine today, were not so well known then. I think they are still worth attention.

I stated the basic argument as follows:

The profit resulting from any business considered abstractly, is no real measure of the merits of that particular business. An operation making $100,000.00 per year may be a very profitable business justifying expansion and the use of all the additional capital that it can profitably employ. On the other hand, a business making $10,000,000 a year may be a very unprofitable one, not only not justifying further expansion but even justifying liquidation unless more profitable returns can be obtained. It is not, therefore, a matter of the amount of profit but of the relation of that profit to the real worth of invested capital within the business. Unless that principle is fully recognized in any plan that may be adopted, illogical and unsound results and statistics are unavoidable . . .

There seems to me still to be no question about that. It is as I see it the strategic aim of a business to earn a return on capital, and if in any particular case the return in the long run is not satisfactory, the deficiency should be corrected or the activity abandoned for a more favorable one.

For sales to outside customers, I recognized in the report that the market would determine the actual price, and if this yielded a desirable return, the business in question might justify expansion. For exclusively interdivisional transactions I recommended that the starting point should be cost plus some predetermined rate of return, but only as a guide. To avoid the possibility of protecting a supplying division which might be a high-cost producer, I recommended a number of steps involving analysis of the operation and comparison with outside competitive production where possible. The point I wish to make here relates not to technique—which other people know better than I do—but to the general principle of rate of return as the measure of the worth of a business. That idea was fundamental in my thinking about management problems.

On the influence of rate of return on decentralization and the relation of the part to the whole, I made several points of which the following seem to me to be of interest.

As to its bearing on organization:

. . . [It] Increases the morale of the organization by placing each operation on its own foundation, making it feel that it is a part of the Corporation, assuming its own responsibility and contributing its share to the final result.

As to its bearing on financial control:

. . . [It] Develops statistics correctly reflecting the relation between the net return and the invested capital of each operating division—the true measure of efficiency—irrespective of the number of other divisions contributing thereto and the capital employed within such divisions.

As to its bearing on strategic investment:

. . . [It] Enables the Corporation to direct the placing of additional capital where it will result in the greatest benefit to the Corporation as a whole.

So far as I know, this was the first written statement of the broad principles of financial control in General Motors.

I continued thereafter to occupy myself with the subject of organization.

In the late summer of 1919 I had gone abroad with a group of General Motors executives to study the overseas prospects of the corporation. In the group were Mr. Haskell, its chairman, Mr. Kettering, Mr. Mott, Mr. Chrysler, Albert Champion, and Alfred T. Brandt, who acted as secretary. On our way over on the S.S. *France* we held regular meetings on overseas matters and at other times met and discussed problems of organization. I can recall that we had such conversations but I cannot recall what was said. Mr. Haskell, it appears, regarded them as being of some importance at the time. At the end of a letter to Mr. Durant on October 10, 1919, shortly after we returned to the United States, he wrote the following:

We started working on organization matters the day we left New York and the entire committee participated in conferences which resulted in an agreement, and a report is being prepared . . . which we believe will be workable and help to lighten all of our burdens. However, these matters can best be dealt with personally rather than in a perhaps already too long communication.

I do not know what Mr. Haskell meant by saying that we agreed, other than perhaps on the need for better organization; my recollection is that there was more disagreement than agreement. Nor do I know of any report on organization that came out of these discussions.

It is a long time to go back in memory and find the precise times and places of things, especially when their importance was not realized at the time. I have instituted searches to verify or correct my memory on origins. I find, for example, that during the year 1919, as a member of the Executive Committee, I along with others performed a number of tasks concerned with organization, and in connection with them developed in a rudimentary way some of the ideas that I wrote up in my general "Organization Study."

One of these tasks was the study of interdivisional business, discussed above. Another was the study of appropriations-request rules, which is discussed in a later chapter. In the midst of this welter of thought and attempted action, and a half year before the actual economic and management crisis began, I drafted the "Organization Study" and circulated it unofficially. It became a kind of "best seller" in the corporation all during 1920; I received numerous letters from executives requesting copies of it, so many, in fact, that I found it necessary to reproduce it in quantity. It had no competition; that is, no other tangible effort was made, so far as I know, to achieve a general solution of the organization problem.

In September 1920 I sent a copy of the study to Pierre S. du Pont, then chairman of the corporation. We had an exchange about it. I wrote:

My dear Mr. DuPont:—
Referring to our conversation the other day, I am enclosing herewith copy of Organization Study worked out about a year ago.

I have reviewed this in the light of development since then and a greater insight in the working of our organization, and I do not see as I would recommend any radical changes except in reference to the additional recommendations . . . which I would not make as I view the situation now.

If you have time to read this Study at all, please bear in mind that it was worked out on a basis of what I thought would be acceptable to all interests rather than what would form an ideal organisation. If it were to be worked out along the latter line, I should be in favor of ultimately appointing an executive in charge of the three groups listed on Page 6; the miscellaneous group other than the Export Corporation and the Acceptance Corporation, ultimately passing into one of the other three groups. This would reduce the number of executives reporting directly to the President, to five, thus giving the President time to study into the broader problems.

Mr. du Pont replied:

Dear Mr. Sloan:
I am glad that you followed up our conversation with a copy of your study of a year ago. At the first opportunity, I shall read this carefully and hope for another discussion on the subject with you.

At the end of November 1920, when Mr. Durant went out and Mr. du Pont became president, the new administration needed a scheme of organization immediately. Mr. Durant had been able to operate the corporation in his own way, as the saying goes, "by the seat of his pants." The new administration was made up of men with very different ideas about business administration. They desired a highly rational and objective mode of operation. The "Organization Study" served the purpose and, as I have related, it was officially adopted, with some revision, as basic corporation policy.

The study was primitive by comparison with present-day knowledge of management. And it was written from the point of view of presenting something that I thought would be acceptable to Mr. Durant. So it was not without constraints. It began as follows:

The object of this study is to suggest an organization for the General Motors Corporation which will definitely place the line of authority throughout its extensive operations as well as to co-ordinate each branch of its service, at the same time destroying none of the effectiveness with which its work has heretofore been conducted.

The basis upon which this study has been made is founded upon two principles, which are stated as follows:—

1. The responsibility attached to the chief executive of each operation shall in no way be limited. Each such organization headed by its chief executive shall be complete in every necessary function and enable[d] to exercise its full initiative and logical development.

2. Certain central organization functions are absolutely essential to the logical development and proper control of the Corporation's activities.

This does not need much interpretation. It asks first for a line of authority, co-ordination, and the retention of the effectiveness of the then prevailing total decentralization. But looking back on the text of the two basic principles, after all these years, I am amused to see that the language is contradictory, and that its very contradiction is the crux of the matter. In point 1, I maximize decentralization of divisional operations in the words "shall in no way be limited." In point 2, I proceed to limit the responsibility of divisional chief executives in the expression "proper control." The language of organization has always suffered some want of words to express the true facts and circumstances of human interaction. One usually asserts one aspect or another of it at different times, such as the absolute independence of the part, and again the need of co-ordination, and again the concept of the whole with a guiding center. Interaction, however, is the thing, and with some reservation about the language and details I still stand on the fundamentals of what I wrote in the study. Its basic principles are in touch with the central problem of management as I have known it to this day.

The next point in the study was how to carry this philosophy into action. I wrote:

Having established the above principles as fundamental, and it is believed that all interests within the Corporation agree as to such principles, the definite objects which it is hoped to attain by this study, are enumerated as follows:—

1. To definitely determine the functioning of the various divisions constituting the Corporation's activities, not only in relation to one another, but in relation to the central organization.

That was a big chew, but it is correct. If you can describe the functions of the parts and the whole, you have laid out a complete working organization, for by implication the apportionment of responsibility for decisions at various levels is contained in the description.

I continued with the second objective:

2. To determine the status of the central organization and to coordinate the operation of that central organization with the Corporation as a whole to the end that it will perform its necessary and logical place.

This is a restatement of the first point, but in reverse—that is, looking from the top down.

The third objective:

3. To centralize the control of all the executive functions of the Corporation in the President as its chief executive officer.

Decentralization or not, an industrial corporation is not the mildest form of organization in society. I never minimized the administrative power of the chief executive officer in principle when I occupied that position. I simply exercised that power with discretion; I got better results by selling my ideas than by telling people what to do. Yet the power to act must be located in the chief executive officer.

The fourth and fifth points speak for themselves:

4. To limit as far as practical the number of executives reporting directly to the President, the object being to enable the President to better guide the broad policies of the Corporation without coming in contact with problems that may safely be entrusted to executives of less importance.

5. To provide means within each executive branch whereby all other executive branches are represented in an advisory way to the end that the development of each branch will be along lines constructive to the Corporation as a whole.

In brief, the study presented a specific structure for the corporation as it existed at that time. It recognized the form of the divisions, each of which was a self-contained group of functions (engineering, production, sales, and the like). It grouped the divisions, according to like activities, and, as I said in my letter to Mr. du Pont, proposed to place an executive in charge of each group. The plan provided for advisory staffs, which would be without line authority. It provided for a financial staff. It distinguished policy from administration of policy, and specified the location of each in the structure. It expressed in its way the concept that was later to be formulated as decentralized operations with co-ordinated control.

The principles of organization in the study thus initiated for the modern General Motors the trend toward a happy medium in industrial organization between the extremes of pure centralization and pure decentralization. The new policy asked that the corporation neither remain as it was, a weak form of organization, nor become a rigid, command form. But the actual forms of organization that were to evolve in the future under a new administration—what exactly, for example, would remain a divisional responsibility and what would be co-ordinated, and what would be policy and what would be administration—could not be deduced by a process of logic from the "Organization Study." Even mistakes played a large part in the actual events, as I shall show; and if our competitors —Mr. Ford among them—had not made some of their own of considerable magnitude, and if we had not reversed certain of ours, the position of General Motors would be different from what it is today.

Although the plan was officially adopted in 1920, expediency was for some time to rule the corporation. The formation of the new Executive Committee was the first outstanding example of this. Its four members, who were charged with the guidance of the corporation, had never before had the responsibility of producing an automobile. The great automotive producers in General Motors had been Mr. Durant, Mr. Nash, and Mr. Chrysler. They had already, by 1921, made their mark in the leadership of the automobile industry, and owing to the turns of fortune which I have described, they were then, or were about to be, numbered among our competitors. Mr. Durant, soon after leaving General Motors, formed another company, Durant Motors, which in its time was to produce several cars, the Durant, the Flint, the Star, and the Locomobile (which he took over). Mr. Chrysler was currently engaged in rescue operations at Willys-Overland and at Maxwell—forerunner of the Chrysler Corporation—and Mr. Nash was operating the enterprise that bore his name.

On the other hand, look at the new management of General Motors. Pierre S. du Pont in his first five years as chairman of General Motors had left the operating end of the business briefly to Mr. Nash and thereafter to Mr. Durant. Mr. Raskob was a financial man. Mr. Haskell's contact with the business was brief and not directly in divisional operations; and he soon dropped out of intimate participation in the new operating responsibility. He died on September 9, 1923. I came nearest to having automotive experience, and though I had spent my life in the industry, I was still undeveloped in car operations. So we were four amateurs, so to speak, in comparison with Mr. Nash, Mr. Chrysler, and Mr. Durant; soon, on the active end, we were three; and since Mr. Raskob was in finance, the highest responsibility for operating the corporation fell upon two of us, Mr. du Pont and myself as his principal assistant. Mr. du Pont and I worked closely together, traveled together, and met with operating executives in Detroit every two weeks. After six months I became a sort of executive vice president in charge of all operations, reporting to Mr. du Pont. But there was no straight and clear line in this matter; at one point, for example, Mr. du Pont added to his burdens and to the complexity of the improvised management by causing himself to be appointed general manager of Chevrolet along with his chairmanship and presidency of the corporation.

If we lacked experience in operations, we did not lack energy in overcoming this deficiency. The Executive Committee worked without respite throughout 1921. We met during that year exactly 101 times in formal session. Between sessions, individually and together, we were absorbed in the innumerable problems of the emergency and of the future, and were constantly on the go visiting the divisions and their plants in Detroit, Flint, Dayton, and elsewhere.

And so, if I were to take stock of the situation as it stood three or four months after the change of administration, I would say that, although we were short on experience, we were long on logic and energy, and we were getting control of the runaway elements of the business, particularly the inventory. Furthermore, we recognized that General Motors had no explicit policy as to the line of cars to be produced, and that that was the next order of business.

GENERAL MOTORS CORPORATION

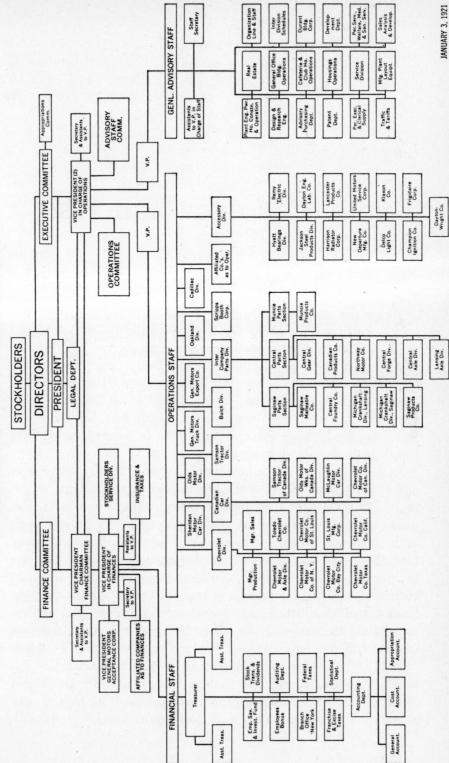

JANUARY 3, 1921

Chapter 4

PRODUCT POLICY AND ITS ORIGINS

A FTER the two great expansions of 1908 to 1910 and 1918 to 1920 —perhaps one should say because of them—General Motors was in need not only of a concept of management but equally of a concept of the automobile business. Every enterprise needs a concept of its industry. There is a logical way of doing business in accordance with the facts and circumstances of an industry, if you can figure it out. If there are different concepts among the enterprises involved, these concepts are likely to express competitive forces in their most vigorous and most decisive form.

Such was the case in the automobile industry in 1921. Mr. Ford's concept of a static model at the lowest price in the car market, expressed in the Model T, dominated the big-volume market then as it had for more than a decade. Other concepts were present, such as the one implied in about twenty makes of cars calculated to have low volume and very high price, and those behind the various cars in intermediate price brackets. General Motors then had no clear-cut concept of the business. It is true, as I have shown, that Mr. Durant had established the pattern of variety in product expressed in the seven lines: Chevrolet (in two very different models with different engines, the "490" standard, and a higher-priced "FB"), Oakland (predecessor of the Pontiac), Olds, Scripps-Booth, Sheridan, Buick, and Cadillac. Of these, only Buick and Cadillac had clear divisional concepts, Buick with its high quality and fairly high volume in the high middle-price bracket, and Cadillac with its permanent endeavor to present the highest quality at a price consistent with a volume that would make a substantial business; and in fact Cadillac and Buick had long been the industry leaders in their price classes.

Nevertheless, there was then in General Motors no established policy for the car lines as a whole. We had no position in the low-price area, Chevrolet at that time being competitive with Ford in neither price nor quality. In early 1921, the Chevrolet was priced about $300 above the Model T (when an adjustment is made for comparable equipment), hence, out of sight from the viewpoint of competition. The fact that we were producers of middle- and high-price cars, so far as I know, was not a deliberate policy. It just happened that no one had figured out how to compete with the Ford, which had then more than half the total market in units. It should be observed, however, that no producer at that time presented a full line of cars, nor did any other producer present a line as broad as General Motors' line.

The spacing of our product line of ten cars in seven lines in early 1921 reveals its irrationality. Our cars and their prices at that time (priced from the roadster to the sedan, F.O.B. Detroit) were as follows:

Chevrolet "490" (four-cylinder)	$ 795 – $1375
Chevrolet "FB" (four-cylinder)	$1320 – $2075
Oakland (six-cylinder)	$1395 – $2065
Olds (four-cylinder "FB")	$1445 – $2145
(six-cylinder)[1]	$1450 – $2145
(eight-cylinder)	$2100 – $3300
Scripps-Booth (six-cylinder)[1]	$1545 – $2295
Sheridan (four-cylinder "FB")	$1685
Buick (six-cylinder)	$1795 – $3295
Cadillac (eight-cylinder)	$3790 – $5690

[1] Six-cylinder engine made by Oakland.

Superficially this was an imposing car line. In the previous year, 1920, we had sold 331,118 U.S.-produced passenger cars, of which Chevrolet accounted for 129,525 and Buick for 112,208, the remaining 89,385 being distributed among the other cars in the line. In total output of vehicle units and in dollar sales, General Motors in 1920 was second to the Ford Motor Company. In the United States and Canada we sold 393,075 cars and trucks as compared with Ford's production of 1,074,336. The total industry factory sales were about 2,300,000 cars and trucks. Our net sales totaled $567,320,603 as compared with Ford's total of $644,830,550.

From the inside the picture was not quite so good. Not only were we not competitive with Ford in the low-price field—where the big volume and substantial future growth lay—but in the middle, where we were concentrated with duplication, we did not know what we were trying to do except to sell cars which, in a sense, took volume from each other. Some kind of rational policy was called for. That is, it was necessary to know what one was *trying* to do, apart from the question of what might be imposed upon one by the consumer, the competition, and a combination of technological and economic conditions in the course of evolution. The lack of a rational policy in the car line can be seen especially in the almost identical duplication in price of the Chevrolet "FB," Oakland, and Olds. Each division, in the absence of a corporation policy, operated independently, making its own price and production policies, which landed some cars in identical price positions without relationship to the interest of the enterprise as a whole.

The presence of Sheridan and Scripps-Booth in the line was, to my mind, without any justification. Neither car had its own motor. The Sheridan, assembled in a single plant in Muncie, Indiana, had the four-cylinder "FB" motor. The Scripps-Booth, made in Detroit, had an Oakland six-cylinder motor, which, I might add, was then no attraction. Both had only modest dealer organizations. Singly or together they added nothing but excess baggage to the General Motors car line. Why then were they there? Scripps-Booth stock had come into the corporation with the acquisition of Chevrolet's assets in 1918. But the car had not developed important volume (about 8000 in 1919 and the same in 1920) and had no reasonable place in General Motors' line. The presence of the Sheridan is a mystery to me. Mr. Durant caused General Motors to acquire it in 1920, doubtless with something special in mind. I am uncertain what. It did not have a strong organization or demand or recognizable purpose in our line.

As for Oakland and Olds, not only were they competing at nearly identical prices, but both of them were growing rapidly obsolescent in design. Take the Oakland. At a meeting in my office on February 10, 1921, Mr. Pratt described the problem of this car as follows: "Oakland is spending [its] efforts in trying to improve [its] product. Some days they produce ten cars and some days they produce 50 cars. The situation is this—they turn out a lot of cars that are not what they should be and then they have to fix them up . . . The power plant has been the great trouble . . ." At the same meeting I said: "There is a lot that enters into this problem. At the present time we are getting 35 to 40 H.P. out of the Oakland motor and the crankshaft is too light for this rate of speed [power], and we have had a lot of poor workmanship together with other things, and the Oakland Motor Car Company over a year ago decided that they would put in a new motor. A new motor plant was authorized a year ago but we had to hold it up when we curtailed our development program . . . It is really a question of management to get this motor in the Oakland so it will pass inspection and be right . . ."

Oakland had sold its high of 52,124 cars in the boom year, 1919; it sold 34,839 in 1920, and, as it turned out, was to sell only 11,852 cars in 1921.

So much for Oakland.

Olds was only a little better off. It had sold 41,127 vehicles in 1919, 33,949 in 1920, and would sell 18,978 in 1921. It would take a new design just to save it.

Cadillac made 19,790 unit sales in 1920. In 1921 it would sell 11,130, and with the big price deflation that had taken place in the United States it would have to find a new optimum of cost, price, and volume.

The hard fact was that all the cars in the General Motors line, except Buick and Cadillac, were losing money in 1921. The Chevrolet Division that year lost about half of its 1920 volume. Its dollar losses at one point in 1921 reached approximately $1 million a month, and for the year as a whole it lost nearly $5 million. So strongly did I feel about the situation that, when someone proposed making changes in Buick's management, where Harry Bassett was successfully carrying on Walter Chrysler's old policy, I wrote to Mr. du Pont: "It is far better that the rest of General Motors be scrapped than any chances taken with Buick's earning power." If that seems like an overextended argument, consider Buick's position. Its sales dropped only moderately from 115,401 in the 1919 boom to 80,122 in the 1921 slump, and what's more, it continued to produce an income. It was Buick that made any kind of General Motors car line worth talking about.

This situation reflected in good part the poor quality and unreliability of the other cars in the line, as compared with the high quality and reliability of Buick and Cadillac; the effect of these factors was intensified by the stress of the general economic slump. Given the fact of the slump and the unavoidability of a general decline in sales, the relative decline of one division as compared with another was a question of management.

The slump had the effect of showing up all kinds of weaknesses, as slumps usually do. General Motors in 1920 had enjoyed 17 per cent of the U.S. car and truck market; in 1921 we were on our way down to 12 per cent. Ford, on the other hand, was in the course of rising from 45 per cent of the market in units in 1920 to 60 per cent in 1921. In other words, Mr. Ford, whom no one had dared seriously to challenge in the low-price field since 1908, was tightening his grip while we were losing in unit volume as well as in the profitability of most of our divisions. All in all, with no position in the big-volume low-price field and no concept to guide our actions, we were in a bad situation. It was clear that we needed an idea for penetrating the low-price field, and for the deployment of the cars through the line as a whole; and we needed a research-and-development policy, a sales policy, and the like, to support whatever we did.

In view of these circumstances, it is hardly surprising that on April 6, 1921, the Executive Committee set up a special committee of the Advisory Staff, made up of experienced automobile men in management, to look into our product policy. This task was to be one of the most significant in the evolution of the corporation. The members of the committee were C. S. Mott, then group executive for car, truck, and parts operations; Norval A. Hawkins, who had been chief of Ford sales before joining General Motors; C. F. Kettering of General Motors research; H. H. Bassett, general manager of Buick; K. W. Zimmerschied, newly appointed general manager of Chevrolet, and myself from the Executive Committee. Since I was in charge of the Advisory Staff when the special committee was formed and the senior member of the committee, its work came under my jurisdiction. About a month later we had completed our study, and on June 9 I presented our recommendations to the Executive Committee, where they were approved and became the adopted policy of the corporation. The recommendations outlined the basic product policy of the corporation, a market strategy, and some first principles; all together they expressed the concept of the business.

The general historical circumstances described above had much to do with the nature of the recommendations. And there were other circumstances in the internal situation in General Motors which influenced what we had to say. In the first place the Executive Committee had instructed the special committee that the corporation intended to enter the low-price field—that is, that it intended to make a competitive challenge to the dominance of Ford. The Executive Committee asked the special committee for advice on this question, and suggested that cars be designed and built in two low-price ranges, the lower of which would compete with Ford. They also asked for a discussion at some later time of other price areas. They excluded, however, any changes in the successfully established positions of Buick and Cadillac.

The seeds of a great controversy in the corporation had been sown a few weeks earlier when the Executive Committee, led by Pierre S. du Pont, decided that the corporation should make its entrance into the low-price field with a new and revolutionary kind of car, discussed in detail in the next chapter. This car appeared to have exciting new potentialities, but I had some reservations about our ability to solve all the engineering problems it raised. Indeed a paramount reason for making a product policy explicit, from my point of view, was to bring the automobile men into the discussion. Other immediate circumstances also had a bearing on that discussion, among them an impending shakeout of the divisions forming the old car line, and a need we all felt for ground rules, that is, for first principles that would be acceptable to all in debate. And in order that the new product policy should be considered not just alone but in its essential relations to the over-all objectives of the corporation, we undertook to draw the whole picture and put all the known pieces into it.

Thus the new management took the opportunity that comes rarely in the initial stage of a business, to stand back and review aims and deal with the matters at hand both in particular and with a considerable degree of generalization. It was not going to be easy to get willing agreement on specific and immediate issues. For example, the idea of the revolutionary car was very much entrenched in the Executive Committee, and I wanted to broaden the concept of the product to the concept of the business. I believe it was for this reason that we on the special committee first idealized the problem. We started not with the actual corporation but with a model of a corporation, for which we said we would state policy standards.

Our aim we said was to chart the true best course for the future operations of this model corporation, recognizing that present actual conditions necessitated sailing off the recommended course temporarily until it became practicable to put any adopted policy standard into full effect. To this end we made the assumptions of the business process itself explicit. We presumed that the first purpose in making a capital investment is the establishment of a business that will both pay satisfactory dividends and preserve and increase its capital value. The primary object of the corporation, therefore, we declared was to make money, not just to make motor cars. Positive statements like this have a flavor that has gone out of fashion; but I still think that the ABC's of business have merit for reaching policy conclusions. General Motors had collected a number of profitless motor cars since 1908, and a few were still being produced. The problem was to design a product line that would make money. The future of the corporation and its earning power, we asserted, depended upon its ability to design and produce cars of maximum utility value in quantity at minimum cost. You can't really simultaneously maximize utility and minimize cost, but it was a manner of speaking for what nowadays we refer to more precisely as the optimizing of conflicting functions. To raise the utility and lower the cost of our cars, one of our first conclusions was that the number of models and the duplication that then existed within the corporation should be limited. By such economizing, which has taken various forms through the years, the corporation, I believe, has rendered the service to the public that all must give in the long run to succeed in business.

The prevailing concept in the Executive Committee was to meet Ford more or less head on with a revolutionary car design. Certainly Ford looked unbeatable by any ordinary means. There may also have been opinion among some in the corporation that to enter the low-price precincts on any basis would waste the resources we had gained elsewhere. In any case, we had given to us in our directive a volume product policy, namely, to sell cars in the low-price area,

where there were buyers. The real question for the special committee was how to do it. Our answer was to accept the concept of a
new car design but to place it in the perspective of a broad product
policy.

The product policy we proposed is the one for which General
Motors has now long been known. We said first that the corporation should produce a line of cars in each price area, from the lowest price up to one for a strictly high-grade quantity-production car,
but we would not get into the fancy-price field with small production; second, that the price steps should not be such as to leave
wide gaps in the line, and yet should be great enough to keep their
number within reason, so that the greatest advantage of quantity
production could be secured; and third, that there should be no
duplication by the corporation in the price fields or steps.

These new policies never materialized precisely in this form—for
example, we always have had in fact duplication and competition
between the divisions—yet essentially the new product policy differentiated the new General Motors from the old, and the new General Motors from the Ford organization of the time and from other
car manufacturers. Naturally we thought that this policy was superior to competing policies in the industry and would win over
them. Again let me say that companies compete in broad policies
as well as in specific products. In the perspective of so many years
gone by, the idea of this policy seems pretty simple, like a shoe
manufacturer proposing to sell shoes in more than one size. But it
certainly did not seem simple at the time, when Ford had more
than half the market with two grades (the high-volume, low-priced
Model T, and the low-volume, high-priced Lincoln), and Dodge,
Willys, Maxwell (Chrysler), Hudson, Studebaker, Nash, and
others had substantial positions in the industry and were making or
preparing powerful bids with other product policies. For all we
knew then, our policy might not have worked best. If the industry
had thought it would work, the others would have adopted it at the
time. The same policy was available to all, but for a number of years
General Motors alone was to pursue it and prove its worthiness.

In drawing the whole picture of the policy we integrated into it
other possible valid criteria—possible, that is, in the sense that they
might be used as individual criteria. For example, the policy we
said was valid if our cars were at least equal in design to the best
of our competitors in a grade, so that it was not *necessary* to lead

in design or run the risk of untried experiments. Certainly I preferred this concept to an irrevocable commitment to replace the then standard Chevrolet with a revolutionary car. Such a car would be fine if it worked, but I preferred to rest first on a broad business strategy; and, as the policy was adopted, it is evident that Pierre S. du Pont also subscribed to the general concept at least in principle. We of the special committee of course acknowledged that General Motors automobiles could reasonably be expected to be made pre-eminent in all grades. We argued that the breadth of the car line would give us this capability, though of course our then 12 per cent of the market gave us no particular advantage in this respect. We figured that in product line and in quality standards we were, or could become, as good as anybody in whatever they were good at and better at what they were not good at.

The same idea held for production, where of course we had to have Ford in mind. We pointed out that it was not *essential* that, for any particular car, production be more efficient than that of its best competitor, or for that matter that the advertising, selling, and servicing methods in any particular product be better than its competitors. The fundamental conception of the advantage to be secured in this business, we said, was expressed by co-operation and co-ordination of our various policies and divisions. It was natural to expect that co-ordinated operation of our plants should result in greater efficiency than was the case when the divisions were working at cross purposes, and the same could be said for engineering and other functions. By raising our own standards in this way, we could reasonably expect to equal the best, in any respect, that our competition in any grade had to offer, and to exceed it in some respects. Under a plan of co-operation, the teamwork could thus attain increased volume at reduced cost. And so, at a time when we sold only a small proportion of all U.S. cars and trucks, we nonetheless believed that, with a federated policy in a business of wide scope, General Motors cars in the future would be made pre-eminent in engineering in all grades, and could similarly achieve unquestioned leadership in production, advertising, selling, and other functions.

Having set forth these concepts, we then approved the resolution of the Executive Committee, which had been passed on to us to study, to the effect that a car should be designed and built to sell for not more than $600; and that another car should be designed and built to sell for not more than $900. The special committee further recommended four additional models, each to be kept strictly within the price range specified. It also recommended that the policy of the corporation should be to produce and market only six standard models, and that as soon as practicable the following grades should constitute the entire line of cars.

(a)	$450 —	$600
(b)	$600 —	$900
(c)	$900 —	$1200
(d)	$1200 —	$1700
(e)	$1700 —	$2500
(f)	$2500 —	$3500

This brand-new, hypothetical price structure, when compared with General Motors' actual price brackets listed earlier in this chapter, will be seen to reduce the car lines from seven to six (or ten to six cars if the Chevrolet "FB" and the Olds "6" and "8" are considered separate cars, as they pretty much were). It opened up one new classification on the low end of the list where we had none. And where we had eight cars in the middle, above the lowest price and below the highest, we now had only four classifications. The new set of price classes meant that the General Motors car line should be integral, that each car in the line should properly be conceived in its relationship to the line as a whole.

Having thus separated out a set of related price classes, we set forth an intricate strategy which can be summarized as follows: We proposed in general that General Motors should place its cars at the top of each price range and make them of such a quality that they would attract sales from below that price, selling to those customers who might be willing to pay a little more for the additional quality, and attract sales also from above that price, selling to those customers who would see the price advantage in a car of close to the quality of higher-priced competition. This amounted to quality competition against cars below a given price tag, and price competition against cars above that price tag. Of course, a competitor could respond in kind, but where we had little volume we could thereby chip away an increase from above and below, and where we had volume it was up to us to maintain it. Unless the number of models was limited, we said, and unless it were planned that each model should cover its own grade and also overlap into the

grades above and below its price, a large volume could not be secured for each car. This large volume, we observed, was necessary
to gain the advantages of quantity production, counted on as a most
important factor in earning a position of pre-eminence in all the
grades.

The product policy also took up specifically the problem of penetrating the low-price field, a special case of the general concept.
The field for cars of the first grade, we noted, was then practically
monopolized by the Ford, and we were trying to invade it. We
recommended that General Motors should not attempt to build and
sell a car of the precise Ford level, as the Ford sold at the lowest
price within the first grade. Instead the corporation should market
a car much better than the Ford, with a view to selling it at or near
the top price in the first grade. We did not propose to compete head
on with the Ford grade, but to produce a car that would be superior
to the Ford, yet so near the Ford price that demand would be drawn
from the Ford grade and lifted to the slightly higher price in preference to Ford's then utility design.

We observed that the converse of this effect would be produced
when the new General Motors low-price car, selling at the top of
the lowest price range in the table ($600), was compared with cars
of competitors in the next higher grade, selling at $750 or slightly
below. Even though the new General Motors low-price car might
not have quite the quality of competing cars selling at approximately
$750, it should be so near the grade of competing cars selling at
the middle of the second price range that prospective buyers would
prefer to save $150 and to yield the comparatively slight preference
they might have for the competing car if the prices were nearly
equal.

The specific competitive aim of the new product policy at that
time is evident in the lowest price classification set up for the
model corporation. In this classification General Motors did not
have a car to offer in April 1921. The only car available in this area
was the Ford. Furthermore, in the second-lowest classification only
Chevrolet and Willys-Overland offered a car. Thus the policy was
directed at supplying a car to be put into competition solely with
the chief product of the then leading car manufacturer in the United
States and the world.

As it happened, actual car prices in all categories fell rapidly in
1921, collapsing the whole price structure that existed in the market

in April, when we formulated the policy. But, while actual levels became different, the aim of the policy remained the same, namely to move into the relatively lower price areas. Indeed, by September 1921 the price of the Chevrolet "490" touring car was down from $820 (January 1921 price) to $525, while the Ford Model T was down from $440 to $355. But the Ford price did not include demountable rims and self-starter, as Chevrolet did, so that on a comparable-equipment basis there was in September only about $90 difference between Ford and Chevrolet. This difference was still relatively considerable, but the Chevrolet was beginning to move in the direction indicated in the product policy. Thus, this policy, by opening up new low-price areas, foreshadowed the challenge that General Motors was actually to make to the dominance of Ford.

The placement of actual products in these price ranges was made by the committee, from bottom to top as follows: Chevrolet, Oakland, a new Buick 4, Buick 6, Olds, and Cadillac. In 1921 we sold Sheridan and took steps to dissolve Scripps-Booth, and in 1922 we dropped the Chevrolet "FB." Only the price-class positions of Chevrolet and Cadillac, as it turned out, were to be permanent.

The core of the product policy lies in its concept of mass-producing a full line of cars graded upward in quality and price. This principle supplied the first element in differentiating the General Motors concept of the market from that of the old, Ford Model T concept. Concretely, the General Motors concept provided the strategy for putting Chevrolet into competition with the Model T. Without this policy of ours, Mr. Ford would not have had any competition in his chosen field at that time.

In 1921 Ford had about 60 per cent of the total car and truck market in units, and Chevrolet had about 4 per cent. With Ford in almost complete possession of the low-price field, it would have been suicidal to compete with him head on. No conceivable amount of capital short of the United States Treasury could have sustained the losses required to take volume away from him at his own game. The strategy we devised was to take a bite from the top of his position, conceived as a price class, and in this way build up Chevrolet volume on a profitable basis. In later years, as the consumer upgraded his preference, the new General Motors policy was to become critically attuned to the course of American history.

But although this concept gave us direction, it was, as it turned out, formulated before its time. It took a number of events in the automobile market to give full substance to its principles. Also, a number of events in General Motors, particularly with respect to research and development—that is, the revolutionary car—were to hold up the application of the concept and keep General Motors in suspense for the next couple of years.

Chapter 5

THE "COPPER-COOLED" ENGINE

LOGICALLY one might suppose that, upon the adoption of the concept of management and the concept of the car business, the new administration should have proceeded forthwith to translate them into realities. Such, however, was not the case. Indeed, for the next two and a half years—that is, for most of the first definable period of the new administration—we departed from and even violated those first principles. In other words, the logic of the mind and the "logic" of history were not of the same order. This chapter is a painful one in the General Motors story, but I see no way to avoid it if I am to account for General Motors' progress. For, as often happens, the lessons of such experience are the best-learned lessons. The years 1921 and 1922 fortunately offered time to spare for a schooling that was to have a considerable part in shaping the future of the corporation.

The problem was one of conflict between the research organization and the producing divisions, and of a parallel conflict between the top management of the corporation and the divisional management. The subject of the conflict was a revolutionary car with an air-cooled engine of Mr. Kettering's design, which Pierre S. du Pont proposed as a replacement for the corporation's conventional cars with water-cooled engines.

The story begins in 1918 when Mr. Kettering began experimenting with an air-cooled engine in one of his workshops in Dayton. An air-cooled automotive engine was not unknown. Earlier ones were then in use in the United States in the Franklin car and others. The principle of air-cooling as we knew it was to draw off the heat of the engine through its walls by attaching fins to the walls and blowing air over them with a fan. The Franklin tried to do this with cast-iron fins. Mr. Kettering proposed to use copper fins, the conductivity of copper being ten times that of cast iron, and to braze or weld the fins to the engine walls. This involved new technology both in engines and in metallurgy. Mr. Kettering found a number of difficult design problems in the area of expansion and contraction of the two metals, but he had in mind and under test, solutions to the problems of design; problems of production were still another matter and of course belonged to a later stage of development.

The air-cooled engine offered an attractive prospect. It would get rid of the cumbersome radiator and plumbing system of the water-cooled engine and promised to reduce the number of parts in the engine, its weight, and its cost, and at the same time to improve engine performance. If it fulfilled all these promises it would indeed revolutionize the industry. But it is a long way from principle to reality in engine design; one has only to observe the years and engineering man-hours taken to develop practical jet and rocket motors, or to note that the water-cooled internal-combustion engine had come to its 1921 level of efficiency after constant development by an entire industry since the late nineteenth century. Nevertheless, though he had been at it only a short time, Mr. Kettering's convictions regarding his new air-cooled engine were optimistic; and he had then a very considerable reputation in the automotive field because of his pioneering work on the self-starter and ignition and lighting systems, and in the aviation field where he was so far ahead as to have experimented with a pilotless plane.

Mr. Kettering came before the Finance Committee on August 7, 1919, to explain the work he was doing on the air-cooled engine and on fuel research—to result later in tetraethyl lead for gasoline (ethyl gas)—at the Dayton Metal Products Company and the Dayton Wright Airplane Company. I had some part in the preliminaries of this meeting. I had known Mr. Kettering since 1916, when his Dayton Engineering Laboratories Company came into United Motors, and had kept in touch with his work. On the day before the meeting of the Finance Committee, Mr. Kettering had met with Harold E. Talbott, president of Dayton Metal Products Company, Mr. Haskell, Mr. Raskob, and myself to work out arrangements for General Motors to purchase the assets of the Dayton companies— Domestic Engineering Company, Dayton Metal Products Company, and Dayton Wright Airplane Company. The thing was wrapped up at the committee's meeting of August 26, 1919. There Mr. Durant and Mr. du Pont reported on the Dayton situation, saying, "that Mr. Charles F. Kettering . . . is the center of this situation; that the obtaining of Mr. Kettering's entire time and attention is of prime importance, it being desired to place him in charge of the new Detroit laboratory . . . and that in the opinion of Mr. Durant, Mr. Haskell, Mr. Sloan, Mr. Chrysler and others Mr. Kettering is by far the most valuable man known to this Corporation for the position . . ." The Finance Committee minutes then say:

The Committee was advised by the President [Mr. Durant] regarding the air-cooled engine which is being developed by the Dayton Metal Products Company and the possible future thereof, it appearing that this invention has as yet not progressed to the point where its success is absolutely assured but that its chances of proving successful are favorable and that in this event our investment will provide a splendid financial return.

So it was that we got Mr. Kettering's services, the Dayton properties, and the air-cooled engine; and a good deal of General Motors' history was set in motion.

More than a year went by and much water went under the bridge, as I have related. On December 2, 1920, shortly after Mr. du Pont became president of General Motors, Mr. Kettering reported to him: "The small air-cooled engine of the Ford type is now ready to push toward a production basis." Mr. Kettering suggested that a few cars be made and tested, and that if they were satisfactory a number of cars, 1500 or 2000, might be made ready for the market in 1921.

A few days later, on December 7, 1920, a party of us made a trip to Dayton to look things over there. Pierre S. du Pont, John J. Raskob, J. A. Haskell, K. W. Zimmerschied, who was general manager of Chevrolet, C. D. Hartman, Jr., secretary of the Finance Committee, and myself, went down together. On the train to and from Dayton we discussed a number of things, among them the air-cooled engine. A record of the discussion says:

After careful consideration it was the consensus of opinion that the new car being developed at Dayton should be tested in adequate numbers and under the most rigorous conditions before undertaking to exploit the type in any degree. When satisfied as to the merits of the product, it will be adapted for the Chevrolet line, and will replace the present 490 model.

The "490" was then the standard lower-priced Chevrolet in our line, potentially though not then actually competitive with Ford. The question of a new engine for it was a big thing, conceivably a decisive one for General Motors in the high-volume market.

It is not surprising, therefore, that on January 19, 1921, at one of its earliest meetings, the new Executive Committee agreed upon making a comparative study of the air-cooled engine and the existing water-cooled Chevrolet "490." It was the consensus of the committee that no material changes in the "490" were possible for the next model year, beginning in the autumn of 1921, "and that it would be well to await future developments in the air-cooled engine before deciding upon the changes to be made for the production year beginning August 1922." Thus we decided to "await" the air-cooled car and in the interim to do nothing to develop the old, water-cooled "490" model. I say "we decided," for the Executive Committee always made decisions as a body.

Two weeks later we moved to a firmer position, resolving "that it is our intention that the air-cooled engine be developed first for a low-priced car and that it be made in the Chevrolet Division, and that Messrs. Kettering and Zimmerschied be informed of this opinion." This was virtually an order, and so far as Chevrolet was concerned the die was cast.

In another two weeks the Executive Committee expanded its position with a proposal to take a second car, the Oakland, into the air-cooled program with a new six-cylinder engine. The Executive Committee, however, noted "great uncertainty" within itself on the question and ordered a report on it from the Advisory Staff, of which I was then the head. If I am not mistaken in memory, the "great uncertainty" among the four of us on the committee was mainly in my mind. This will become clear later. But the committee was led with a firm hand by the president, Mr. du Pont. He pressed for the air-cooled program, upon the advancement of which he had by this time set his mind.

Another week later, on February 23, 1921, at a meeting from which I was absent, the Executive Committee moved on quickly to new decisions: "It was assumed," the minutes say, "that the 4 cylinder air cooled car now under study and development would occupy the lowest price field; that second to this would be a 6 cylinder air cooled car, selling in the neighborhood of $900. to $1000." Mr. Kettering was ordered to "proceed with the design and construction of the 6 cylinder air cooled car." But, the committee said, "no quantity production should be attempted until success had been established, by a thorough test of a few [trial] cars." Mr. Kettering, who was present along with Mr. Mott and Mr. Bassett, said he expected to know the merits of both cars by July 1, 1921, and that preparations for the manufacture of the air-cooled "4" could be started on August 1 with a view to bringing out the car about January 1, 1922. Mr. Zimmerschied of Chevrolet was called in and told about the program for his division. He demurred, saying he desired to prepare for production of the air-cooled "4" in August 1922. He said he had improved the water-cooled "490" and had designed a new body for it. The Executive Committee and the Chevrolet Division were thus revealed as moving in different directions.

Mr. Kettering had test cars of both types in operation in Dayton in May 1921 and reported that either the "4" or "6" could be first to come out. On June 7 the Executive Committee agreed that a small manufacturing section—a kind of pilot operation—should be created at the General Motors Research Corporation (later called our Research Laboratories) in Dayton, with a maximum production of not more than twenty-five cars a day.

About this time Mr. Zimmerschied's reservations regarding the air-cooled Chevrolet crystallized, and the divisional problem, so to speak, thereby came to the foreground, where it was to remain for some time. Circumstance had dictated that Buick, which was doing well, should be left for the time being more or less in its former, wholly decentralized state, and with its own program. But notwithstanding our concept of organization and directly contrary to it, expediency was permitted to centralize the affairs of other divisions. This trend was made emphatic by the decision of the top officers to impose a radical car design upon two divisions, Chevrolet and Oakland. The Executive Committee thus made both the policy and the program for these divisions on the most significant question that can come before a division, namely its engine and car design. The Executive Committee had that privilege, and in the circumstances it elected to exercise it. The difficulty lay not only in the question of whether the decision regarding the new car was sound, but in how to get it carried out where it had to be carried out, namely, in the divisions. In extenuation of what was done, I should say that this was the first time, to my knowledge, in the history of General Motors that intimate co-operation was called for between the Research Corporation and the divisions on an important problem, and no established means existed by which this co-operation was to function. Since the initial production as well as the creation of the design was assigned to Mr. Kettering's research group in Dayton and the actual mass production was assigned to the divisions, the responsibilities were blurred. Mr. Zimmerschied wanted to know who was adviser to whom on production: Research to the car division or the car division to Research? Even if there had been no question as to the merits of the new design, this would have represented a problem in management. As it was, there was skepticism at Chevrolet about the new engineering design, and anxiety at the Dayton laboratories that the car divisions would change the design. Divisional engineers and the general managers traveled back and forth between their home bases and Dayton, and in the course of these visits Mr. Kettering observed that George H. Hannum, general manager of Oakland, was more sympathetic to the new car. Mr. Kettering also thought that he could have the air-cooled "6" ready for Oakland by the end of the year.

I was in Paris during the first part of July 1921, and on my return all four of us on the Executive Committee again traveled together to Dayton, arriving there on July 26. We met informally with Mr. Kettering and Mr. Mott, who was then group executive for the car divisions. Mr. Kettering's enthusiasm for the new car was stronger than ever: ". . . it is," he said, "the greatest thing that has ever been produced in the automobile world." Mr. du Pont left no doubt of his faith in this judgment. Mr. Kettering again noted the differences between the attitudes at Chevrolet and Oakland. Naturally he was anxious to work more closely with the division that expressed the greater sympathy, namely, Oakland. A transcript of the meeting in Dayton says: "It was finally recommended that the 6 cyl. car be pushed ahead and that the 4 cyl. car be held up for the time being as it was felt that they could profit by their experience on the '6' when producing the '4' . . ." Mr. Zimmerschied of Chevrolet, it was believed, could be sold on the air-cooled "4" engine after the validity of the "6" was established. Chevrolet anyway, Mr. Mott said, had an inventory of about 150,000 "490's" which still needed to be liquidated.

This temporizing attitude toward Chevrolet was not permitted to last long. A few weeks later Mr. du Pont presented to the Executive Committee a general review of the product situation in General Motors with proposals for a definitive corporation program. He reaffirmed the decisions regarding the air-cooled "6" for Oakland. When he came to Chevrolet, he wrote: "It [the '490'] is not to be continued in production beyond the time necessary to reduce inventories and commitments. Immediate decision upon a new car for permanent manufacture is necessary." The air-cooled "4," he said, was to be "the adopted standard for the Chevrolet Division unless a definite change of policy should be made," and it should be ready for production before May 1, 1922. The Executive Committee as a body concurred.

The development work on the new engine continued at Dayton through the fall of 1921, and at the same time studies were made concerning new plants, conversion of plants, and marketing programs for the air-cooled cars. As the time for the delivery of the first test car from Dayton to the Oakland Division grew near, there was a growing atmosphere of expectancy in the New York and Detroit offices. Mr. du Pont wrote to Mr. Kettering, "Now that we are at the point of planning production of the new cars I am beginning to feel like a small boy when the long expected circus posters begin to appear on the fences, and to wonder how each part of the circus is to appear and what act I will like best."

Specific dates for the Oakland schedule were officially set by the Executive Committee on October 20, 1921, as follows:

Production of the existing water-cooled car to be stopped on December 1, 1921.

New air-cooled cars, made in Dayton, to be introduced at the New York Automobile Show in January 1922.

Production of the new car to begin at the Oakland Division in Pontiac, Michigan, in February at one hundred a day and to increase thereafter.

No further questions on program remained, it seemed.

The first air-cooled car then was sent from Dayton to the Oakland Division for test. This was the first evaluation of the validity of the air-cooled car outside of the test cars operated by Mr. Kettering in Dayton. There was a pause, and then shock. Word came that the car had failed its tests at the Oakland Division.

On November 8, 1921, Mr. Hannum wrote to Mr. du Pont:

With the changes that are necessary to make this a real job, it is going to be impossible to get into production in the time specified, in fact, to get this car to the point where, after all tests are complete and we are ready to put our O. K. on same, it will take at least six months.

To bridge the time when the present allotment of the old models are completed, which will be about Dec. 15th, and the time we bring in the Air Cooled Car, we are planning on bringing in a complete new [water-cooled] line . . .

I want to say further the changes which we have in mind for the Air Cooled Job have not changed my views of the proposition in the least, as I believe, when we get the first job on the road, with the changes incorporated, there will be a great change in the test reports.

Thus in less than a month the adopted schedule of the corporation was overthrown and the whole situation with respect to Oakland and the future General Motors product line had profoundly changed. There was disappointment and alarm in New York and pessimism in Detroit, Flint, and Pontiac concerning the outlook for the air-cooled car. Between Dayton and the manufacturing divisions controversy and confusion arose over the testing of the new car; there was no meeting of minds between Mr. Kettering's designers on the one hand and the divisional engineers and general managers on the other. Mr. Kettering felt fatigue and was so discouraged that the Executive Committee, upon officially canceling the Oakland air-cooled schedule on November 30, 1921, sent him a letter of confidence, as follows:

Dear Kettering:—

It is most important in our opinion that your mind be kept free from worries foreign to the development of the air cooled car and other laboratory work.

In the development and introduction of anything so radically different from standard practice as the air cooled car is from the regular water cooled job, it is quite natural that there should be a lot of "wiseacres" and "know-it-alls" standing around knocking the development.

In order that your mind may be completely relieved as to the position of the undersigned with respect to the air cooled development, we beg to advise as follows:—

1st. We are absolutely confident in your ability to whip all problems in connection with the development of our proposed air cooled cars.

2nd. We will continue to have this degree of confidence and faith in you and your ability to accomplish this task until such time as we come to you and frankly state that we have doubts as to the possibility or feasibility of turning the trick and you will be the first one to whom we will come.

We are endeavoring in this letter to use language such as will result in complete elimination of worry on your part with respect to our faith in you and this work and if this language fails to create this result, then won't you kindly write us quite frankly advising in what respect we have failed?

Due to the fact that criticisms are bound to continue until the air cooled cars are in active production and use, would it not be well for you to agree with us that at any time you have occasion to pause and wonder about our faith and confidence in you and this development, that you will pull this letter out of your desk and read it again, after which you will write to us in consideration of our frankly stating that we will write to you first in case of any doubt?

The letter was signed individually by the four members of the Executive Committee and by C. S. Mott, who as I have said was the group executive for the car divisions.

The crisis passed. The president's faith in the new engine was restored, Mr. Kettering revived his interest and energies, and the scene shifted from Oakland to Chevrolet.

On December 15, 1921, the Executive Committee proposed a strong effort to get the Chevrolet air-cooled "4" into production by September 1, 1922. To reconcile the divisions and research, O. E. Hunt, chief engineer of Chevrolet, and B. Jerome and E. A. De Waters, chief engineers representing Oakland and Buick, respectively, were sent to Dayton to collaborate with Mr. Kettering on the design of the air-cooled "4" and "6." Daily test reports were requested to be sent to the division managers and to the president.

The year 1921 closed with no definable progress in the General Motors product line.

These events bothered me to the extent that I attempted to raise them to a higher level in my mind with a view to taking them up with the Executive Committee. I did not feel strongly one way or the other about the technical question of an air-cooled versus a water-cooled engine. That was an engineering matter, for engineers. If I have any opinion today it is that Mr. Kettering may have been right in principle and ahead of his time, and that the divisions were right from a development and production standpoint. In other words, in this kind of situation it is possible for the doctors to disagree and still all be right. From a business and management standpoint, however, we were acting at variance with our doctrines. We were, for example, more committed to a particular engineering design than to the broad aims of the enterprise. And we were in the situation of supporting a research position against the judgment of the division men who would in the end have to produce and sell the new car. Meanwhile, obsolescence was overtaking our conventional water-cooled models and there was nothing in the official program to protect their position.

Late in December 1921, having in mind the breakdown of the test at Oakland and the problems that the proposed new car had created, I wrote some notes to myself to clarify in my mind the problems of the corporation, with a view to discussing them with Pierre S. du Pont. Regarding the Dayton situation, I said:

I believe that considerable time has been lost in the development of the air-cooled car through lack of appreciation, undoubtedly on the part of all of us, that certain fundamental facts do not, to any extent, subscribe to the contentions of Mr. Kettering—that everybody in General Motors must be sold on the details of his proposed car. I believe that if he had developed a car and demonstrated its performance or it had demonstrated its performance in the hands of independent observers and that he had left the production of the car to others as a principle, that we would have been farther ahead. I think we have made a mistake in putting it all up to Mr. Kettering and not recognizing his particular and peculiar situation. I believe that the Corporation needs and the industry needs advanced engineering. We are not going to get advanced engineering from a mediocre mind such as the average of our engineers compared with that of Mr. Kettering. Advanced engineering always, like advanced everything else, brings down upon it the discredit of ridicule of minds who cannot see so far. For all this reason, such engineering must be demonstrated in such a way that the facts must be accepted rather than theories. I do not think that there would have been any trouble in Oakland or that any changes would have been suggested had Mr. Kettering waited until he had a car that would demonstrate a reasonable satisfactory performance. I fear that the way this is working will result in the loss of a great many of the ideas that we need so badly and can only accept from a man of Mr. Kettering's marvelous ability.

The writing of this memorandum served mainly to mark a turning point in my conduct concerning the air-cooled engine. I began then to pursue a dual policy: first, continuing to support Mr. du Pont's and Mr. Kettering's hopes for the new car, and second, giving support to the divisions in the development of alternate programs of the conventional water-cooled type. And, incidentally, on the side, for a while Mr. Zimmerschied and I looked into a new "Muir" steam-cooling system, which never went into production. While Mr. du Pont had no enthusiasm for alternatives to the air-cooled engine, he did not forbid my taking this position. We simply worked along somewhat different lines. But such a situation between the two leading members of the operating organization was not entirely comfortable and could not last forever.

For the next sixteen months the air-cooled car continued to distract the corporation and to keep its leading officers in a state of tension over the question of what the future product of the corporation was to be.

At the beginning of 1922, the pressure on Chevrolet for the new car was increased, while that on Oakland was somewhat relieved. I took a first step toward the compromise which I felt was necessary to protect the corporation in the event of failure of the new program, and to bridge the gap that had opened between top management and the divisions. As vice president of operations I held a meeting in my room in the Hotel Statler in Detroit on January 26, 1922, with Mr. Mott (car group executive), Mr. Bassett (Buick), and Mr. Zimmerschied (Chevrolet), and reached an understanding that the official air-cooled program for Chevrolet was to be advanced, but with caution. The official program required that the experimental air-cooled "4" models under development at Dayton, "if proper, should be put in production by the Chevrolet Division as of September 1, 1922," that is, just seven months away, though the Chevrolet management had not yet received a test car from Dayton. We agreed, however, "that there is nothing before the Corporation or the Chevrolet Division at the present time to justify the positive conclusion that the air-cooled car should be put into production on the date specified," but that on April 1, 1922, after tests had been made, we could determine a safe program. At the same time we agreed that "a second line of defense should be prepared—this being only a conservative policy." The second line of defense was a parallel effort in the division to improve the existing water-cooled Chevrolet.

As to Oakland, on February 21, 1922, I reported to the Executive Committee and obtained approval to postpone a new schedule for the air-cooled "6," production of which had been canceled. For Oakland then we agreed:

1. To continue its recently established [water-cooled] models for a period of a year and a half, ending June 30, 1923.

2. To eliminate from consideration, as far as Oakland is concerned, the introduction of any air cooled model previous to that date.

3. That any design that Oakland may develop in the meantime will be in accordance with the program of designs already established by the Corporation.

4. That if the economic position of the Oakland models change[s] to the extent that the Division is unable to break even, steps will have to be taken at that time as seem best in view of all the circumstances prevailing at that time.

Since the Research Corporation at Dayton was the only substantial corporation-wide, staff engineering group in General Motors at the time, and it was occupied with the air-cooled-engine experiment, the advanced engineering for the water-cooled models devolved largely upon the divisions. All of the car divisions at that time were in need of advanced engineering staff work to make and keep their conventional cars competitive. At Chevrolet, Oakland, and Olds the need was acute. In other words, the divisions had to attend not only to their principal business of engineering, manufacturing, and selling current models, but to their own staff work on forward engineering as well. Not that matters had been any different in this area previously, but it was our intention to provide for comprehensive engineering staff work for the corporation. From the way in which the Research Corporation chose to operate—that is, as a long-range idea organization centering upon Mr. Kettering's unusual capabilities—it was evident that a gap had opened between his important function and the bread-and-butter type of advanced engineering. I did not then know that a historic distinction was being made in General Motors, but I saw the gap before me and on March 14, 1922, obtained approval of a policy of seeking outside engineering designs for the divisions. This policy would never solve the problem but it would help; many years would pass before the problem was entirely understood and met. Among those whom I consulted at that time was Henry Crane, who later came into the corporation as technical assistant to the president and contributed importantly to the corporation's engineering progress, especially in the design of the Pontiac car. O. E. Hunt had only recently—in October 1921—been brought by Mr. Zimmerschied into Chevrolet as chief engineer and I was not yet familiar with his fine capabilities.

The compromise between the air-cooled and water-cooled developments at Chevrolet was an uneasy one. It was soon accompanied by a change in management. On February 1, 1922, at Mr. Mott's suggestion, William S. Knudsen, who had formerly been Ford's production manager, was brought into the corporation's Advisory Staff and assigned as manufacturing assistant to Mr. Mott. Mr. Knudsen visited Dayton and on March 11 made a report on the air-cooled car, in which he recommended "that the car be put in production at once." He advised me, however, that he meant that production should be started in a small way to test the car both commercially and technically. On March 22 Mr. du Pont obtained the agreement of the Executive Committee to remove Mr. Zimmerschied from his post as general manager of Chevrolet and make him assistant to the president of General Motors; and to appoint Mr. Knudsen as vice president of operations at Chevrolet. Mr. du Pont also proposed to make himself general manager of the Chevrolet Division, while remaining chairman and president of the corporation, and it was agreed.

On April 7, 1922, at the president's request, we officially named the experimental development the "copper-cooled" instead of the "air-cooled" engine. Mr. du Pont wished to differentiate it from other systems of air-cooling. But Mr. Kettering continued to say "air-cooled."

Preparations for tooling up for production of the copper-cooled Chevrolet "4" began, with manufacture expected to start about September 15, 1922, at ten cars a day, increasing to fifty a day by the end of the year. The Canadian organization, too, was instructed to develop and introduce a copper-cooled "4." But the spring of 1922 passed without bringing any reality to the new programs. The copper-cooled engine remained under test at Dayton.

Spring sales of cars showed 1922 to be a year of fair recovery, and the Chevrolet "490," underdeveloped as it was in engineering design, was selling again. At a meeting in Detroit in May 1922—at which Mr. du Pont, Mr. Mott, Mr. Knudsen, Colin Campbell, then sales manager of Chevrolet, and I were present—Mr. Mott, with my support, proposed another compromise—namely, to put the new Chevrolet bodies, designed for the copper-cooled car, on the old "490" chassis in the fall, to make certain that we would have something new to sell for the next model year. Mr. Campbell opposed this, saying he was afraid to load up the dealers with "490's" during the winter and then give them copper-cooled cars in the spring of 1923. Again I tried to advance the policy of a dual program, saying: ". . . we should use the copper cooled car as an experiment until April 1st [1923]. Then, if it has become successful and is holding up in the field, increase production on the copper cooled jobs and on August 1st [1923] bring in the car as the sole product of the Chevrolet Division. If the car were not successful, we could continue to manufacture the 490s." The differences thus were laid on the table, but nothing was decided.

The parallel programs and proposals for programs created inevitable tensions in the corporation. Mr. Kettering continued to feel that the divisions were dragging their feet. Oakland, he observed, was now several months behind Chevrolet in the copper-cooled development, and Chevrolet plans, he said, were inadequate. He said in May of 1922 that he was working best with Robert Jack, chief engineer of Olds. Mr. du Pont supported Mr. Kettering's opinion of Chevrolet's plans and in June proposed a stiffening of the copper-cooled program at that division. Since chassis and body changes for the new engine were expected to be complete in the fall, and the change-over then would be concerned with the engine only, he recommended that production of the copper-cooled Chevrolet be scheduled for the forthcoming winter.

In September production had not begun, but the official expectations were optimistic. The plan for Chevrolet was to have a monthly capacity of 30,000 water-cooled and 12,000 copper-cooled cars by March 1923 and to convert the entire water-cooled production into copper-cooled by July or, at the latest, October 1923.

In November, Mr. Kettering noted a lack of interest in the copper-cooled car at Olds as well as at Oakland. I said to Mr. du Pont that I was fearful of the outcome of committing three main divisions to a new, untried engineering car design. Mr. du Pont pointed out to me that the decision had been made by the Executive Committee some months ago "and that the only decision left was the question of a change of front, or the abandonment absolutely of all experiments with water cooled and steam cooled cars." He agreed, however, that there would be no final determination with regard to Chevrolet until May 1, 1923. He then proposed that the Olds program be converted exclusively to copper-cooled.

Mr. du Pont's and my views were then expressed on November 16, 1922, in this compromise resolution of the Executive Committee:

RESOLVED, That the copper cooled program shall be as follows:

1. That the product of the Olds Division as of August 1st, 1923, shall be a six cylinder copper cooled car . . . All experiments and developments of water cooled motors shall be discontinued from this date (November 16th, 1922).

2. The Chevrolet Motor Division will proceed with the development of its copper cooled model cautiously, with a view to determining all factors involved, both commercially and technically, always recognized as being present in the development of any new product, in such a way that the hazard to the Corporation is at all times kept at a minimum.

3. The policy of the Oakland Division will be hereafter determined, but under no circumstances shall the Oakland Company put in production a copper cooled car of any kind or description until the position of the copper cooled car as a type is determined in a broad way by actual experience in the field of a sufficient number of cars, such experience being both of a technical and commercial nature.

Thus at the end of 1922 we were committed exclusively to the copper-cooled program at Olds, to a dual program at Chevrolet, and Oakland was exempted until the new car had proved itself. In December, Mr. Knudsen began to manufacture 250 copper-cooled cars at Chevrolet. The year 1922, like 1921, ended with uncertainty as to what the engineering design of the General Motors product was to be.

At the New York Automobile Show in January 1923 the copper-cooled Chevrolet—chassis and motor—was unveiled. It was priced at about $200 above the standard, water-cooled Chevrolet (now called the "Superior" model), and was the sensation of the show.

The schedule of the Chevrolet Division called for the manufacture of 1000 copper-cooled cars in February, with the monthly rate to increase to 50,000 in October. The only question that seemed to remain at the beginning of the new year regarding the water-cooled car was the exact date on which it should be abandoned.

But troubles appeared in the course of production and Chevrolet copper-cooled cars failed to appear in February in large numbers.

Two decisive events occurred simultaneously during the months of March, April, and May 1923. First, we found ourselves in the greatest boom year up to that time in automobile history, the beginning of the industry's first four-million car-and-truck year. Second, difficulties in production had slowed the manufacture of copper-cooled Chevrolets to a walk, and the few copper-cooled Chevrolets that were on the road and being checked by the division produced a large number of reports of troubles, indicating that they were still experimental, unproved, and in need of further development. The question of what to do required no great act of mind. The only Chevrolet we had to sell was the old, conventional water-cooled model. Although it was not a high-performance automobile, even for those days, the Chevrolet water-cooled "Superior" model had been improved and it was a workable car. It ran up record sales that spring.

One could feel that a new era in the demand for automobiles had opened up, and it was imperative that the corporation settle upon its product program for a future that would present itself but once. On May 10, 1923, Mr. du Pont resigned as president of General Motors and on his recommendation to the board I succeeded him in that office. We continued to disagree on the merits of the copper-cooled program, but it was left to me as chief executive officer to make the decisions.

At Olds, in accordance with prevailing policy, all work on the water-cooled car had stopped; the inventory of cars was being sold off at a loss of about fifty dollars a car while the division waited to go into production of the new copper-cooled "6" on August 1, 1923. But the troubles with the copper-cooled Chevrolet clearly threatened the validity of this program.

As president I was of course chairman of the Executive Committee—which was enlarged to include Fred Fisher, head of Fisher Body, and Mr. Mott—and at the first meeting at which I presided on May 18, 1923, I took up the Olds question. I stated the facts about the Olds situation and said: ". . . the continued delay in producing the Chevrolet copper-cooled car is a constant reminder of the uncertainties and the difficulties in engineering and manufacture which would most certainly delay the program and might lead to serious embarrassment to the Olds Motor Works organization at the factory and throughout the world." After a discussion with Mr. Kettering, Mr. Knudsen, and Mr. Hunt, we appointed a committee of three engineers—A. L. Cash, general manager of Northway, an engine-producing division of General Motors, Mr. Hunt, chief engineer of Chevrolet, and Mr. De Waters, chief engineer of Buick—and instructed them to report on the status of the six-cylinder copper-cooled engine. They presented their report to the Executive Committee at a meeting on May 28, 1923, from which Mr. du Pont, Mr. Haskell, and Mr. Raskob were absent. The report was the main business of the meeting. The engineers said:

That the [copper-cooled "6"] engine pre-ignites badly after driving at moderate speeds in air temperatures from sixty to seventy degrees. That it shows a serious loss of compression and power when hot, though the power is satisfactory when the engine is warming up from the cold condition.

These major difficulties plus several minor ones which can be reported in detail, if you so desire, lead us to the conclusion that the job is not in shape for immediate production. We recommend that we set it aside for further development and it be left out of consideration as far as immediate production is concerned.

Upon hearing this report the Executive Committee canceled the prevailing copper-cooled program at Olds and instructed the division to proceed with the development of a water-cooled engine that would be able to function on the copper-cooled chassis. We expressed confidence in the principle of copper-cooling as a longer-range development, and assigned the copper-cooled "6" engine to Mr. Cash for development at the Northway Division.

At Chevrolet 759 copper-cooled cars had been produced, of which 239 were scrapped by the production men. Of the balance, 500 were delivered to the sales organization. Of these about 150 were used by factory representatives. Something over 300 were sold to dealers, of which about 100 went to retail buyers. In June 1923 the Chevrolet Division decided to recall all of these copper-cooled cars from the field.

On June 26, 1923, in a letter to me, Mr. Kettering proposed to take the copper-cooled engine out of General Motors. He wrote:

We started out to do a perfectly definite thing, which has been done, and it is just the same now as it was a year ago, but in the transition stage certain factors have entered into this, which have confused the thing to the point where, unless things can be clarified, I believe the whole proposition should be dropped. If we cannot get some practical way of commercializing this product, in our own organization, I should like very much to discuss with you the possibility of taking this outside of the corporation and this is a thing which has come up within the last week. I am sure I can get capital and pretty much of an organization to go do this job the way in which I know it can be done.

It appears that he did not understand then that the copper-cooled Chevrolets had been withdrawn. Four days later, upon his learning of this decision, Mr. Kettering wrote to me again and proposed to resign from the corporation:

I have definitely made up my mind to leave the Corporation unless some method can be arranged to prevent the fundamental work done here from being thrown out and discredited through no fault of the apparatus . . .

I am perfectly sure that we can take any proposition and make out of it a 100% success, provided we do not have to overcome an organized resistance within the Corporation. This is impossible unless the Executive Committee can take it upon themselves to force through an Executive order when they know it is going to be of value to the Corporation.

I regret very much that this situation has developed. I have been extremely unhappy and know that I have made you and Mr. du Pont equally unhappy by my frequently discussing this matter with you. I am not temperamentally constituted where I can sit down and do nothing. I have never failed in any proposition that I have undertaken yet. The work here at the Laboratory, I realize, has been almost 100% failure, but not because of the fundamental principles involved. Enough may have come out of the Laboratories to have paid for their existence but no one will care to continue in Research activities as the situation now stands.

My only regret, in severing my connection with the Corporation, would be the wonderful association I have had with yourself, Mr. du Pont, Mr. Mott and others. There are many possibilities for work of the kind which I can do in industries where the problems which exist in getting new things over, are not quite as difficult as in the motor industry. Therefore, I hope, after reading this, that you can formulate some definite plan whereby either the situation within the Corporation can be cleared up or I can be relieved of my present duties. I would like to have some definite conclusion reached on this as soon as possible, as I would like to formulate definite plans.

Mr. Kettering was always very frank. In our forty years of friendship and association, he always spoke his mind clearly to me and I spoke the same way to him. I think that this was our worst moment. His biographer T. A. Boyd, has written: ". . . the discontinuance of the copper-cooled Chevrolet in the summer of 1923 was a staggering blow to him. It was then that his spirits reached the lowest point in his research career." I knew that. But I was as certain of the position I felt I had to take as he was of his, and of course we had different responsibilities. Management involves more than technical problems. I could not, as I saw it, in the face of an expanding market hold up the programs of the corporation for an uncertain development. If I had done so I do not believe there would be a General Motors today; we would have missed the boat. Furthermore, however sound the engine might have been in principle, it was not my policy then or at any time afterward to force on the divisions a thing of this kind against their judgment. On this question (though not on any other) there had unfortunately opened a wide gap in the corporation, with Mr. Kettering, his laboratories, and Mr. du Pont on one side, and myself and the divisions on the other. I was anxious to close it.

My problem was to reconcile Mr. Kettering's natural reactions and enthusiasm for his new idea with the realities in the case. The copper-cooled car had failed to meet the test of validity. It had failed at Oakland. It had been adjudged as needing further development by a joint study made by the chief engineers of Buick, Chevrolet, and Northway—a highly competent group. Sample cars produced by Chevrolet and sent into the field had been withdrawn because of various defects. The problem was complicated by the uncertainties of a new chassis as well as a new engine. We had to recognize that research engineers had little experience, relatively speaking, in chassis design as compared with the engineering staffs of the operating divisions. I had of necessity to respect all these facts and circumstances.

On July 2, 1923, I wrote Mr. Kettering a letter, from which I quote the following:

1. You say that you learned the day before yesterday that all Chevrolet cars were to be taken off the market. Now, you recollect in Mr. du Pont's office in Detroit it was agreed that the copper cooled Chevrolet car would be discontinued so far as further assembly is concerned and

assembly would not be started again until Messrs. Knudsen, Hunt and yourself reported to us that it was satisfactory to do this. You were a party to this you recollect, and it seemed after a very lengthy discussion in which many technicalities were brought up, that this was the right thing to do. At the same conference it was agreed that for the sales year beginning August 1st the copper cooled car would be continued and Mr. Campbell was authorized to write contracts both ways. You recollect that. Therefore, as a matter of fact, the Chevrolet position as agreed to at that conference is; first, that they would sell both cars during the sales year of 1923–4 and second, that no copper cooled would be assembled until it was further authorized. Therefore, you can see that they are in a rather embarrassing position. They are told that there will be two cars and yet they can only produce one. I just mention this so that there will be no misunderstanding.

2. It was called to my attention recently that there were 143 copper cooled cars out in the territory and it appeared to be desirable to withdraw them and reassemble them. In other words, it was thought desirable, in view of the fact that there were more or less complaints, not dealing with the engine particularly but dealing with the whole car, that they should be taken in and an adjustment made. There was nothing said that it was due to engine trouble or anything else. It simply seemed, all things considered, to be the desirable thing to do. You must appreciate that when these things are done the policy has to be worked out in detail and it is sometimes impossible to get all of the many people that have to carry out the thing to thoroughly understand and properly present the real reasons behind the policy.

I pass over matters which are not essential here and go on to the conclusion of my letter:

7. I do not agree with you that the situation is in any sense hopeless. I have great confidence in our organization, speaking of it as a whole. I think they are entitled to the credit that is due them and they are also entitled to the discredit of their shortcomings, if I might put it so. The great trouble is that there is an apparent lack of confidence in this copper cooled car and notwithstanding that the executives of the Corporation and the Executive Committee have tried to do their best to get it across, the fact that our Divisions have not believed in it so far has made it practically an impossible problem. That, as I see it, is the real problem before us. It is not the merits of the case and days and weeks spent over it will not alter the situation. What we have got to do is to make our people see the thing as you see it and with that accomplished then there will be nothing more to the problem. I do not think that forcing the

issue, is going to get us anywhere. We have tried that and we have failed. We have got to go at it in a different manner if we are going to succeed.

I have quoted from this letter at some length because of the various matters it brings up, most of which are self-evident, at least as to what my position was.

In an effort to relieve the tension I proposed a new development program for the copper-cooled car.

It appeared clear that one basic mistake was a divided responsibility. The Executive Committee, the operating divisions, and the Research Corporation, all with different viewpoints both within themselves and with each other, were trying to do an administrative job. It was clear that we now must get back to sound principles, concentrate the responsibility in a single place, and support that effort. My plan was to create an independent pilot operation under the sole jurisdiction of Mr. Kettering, a kind of copper-cooled-car division. Mr. Kettering would designate his own chief engineer and his production staff to solve the technical problems of manufacture, and his organization would market the copper-cooled cars. They would make a few, or many, as the circumstances dictated. Such a program would provide Mr. Kettering a free hand, without interference, to demonstrate successfully the validity of the concept in which he had so much confidence.

To appraise the new approach I called a meeting of Fred Fisher, Stewart Mott, and myself. We all were sympathetic to this proposed solution of the problem. I quote from a memorandum I sent to Mr. du Pont on July 6, 1923:

Mr. Fisher, Mr. Mott and myself had a long talk yesterday regarding a policy that would be more constructive and more fundamental than the one we have been pursuing heretofore. We feel that in forcing the Divisions to take something they do not believe in and in which there are certain argumentative points yet to be demonstrated, is not getting us anywhere and with the divided responsibility between the Chief Engineer and Mr. Kettering we are not going to get anywhere unless the responsibility is positively assured in the hands of one or the other party. We are most anxious to practically demonstrate the commercial value of the proposition and believe that the solution, practically determined upon subject to your approval, is the only way out.

We have discussed the matter with Mr. Kettering at some length this morning and he agrees with us absolutely on every point we make. He appears to receive the suggestion very enthusiastically and has every confidence that it can be put across along these lines. The plan is based upon the following principles:—

1. That as we stand today our efforts to commercially develop the copper cooled have resulted in a total loss and we feel that we are worse off than we were two years ago on account of the resistance which has been set up on account of our repeated failures.

2. That the engineering responsibility for putting the job across must be definitely centralized in one man.

3. That we feel that the only way to get the desired result is to establish an independent Operation with the sole purpose of commercially demonstrating the copper cooled idea.

4. Therefore, we have decided to set up a new Division at Dayton using a part of the Research Plant, especially that part which is being vacated by the Aeroplane Division, and we will set up an organization there which will be more or less of an assembly proposition. Mr. Kettering will have complete charge of the engineering side of it, operating through a Chief Engineer whom he will appoint.

5. The new Operation will take over the four cylinder copper cooled engine and probably the six cylinder Olds and will market these two copper cooled jobs under their own name, starting with five or ten a day and building up as the demand increases.

6. All tool equipment and inventory already developed will be available except so far as Mr. Kettering may determine to make changes.

7. The Operation will be of a specialty nature, putting an extra long price on the job on account of the comparatively small production and special nature of the power plant, adding attractive features to the body which we feel sure will get the job across.

Mr. Fisher, Mr. Mott and myself feel that this is the only way out and place the responsibility where it belongs and eliminate all confusion with the other Divisions who can go ahead about their business in their own way as they have very big problems to work out to maintain their present position for the future. I believe that it is useless to attempt to establish an agreement between Mr. Kettering and Mr. Hunt or Mr. Kettering and anyone else on these various technical points involved in the copper cooled development. They never will agree and one or the other must be required to work the thing out largely in his own way along lines that commend itself to his judgment.

Mr. du Pont did not approve of this plan to segregate the copper-cooled development from the divisions and their large sales organizations, but in the end he accepted it. With the burden of the copper-cooled development placed in Dayton under Mr. Kettering's jurisdiction, and the car divisions cleared to proceed on standard water-cooled programs, I wrote on July 25, 1923, a memo of review to the members of the Executive Committee, from which I quote the following:

Two and a half years have elapsed since the reconstruction of General Motors commenced and in that time, due to the jam we have got into on account of the copper cooled, the position of our Chevrolet car has not made the progress that I think it should have made. Certainly every step that has been taken has been carefully considered and many reasons could be ascribed to this result and probably there would be some difference of opinion as to what really has contributed to the cause, but nevertheless the fact remains, and the object of this memorandum is to simply point out certain advantages that would accrue had we an intensively developed model at this time or what we can expect to gain by getting such a model at the earliest possible moment. Undoubtedly all these advantages, or certainly the most important ones would be available if the power plant was copper cooled as well as water cooled because I do not think that the real difference between the two designs would be material other than that the copper cooled would eliminate water which, if all other conditions were the same, would undoubtedly be a step in advance.

This memorandum was not a mere expression of regret for lost time but a preamble to a new program of advance with new designs for the water-cooled Chevrolet that would be put into competition in the low-price, high-volume market in accordance with the product plan of 1921.

The copper-cooled car never came up again in a big way. It just died out, I don't know why.[1] The great boom was on and meeting the demand for cars and meeting the competition with improved water-cooled car designs absorbed our attention and energies.

Mr. Kettering and his staff went on to their great achievements in creating and developing tetraethyl lead, high-compression engines, nontoxic refrigerants, the two-cycle diesel engine which was to enable General Motors to revolutionize the railroads, and innumerable other inventions, refinements, and developments which

[1] Many years later the state of the art of the air-cooled engine improved to the point where application of its principles to automobiles became practicable. An example of such an engine made of aluminum is in the modern Corvair built by Chevrolet.

are everywhere to be found in automobiles, locomotives, airplanes, and appliances.

The significant influence of the copper-cooled engine was in what it taught us about the value of organized co-operation and co-ordination in engineering and other matters. It showed the need to make an effective distinction between divisional and corporate functions in engineering, and also between advanced product engineering and long-range research. The copper-cooled-engine episode proved emphatically that management needed to subscribe to, and live with, just the kind of firm policies of organization and business that we had been working on. Altogether, the experience was to have important consequences in the future organization of the corporation.

Chapter 6

STABILIZATION

THE change in the presidency of General Motors in the spring of 1923, when Pierre S. du Pont resigned and I succeeded him, marked the end of the first period of the modern corporation. Despite the delay in the product program, the corporation in this period achieved general stability, which at that time represented its greatest need. This, in part, was made possible by the passing of the slump of 1920–21, but the foundation of the achievement itself belongs to Mr. du Pont. To him more than to any other individual must be assigned the credit for rescuing the corporation in its time of need and guiding it into a broad position of strength. It was when he recognized that the management of the corporation was again able to continue on its own feet that he made his own decision to turn the operating leadership over to the automobile men. He took this action in the following way.

An annual meeting of the shareholders took place on April 18, 1923, and elected a board of directors to hold office for the ensuing year. The next day, April 19, the directors held an organization meeting and re-elected the same officers, including Mr. du Pont as president, and the standing committees, to serve for another term. Almost all members of the board thought that we were set for a year. I certainly did. But it was not so.

On May 10, after a regular meeting, Mr. du Pont called a special meeting of the board and after asking Mr. Mott to act as chairman, presented his resignation as president of the corporation. Thereupon the board adopted unanimously the following resolution:

On motion duly made and unanimously carried, it was

RESOLVED, that the resignation of Mr. Pierre S. du Pont as President be accepted, and it was further

RESOLVED, that in accepting Mr. du Pont's resignation as President the Directors wish to place on record their appreciation of the invaluable services that he has rendered the Corporation during the past two and one-half years, and also to recognize the sacrifices that he made in taking over the duties of the presidency. During his incumbency of this office the affairs of the Corporation have been brought to a high state of prosperity and the Directors wish to express deep regret that he has decided to retire from this office. They are gratified to know that he is not in any way to disassociate himself from the Corporation, but is to continue active participation in the direction of its affairs as Chairman of its Board of Directors.

The meeting then proceeded to the election of a president to fill the vacancy. Mr. du Pont nominated me and I was elected. Subsequently, I was also elected chairman of the Executive Committee. Although Mr. du Pont's resignation at that time was not expected, it had been understood when he took office that it would be for a limited time, and that during his term he would transfer many of his operating duties to vice presidents. He had in fact done so.

No one can appraise Mr. du Pont's conspicuous service to General Motors in the critical period in which he served as intimately as I can. I was very close to him throughout his entire presidency; we traveled together, we attended meetings together, and we counseled together on all the problems that arose. Mr. du Pont had come out of retirement to become head of a complex enterprise which was in financial difficulties, and one in which he had little practical experience. The enterprise was decimated by resignations, its market position was declining, and its management's faith in itself and the future of its opportunities was shaken. Yet the mere fact that Mr. du Pont was there at the head of the enterprise changed the psychology of the whole situation, so to speak. The banks were reassured; the organization's faith in its future was renewed; the shareholders were encouraged; all of us in the corporation determined not only to carry on but to capitalize the vast opportunity inherent in the very nature of our business, and in this we were inspired by our faith in the new and distinguished leadership of Mr. du Pont.

His administration was an active one for him. He withdrew from his home in Pennsylvania, just outside Wilmington, Delaware, in which he took pride and satisfaction, and divided his time between New York and Detroit in alternate weeks. He made frequent trips into the field to inspect the properties and to discuss problems that could be better evaluated on the spot. Days were spent in inspection and observation, nights in discussion; and even then it was hard to keep up with the problems. Mr. du Pont's administration might be called one of evaluation and construction. As a result we were able to identify the elements of the business and, through the process of much trial and many errors, to construct the foundation upon which the modern corporation has been built.

Mr. du Pont's administration adopted in principle a sound scheme of organization and in principle a sound approach to the product line. At the same time, system was introduced into accounting and finance. A most comprehensive incentive plan was developed by John J. Raskob and his former du Pont associate Donaldson Brown, and it was supplemented by an opportunity for the more important executives to participate in the financial gains of the business. The plan for executive participation known as the Managers Securities Plan (described in a later chapter) was made possible by Mr. du Pont's belief in the validity of a partnership relationship between shareholders and executives. Mr. du Pont also liquidated unprofitable divisions, such as Samson Tractor, and guided a vast financial reorganization that put the corporation on a sound and solid basis.

An administration may also be measured by the caliber of the men brought in or retained by it. In or associated with the corporation in one place or another in 1923 was a large number of men who were to make a mark in American industrial history. Some of them had already begun to make it. There were the Fisher brothers, led by their dean, Fred Fisher. In Anderson, Indiana, as factory manager of the Remy Electric Division, was young Charles E. Wilson, who would one day be president of the corporation and afterward Secretary of Defense of the United States. James D. Mooney was vice president in charge of General Motors' overseas business. Down at Dayton, in charge of Delco Light, was Richard H. ("Dick") Grant, who would guide Chevrolet's sales through the twenties, and so become the top salesman in the United States. The comptroller of the AC Spark Plug Division was Harlow H. Curtice, who would be president during the great post-Korea expansion of General Motors. There was William S. Knudsen, who directed Chevrolet for some years before he, too, served as president of the corporation. John Thomas Smith was general counsel; he was later to serve on the Executive Committee, and I might say that his advice and influence in the corporation were of a very high order in moral and public-policy matters as well as in the law. The manager of manufacturing for Chevrolet was K. T. Keller, later to be president and chairman of the Chrysler Corporation. Albert Bradley, who would one day be chairman of General Motors, was then a young and important member of the Financial Staff. And so on; these and many others, together with those I have mentioned earlier—notably Charles S. Mott, Charles F. Kettering, John J. Raskob, Donaldson Brown, and John L. Pratt, the latter three of whom came from the du Pont organization—were a great team of experienced or promising automobile and financial men.

As to myself, I recognized that my election to the presidency of the corporation was a big responsibility and a business opportunity that comes to few. I resolved in my own mind that I would make any personal sacrifice for the cause, and that I would put forth all the energy, experience, and knowledge I had to make the corporation an outstanding success. General Motors has been for me a dedicated activity ever since, perhaps to a fault. My becoming president involved few changes in the activities for which I had been responsible as vice president in charge of operations. The work flowed on without a break. I became president under the auspicious fact that many of my basic views had become the accepted policy of the corporation. The period of development lay ahead.

But to Pierre S. du Pont must go the credit for the very survival of General Motors and for laying the foundation of its future progress.

Chapter 7

CO-ORDINATION
BY COMMITTEE

THE atmosphere in the corporation in the fall of 1923 was one of excitement at the prospect that the industry's first four-million car-and-truck year had opened up, and there was a great desire for reconciliation of the organizational issues raised by the copper-cooled engine. The experience with that engine had a profound effect on General Motors. At the same time the power of the great demand for automobiles acted as a disciplinary force. It was clearly time to gather ourselves to meet the challenge of the boom twenties, and to gather meant to co-ordinate.

The problem of co-ordination was one of developing the practical means of relating the various functions of management. We had the principles of organization which were laid down in the "Organization Study" of 1919–20. We needed now concretely to co-ordinate such very different bodies in the corporation as the general office, the research staff, and the decentralized divisions. The divisions in General Motors are self-contained units combining the functions of engineering, production, and sales—the profit-creating activities, in other words. Corporation staff work in each of these functions cuts across these divisional units. For example, the function of staff engineering is potentially and sometimes immediately related to the engineering activities of any or all of the self-contained operating divisions. The junctures between staff and line are critical, as we had learned the hard way. The experience with the copper-cooled car showed what a paralyzing effect one of these junctures could have if it were turned into a battlefield.

The broad problem of co-ordination and decentralization began at the top of the corporation, and was now my responsibility. What I did about it I had already begun to do in the first period of the new administration. In my notes on the situation in the corporation, which I had written at the end of 1921, I introduced the question of decentralization in relation to the activity of the top executive group. First I set down a declaration of principle, as follows:

. . . That I approached the matter [of organization] from the standpoint of a thorough belief in a decentralized organization. I still, after a year's experience, [am] just as firmly of the same belief that a decentralized organization is the only one that will develop the talent necessary to meet the Corporation's big problems, but certain things, notwithstanding a decentralized organization, must be recognized and I appreciate these much more than I did before . . .

The main questions, I said, looking forward to the liquidation of the emergency of 1921, were related to the Executive Committee itself, the highest body in the operating structure. These questions were: the role of the Executive Committee as a policy-making group, the representation from the operating side, and the need for authority in the person of the president. I wrote:

a. That the Executive Committee [should] confine itself more particularly to principles which should be presented to it by the [operating organization], properly developed and thoughtfully carried out rather than to constitute itself as it is now, a group management.

This needs little explanation in view of what I have already related. But let me say that, though I have often been taxed, by people who do not know me, with being a committee man—and in a sense I most certainly am—I have never believed that a group as such could manage anything. A group can make policy, but only individuals can administer policy. At that time, and in particular in relation to the copper-cooled engine, the four of us on the Executive Committee were, in my opinion, trying to manage the divisions.

My next point was not specifically aimed at the lack of automotive experience, but at the need for integration of the top executive committee and the operating organization:

b. The Operating side on the Executive Committee is not strongly enough represented. This should be corrected by the increase of the Executive Committee, and I suggest Messrs. Mott, McLaughlin and Bassett as additional members. The Executive Committee to meet not oftener than every two weeks and perhaps once a month.

I then proposed that the president should assume not less but more authority. This is not as surprising as it may seem at first sight, for it followed the principle that an individual and not a group should administer. In actual fact general operations had devolved on me at the time I was vice president of operations, and we had a situation of confused authority. I wrote as follows:

c. Whoever is in charge of Operations should be designated with real authority to be used in case of an emergency. It will probably be best if the President of the Corporation could absolutely have charge of Operations. If this is not feasible, somebody should be so appointed and whoever has charge should develop a reasonable organization to contact with the Operations side as well as the Executive Committee.

I then gave examples of the distinction between policy and administration. Over-all pricing policy, I said, should be reserved to the Executive Committee. Obviously, since we were working with divisional price classes, we were not likely to want Cadillac to produce a car in the Chevrolet price class.

And on the question of Executive Committee action on the character and quality of product, I wrote as follows:

It would seldom be suitable for the Executive Committee to approve the specifications of contemplated product, or even the principal characteristics unless they be of peculiar significance as involving the entry into new fields, or the possibility of undermining the position of existing profitable lines. The Executive Committee should treat with the question from the standpoint of policy and in the direction of regulating the general quality of product of divisions respectively so as to gain a wholesome distribution of product by class ranges, and the avoidance of undue interference between divisions. A carefully designed policy should be enunciated that will convey to each division a complete understanding of the general quality of product that should be attained or maintained and all major alterations of design should be submitted to the Executive Committee for approval from this standpoint. The Executive Committee should not attempt to pass upon the mechanical features, but must rely upon some competent individual or body in the operating organization.

In general, the activity of the Executive Committee should be guided along the lines of establishing policies and laying the same down in such clear cut and comprehensive terms as to supply the basis of authorized executive action . . .

I cannot recall how Mr. du Pont expressed himself on these proposals. I think he must have agreed, for he co-operated in bringing them into effect. In 1922 he caused to be elected to the Executive Committee Mr. Mott and Fred J. Fisher, both experienced in operations. And later, in 1924, when I was its chairman, he concurred in adding Mr. Bassett, Mr. Brown, Mr. Pratt, Charles T. Fisher, and Lawrence P. Fisher, making ten in all, seven experienced in operations, two in finance, and Mr. du Pont himself. The Executive Committee thus achieved an identity with the operating organization, which, under one title or another, it has maintained ever since. Eventually the Executive Committee limited itself to policy matters, and left administration to the president.

Now the question of the relation of the staff, line, and general officers. I shall describe here the steps which, when completed, put form into the organization.

Two early steps, one in the area of purchasing, the other in advertising, assisted in pointing the way to a practical form of organization. The setting up of the General Purchasing Committee was a task I undertook in 1922. There are two things about this committee which it is important to consider. One was its value or lack of it in its own right; the other was its incidental value as a lesson in co-ordination, which is more germane to the story here.

Centralized purchasing was not an original idea with us. In those days it was considered to be an important industrial economy, and in some circumstances I believe it was. I had experience with volume economies at Hyatt as a supplier to Ford. But centralized purchasing, in which a single purchasing office executes contracts involving more than one division of an enterprise, was an oversimplified notion, as we discovered. The problem for General Motors, as I saw it in 1922, was to get the advantages of volume by buying on general contracts such items as tires, steel, stationery, rags, batteries, blocks, acetylene, abrasives, and the like, and at the same time to permit the divisions to have control over their own affairs. In a preliminary memorandum I argued that co-ordination of purchasing would save the corporation an estimated five to ten million dollars a year; that it would make it easier to control—especially to reduce—inventory; that in an emergency one division could obtain materials from another, and that the corporation's purchasing specialist could take advantage of price fluctuations. I conceded, however, the peculiar difficulties that arise "when one considers the extremely technical character of practically all the Corporation's product and recognizes that we are dealing with many personalities and viewpoints developed through years of contact with certain products as compared with others." In other words, it was a question of acknowledging the natural constraints of decentralization that were built into both the technology of the product and the minds of the managers. The latter were not long in making precisely this point when I first proposed to have a purchasing staff do the co-ordinating. They gave as argument their long experience, the variety of their requirements, and the loss of divisional responsibility in an area which could affect their ability to carry out their car programs.

To meet these objections I proposed the General Purchasing Committee, with a membership drawn mostly from the divisions. The divisions supported the proposition when they learned that they would be represented and would participate in deciding on policy and procedures for purchasing, determine specifications, and draw up contracts, and that their decisions in the committee would be final. Thus it was arranged that in the committee the representatives of the divisions had the opportunity to draw the balance between their special needs and the general interest. A corporation purchasing staff was to administer, but not dictate, the committee's decisions; that is, the relation of committee to staff was to be that of "principal and agent." The Purchasing Committee lasted about ten years and worked reasonably well during that time. But a number of limitations on its value arose:

The first was that quantities of any particular product needed for one division were generally large enough to justify the supplier giving the lowest possible price to that division.

The second was the question of administration. For instance, if the corporation made a contract available to all divisions it sometimes happened that a supplier who did not get the contract would go to one of the divisions and make a lower price, even though he had participated in the original offering. That would cause confusion and unhappiness.

Third, a large number of parts and supplies to be purchased had no common denominator. They were special items applicable to a particular engineering concept.

Therefore, I think the General Purchasing Committee itself cannot be cited as an unqualified success. It caused us, however, to make a strong effort to standardize articles where possible. This and the description of standardized production were very important matters. The General Purchasing Committee's real and lasting success was in the area of standardization of materials.

Also, this committee provided our first lesson in co-ordination. It was our first experience of interdivisional activity, combining line (at the level of a divisional function), staff (a general purchasing section), and general officers (I was the first chairman of the committee). Two years later, reviewing its work, I wrote:

. . . The General Purchasing Committee has, I believe, shown the way and has demonstrated that those responsible for each functional activity can work together to their own profit and to the profit of the stockholders at the same time and such a plan of co-ordination is far better from every standpoint than trying to inject it into the operations from some central activity.

The next significant step toward co-ordination was in the area of advertising. I had had some consumer studies made in 1922, and we found that people throughout the United States, except at the corner of Wall and Broad streets, didn't know anything about General Motors. So I thought we should publicize the parent company. A plan submitted to me by Barton, Durstine, and Osborn, now BBDO, was approved by the Finance Committee and by our top executives. But since divisional matters would come into the picture, I asked both divisional personnel and other executives in Detroit for their viewpoints on the propriety of such a program. It was agreed that the plan was worthwhile, and Bruce Barton was given full responsibility for conducting the campaign. We then formed the Institutional Advertising Committee, consisting of car-division managers and staff men, to assist Mr. Barton and "to effect the necessary co-ordination with other phases of the Corporation's publicity." I made a rule that if any advertising theme dealt with a particular division, it must have the approval of that division. It was another little lesson in divisional relationships.

The really big step forward in co-ordination, however, followed from the copper-cooled-engine experience. When that issue was concluded with the parties to it divided against one another—particularly the research engineers on the one hand and the divisional engineers on the other—something had to be done to heal the wounds, and to resolve this fundamental conflict between those seeking new concepts and those with the responsibility for producing automobiles. First of all, what was needed was a place to bring these men together under amicable circumstances for the exchange of information and the ironing out of differences. It seemed to me preferable that such a meeting of minds should take place in the presence of the general executives, who would in the end have to make or approve the big decisions on forward programs.

Rather than try to give the picture wholly through recollection, in which it might well be supposed that I would share in the human failing of making it seem more logical than it was, I shall quote here at length a proposal—the key statement, I believe, in the whole affair—which I wrote and circulated to a number of executives of the corporation and obtained approval of during September 1923:

I have felt for a long time past that if a proper plan could be developed that would have the support of all those interested that a great deal could be gained for the Corporation by co-operation of an engineering nature between our various Operations, particularly our Car Divisions, dealing as they do in so many problems having the same general characteristics. Activities of this type have already been started in the way of purchasing and have been very helpful and I am confident that as time goes on will be justified in a great many different ways beside[s] resulting in very material profit to the Corporation. The activities of our Institutional Advertising Committee have been constructive and Mr. du Pont remarked to me the other day after one of those meetings that even if it was assumed that the value of the advertising was negligible the other benefits accruing to the Corporation by the development of a General Motors atmosphere and the working together spirit of all members of the Committee representing the various phases of the Corporation's activities . . . the cost was well justified. I am quite confident that we all agree as to these principles and assuming that is the case and there is no reason why the same principle does not apply to engineering, it appears to me to be well worth a serious attempt to put the principle into practical operation. I am thoroughly convinced that it can be made a wonderful success. I believe, therefore, that we should at this time establish what might be termed a General Technical Committee which Committee would have certain powers and functions which should be broadly defined at the start and amplified in various ways as the progress of the work seems to justify.

Before attempting to outline even the general principles upon which I believe a start could be made, I think it should be very clearly set forth and distinctly understood by all that the functions of this Committee would not in any event be to deal with the specific engineering activities of any particular Operation. According to General Motors plan of organization, to which I believe we all heartily subscribe, the activities of any specific Operation are under the absolute control of the General Manager of that Division, subject only to very broad contact with the general officers of the Corporation. I certainly do not want to suggest a departure even to the slightest degree from what I believe to be so thoroughly sound a type of organization. On the contrary I do believe and have believed for a long time that one of the great problems that faces the General Motors Corporation was to add to its present plan of organization some method by which the advantages of the Corporation as a whole could be capitalized to the further benefit of the stockholders. I feel that a proper balance can and must necessarily be established in the course of time between the activities of any particular Operation and that of all our Operations together and as I see the picture at the moment no better way or even as good a way has yet been advanced as to ask those members of each organization who have the same functional relationship to get together and decide for themselves what should be done where coordination is necessary, giving such a group the power to deal with the problem where it is felt that the power can be constructively applied. I believe that such a plan properly developed gives the necessary balance between each Operation and the Corporation itself and will result in all the advantages of co-ordinated action where such action is of benefit in a broader way without in any sense limiting the initiative of independence of action of any component part of the group.

Assuming that this is correct in principle, I might set forth specifically what the functions in the case of the General Technical Committee would be, although this discussion would, I think, apply equally well to other Committees dealing with all functions common to all manufacturing enterprises.

1. The Committee would deal in problems which would be of interest to all Divisions and would in dealing with such matters largely formulate the general engineering policies of the Corporation.

2. The Committee would assume the functions of the already con-

stituted Patent Committee which would be discontinued and in assuming these functions would have the authority to deal with patent matters, already vested in the Patent Committee.

3. The Committee would not, as to principle, deal with the specific problems of any individual Operation. Each function of that Operation would be under the absolute control of the General Manager of that Division.

It is to be noted that the functioning of the Patent Section, Advisory Staff, differs materially from that of any other staff activity and is in a sense an exception to General Motors plan of organization in the fact that all patent problems come directly under the control of the Director of the Patent Section. In other words, all patent work is centralized. The Patent Procedure provides, however, for an Inventions Committee and for co-operation with the Director of the Patent Section and the dividing under certain conditions of responsibility in patent matters. In view of the fact that the personnel of the Inventions Committee must necessarily largely parallel that of the General Technical Committee it is thought advisable to consolidate the two for the sake of simplification.

There is also to be considered the functions of the General Motors Research Corporation at Dayton. I feel that up to the present time the [General Motors] Corporation has failed to capitalize what might be capitalized with a proper system of administration, the advantages that should flow from an organization such as we have at Dayton. In making this statement I feel that there are a number of contributing causes, the most important being a lack of proper administrative policy or, I might say, a lack of getting together which it is hoped that this program will provide not only, as just stated, for better co-ordination with the Research Corporation but better co-ordination also among the Operating Divisions themselves. I believe that we would all agree that many of our research and engineering problems in Dayton can only be capitalized through the acceptance and commercializing of same by the Operating Divisions. I fully believe that a more intimate contact with what the Research Corporation is trying to do will be all that is necessary to effect the desired result and strengthen the whole engineering side of the entire [General Motors] Corporation.

It is my idea that the General Technical Committee should be independent in character and in addition to developing through its Secretary, as hereafter described, a program for its meetings, which it is believed would be helpful and beneficial to all the members of the Committee, would conduct studies and investigations of such a character and scope as its judgment would dictate as desirable and for that purpose would use the facilities of the Research Corporation or of any Operating Division or of any outside source that in its judgment would lead to the most beneficial result. Projects of this character would be presented to the Committee by any member of the Committee itself, by the Research Corporation or by any member of the General Motors Corporation through the Committee's Secretary. Beginning January 1, 1924 the cost of operating the General Motors Corporation will be under the control of a budget system and funds will be provided in that budget to cover this purpose.

I have presented the above ideas at an Operations Committee meeting of which all the General Managers of the Car Divisions primarily interested in this matter and the Group Vice Presidents are members and they all seemed to think that the step was a constructive one and would have the support of all.

In order, therefore, that all the above may be crystallized in a few principal points which will be sufficient to form a starting point, I propose the following:—

1. That co-operation shall be established between the Car Divisions and the Engineering Departments within the Corporation, including the engineering and research activities of the General Motors Research Corporation and that co-operation shall take the form of a Committee to be established to be termed the General Technical Committee.

2. The Committee will consist as to principle, of the Chief Engineers of each Car Division and certain additional members . . .

Thus formed, the General Technical Committee became the highest advisory body on engineering in the corporation. It brought together the very persons who had parted over the copper-cooled engine: the divisional chief engineers, including, notably, Mr. Hunt; staff engineers, including, notably, Mr. Kettering; and a number of the general officers of the corporation, including myself as the committee's chairman. It was, as my proposal stated, an independent staff organization with its own secretary and budget. It held its first meeting on September 14, 1923. I was pleased to sit among those fine men—Mr. Kettering, who had the research responsibility; Mr. Hunt, who had a production-engineering responsibility at Chevrolet; Henry Crane, who was my assistant on engineering matters; and the others—all of whom met in a friendly atmosphere and entered afresh into the future development of the automobile.

The General Technical Committee raised the prestige of the engineering group in the corporation and supported its efforts to acquire more adequate facilities and personnel. Its activities emphasized the importance of product integrity as the basic requirement for the future success of the business. It had a remarkable effect in stimulating interest and action everywhere in the corporation in matters of product appeal and product improvement, and produced a free exchange of new and progressive ideas and experience among division engineers. In short, it co-ordinated information.

A number of specific functions were given to the General Technical Committee. For a while it dealt with patent matters, but these were soon turned over to a special New Devices Committee. More important was the committee's role as a kind of board of directors of the great new Proving Ground that we built at Milford, Michigan. Testing had clearly become a crucial question for the future of our products. The Proving Ground, with its controlled conditions, was the logical step away from testing on public roads, which the industry up to that time had practiced. The committee saw to it that the Proving Ground developed standardized test procedures and measuring equipment, and that it became the corporation's center for making independent comparisons of division products and the products of competition. Although engine testing was not assigned to the Proving Ground, the committee was charged with developing an engine test code that would produce uniformity in the engine-testing practices of the various divisions.

And yet the General Technical Committee was the mildest kind of organization. Its most important role was that of a study group. It got to be known as a seminar. Its meetings usually were opened with the reading of one or two papers on a specific engineering problem or device, and these would then be the center of a general discussion. Sometimes the committee's discussion would conclude with the approval of a new device or method, or a recommendation on engineering policy and procedure, but more often the results were simply that information was transmitted from one to all. The members returned to their divisions with a broader understanding of new developments and current problems of automotive engineering and with knowledge of what their associates in other areas of the corporation were doing.

In its reports, papers, and discussions the General Technical Committee studied such short-range engineering problems as those concerning brakes, fuel consumption, lubrication, changes required in the steering mechanism as a result of the development of four-wheel brakes and "balloon" tires (this led to a subcommittee conferring with the rubber companies), and the condensation of products of combustion that resulted in internal rust and oil sludge (which was finally eliminated by proper crankcase ventilation). In 1924 and 1925 the committee gave attention to the education of the dealers and sales departments on the advertising and sales value of current engineering developments. I asked the committee to develop a series of criteria by which "car value" of the different makes and models might be objectively determined. In 1924, too, I gave the committee the task of setting up the broad specifications of the different cars to assist in our efforts to keep the several General Motors' cars distinct and separate products and in a proper price and cost relationship to one another.

Mr. Kettering's staff made most of the long-range investigations and submitted most of the reports during the early years of the committee. They discussed such matters as control of cylinder-wall temperature, cylinder heads, sleeve-valve engines, intake manifolds, tetraethyl lead for gasoline, and transmissions. Fundamentally the subject matters were fuels and metallurgy, the two areas which have furnished the most important improvements in the performance of the automobile since that time.

A meeting on September 17, 1924, in which the subject of transmissions was considered, is a good example of the committee at work. I rely on the minutes for this description. Mr. Kettering began by describing the relative merits and demerits of various types of transmissions. This was followed by a long discussion on the practicality of the inertia-type transmission from an engineering standpoint. Mr. Hunt discussed the different types from the "commercial angle." The growing traffic problem, he said, was calling for a car which "has real acceleration, and in addition it has to have real brakes." After some give and take around the table, I closed this part of the meeting by saying: "I take it that the sentiment of the Committee is something like this: First, that we should look to the ultimate, which is directly a Research problem, and that the inertia type [transmission] is the one which offers the greatest possibilities.[1] This being strictly a Research problem, should not the Committee charge Mr. Kettering with doing everything possible toward its development? . . . Second, for the present we must have minimum inertia and minimum friction in our clutch and transmis-

[1] The inertia-type transmission did appear to have great possibilities technically, but in actual performance it did not prove to be sufficiently smooth or long-lived to warrant production.

sion elements at our various divisions, and this problem is their own."

In such manner we separated the function of the Research Corporation from that of the divisions. The divisions in those days, however, also had long-term projects; Chevrolet, for example, developed a six-cylinder low-priced car.

That summer I wrote Mr. Kettering about a session of the Technical Committee in Oshawa, Canada. This passage gives the general idea:

. . . We had a splendid meeting not only so far as the meeting itself went but the boys stayed over Saturday and some of them Sunday and some went fishing and others played golf and that helps a lot in bringing men who are thinking in the same direction, more closely together. I can't help but feel, considering the magnitude of our picture and all that sort of thing, that this co-operation in engineering is working out just splendidly. We must be patient, but I am sure that as time goes on we are going to be fully repaid for the way we have handled it as compared with a more military style which I do not think would have ever put us anywhere.

The interdivisional committee, tried in a rudimentary way in purchasing and advertising, and applied more intensively in the General Technical Committee, was the first big idea for co-ordination in the corporation. We went on from the General Technical Committee to apply the concept to most of the principal functional activities of the divisions. The next interdivisional committee to be formed was in sales. The sales area was relatively unexplored, for the industry in the mid-twenties for the first time had entered its commercial phase. I therefore arranged to set up the General Sales Committee, made up of the sales managers of the car and truck divisions, sales-staff members, and general officers of the corporation. As its chairman, I opened its first meeting on March 6, 1924, with the following remarks:

While General Motors is definitely committed to a decentralized plan of operation, it is nevertheless obvious that from time to time general plans and policies beneficial to the Corporation and its stockholders, as well as to the individual divisions, can best be accomplished through concerted effort.

The necessity for concerted action on the broader phases of our activities is emphasized by the likelihood of some of our competitors merging their interests—perhaps in the near future. This, as you know, is the trend of the industry. Narrowing profits will add impetus to such a tendency and under the highly competitive conditions of the near future we may expect a decidedly different situation in the field.

General Motors, as you know, has made quite a lot of progress in lining up its products into different price groups, which, relatively speaking, are non-competitive. From the standpoint of design and manufacture we have, through the cooperation of our Division Managers and Engineers, made wonderful progress in the direction of coordination.

Much is to be gained through a similar coordination of sales activities. I think that we, in General Motors, have all got to recognize that the "neck of the bottle" is going to be the sales end. This is perfectly natural in any industry; it eventually gets down to the sales end, and certainly the automotive industry is beginning to reach that period—if it has not already arrived.

It is our idea that this Committee will take in hand all those major sales problems which [a]ffect the Corporation as a whole. It is your Committee. You can feel perfectly free to bring up any sales problems that seem to require general discussion and concerted effort. Whatever general policies or actions you may decide upon will be fully supported by the parent Corporation.

We should, I believe, confine our discussions in these meetings to problems of common interest [a]ffecting all divisions. Realizing that all of you men are extremely busy we will try to keep away from details—dealing only with the basic problems. We will do everything in our power to make the sessions business-like and to the point. No time will be taken to prepare papers, etc. unless in some instances you may wish it that way. Mr. [B. G.] Koether [director, Sales Section] will serve as Secretary of the Committee. He has a Staff which can be expanded if necessary, and whose services are entirely at your command.

We have not developed any definite programs for these meetings because we want to leave such matters to you, realizing that you are in a better position to know just what problems require the most urgent attention and while we may suggest a number of things from time to time it is entirely up to you to act upon such suggestions as you may see fit . . .

The chairmanship of the General Sales Committee was later given to Donaldson Brown, vice president of finance, because of the bearing of statistical and financial controls on production and sales problems. Co-ordination in sales thus extended to the Financial Staff.

After a study of the interdivisional type of committee by Mr. Pratt in late 1924 confirmed in the minds of everyone that this was the best form of co-ordination we had found up to that time, it was made more or less official and was extended to works managers and the power and maintenance staff. Something of the same sort of co-ordination was extended to the very top level of management —but with a difference.

The reader will recall that under Mr. Durant the Executive Committee was composed largely of division managers who campaigned there for the interests of their respective divisions. When we formed the new temporary Executive Committee of four, we placed the former members, mainly the division managers, in an advisory operations committee. For some time, while the emergency was being liquidated, this advisory committee was not regularly active. After I became president and the Executive Committee was enlarged again, it included at different times one or two division managers, depending on circumstance, or motivated by the thought that the largest car division should have representation there. But these were exceptions, not the rule, for I believed in principle that the top operating committee should be a policy group detached from the interests of specific divisions. In other words, it should contain only general executives. Holding this view, after I became president I felt that something should be done to bring the general managers into contact in a regular way with the members of the top operating policy group. I therefore reactivated the Operations Committee and had placed on it all the general operating officers on the Executive Committee and the general managers of the principal divisions, thus making it the major point of regular contact between the two types of executives. The Operations Committee was not a policy-making body but a forum for the discussion of policy or of need for policy. The Operations Committee would receive a full set of data on the performance of the corporation and would review that performance. The word "forum" may suggest something idle, but I assure you that in this case it does not mean that. In a large enterprise some means is necessary to bring about a common understanding. It is perhaps sufficient to note that, with all of the members of the top operating policy group present, an agreement on a policy, suggested say by a division manager, would be tantamount to acceptance on the operating side of the corporation.

In sum then, the whole picture of co-ordination in 1925 and for a number of years thereafter was as follows: The interdivisional-relations committees gave a measure of co-ordination to the functions of purchasing, engineering, sales, and the like. The Operations Committee, including the general managers, appraised the performance of the divisions. The Executive Committee, with contacts in all directions, made policy. It sat at the head of operations, responsible to the board of directors—indeed it was a committee of the board—but beholden to the Finance Committee for its larger appropriations. On the operating side the Executive Committee was supreme. Its chairman was the president and chief executive officer of the corporation; and he had all the authority he needed to carry out established policy. This was the new General Motors scheme of management from which developments down to this day, through much evolution, have been derived.

GENERAL MOTORS CORPORATION

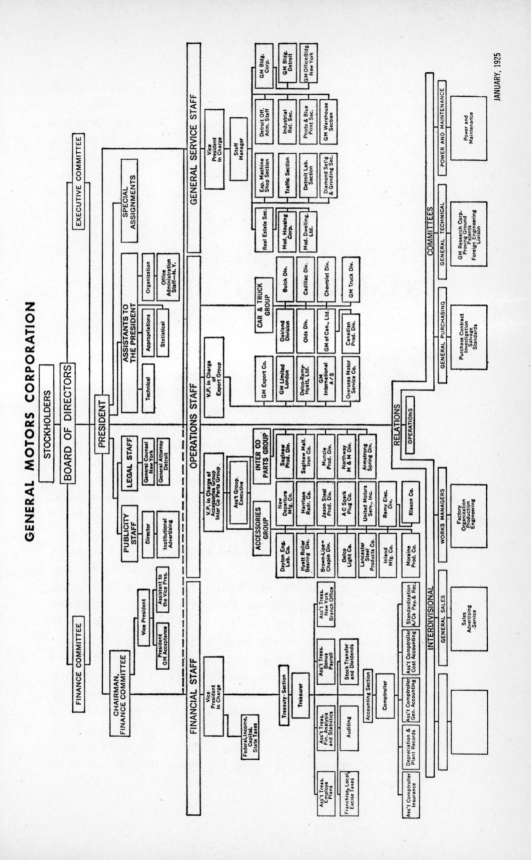

JANUARY, 1925

Chapter 8

THE DEVELOPMENT OF
FINANCIAL CONTROLS

THE development of co-ordination by committee in the early 1920s was accompanied by co-ordination of another order, namely that of financial control. General Motors' progress, I believe, was largely the result of advances the corporation made in this area of management, along with those in organization and product policy. Our modern financial policies, like those in organization, came out of the ruins of 1920.

For the leading members of the new administration that took over the corporation, the necessity of providing new forms of financial control was doctrine. The question was what they should be and how to put them into effect. The specific forms of financial control in General Motors were introduced in good part by Donaldson Brown, who came to General Motors from the du Pont Company at the beginning of 1921, and Albert Bradley, his young associate who came to General Motors in 1919 and who was to succeed Mr. Brown as the top financial officer and later to succeed me as chairman of the board. Their contributions to financial thought have long been recognized. They wrote papers on the subject which are classics of the 1920s, and at the same time put their concepts into practice in General Motors. Frederic G. Donner, present chairman and chief executive officer; George Russell, executive vice president, and other gifted members of the Financial Staff rose out of this great school of finance to make their own contributions in their long service to the corporation. Although I wrote on the subject of finance in the form of reports, particularly in connection with inter-divisional business and appropriations, my experience was mainly from the operating side. My responsibility involved the application of financial method, for finance could not exist in a vacuum but had to be integrated with operations.

I think I have made clear that Mr. Durant had no systematic financial methodology. It was not his way of doing business. And yet modern financial concepts were brought into General Motors during his administration. Mr. Durant was instrumental in arranging for the du Pont executives to come on the Finance Committee and take the responsibility for that aspect of the corporation's affairs. I believe the outstanding benefit General Motors derived from the du Pont association—apart from their general position as a responsible shareholder serving on the board of directors—was in the financial area. A number of du Pont men experienced in accounting and finance came to General Motors in the early years and assumed key positions.

Mr. Brown was one of these men. A word on his background, as he has told it to me: He was in the sales department of the du Pont Company for a number of years during the early part of this century. In 1912 he was taken into the office of one of the du Pont general managers as an assistant without portfolio. That was when Coleman du Pont was president of the du Pont Company. The general manager of this department was handicapped seriously by bad health and had to be out of the office for a period. At that time the du Pont Executive Committee was seeking a realistic report on the efficiency of the operating departments of the company, then engaged almost wholly in manufacturing explosives: blasting powder, dynamite, and the like. Mr. Brown took upon himself the job of developing a method to reveal the desired facts about the several activities under the general manager. The method he chose emphasized the importance of capital turnover as well as profit margin in calculating return on investment. Mr. Brown passed his report on to the chief executives and it made such an impression on Coleman du Pont that he recommended that Mr. Brown be transferred to the Finance Department. Pierre S. du Pont was then treasurer, and Mr. Raskob was assistant treasurer. Mr. Raskob made Mr. Brown the junior assistant treasurer—"very junior" Mr. Brown says. I guess he was, with Mr. Raskob around. But eventually Mr. Raskob succeeded

Mr. du Pont as treasurer, and Mr. Brown succeeded Mr. Raskob in that post when Mr. Raskob went into General Motors. Mr. Brown brought economists and statisticians into the du Pont Company, a practice that was unusual in those days. Thereafter when the du Pont Executive Committee met with the du Pont general managers, Mr. Brown displayed charts on the efficiency of divisional performance, a technique of presentation which he initiated.

At Mr. Raskob's request Mr. Brown came to General Motors on January 1, 1921, as vice president in charge of finance. He and I shared similar views on the value of detailed, disciplined controls in the operation of a business. From the time of his arrival in the corporation we recognized this affinity and began a long and congenial relationship.

The du Pont group, after coming into the corporation in 1917, had made an effort to apply the principle of return on investment in appropriating funds to the operating side of the corporation. Yet Mr. Raskob, though he had the right idea in general, was not prepared with the instrumentation for General Motors. I have described in an earlier chapter how, during the expansion of 1919, difficulties arose owing to the loose manner in which appropriations were made, and how the inventory runaway and shortage of cash brought crisis to the corporation in the slump of 1920. These three emergency problems—overruns on appropriations, inventory runaway, and the resulting cash shortage—exposed the lack of control and co-ordination in the corporation. It was in the effort to meet these specific emergency problems that new methods of financial co-ordination and control were developed in General Motors.

Financial method is so refined today that it may seem routine; yet this method—the financial model, as some call it—by organizing and presenting the significant facts about what is going on in and around a business, is one of the chief bases for strategic business decisions. At all times, and particularly in times of crisis, or of contraction or expansion from whatever cause, it is of the essence in the running of a business. The situation in 1920 proved this negatively and we were to prove it positively in the subsequent critical years.

I have related how, in 1919 and 1920, in the absence of a system for control of appropriations, each division manager got his maximum request satisfied, without real effort on the part of the corporation to evaluate the request or to reconcile the total amount of all requests with the available funds. This, together with overruns on appropriations and the inventory rise, represented a drain on available funds which had to be met in some way. To get the money we sold common stock, debenture stock, and preferred stock, though not so easily or in such amounts as we expected; and before the year 1920 was out we had to borrow about $83 million from banks. From then through 1922 we charged against income of the corporation about $90 million for extraordinary write-offs, inventory adjustments, and liquidation losses, an amount equal to about one sixth of the total assets of the corporation. Financial control at this juncture was not merely desirable, it was a necessity. To survive we had to pull back from the brink and find a general solution.

The story of how we did it falls into two parts. The first part concerns how the corporation curtailed the excessive freedom of the divisions, which had gone so far as to jeopardize the survival of the corporation, and how we established control over them. The immediate remedies inevitably were centralizing in character, for the corporation could not afford to let its divisions continue to make the kind of mistakes they were making: the weak divisions threatened the existence of the strong ones, and the strong ones themselves were operated more for their own than the corporation's interest. These centralizing remedies—largely operating controls—created a temporary distortion in our general policy which later had to be corrected in order to return to a workable decentralization. The second part of the story involves the development of the financial instruments which made it possible to establish decentralization with co-ordinated control.

Effecting Corporate Control: Appropriations for Capital Spending

Just before the economic collapse of 1920, that is, in June of that year, the Committee on Appropriation Request Rules, which had been formed at the end of 1919 and of which I was chairman, gave its report to the Executive Committee. This report, prepared by Mr. Pratt, Mr. Prentis, and myself, marks a historic turning point in the development of appropriations procedures in General Motors.

The core of our concept lay in the determination of the propriety of proposed projects. Four principles were to be satisfied, which we stated as follows:

a. Is the Project a logical or necessary one considered as a commercial venture?

b. Has the Project been properly developed technically?

c. Is the Project proper, considering the interest of the Corporation as a whole?

d. What is the relative value of the Project to the Corporation as compared with other Projects under consideration, from the standpoint not only of the return on the necessary capital to be invested, but of the need of the particular Project in supporting the operations of the Corporation as a whole?

Bearing down on the main weakness of the corporation in this area at that time, we said in the report:

. . . a very careful consideration of the subject on the part of your Committee leads it to the inevitable conclusion that at least so far as the larger Projects are concerned, an independent impartial review and checking of all phases of [the] proposed project outside of the Division or Subsidiary itself, is essential and will be found more and more so as time develops and the operations of the Corporation become more interwoven and complex.

This procedure required a review by an appropriations committee before submission of a request to the Executive Committee or Finance Committee for approval, and a policy review by the latter committees. We defined the scope of their review as follows:

It appears to your Committee that the members of such committees [Executive and Finance] should be interested in the Projects as a matter of general policy and that their passing of such Projects should be a matter of financial returns or necessity of the Projects to the general development of the Corporation rather than from the standpoint of the particular type of lathe or milling machine, or how many such lathes or milling machines are essential to the proper development of the proposed Project.

Following this line of reasoning, we allowed certain small amounts of expenditure to be authorized by the general manager of a division on his own. For larger amounts, we proposed a detailed procedure on the development and follow-up of supporting data, and, in this connection, we proposed to bring together the two main branches of the corporation: "Your Committee recognizes the necessity of determining proper co-ordination between the Financial and Operating Staffs as regards expenditures . . ." And to be specific we recommended that an appropriations manual be developed for the corporation setting forth in detail the kind of information the divisions and subsidiaries should present to demonstrate the desirability of a proposed expenditure both from an engineering and an economic standpoint.

The Executive Committee approved our recommendations in September 1920 and requested that the manual be prepared. This manual, approved by the Executive and Finance committees in April 1922, established the first well-defined capital-appropriation procedure in General Motors. It called for an appropriations committee, functioning under both the Finance and Executive committees, to have general charge of all appropriation matters and co-ordinate programs involving more than one division. The divisions were to make monthly reports of construction in progress to the appropriations committee, which in turn would present a combined report each month to the Finance Committee. Each appropriation request was to receive consideration and analysis from a corporation as well as a divisional standpoint before any commitment was made. Proper records were to be kept of expenditures and approvals for expenditures, and uniform treatment was to be given to appropriation requests throughout the corporation. In short, we were for the first time to get accurate and orderly information. After that it would be a matter of business judgment whether to grant a request. Changes in this procedure have been made from time to time, and an appropriations committee as such was discontinued long ago. However, in its essentials, this is still the way capital appropriations are approved in General Motors.

Cash Control

We were short of cash in 1920 because we spent a lot of money on the future and did not take in enough in the present. Hence the bank borrowing, which reached a maximum of about $83 million at the end of October of that year. For some time afterward cash was a question of conservation.

The way cash was handled at that time is almost unbelievable. Each division controlled its own cash, depositing all receipts in its own accounts and paying all bills from those same accounts. Since only the divisions sold products, none of these cash receipts flowed directly to the corporation itself. We had no effective procedure for getting cash from the points where we happened to have some to the points where we happened to need some. When the corporation, as an operating company, had to pay dividends and taxes, and such items as rent, salaries, and other expenses of the general staff, the usual procedure was for the treasurer to request cash from the divisions. That was not so simple as it sounds, however, for the divisions, operating independently, tried to keep their cash balances high enough to satisfy their own peak requirements. Therefore, when they had more cash than they needed at the moment, they were not eager to turn it over to the corporation.

I remember that Buick, for example, at that time was very loath to give up its cash. This profitable division was, of course, the most prolific source of cash for the corporation, and long experience had made Buick's financial staff highly adept at delaying its report of the cash they had on hand. Buick made a practice of maintaining large cash balances in its factory sales branches. The amounts of these balances were not ascertainable at headquarters until Buick had submitted its monthly financial statement for the division as a whole—and this was usually a month or two after the fact. When the corporation needed cash, the treasurer, Meyer Prentis, would try to guess how much Buick actually had and how much of it he could probably get from them. Then he would go to Flint, discuss whatever other questions might be outstanding between Buick and headquarters, and at last casually bring up the subject of cash. Buick's financial people would invariably express surprise at the size of Mr. Prentis' request and occasionally would try to resist the transfer of such a large amount. Naturally, this cat-and-mouse game did not result in the most efficient utilization of funds, especially when some divisions had more operating cash than they needed, at the same time that other divisions were short of operating cash.

In 1922 we changed all this by setting up a consolidated cash-control system. This was a new concept for a large corporation. Depository accounts were established in some one hundred banks in the United States, and all incoming receipts were deposited in these accounts to the credit of General Motors Corporation. All withdrawals from them were administered by the central Financial Staff; the divisions had no control over cash transfers from these deposit accounts.

Under this system transfers between banks could be made quickly and automatically. The Financial Staff of the corporation set fixed minimum and maximum balances for these local deposit accounts, based on the size of the bank and the activity of the account. Whenever the amount in any one account rose above the maximum, the excess over the fixed minimum was automatically transferred by Federal Reserve telegraph to one of a number of central reservoir banks. The accounts in these reservoir banks were also administered by the Financial Staff. Divisions needing cash for their own requirements could apply to headquarters for transfer by telegraph. In two or three hours excess funds in one city could be made available to a division needing them in another city at the other end of the country.

Cash in transit also was reduced by putting an end to cash payments between divisions. We set up an intracorporation settlement procedure under which the Financial Staff at headquarters acted as a clearinghouse for the settlement of interdivisional claims and payments. Intracorporation settlement certificates were exchanged instead of cash.

At this time, too, we began calculating a month ahead what our cash would be each day of the month, taking into account the sales schedule, payrolls, payments for materials, and the like. Against this projected curve we compared each day the corporation's actual cash balances. A divergence of the actual curve from the projected curve would be the signal to find the reasons for such divergence and to take corrective action at the appropriate level of operations.

A side effect of the new cash system was that it broadened the supply of credit available to General Motors. By establishing good working relationships with a large number of banks we were able to develop extensive lines of credit which could be drawn on if the need arose. By reducing our cash balances in banks, this system also enabled us to invest the excess cash, principally in short-term government securities. Thus we earned an income on money formerly kept as cash and so increased the efficiency with which we used our capital.

A number of people contributed to the creation of the cash plan. The need for it was seen by Mr. Raskob. He requested the preparation of the plan from Mr. Prentis, who, with the assistance of many others, drafted its broad outline. In general the technique they developed is still used by General Motors to control cash.

Inventory Control

The worst of the emergency problems was the inventory. I have related how uncontrolled purchases of raw and semifinished materials by the division managers had reached a total of $209 million by October of 1920, exceeding the Executive and Finance committees' maximum allotment by $59 million and far exceeding the amount that could immediately be used in the plants; and how the Finance Committee, on a temporary emergency basis, had taken control of inventories away from the operating divisions and on October 8, 1920, appointed an inventories committee, headed by Mr. Pratt, who was on Mr. Durant's staff, to bring the inventories under control.

John L. Pratt was one of the finest business executives I have ever known. He was originally a civil engineer. In 1905 he joined the du Pont Company, where he worked on the layout and building of plants. In 1918 he was made head of a section of the du Pont Development Department which at that time gave assistance to General Motors. He came into close association with Mr. Durant, and in 1919, at Mr. Durant's request, came to General Motors as assistant to Mr. Durant. Mr. Pratt did a number of high-level jobs for General Motors and had a large responsibility in getting Frigidaire going and in building it up in later years. He also succeeded me as head of the accessory divisions. For many years, on the operating side, Mr. Pratt, Mr. Brown, and I worked on the same floor and were in touch with each other on all the problems that came up. Mr. Pratt was, you might say, a stand-in for me when I was president. He had a great capability for handling large problems with plainness and simplicity. He could get to the point.

"The first step of the Inventories Committee" in the crisis of 1920, Mr. Pratt later wrote to Mr. Raskob, "was to send out, under the signature of the President of General Motors Corporation, a letter instructing all General Managers to buy nothing; to stop shipment of all purchases released—until the Inventories Committee could review the situation with each individual General Manager and decide on what material would be received and what would not be received . . . most of the work was done by sitting down with the General Managers in their own offices and going over their inventory situation with them in detail."

The general managers negotiated with the suppliers, and I know of only one instance—in the tractor business, not in the automobile business—in which there was litigation. Then the divisions were put under a system of controls. The original memorandum by Mr. Pratt described the procedure as follows: "After the flow of incoming material was stopped each General Manager submitted a monthly budget to the Inventories Committee which showed estimated sales for the next four months and the estimated materials and payrolls that would be required for production to meet the estimated sales. These budgets were carefully scanned by the Inventories Committee and discussed with the General Managers, and when an agreement had been reached material for one month's production at a time was released by the Inventories Committee." In this way they gained control over runaway inventories, reduced them, and conserved cash. For example, the level of inventory was reduced from the high of $215 million at the end of September 1920 to a low of $94 million at the end of June 1922, and the turnover of inventory was increased from about twice a year in September 1920 to over four times in June 1922.

Mr. Bradley has observed to me that the essential thing we learned from this experience was that the only way to cut back inventories—particularly in a time of declining business—is to reduce purchases and commitments for materials and supplies. Obvious? Not entirely. Anyway it took us a long time to learn this from experience. In those days the general managers tended to be optimists, as most executives in the selling end of the automobile business were and perhaps still are. They always expected that sales would increase and thereby bring the inventories in line. When the expected sales failed to materialize, a problem arose to which there could be no entirely pleasant solution. Hence we learned to be skeptical of expectations of increased future sales as a solution to a rising inventory problem. We took the position that actual inventories, purchases, and commitments should be reduced, knowing that we could increase them later if that were warranted by actual sales.

The emergency measures I have described established that the corporation was in charge of the corporation, so to speak. But centralization of this kind was not in accord with our ideas for permanent ways of doing business in General Motors. We soon turned again toward decentralization.

Donaldson Brown proposed a long-range policy of inventory control in a report to the Finance Committee on April 21, 1921, as follows:

It is believed that the emergency which existed at the time the Inventories Committee was formed has passed sufficiently to do away with this committee and place control of inventories where it belongs with other operating problems under the Vice President in charge of operations.

The function of the Inventories Committee has been to pass upon production schedules according to which deliveries of materials as required might be arranged for by the operating units, and in specific cases to authorize or disapprove the taking in of materials beyond the needs of current operations.

The operating units themselves must of necessity be looked to as the primary seat of control of inventories. The interposition of an Inventories Committee under the jurisdiction of the Finance Committee, with its delegated powers in the direction of inventory control affords a condition of dual responsibility which in normal conditions is unwholesome and objectionable . . .

In other words, it was time to abandon emergency measures in this area and to develop broad policies and practices. The important thing was to determine an inventory policy that could be expected to avoid a repetition of the 1920 crisis. To this end Mr. Brown proposed to establish a new relationship between financial policy and the operating organization. He wrote:

Insofar as the whole [inventory and commitments] involves the matter of working capital requirement the Finance Committee must have its voice reflected in the control, but this had better be by way of rules covering points of general policy rather than by any attempt at direct action. Moreover it would seem logical and sound in organization principle, for the Vice President or Chief Executive in charge of operations to be looked to to see that the divisions effectually control inventories to accord with Finance Committee policies or good business practice.

The financial department of the company is intimately concerned in the matter and should be expected to follow the situation closely at all times so that through the regular financial forecasts or by other reports the Finance Committee shall be as fully informed as possible of the company's position and prospective capital requirement.

These observations outlined the first tangible steps for a new financial-control system in General Motors. They were approved by the Finance Committee in May 1921 and so became the policy of the corporation. The Inventories Committee was disbanded and the administration of inventories was returned to the divisions. The instrumentality of control then became the divisional four-month forecast of expected business, which came to me as vice president in charge of operations; that is, it came to me after mid-1921. This forecast was the key to inventory control and it was my responsibility to review and approve it. Thus the division managers still bought the materials, but they were permitted to buy only enough at a time to make the number of cars and trucks specified in their approved production schedules.

Production Control

It should be understood, however, that conceptually and in practice these measures, growing out of the 1920–21 crisis, concerned mainly the control of unfinished goods and commitments for them. There remained to be solved the more formidable problem of controlling the inventory of finished products. This involved not only the problem of selling the cars on hand, but of controlling the level of car production. To assist in this aim we enlarged the scope of the four-month forecasts, mentioned above, to include plant investment, working capital, and outstanding inventory commitments as well as estimated sales, production, and earnings. These enlarged forecasts originated in the divisions and were to be in my hands on the twenty-fifth of each month. They covered the current month and each of the three ensuing months. After consulting with the vice president in charge of finance, I approved or modified the production schedule for each division in the light of these forecasts.

For some years this arrangement brought Mr. Brown and myself into a continuous relationship, both before and after I became president. My approval of the production schedule constituted authority for the division managers to proceed with production and to purchase or contract for deliveries of materials.

This procedure introduced the first serious effort at forecasting in General Motors. The only forecasts of any sort before the emergency of 1921 had been prepared by the treasurer for the Finance Committee. His forecasts, which covered sales, earnings, working capital, and cash position for the corporation as a whole, were useful in general financial planning. However, they did not represent the divisions' own estimates of expected operating results; indeed they did not even include divisional breakdowns. The division managers, therefore, could hardly be held accountable for fulfilling forecasts made by an authority remote from them, and so the forecasts were of little value in appraising and controlling divisional operating plans. And since the treasurer's forecasts of sales were nothing more than an assumption made at a distance from the customer, their accuracy was not great.

The new administration in 1921 likewise had very little data on which to base a production schedule, but we had to proceed anyway. In the nature of the business we had to build up stocks for spring demand. Then in June and July, three or four months before the end of the model year, we had to estimate sales for the balance of the model year, to be out of stock of cars of the current model, or nearly so, when the new model came in. This estimate could not be changed, since upon it we had to base calculations to get the right amount of materials. Our estimating procedure has evolved over the years, but in principle we still do the same thing.

The key element in the forecast, of course, was expected sales, from which the number of cars and trucks to be produced was determined. The level of production required to yield a given number of cars ready to sell on a given date, and the quantity of materials required to support that production, could be determined accurately by a purely technical calculation, relatively easy to make. The real problem was to forecast how many cars we could expect to sell.

It was in an effort to make the sales forecasts as accurate as possible that we put the responsibility for them directly on the division managers, since they were closer to the consumer and therefore the most likely to be well informed on sales trends. Beginning in 1921 I asked the division managers to give me reports of their actual unit production and sales at the factory for ten-day periods ending on the tenth, twentieth, and final day of each month. And I asked them to report, at the end of each month, how many unfilled orders for cars they had, how many finished cars they had in their plants, and how many cars they estimated their dealers had on hand. At that time such reports—although they were raw estimates of dealer stocks—were a novelty, and for a few years they provided the only factual basis for determining car-production requirements in General Motors.

The big gap in our information system at headquarters and in the divisions was at the retail level. We knew how many cars and trucks our divisions were selling to our dealers, but we did not know the current rate at which those vehicles were being resold to the public. We were not in touch with the actual retail market. The division managers gave me monthly reports on the number of cars in the hands of their dealers, but most of them estimated dealers' inventories without asking the dealers themselves to supply current data. This method—or lack of it—limited our sensitivity to changing market trends and required the staff at headquarters to base its sales forecasts on figures that were not only weak but also several weeks old. Such a time lag could be dangerous. It became, in fact, the source of a new crisis.

Beginning in 1922 I asked the division managers to submit at the end of each year estimates of their expected operating results for the year to come, along with the regular four-month forecasts. These annual estimates were really three different forecasts in one, for I requested them to predict for the coming year what their sales, earnings, and capital requirements would be on the basis of expectations that were pessimistic, conservative (that is, most likely), and optimistic. These compilations were not regarded as commitments—fortunately, for they did not prove to be very accurate. The shorter-term forecasts had a good accuracy record, and the long-term forecasts were fairly good for 1922 and 1923 but proved to be much too high for 1924. Even the pessimistic forecasts for that year were too high.

There was cause. The year 1923 had been so good that some of our car divisions, particularly Chevrolet, had lost potential sales because they were unable to supply the ultimate consumer with cars when required. Most of the division managers projected this experience onto the prospects for 1924 and resolved not to miss any more sales because of underproduction. They set high production rates for the early part of 1924. Some of the division managers, toward the end of 1923, asked permission to exceed their approved production requirements during the winter for the expected spring demand. I recommended that the Finance Committee approve this request and the committee did so.

Although I thus shared the belief that an increase in sales was to be expected, I also held the view that some of the divisions were planning to build more cars than a moderate improvement in sales would justify. I asked several of the division managers to reconsider their production schedules. In each case their reply was that in their opinion the schedule was justified.

Signs of distress began to appear early in 1924. In a report to the Finance and Executive committees dated March 14, 1924, I pointed out that the corporation and the industry as a whole had what was probably a larger number of unsold cars in the hands of dealers, distributors, and branches than at any previous time. Comparison of unit sales and production figures for the four-month period October 1, 1923, to January 31, 1924, with the corresponding figures for the year before showed that our production had increased about 50 per cent while our sales to the ultimate consumer had declined about 4 per cent. Here the time lag entered. I did not get these figures until the first week in March 1924.

I warned the managers of the divisions of the growing danger, and at Chevrolet and Oakland I insisted upon immediate and drastic curtailment of production schedules. The division managers complied reluctantly. As late as the end of March a couple of them still held that their disappointing sales figures were entirely the result of bad weather and that, as soon as the weather improved, brisk selling would justify their original production rates.

At that time I was concerned not with current stocks but with the possibility that a dangerous surplus might develop by July 1. Mr. Brown's figures indicated that all was not well, and although I was impressed by them I hesitated to overrule the divisional people who had the responsibility for selling. There will always be some conflict between the figure men and the salesmen, since the salesmen naturally think they can do something about a statistical situation, as they often can. I got in the middle here—between Mr.

Brown and the divisions—as I often did in the presence of conflicting representations of reality. But then in May 1924 Mr. Brown and I made a trip into the field to discuss distribution problems with the dealers in their places of business, and on that trip I came to know beyond doubt that the March cutbacks had been inadequate and that overproduction was not just a possibility for July but already a certainty. It is not often that the chief executive of a large corporation himself discovers visible overproduction by a physical check of the inventory. But automobiles are big units easy to count. In St. Louis, my first stop, in Kansas City, and again in Los Angeles, I stood in the dealers' lots and saw the inventories parked in rows. The figure man in this instance was right and the salesmen were wrong. Everywhere the inventories were excessive.

I then issued one of the few flat orders I ever gave to the division managers during the time I served as chief executive officer of General Motors. This order directed all division managers to curtail production schedules immediately—the over-all total reduction for the corporation amounted to about 30,000 units a month. By cutting production schedules drastically we were able to reduce dealer stocks to manageable proportions in a few months' time, but not without considerable economic hardship to the employees of the corporation who were laid off.

On June 13, 1924, I was taken to task by the Finance Committee for not having anticipated and prevented this overproduction. The committee adopted a resolution requesting me to explain how our production schedules were developed and who was responsible for the excessive number of General Motors cars in dealers' hands during the spring and summer, and what we proposed to do to avoid a repetition of such an event. The committee stated its questions as follows:

First. What plan of procedure has heretofore been followed in developing production schedules?

Second. What was the justification of a production schedule of 101,209 cars for April as indicated by the February 25th forecast recognizing that the stock of cars in the field was approximately 236,000 as of the end of February?

Third. Why were steps not taken earlier by the Operating Divisions to drastically curtail their production more in line with the unsold stocks of cars in the field and the consumer demand?

Fourth. What steps will be taken to assure effective control of production schedules in the future to guard against over-production?

Fifth. In what way will the Finance Committee be informed as to the general aspect of the situation enabling it to determine whether monthly forecasts are predicated upon a volume of sales to consumers which is in harmony with the Committee's judgement of general business conditions?

In my reply to the committee on September 29, I censured some of the divisions, particularly Chevrolet and Oakland. I pointed out that Cadillac was the only division that had been guided in any way in its production planning by sales to ultimate consumers. The other divisions had developed their production schedules in various ways, generally following the notion that the responsibility from the sales standpoint ceased with the delivery of the product to the dealer or distributor and that the corporation had no further interest in the situation. Our response to the events of 1924 formed a turning point in the development of our procedures for control of our production schedules. I described the situation at that time in a report to the Finance Committee:

First: That up to the first of July, 1924, or thereabouts, production schedules were developed in various ways, based largely on the theory that the responsibility from the Sales standpoint ceased with the delivery of the product to the dealer or distributor, and that the Corporation had no further concern in the transaction, and as long as dealers and distributors could be forced to take cars, the situation was regarded as entirely healthy and constructive.

Second: That no real study of the fundamentals had ever been made. By this is meant that although information as to the sale of cars to consumers—man[i]festly the real index—had been available in a more-or-less satisfactory form during the past two years, this fundamental data had never been developed and capitalized as a guide in the preparation of production schedules.

Third: That July 1st, 1924, a procedure was developed, which, it is believed, places production schedules on an entirely scientific basis, and founded on a real fundamental index. Accountability for the development of such schedules is now definitely established between the Operating Divisions and the Corporation itself, the latter satisfying itself as to the constructiveness of same. A copy of this Procedure entitled "Monthly Forecast of Deliveries to Consumers, Production, Inventory and Sales", has already been submitted to your Committee, but to make this report complete, that section of it dealing with an analysis of production requirements based on forecast of deliveries to consumers, is appended as "Exhibit A".

Fourth: The lack of a proper and fundamental development of production schedules was in no sense limited to General Motors Divisions, for, as a matter of fact, the same method was being followed by the entire industry. This situation is one of the causes contributing to the present economic condition of the average automotive dealer, which condition was reported to your Committee by the undersigned following the field trip taken during the month of May.

Fifth: After due consideration, the undersigned, on behalf of the Corporation, issued a statement which, as evidenced by comments received from dealers and distributors, and by editorials in the automotive press, has been recognized as performing a valuable service and establishing a precedent which other automotive manufacturers will be inclined to follow in future.

In my statement to the Finance Committee then, I summed up my personal feelings:

(a) That it is rather a reflection on the General Motors Corporation, and equally so on the industry as a whole, that nothing of this kind has been accomplished before, nevertheless, like many other important considerations which have not yet been developed as logically as they might be, this should be looked upon as a natural happening in an industry which is not yet thoroughly stabilized.

(b) There is no question in my mind but that General Motors now has absolute control of its production schedules. I feel further that the policy inaugurated by General Motors, as evidenced by the Corporation's Dealer policy, and by similar statements on the part of other manufacturers, cannot help but assist the economic position of dealers and thus be a great help to the industry of which General Motors is such an important part.

I have recounted this episode of 1924 because of its consequences, for it marked the beginning of reasonably effective production control in General Motors. In a certain very important sense, this involved the reconciliation of the work of two kinds of persons in General Motors—essential, I should think, in any corporation with a nationally distributed consumer product. One kind is the sales manager with his natural enthusiasm, optimism, and belief that he can, by his efforts, influence total sales. The other is the statistical person who makes his analyses objectively on broad general evidence of demand. Resolving the conflict between these two viewpoints would give one an idea, for example, of how many cars one should expect dealers to stock. This conflict was especially acute in those days when we had not yet solved the problem of reconciling production levels with seasonal peaks in sales. And of course behind this was the basic problem of controlling production.

Two things were involved: first, the art of forecasting, and second, shortening the reaction time when a forecast proved wrong, which can be expected to happen even in the present day of complex mathematical forecasting technique.

Since we at headquarters had begun to develop techniques of fact-finding and analysis, we were in a better position than the divisions to forecast total industry demand and total sales of our products for the entire model year. And since production, the level of dealer inventories, and general financial planning all depend to a large extent on the outlook for the entire model run, we decided in 1924 to establish an official corporation-wide estimate of consumer demand—that is, an estimate of the number of cars in each price group likely to be sold to the public during the coming year by the entire automotive industry—and to have this correlated with the division managers' forecasts, keeping in mind the percentage of each price group that General Motors might reasonably be expected to obtain. This corporation-wide estimate was based upon actual experience of sales during the past three sales years and an appraisal of the general business outlook for the coming year.

We took the first actual step in putting limits on the divisions in the spring of 1924. Mr. Brown and I worked out along the above lines an estimated volume of business for the second half of the year for the corporation as a whole and for each division. We called this expectation of sales volume the "index volume," that is, the volume to be regarded as the pointer for a twelve-month period. After the index volume had been approved by the Operations Committee, I issued a general letter to the division managers on May 12, 1924, asking that their forecasts for the last six months of 1924 be based on that index. This letter read, in part:

Heretofore in asking for these estimates [the divisional sales forecasts] the basis upon which they have been considered i.e., the volume of business, has been left to the individual judgment of each Operating Division. This time, and dealing with the second half [of the year], I believe we are taking a constructive step forward. I mean by this that the Operations Committee has determined, as a group, the probable trend of business for the manufacturing year beginning July first . . . That being the case, we are able to supply specific information which will assist our Divisions in more accurately forecasting their operating results.

. . . We have in General Motors, I believe for the first time and dealing now with the Corporation as a whole, a definite and logically expressed viewpoint as to what the probabilities are a year hence. Of course the trend may change. It may improve, and I personally believe it will. It may decline but I hardly think that possible. If either takes place an adjustment will be made from month to month in such [m]anner as to eliminate the extreme peaks and declines that have heretofore been characteristic of the industry and of General Motors.

Now what did this tale of internal conflict over statistics come down to? Essentially it was a matter of statistical controls versus salesmanship, which was brought to a head in 1924 by a recession in the general economy following directly upon the boom year of 1923. At that time the salesmen and the general managers were caught in the illusion of riding the wave. In our then excessively decentralized scheme I let them ride. Actually, however, this was not a mere bias in favor of the salesmen, for I had no convincing information with which to counter their intuitions. The information, as I have said, was weak and late. The information was weak because it was neither accurate nor comprehensive enough. It was arrived at by inference from dealer stocks and unfilled orders. This was good enough over a period of time, but the critical trouble was precisely the length of the period. We knew nothing about the most recent five or six weeks of our car sales, and this gap therefore was filled with the speculations of the protagonists—the statisticians with their trend lines on the one hand, and the salesmen with their optimistic intuitions on the other. I was, as I have said, in the middle without any means to judge the contending claims—not a comfortable position for a chief executive officer.

Hence the need first to limit the divisions with a forecast of sales for the model year. But since this expectation could easily be upset by actual developments in the market, there was further need for a corrective device which would enable us to retreat from (or advance beyond) the expectation, and thereby also readjust the expectation. And remember this, that in the automobile industry you cannot operate without programing and planning. It is a matter of respecting figures on the future as a guide. The essential elements are the forecast and the correction, each equally critical. For upon the forecast for the model year, made several months before that year begins, depend the plans and outlays for tooling and other preparations for the level of actual production. After the model year begins, this forecast (the index volume), although often revised, is the guiding mark for six to eight months, after which the model year is closed out by a final unalterable decision on production. The tooling, of course, is unalterably settled ahead of time. But after the model year begins, we depend upon the accuracy of current information and the swiftness with which we receive it as the control mechanism with which to make other essential corrections. These were the lessons of 1923–24, and they led to the following actions.

We worked out in 1924 and 1925 a system of statistical reports to be sent by the dealers to the divisions every ten days. The core of these reports was the information on dealers' sales of cars and trucks to consumers during ten-day periods, together with deliveries of used cars to consumers and the number of both new and used cars on hand in dealers' lots. Used-car inventories were important because if they backed up in the hands of dealers they would block the sale of new cars. With this information in hand each ten days, the divisions thereafter had an up-to-date, comprehensive picture of the situation in the field. The divisions and the headquarters staff were then able to take corrective action and make new forecasts with greater accuracy.

As a further aid to sales forecasting, we used independent data on retail sales to supplement the ten-day reports from dealers. Since the end of 1922, we had obtained from the R. L. Polk Company regular reports on new-car registrations (these reports were also available to others in the industry). The whole procedure thus put production and scheduling on a more disciplined basis and clearly defined the accountability of the operating divisions and of the corporation management for the development of production schedules.

We have endeavored always to refine and improve our techniques in the area of estimating retail demand, and the Distribution and Financial staffs have achieved some success in the field of market analysis. In 1923 the Sales Section undertook a comprehensive study of the total automobile market, based on the then prevailing concept that there was a "pyramid of demand" (formulated by Mr. Bradley in 1921). The study attempted to provide information on the size of the total market for the next few years, the market potential in the various price classes, the probable effect of price reductions on the size of the market, the competitive relationship of new and used cars, and when the so-called "saturation point" would be reached in the market. The findings of this study underestimated the future growth in the market—but its comprehensive approach to the problem represented a significant advance in market-analysis techniques in the automobile industry. The analysis of market potential by price class, in particular, was an important concept that had not previously been developed to a satisfactory degree. Also, the 1923 study clearly demonstrated the relationship between potential automobile demand and the distribution of income in the United States. With this knowledge we were able to give more meaningful recognition to the pyramid of demand in planning our sales strategy and productive capacity.

The 1923 study failed to gauge accurately the future growth of the market largely because it underestimated the effect of two important factors on new car sales. One of these was the process of continuous product improvement which stimulated consumer demand by providing increasing values for the customer's dollar. The other was the continued growth of the economy and the effect of general economic conditions on the sales of the industry in any specific year. In this latter connection Mr. Bradley later introduced into the consideration of market potential the concept that there was a definite relationship between car sales and over-all economic activity. He and his staff continued their interest in the question of the ups and downs of the automobile business in relation to the business cycle and saw that when business, and hence national income, was on an ascending trend, car sales increased at an even faster rate than income; and when business was on a declining trend, sales decreased at a faster rate than income. As additional statistical material on the over-all economy became available, we were able to refine our techniques and demonstrate the remarkably close correlation between car sales and personal income, a correlation that still exists today for car sales and disposable income after taxes.

To return then to the problem of production control: Once the total year's production of a division had been forecast, the division manager's problem was to spread that production out over the year to maintain his output at as even a rate as possible while still allowing for seasonal fluctuations in sales. This was not easy. The automobile business is still seasonal to some extent, and it was very much so in the early 1920s before we had improved roads, the closed car, and such devices as financial incentives to dealers to increase their trade-in allowances during slack periods.

From the standpoint of the dealer's convenience and the most economical control of finished-goods inventory, the factory should have varied its output to conform to seasonal demand. Such a practice would have reduced the risk of obsolescence and the cost of storing finished products for both dealer and manufacturer. On the other hand, absolutely level production—or the nearest to it that could be attained—was ideal from the standpoint of efficient utilization of plant and labor and from the standpoint of the employee's welfare. Since considerations of economical distribution and economical manufacture were thus diametrically opposed, planning and judgment were required to find a reasonable balance between them.

The headquarters staff assisted the division managers in this task with a seasonal analysis of the year's sales estimate, and a computation for each division of an absolute minimum working stock to be maintained and the maximum seasonal excess over that minimum that was allowable at the end of each four-month forecast period. And every ten days, when the reports from the dealers came in, each division manager compared his actual results with the forecast for the month and reviewed his production and purchasing schedule. This was the heart of the matter. If sales were running behind the forecast, production was reduced. If sales were booming, he could, within the limits of his plant capacity, increase his output. Each month he adjusted his forecast for the next four months to conform to the current sales trend. Thus, instead of laying down a hard-and-fast production schedule four months ahead and sticking to it, whatever the actual trend of retail demand, we were able to change production schedules when sales indicated to the management that such a change was necessary. We were able to keep production in line with the indicated retail demand while still keeping the accumulation of finished products in the hands of both divisions and dealers no lower than the desired minimum.

Thus the more important thing in the end was not the correctness of the index for the model year but the sensitivity to actual market changes through prompt reports and adjustment. The objectivity and systematic use of the information had a co-ordinating influence upon the headquarters staff and the divisions of the corporation. It reduced the possibility of irrational conflict such as that of 1924. It also operated as a basic control on expenses, employment, investment, and the like.

The effects of the new forecasting and scheduling were apparent in operating results. Materials inventories were kept to a minimum. In 1921 total inventories of materials, goods in process, and finished goods turned over about two times. By 1922 the turnover had increased to four times, and by 1926 to nearly seven and one-half times. An even greater improvement was shown in the turnover of productive inventory (total inventory less finished product), which reached ten and one-half times annually by 1925.

Progress was made, too, in stabilizing employment. But the problem of keeping production at a stable level is still unsolved today and very likely will remain so, owing in part to the incompletely solved problem of forecasting sales in the uncertain future. Other problems—the variations in the level of demand, both cyclical and seasonal, and the influence of the model change and the buying habits of the general public—have also had much to do with keeping production from remaining stable. As a matter of fact, we could achieve perfect forecasting and still find ourselves unable to stabilize production much more than we can today.

The closer alignment of current production schedules with the movement of the final product into the hands of consumers also improved the turnover of dealers' inventories and hence their profit position. In 1925 the turnover of new-car inventories in the hands of General Motors dealers throughout the United States was twelve times, approximately 25 per cent greater than in any previous year.

Our production-control system was essentially complete in 1925. Since then progress in this area has been a matter of refinements.

The Key to Co-ordinated Control of Decentralized Operations

Having thus established techniques of control in the particular areas of appropriations, cash, inventory, and production, the general question remained: How could we exercise permanent control over the whole corporation in a way consistent with the decentralized scheme of organization? We never ceased to attack this paradox; indeed we could not avoid a solution of it without yielding both the actual decentralized structure of our business and our philosophy of approach to it. I have dealt in earlier chapters with the organization aspect of the question as it was developed in theory and practice in General Motors in the early 1920s. But that alone was not enough. It was on the financial side that the last necessary key to decentralization with co-ordinated control was found. That key, in principle, was the concept that, if we had the means to review and judge the effectiveness of operations, we could safely leave the prosecution of those operations to the men in charge of them. The means as it turned out was a method of financial control which converted the broad principle of return on investment into one of the important working instruments for measuring the operations of the divisions. The basic elements of financial control in General Motors are cost, price, volume, and rate of return on investment.

A word on rate of return as a strategic principle of business. I am not going to say that rate of return is a magic wand for every occasion in business. There are times when you have to spend money just to stay in business, regardless of the visible rate of return. Competition is the final price determinant and competitive prices may result in profits which force you to accept a rate of return less than you hoped for, or for that matter to accept temporary losses. And, in times of inflation, the rate-of-return concept comes up against the problem of assets undervalued in terms of replacement. Nevertheless, no other financial principle with which I am acquainted serves better than rate of return as an objective aid to business judgment.

This principle had governed the thinking of the Finance Committee of General Motors since 1917, as it had governed the thinking of the du Pont people and certain other businessmen in the United States before that time. I do not know the origin of the principle itself. Even the least sophisticated investor measures his profits from stocks, bonds, or savings accounts in terms of what he puts into them. So, too, I imagine, every businessman evaluates profits in terms of his total investment. It is a rule of the game, so to speak. There are other measures for the running of a business; for example, profit on sales, and penetration of the market, but they do not supersede return on investment.

However, the question is not simply one of maximizing the rate of return for a specific short period of time. Mr. Brown's thought on this was that the fundamental consideration was an average return over a long period of time. Under his concept General Motors' economic objective was to produce not necessarily the highest attainable rate of return on the capital employed, but the highest return consistent with attainable volume in the market. The long-term rate of return was to be the highest expectation consistent with a sound growth of the business, or what we called "the economic return attainable."[1]

When Donaldson Brown came to General Motors he brought with him a financial yardstick. It was a method of crystallizing facts bearing on the efficiency of management in the various phases of the business, such as inventory control, plans for capital investment in relation to expected demands on production, cost control, and the like. In other words, Mr. Brown developed the concept of return on investment in such a way that it could be used to measure the effectiveness of each division's operation as well as to evaluate broad investment decisions. His concept can be expressed in the form of an equation for computing return on investment, and it is still one of the measures used by the du Pont Company and General Motors to evaluate divisional performance. This book, however, is not the place for such technicalities as formal equations. I shall touch only on general concepts of financial control.

Rate of return, of course, is affected by all the factors in the business; hence if one can see how these factors individually bear upon a rate of return, one has a penetrating look into the business. To obtain this insight, Mr. Brown defined return on investment as a function of the profit margin and the rate of turnover of invested capital. (Multiplying one by the other equals the per cent of return

---

[1] Mr. Brown put it this way:

"A monopolistic industry, or an individual business under peculiar circumstances, might maintain high prices and enjoy a limited volume with very high rate of return on capital, indefinitely, at the sacrifice of wholesome expansion. Reduction of price might broaden the scope of demand, and afford an enlargement of volume highly beneficial, even though the rate of return on capital might be lower. The limiting considerations are the economic cost of capital, the ability to increase supply, and the extent to which demand will be stimulated by price reduction.

"Thus it is apparent that the object of management is not necessarily the highest attainable *rate of return* on capital, but rather the highest return consistent with attainable volume, care being exercised to assure profit with each increment of volume that will at least equal the economic cost of additional capital required. Therefore the fundamental consideration is the economic cost of capital to the individual business." ("Pricing Policy in Relation to Financial Control," *Management and Administration*, February 1924.)

on investment.) If this seems obscure, pass over it and note only that you can get an increase in return on investment by increasing the rate of turnover of capital in relation to sales as well as by increasing profit margins. Each of these two elements—profit margin and rate of turnover of capital—Mr. Brown broke into its detailed components, a case, you might say, of aggregating and de-aggregating figures to bring about a recognition of the structure of profit and loss in operations. Essentially it was a matter of making things visible. The unique thing was that it made possible the creation, based on experience, of detailed standards or yardsticks for working-capital and fixed-capital requirements and for the various elements of costs. To get standards for commercial expense and manufacturing expense, Mr. Brown used past performance modified by plans for the future. The yardsticks thus established were compared with actual performance. The heart of the financial-control principle lies in such comparisons. Mr. Brown was able to set up tables showing, for example, how the sizes of the inventory and working capital were affecting the turnover of capital in the different divisions, or to what extent selling expenses were a drag on profits.

To make this concept work, each division manager was required to submit monthly reports of his total operating results. The data from these reports were put on standard forms by the central financial office in such a way as to provide the standard basis for measuring divisional performance in terms of return on investment. Each division manager received this form, which spelled out the facts for his division. For a number of years this gave each division its rank in the corporation on a rate-of-return scale.

The divisional return-on-investment reports were constantly studied by the top executives. If the indicated results were not satisfactory, I or some other general executive would confer with the division managers about the corrective action to be taken. When, as chief operating officer, I visited the divisions, I carried a little black book in which was typed in a systematic way both historical and forecast information about each division of the corporation, including, for the car divisions, their competitive position. The figures did not give automatic answers to problems. They simply exposed the facts with which to judge whether the divisions were operating in line with expectations as reflected in prior performance or in their budgets.

The early return-on-investment form, which with some modifications is still used in General Motors, was the first step in educating our operating personnel in the meaning and importance of rate of return as a standard of performance. It provided executives with a quantitative basis for sound decision making, and thereby laid the foundation for what was to be one of General Motors' most important characteristics, namely, its effort to achieve open-minded communication and objective consideration of facts.

In the beginning many limitations in our method were evident. The reports, for example, were not usable for evaluation and comparison until they were set up on a uniform and consistent basis. Uniformity is essential to financial control, since without it comparisons are difficult if not impossible. One of the immediate tasks, therefore, was to strengthen the accounting organization, both centrally and within the divisions, and to institute standard accounting practices throughout the organization. The classification of accounts throughout the corporation was standardized on January 1, 1921. A standard accounting manual, specifying a uniform set of procedures, became effective throughout the corporation on January 1, 1923. To co-ordinate financial organizations of the divisions and the central Financial Staff, we reaffirmed in 1921 the principle of dual responsibility for the divisional comptrollers, which had been introduced in 1919 to make those comptrollers responsible not only to their divisional general managers, but to the corporation comptroller as well.

The development of a uniform accounting practice enabled us to analyze the internal condition of each division and to compare one division's operating performance with another's. But what is equally important, the uniform accounting practice created guidelines, with some exceptions, for overhead-cost accounting, both for actual costs of production and for developing yardsticks for evaluating operating efficiency.

The Concept of Standard Volume

While we had developed and applied the concept of return on investment and had made progress in standardizing our procedures, before 1925 we had no well-defined governing objective against which to measure our results. As a practical matter, because of the influence of changing volume, our results showed wide fluctuations from year to year, which made an evaluation particularly difficult. Therefore, beginning in 1925, we adopted a concept developed by Mr. Brown which related a definite, long-term return-on-investment objective to average or "standard-volume" expectations over a number of years. We took the view that the existence of such a desired long-term return-on-investment goal would provide a useful yardstick for evaluating operating efficiency and the effect of competitive pressures on pricing. With this approach we were not likely to lose sight of the long-run earnings objective and, in evaluating our prices, we would always be aware of the extent to which competition was preventing the attainment of the objective. The concept which Mr. Brown developed, of course, was only a theoretical one because operating results are determined by the interplay of actual prices, competitively determined, and the total costs incurred in the particular year regardless of volume. However, by applying a yardstick, unaffected by short-term volume fluctuations, we could isolate the extent to which we were deviating from our long-term profit goal and make a thorough evaluation of the underlying causes. The concept is a good illustration of our management philosophy of defining a soundly conceived theoretical reference to guide us in the practical management of our affairs.

The standard-volume concept is a method for viewing the long-range performance and potential of our business and its divisions, based on average volume over a number of years. In establishing this policy in the form of a procedure, I wrote in May 1925:

. . . What concerns our stockholders is a return year in and year out, the average of which represents a fair measure of the possibilities of the business in which we are engaged. It is believed the establishing of the principles outlined in this Procedure will lead to this result.

It must be agreed that no definite rule for establishing prices can ever be rigidly adhered to. That is in no sense intended. It is believed, however, that a development of standard prices reflecting proper relation to cost, volume, and return on capital employed, will be most useful in guiding the Corporation toward determining what should be done in each individual case.

There are these elements in the standard-volume approach: volume, costs, prices, and rate of return on capital. At a given volume, cost, and price—theoretical but founded on experience—you can compute a desired rate of return. If, in fact, the anticipated return does not result, it may be because competition dictated a different price, or somewhere the costs were out of line, suggesting a look at the costs. You may find fifty men sitting on a roof somewhere because of a mixup in a plant. That's not typical, but it actually happened once. The calculation of return on investment itself tells you what to expect if the volume is higher or lower than the adopted standard unit volume.

The chief theoretical contribution of Mr. Brown and Mr. Bradley in this area was in the way they made allowance for the effect on unit costs of variations in rates of production over the years. As long as material costs and wage rates are fairly stable, direct costs of production tend to remain constant per unit, regardless of volume. Every car produced contains a certain amount of steel. It also has an engine, wheels, tires, battery, and so on. A certain number of man-hours of labor is required for manufacturing and assembly. Our production engineers and cost estimators could determine the amount paid for each purchased part, the quantity of various kinds of raw material used, and the hours of labor required in manufacturing and assembly operations.

Fixed overhead costs, of course, behave very differently. These fixed costs include supervision, maintenance expenses, and depreciation; tooling, styling, and engineering costs; administration expenses and insurance, and local taxes. With plant facilities established at any given capacity, the total amount of such fixed costs is relatively constant, regardless of the level of operations. Hence, fixed overhead costs per unit vary inversely with volume; they increase as volume falls, and decrease as volume rises. For complete accuracy this concept needs to be qualified by the semifixed costs which do not come down automatically with increased volume. But, in general, unit costs will go up in years of low volume and, conversely, they will go down in years of high volume.

In order to avoid the influence of fluctuating volume on the unit costs to be used as yardsticks, unit costs were developed on a standard-volume basis. Standard volume may be defined as the estimated rate of operations at the normal or average annual utilization of capacity. This capacity must be large enough to meet the cyclical and seasonal peaks which are characteristic of the automobile industry. Standard volume takes into account the necessity of operating the business at various levels of volume and over a period of many years. In actual practice standard volume in General Motors proved to be close to the actual average utilization over a period of years, although the individual years varied.

The standard-volume costing concept permitted us to appraise and analyze our costs from one year to the next on a basis unaffected by changes in volume at a given plant capacity. Changes in these unit costs reflected changes only in wage rates, material costs, and operating efficiencies and were not affected by year-to-year changes in volume. Even more importantly, unit costs at standard volume gave us a bench mark against which to evaluate our cost-price relationship. They also provided a consistent set of unit-cost data against which to compare actual unit costs and thus served as a gauge of the efficiency of our performance from one month to the next as well as from one year to the next.

It is important to recognize that the standard-volume concept of costing also enabled us to establish detailed operating standards for manufacturing expenses. Our uniform accounting practice made it possible to make an allocation to each department in a plant, of the indirect manufacturing expenses, or what we call "burden." Burden commonly includes three types of costs: first, fixed-burden costs such as rentals, insurance, depreciation and amortization, which in general remain constant regardless of the level of operations; second, semifixed costs, such as supervisors' salaries, which are also fixed within a reasonable range of production; and finally, variable-burden costs, which tend to vary directly with the level of production, such as labor related directly to manufacturing, cutting tools, packing and shipping supplies, lubricants, and maintenance. All of these expenses vary from department to department and allocating them properly in computing the cost of goods produced is a difficult part of any cost system in a manufacturing company. To do this, the indirect costs are related to direct productive labor; the latter can be determined on the basis of time studies and known wage rates. The fixed and semifixed portions of costs can be translated into per unit terms through the standard-volume approach. The variable unit costs (direct labor, materials, and burden) are based on past operating experience, current material costs, and wage rates. This classification of manufacturing costs thus segregates the areas where expenses can be controlled by the divisional management. By comparing actual results with the yardsticks established for these items, pressure was exerted to maintain the efficiency required to attain the cost objectives. The guiding principle was to make our standards difficult to achieve but possible to attain, which I believe is the most effective way of capitalizing on the initiative, resourcefulness, and capabilities of the operating personnel.

It is obvious that, with stable material costs and wage rates, if our bench mark showed that unit costs were high in relation to price, efficiency had been reduced. Because of competitive resistance to price increases, profits could be maintained only by reductions in unit costs. If there was a general rise in what industry paid for materials and labor, competitive forces might allow prices to rise. This was likely if consumer demand for cars was strong. Without higher prices under the circumstances, the automobile industry could not long continue to supply the cars that the market wanted. However, even in this case the individual manufacturer was under pressure to reduce his unit costs, since competition would probably not allow price increases sufficient to recover the full cost increase.

An alternative approach to our standard-volume policy would have been to evaluate prices strictly in terms of actual unit costs at actual or anticipated production levels. Because our fixed costs were so large, this would have meant that unit costs would drop in times of high volume and increase during periods of low production. Any attempt to raise prices during periods of low volume, even if competition permitted, to recover the higher unit costs could have deflated sales still further, with the result of still lower profits, less employment, and a generally depressive effect on the economy. Operating as we did in a highly cyclical industry, the use of the actual unit-cost type of evaluation would have been socially and economically unsound. I want to make clear, however, that in any given year our income, which had to reflect all actual costs, was importantly affected by the volume attained. Fixed costs had to be met whether business was good or bad. If our volume fell below standard, only a portion of our total fixed costs could be allocated to the unit cost of production, but the unallocated remainder would have to be deducted in arriving at reported income. Conversely, if volume was above standard, total income would be increased because the fixed costs would be distributed over a greater number of units produced.

It should be apparent from the foregoing that profit is residual, based upon the ability of the manufacturer to keep his costs below the sales price established in a competitive market. That is, profit represents the difference between the price which can be obtained in the competitive market, and total cost. And it is substantially affected by volume. We can estimate very closely what our profit per unit should be at standard volume, but this is not the same as knowing what our actual profit will be when actual volume is realized. Profit is a variable, and a volatile one, in the automobile business.

The need for financial controls grew out of crises. Controls were brought in to ensure that crises did not recur. Their effectiveness was demonstrated particularly in the depression year 1932. The corporation's U.S. and Canadian unit volume in that year was 50 per cent less than that of 1931, and 72 per cent below the high of 1929. But the corporation was not demoralized as it had been in 1920 and it stayed in the black. Not many corporations did as well.

Financial control as worked out by General Motors gave the corporation a review of operations that reduced the need to administer operations from the top. Central-office management was able to know whether the decentralized management was operating well or poorly and had a factual basis for a judgment regarding the future of any particular part of the business. We had the fundamentals of this system worked out just in time for one of the greatest changes that has ever taken place in the automobile market.

Chapter 9

TRANSFORMATION OF THE AUTOMOBILE MARKET

B Y the middle of the 1920s General Motors had accomplished
some things, but apart from survival and reorganization, they
were more in the realm of the mind than of reality. We knew,
as I have related, the strategy with which we proposed to approach
the car business, how we proposed to manage the enterprise finan-
cially, and the relationships we wanted to establish among persons
in different roles. But by the end of 1924 little of this was reflected
in our activities in the automobile market. That our volume of
business had increased after the slump of 1921—and especially in
1923—could be attributed less to our own wits than to the improvement in the general economy and the rising demand for automobiles. While internally we had made much progress, externally
we had marked time. But the time had come to act.

Now it so happened—luckily for us—that during the first part of
the 1920s, and especially in the years 1924 to 1926, certain changes
took place in the nature of the automobile market which transformed it into something different from what it had been all the
years up to that time. (Seldom, perhaps at only one other time in
the history of the industry—that is, on the occasion of the rise of
the Model T after 1908—has the industry changed so radically as it
did through the middle twenties.) I say luckily for us because as a
challenger to the then established position of Ford, we were favored by change. We had no stake in the old ways of the automobile business; for us, change meant opportunity. We were glad to

bend our efforts to go with it and make the most of it. We were prepared, too, with the various business concepts which I have described, though I must say we saw them as merely *our* way of doing business and not as having any general application or logical involvement in the future of the industry.

To set the scene, let me divide the history of the automobile, from a commercial standpoint, into three periods. There was the period before 1908, which with its expensive cars was entirely that of a *class* market; then the period from 1908 to the mid-twenties, which was dominantly that of a *mass* market, ruled by Ford and his concept of basic transportation at a low dollar price; and, after that, the period of the mass market served by better and better cars, or what might be thought of as the *mass-class* market, with increasing diversity. This last I think I may correctly identify as the General Motors concept.

All three of these periods have in common the long-expanding American economy, the horizon of each period having been formed by the respective degrees of that rise and its spread through the population. The willingness of the relatively few who could afford them to buy expensive though unreliable cars—by today's standards—enabled the industry to get going. Then when a large number of individuals were able to afford a few hundred dollars of expenditure, they made possible the development of the inexpensive Model T (it is possible that such a market was long waiting for the offering of a car like the Model T). As the economy, led by the automobile industry, rose to a new high level in the twenties, a complex of new elements came into existence to transform the market once again and create the watershed which divides the present from the past.

These new elements I think I can without significant loss reduce to four: installment selling, the used-car trade-in, the closed body, and the annual model. (I would add improved roads if I were to take into account the environment of the automobile.) So imbedded are these elements in the nature of the industry today that to conceive of the market without them is almost impossible. Before 1920 and for a while thereafter the typical car buyer was in the situation of buying his first car; he would buy it for cash or with some special loan arrangement; and the car would be a roadster or touring car, most likely of a model which was the same as last year's and could be expected to be the same as next year's. This situation was not to change for some years and the change would not be sudden except at its climax. For each of the new elements of change had a separate beginning and rate of development before they all interacted to cause complete transformation.

Installment selling of automobiles in regularized form first appeared in a small way shortly before World War I. This form of borrowing, or inverse saving, when placed on a routine basis, enabled large numbers of consumers to buy an object as expensive as an automobile. The statistics of installment selling in those days were very poor, but it is clear that it grew from some very low level in 1915 to around 65 per cent for new cars in 1925. We believed that with rising incomes and the expectation of a continuance of that rise, it was reasonable to assume that consumers would lift their sights to higher levels of quality. Installment selling, we thought, would stimulate this trend.

As the first car buyers came back for the second round and brought their old cars as down payments, the custom of trading was established. That the industry was engaged in a trading business had revolutionary significance not only for dealer arrangements but for manufacturing and the whole character of production, since dealers usually had to sell to a man who already had a car with mileage left in it.

The statistics for used-car trade-ins before 1925 are as poor as those for installment selling. It stands to reason, however, that there was some kind of upward curve in used cars traded from World War I on, if only because there were relatively few cars in existence before that time. Until some unknown date in the early 1920s, the majority of car buyers were buying their first car. The total number of passenger cars in operation in the United States from 1919 through 1929 rose by years in millions approximately as follows: 6, 7.3, 8.3, 9.6, 11.9, 13.7, 15.7, 16.8, 17.5, 18.7, 19.7. The industry, on the other hand, produced in those years passenger cars for domestic and export markets in approximate millions as follows: 1.7, 1.9, 1.5, 2.3, 3.6, 3.2, 3.7, 3.7, 2.9, 3.8, 4.5.[1] This production was enough to cover both the growth in numbers and the scrappage. The used car was traded perhaps two or three times on the way to

---

[1] The figures above are for passenger cars only. The full production of all vehicles, cars and trucks, for 1919 through 1929, was as follows: 1.9, 2.2, 1.6, 2.5, 4, 3.6, 4.3, 4.3, 3.4, 4.4, 5.3.

the scrap heap. So I assume there must have been a rising curve of used-car trade-ins.

The closed body was a specialty and mainly a custom-job affair before World War I. In the years 1919 through 1927, in round numbers by years, the industry sold closed cars in the following uninterruptedly rising percentages: 10, 17, 22, 30, 34, 43, 56, 72, and 85.

Of the annual model I shall say more later; suffice it to say here that in the early twenties it was not a formal concept as we know it today, except as it was negatively expressed in Ford's concept of a static model.

We were not unconscious of the unfolding of these four elements when the administration of General Motors changed in 1921. We started GMAC in the installment financing field in 1919. We had an interest in Fisher Body, which made closed bodies. As large sellers of medium- and high-price cars, we met the used-car trade-in early. And we tried to make our models more attractive each year. Yet we did not see the movement—especially the interaction—of these elements in the whole automobile market as I can see it today looking back. We saw them then as uncertainties, unknowns, and trends, in the form of figures to study at a desk. However, the plan of campaign laid down in the product program of 1921 logically fitted better and better the unfolding situation.

It was that plan, policy, or strategy of 1921—whatever it should be called—which, I believe, more than any other single factor enabled us to move into the rapidly changing market of the twenties with the confidence that we knew what we were doing commercially and were not merely chasing around in search of a lucky star. The most important particular object of that plan of campaign, which followed from its strategic principles, was, as I have said, to develop a larger place for Chevrolet between the Ford car below and the medium-price group above, a case of trying to widen a niche. That was all, in the beginning, despite the completeness of the plan with regard to the whole market.

There was the pause while we settled the copper-cooled-engine matter, in which we gave up the commercial-mindedness of our original strategic plan to pursue an engineering dream. We were rescued from that folly by the four-million car-and-truck year of 1923, which absorbed some 450,000 Chevrolets, and we saw the illusions of the upward swing of that year dashed in the recession of 1924. It was thus made clear to us that the plan of 1921 would have meaning only if meaning were given to it in the design of the product itself.

Certain facts of failure in particular were impressed upon us. During the year 1924, while the industry's passenger-car sales in the United States fell 12 per cent, General Motors' sales fell 28 per cent. Of the industry's decline in sales of about 439,000 car units, almost half was represented by the decline in General Motors' car sales. Our share of the passenger-car market in units dropped from 20 per cent to 17 per cent, while Ford's share went up from 50 per cent to 55 per cent. Some of the General Motors decline was in Buick and Cadillac, as was to be expected of higher-priced cars in a period of economic recession. (Olds increased, Oakland was unchanged.) But most of it was in sales of the Chevrolet, which fell 37 per cent while sales of its opposite number, the Ford, fell only 4 per cent. Of course, what happened was not due entirely to the events of 1924, including some bad management, but to the recession of that year combined with earlier events. The lag between automotive design and production is a peculiar feature of the automobile industry. The events in a current year are always in part due to decisions taken from one to three years earlier. Hence the extent of the Chevrolet slump of 1924 could properly be laid to the retarded development of Chevrolet's design during the previous three years. Among other things, it had an infamous rear end; but there is no use specifying its deficiencies. The curious thing was that there we were with a plan that rested upon the concept of better and better cars, with a bigger package of accessories and improvements beyond basic transportation, and the concept of a Chevrolet at a higher price that would be so compellingly attractive as to draw buyers away from the Model T. It would be difficult to find a wider margin between aspiration and realization than that represented by the plan of 1921 and the Chevrolet of 1924. Nevertheless, we did not alter the original plan, perhaps because we knew better than anyone the causes of our decline.

Indeed from the time the copper-cooled-engine program was abandoned, in the summer of 1923, Chevrolet's engineers, headed by Mr. Hunt, had worked intensively on redesigning the old car into a new model, known as the K Model, for the 1925 model year. The K Model had among its new features a longer body, increased leg room, a Duco finish, a one-piece windshield with automatic wipers on all closed cars, a dome light in the coach and sedan, a Klaxon horn, an improved clutch, and a sound rear-axle housing in place of the old one which had given so much trouble. It was far from being a radically new car but it was much better than it had been, and in the particulars noted above it gave the first real expression of what we had in mind to do. The K Model came on a rising market in 1925 and recovered Chevrolet's position sharply with factory sales of 481,000 cars and trucks, a 64 per cent gain over 1924 and a level 6 per cent above the 1923 peak.

Ford's sales held about even in 1925 with a volume of about two million cars and trucks. But since the market as a whole in that year rose substantially over 1924, Ford's share declined relatively from 54 to 45 per cent, a sign of danger, if Mr. Ford had chosen to read it. Yet he still held almost 70 per cent of the low-price field, and his touring car, priced at $290—without a starter or demountable rims—seemed unbeatable in that area. The Chevrolet touring car in 1925 was selling at $510, though with its extras it was not exactly comparable with the Ford. The Ford sedan—with starter and demountable rims—then sold at $660; the Chevrolet K Model at $825. Chevrolet's dealer discount was larger than Ford's, which made a difference in trading.

Chevrolet's internal statement of policy at this time was that it was our objective to get a public reputation for giving more for the dollar than Ford. As a matter of fact, when the Ford and Chevrolet were considered on a comparable-equipment basis, the Ford price was not far below that of Chevrolet. On the quality side we proposed to demonstrate to the buyer that, though our car cost X dollars more, it was X plus Y dollars better. Too, we proposed to improve our product regularly. We expected Ford, generally speaking, to stay put. We set this plan in motion and it worked as forecast.

Nevertheless, despite the success of the K Model Chevrolet, it was still too far from the Ford Model T in price for the gravitational pull we hoped to exert in Mr. Ford's area of the market. It was our intention to continue adding improvements and over a period of time to move down in price on the Model T as our position justified it.

As we said in our product policy of 1921, any given car was related to other cars that impinged upon it below and above in price and engineering design. Hence when looking at the Chevrolet in relation to the Ford below it, it was logical to consider equally what might happen to Chevrolet as a result of similar actions by competitors above it. This question was very much on our minds while the Chevrolet 1925 K Model sedan was being prepared during the year 1924, and for good reason.

A glance at the General Motors price list that year shows that we had still to realize the ideal or theoretical list set up in the 1921 plan. The list for the still-dominant touring cars in 1924 was as follows: Chevrolet, $510; Olds, $750; Oakland, $945; Buick "4," $965; Buick "6," $1295; and Cadillac, $2985.

The most obvious gaps in this line were between the Cadillac and Buick "6" at the top and between the Chevrolet and Olds at the bottom. To fill the gap between the standard Cadillac and the Buick "6," I proposed that Cadillac study the possibility of making a family-type car to sell at about $2000, which eventually resulted in the famous La Salle car, introduced in 1927. From the strategic standpoint at that time, however, the most dangerous gap in the list was that between the Chevrolet and the Olds. It was big enough to constitute a volume demand and thereby to accommodate, on top of Chevrolet, a competitor against whom we then had no counter. It was therefore an important gap to fill both offensively and defensively; offensively because there was a market demand to be satisfied there, and defensively because competitive cars could come in there and come down on Chevrolet as we planned for Chevrolet to come down on Ford. On this reasoning, we made one of the most important decisions in the history of General Motors, namely to fill the gap above Chevrolet with a brand-new car with a new six-cylinder engine. We had come to believe from an engineering standpoint that the future favored sixes and eights. However, to make the strategy effective, it would be necessary to fill the gap with a car that also had some volume economies. Otherwise, because the new car would draw some volume away from Chevrolet, reducing its economies, a loss would result for both cars. We concluded, therefore, that the new car must be designed in physical co-ordination with Chevrolet so as to share Chevrolet's economies, and vice versa.

The idea for such a car was first discussed by Mr. Hunt, Mr. Crane, and myself a few months after I became president. We had learned something of value in trying to make dual-purpose bodies and dual-purpose chassis for the copper-cooled and water-cooled engines in the period of uncertainty in those matters. We talked now about the development of a six-cylinder car based on the use, if possible, of such Chevrolet body and chassis parts as would fit the new design. As a "6," it would be a smoother-running car than the Chevrolet "4" and would require a longer wheel base, greater engine displacement and horsepower, and increased car weight. A longer and deeper frame, a heavier front axle, and a short-stroke six-cylinder L-head engine, proposed by Mr. Crane, were the principal new units in the design.

While the corporation's engineering committee worked on the design, I remained uncertain where to place the car in the divisional picture. Mr. Hannum, general manager of Oakland, wrote to me proposing that his division undertake the development phase of the work. My reply to him, on November 12, 1924, shows how I felt about the new car then, from the point of view of co-ordination with Chevrolet and of competition. I quote:

Your letter of October 11th reached me in Detroit but I did not have, you will remember, a clear viewpoint with relation to the so-called Pontiac car. I have been, in a way, up in the air on the Pontiac car development and did not reply to your letter although I read it over several times very carefully pending a crystallization of a viewp[o]int on what appeared to be the best policy to pursue.

I am thoroughly convinced, and have been from the beginning, that there was a place for such a car and, second, that if General Motors didn't go in there someone else sooner or later would. If the whole field was left to General Motors I do not know as I would be so anxious about it but, of course, fortunately for us, I presume it is not, therefore, we must give weight to what the other fellow is likely to do.

One very difficult thing has developed in all the discussions there have been and that is the tendency to get away from the Chevrolet part of the idea. Every time it comes up some one wants to make something different and the result of that is that if everybody had their way we would have a second Olds or probably an Oakland car, more likely a second Buick or Cadillac. In other words, we are never going to make a success I think you will agree with me unless we st[i]ck to the principle, namely, a Chevrolet chassis with a six-cylinder engine.

That being the case, I have definitely come to the conclusion that the only thing to do in order to work along the lines of least resistance is to have the development undertaken by the Chevrolet Engineering organization, because in so doing there will be every tendency to use what we can of Chevrolet as against the other method—the tendency to use something different, due to the natural and very proper tendency of an independent engineer to inject his own personality and ideas into the picture, perhaps to the detriment of the car but certainly not to the detriment of this particular development, which must follow along Chevrolet lines if we are going to capitalize Chevrolet components, plants and assembly plants, either at the beginning or at some future date when volume justifies same.

Therefore, I have been discussing the matter with Mr. Knudsen and feel that we should turn over to Mr. O. E. Hunt, his Engineer, all that we have accomplished, let him weigh it carefully, let him undertake to work out for us a six-cylinder engine along constructive lines, recognizing, as he does, what the picture has got to be. As a matter of fact, Chevrolet should be experimenting with engine developments on its own account and these two things should work along concurrently . . .

On the same day, I crystallized my thoughts on the subject in a report to the Executive Committee under the title, "Status of the Pontiac Car So-Called." I quote from this report the passages relating to costs, competition, co-ordination, and assignment in the corporation, these being the final questions to be resolved in a decision:

Mr. Brown has had his Staff develop some costs which, although not in any way conclusive, appear to demonstrate what we have felt was reasonable, namely, that even loading the cost with such overhead as it should logically carry, that is, on a basis of equal distribution with other items, there remains considering a list price of something like $700, a profit which will give us a very excellent return on the capital employed. This data has been laid down using figures on the Olds engine, the cost of which we know to be excessive and which for that reason will probably not be used. Looking at the development from the standpoint of the economic cost or real profit to the stockholders, the result is very satisfactory and of such a nature as really requires us to go ahead.

In addition to the above, information not conclusive seems to indicate that one or two of our competitors are going to attempt the same thing which brings us to the consideration that although this development will probably take business from both Olds and Chevrolet, it will be better that we take business from our own Divisions than have competitors do so. It looks now as if both things would ultimately happen.

We have been working on this proposition for about a year and I am frank to say we have made little headway. It seems as if every time we bring it up for discussion that an uncertainty develops in the minds of the Executive Committee as to its practicability. I have come to the definite conclusion that we are never going to get anywhere along the lines we must proceed to make it a success if we have it developed by an independent engineering department or by the Oakland Division where it was originally started. I am further definitely of the opinion that the only chance for success is to have it developed in the Chevrolet Division. Under such auspices coordination as to the chassis will come about as a natural course of events and there will be no tendency to introduce this and that difference simply because the engineer wishes very naturally and properly to inject his own personality into the picture. In other words, it will logically follow a development it has got to follow if we are to come through at all.

The thing especially worth noting in this report is the consideration given to the question of co-ordinating the manufacture of one car with another. For the Pontiac represented the first important advance in co-ordinating the physical product in manufacturing. Physical co-ordination in one form or another is, of course, the first principle of mass production, but at that time it was widely supposed, from the example of the Model T, that mass production on a grand scale required a uniform product. The Pontiac, co-ordinated in part with a car in another price class, was to demonstrate that mass production of automobiles could be reconciled with variety in product. This was again the opposite of the old Ford concept, which we persistently met and opposed at every turn. For General Motors, with its five basic price classes by car makes and several subclasses of models, the implication of the Pontiac idea was very great for the whole line. If the cars in the higher-price classes could benefit from the volume economies of the lower-price classes, the advantages of mass production could be extended to the whole car line. This gave new significance to the product plan of 1921, and was in fact eventually applied in varying degrees by all the General Motors car divisions.

The proposed Pontiac was assembled and road tested at Chevrolet and then assigned back to Oakland with full responsibility to that division for its final development, production, and ultimate sale as a companion car to the Oakland. We scheduled it for the model year 1926.

During the time of this development, another more or less independent event took place which was profoundly to influence the fortunes of the Pontiac, the Chevrolet, and the Model T. In 1921 Roy Chapin of the Hudson Motor Company had introduced the Essex coach at a price of $1495, or $300 above the Essex touring car.

This was a relatively smaller price difference for the closed body than had been the case for the lines of other manufacturers. By 1923 the Essex "4" coach had been reduced to $1145. Early in 1924 the Essex "6" superseded the "4" and came on the market at a price of $975 for the coach model, which was $125 over the touring-car price. In June of that year prices were increased to $1000 for the coach and $900 for the touring car. Then, beginning in 1925, Mr. Chapin cut the price of the coach model to $895, or $5 below the touring-car model. Nothing like that had ever been seen before in the automobile industry, and the Essex coach had a considerable vogue. This suggested that closed cars, priced on a volume basis, could in the future dominate even the low-price field.

Such a development doubtless was inevitable, but in fact the Essex competition stimulated us in two matters at once, first our general closed-body development, and second, our preparations for the forthcoming Pontiac car.

General Motors had already been changing over to closed bodies. On September 18, 1924, the Executive Committee "expressed the sentiment that our Managers should be cautioned to be very careful about open car schedules as the trend seems to be very rapidly turning to closed jobs." In October we raised the proportion of our production of closed cars from about 40 per cent, where it had been for most of that year, to 75 per cent for November. A year later, at the end of 1925, the proportion of closed-car production for the corporation as a whole was up to almost 80 per cent.

I do not recall that the Essex coach influenced the Pontiac program directly, but the Essex and the future Pontiac were clearly to be competitors, and in point of fact we designed our first Pontiac cars exclusively with closed bodies, a coupe and a coach.

In the Executive Committee meeting of September 30, 1925, I reported confidently: ". . . when the 'Pontiac' car comes out in December it will give us everything for which we have been working, namely, the lowest priced 6-cylinder car that is possible, constructed with Chevrolet parts."

At the Executive Committee meeting of October 21, 1925, I reported on the over-all situation of growing tension in the market. From the minutes of the meeting I glean the following: "Attention was called to the fact that the Essex is attacking the Chevrolet market from the top while the Ford Company (whose policy now

seems to be that of improving the quality of its car rather than reducing the price) is a strong competitor on the other side."

The Pontiac went on the market on schedule for the model year
1926 with the coach priced at $825, that is, about halfway between
the Chevrolet coach, priced at $645, and the Olds coach, priced at
$950; and the gap in our car line was closed.

That event settled General Motors' basic car positions for many
years. The Cadillac and the Buick were first and second from the
top of the price pyramid. Chevrolet was always the base of the pyramid. The Oakland organization, which produced the Pontiac car,
later became the Pontiac Division, and the manufacture of Oakland
cars was discontinued. The Pontiac became a distinctive car in its
own right while maintaining its original economies. That put Olds
between Pontiac and Buick, making the basic price line: Chevrolet,
Pontiac, Olds, Buick, and Cadillac, more or less as it is today.

I shall not deal here with the evolution of all the cars in the line
in the 1920s. I observe only that Olds and Oakland were not very
lively lines. Buick, though always basically strong, had its ups and
downs. Cadillac, as always, was strong in its price class, though it
was superseded as sales leader for a time, beginning in 1925. I pass
over the interesting record of these divisions to concentrate upon
the most important changes that took place in that period, namely,
those in the low-price, high-volume area where we were seeking a
position against Ford.

The last decisive element in this competition, I believe, was the
closed body, which itself was by far the largest single leap forward
in the history of the automobile since the basic car had been made
mechanically reliable. The closed body expanded the use of the
automobile by making it a comfortable all-year-round vehicle,
and added substantially to the price of the product. The 1925
Model K Chevrolet coach sold for 40 per cent and the sedan for
57 per cent more than the roadster.

Although the Essex was the first spectacular demonstration of
volume production of a closed car at a price comparable to an open
car, the price of both Essex cars was still relatively high. The Essex threatened the Chevrolet from the top, but was not really in the
low-price field. Although Chevrolet in 1925 was still higher priced
than Ford, it had a very good position in the low-price closed-car
field, partly because of its relationship to Fisher Body.

A few words about Fisher Body, which had the responsibility for building most of General Motors' car bodies. General Motors, as I said earlier, acquired a 60 per cent interest in the Fisher Body Corporation in 1919, with arrangements that Fisher supply all General Motors' passenger-car body requirements that it could. In 1926 we purchased the remaining 40 per cent interest in Fisher Body and absorbed it into General Motors as a division. There were a number of reasons for doing this. As early as February 3, 1925, in the Executive Committee, "Attention was called to the fact that Chevrolet's sales are at present limited by its ability to produce new models, which is largely determined by the ability of Fisher Body Corporation to supply closed bodies." There were operating economies to be gained by co-ordinating body and chassis assemblies, and with the closed body becoming dominant in the industry, it seemed sensible to bring the body operation entirely under the General Motors roof. And it was felt desirable also to bring the Fisher brothers into closer relationship with our organization.

The story of the Fisher brothers is a remarkable family saga which I hope they will sometime record. I do not know it far back by personal association, since I came into the industry through the chassis, so to speak, while they were fabricating bodies. But I knew of them as skilled artisans with a background in the carriage industry. The Fisher Body Company was organized in 1908, the Fisher Closed Body Company—with an order for 150 Cadillac bodies—in 1910, and the Fisher Body Company of Canada in 1912. The three companies were brought together in the Fisher Body Corporation in 1916. They had made bodies for several automobile companies, including Buick and Cadillac. I first came to know Fred J. Fisher well when he came on the General Motors Executive Committee in 1922, and he was a valued member of that early team. In 1924 he was made a member of the Finance Committee. In that year Charles T. and Lawrence P. Fisher were made members of the Executive Committee and in 1925 I appointed the latter to head Cadillac. The other brothers, William A., Edward F., and Alfred J., remained with Fisher Body Corporation, with William A. as its president. Lawrence P. Fisher played an outstanding part in the evolution of styling in General Motors, a story I tell in a later chapter.

As the closed body developed rapidly from 43 per cent of the industry in 1924 to 72 per cent in 1926 and 85 per cent in 1927, Chevrolet's percentage of closed-body production rose from about

40 per cent in 1924 to 73 per cent in 1926 and on to 82 per cent in 1927. A big change in every respect.

The rise of the closed body made it impossible for Mr. Ford to maintain his leading position in the low-price field, for he had frozen his policy in the Model T, and the Model T was pre-eminently an open-car design. With its light chassis, it was unsuited to the heavier closed body, and so in less than two years the closed body made the already obsolescing design of the Model T noncompetitive as an engineering design. Mr. Ford, nevertheless, put closed bodies on the Model T and sold 37.5 per cent of his production in this form in 1924. Although the market for closed bodies rose sharply in the next three years, he sold only 51.6 per cent in 1926 and only 58 per cent in 1927, while Chevrolet's sales of closed bodies during that period rose to 82 per cent.

From 1925 to 1927 the Chevrolet, as its cost position justified a lower price, became more competitive with Ford, as we had hoped, the Chevrolet two-door coach going in that period progressively from $735 to $695 to $645 to $595, while the Ford Tudor Model T went from $580 in 1925 to $565 in June 1926, and to $495 in 1927. Thus the old strategic plan of 1921 was vindicated to a "T," so to speak, but in a surprising way as to the particulars. The old master had failed to master change. Don't ask me why. There is a legend cultivated by sentimentalists that Mr. Ford left behind a great car expressive of the pure concept of cheap, basic transportation. The fact is that he left behind a car that no longer offered the best buy, even as raw, basic transportation.

It was not difficult to see in 1925 and 1926 that Chevrolet was closing in on Ford. In 1925 Chevrolet had about 481,000 U.S. factory sales of cars and trucks, while Ford had approximately two million factory sales. In 1926 Chevrolet moved up to about 692,000 factory sales of cars and trucks, while Ford moved down to about 1,550,000. His precious volume, which was the foundation of his position, was fast disappearing. He could not continue losing sales and maintain his profits. And so, for engineering and market reasons, the Model T fell. And yet not many observers expected so catastrophic and almost whimsical a fall as Mr. Ford chose to take in May 1927 when he shut down his great River Rouge plant completely and kept it shut down for nearly a year to retool, leaving the field to Chevrolet unopposed and opening it up for Mr. Chrysler's Plymouth. Mr. Ford regained sales leadership again in 1929, 1930, and 1935, but, speaking in terms of generalities, he had lost

the lead to General Motors. Mr. Ford, who had had so many brilliant insights in earlier years, seemed never to understand how
completely the market had changed from the one in which he made
his name and to which he was accustomed.

Go back for a moment to the first four-million car-and-truck
year, 1923. From then to 1929, setting aside variations in the years,
there was a seven-year plateau in new-car sales. And yet the total
number of cars in use, as I have shown, continued to rise. While the
total market, including used cars, expanded, the new-car market
leveled off, and, as I have said, the role of the new car was to cover
scrappage and growth in car ownership. Meanwhile the used cars
at much lower prices dropped down to fill the demand at various
levels for basic transportation. Mr. Ford failed to realize that it was
not necessary for new cars to meet the need for basic transportation. On this basis alone Mr. Ford's concept of the American market did not adequately fit the realities after 1923. The basic-trans-
portation market in the United States (unlike Europe) since then
has been met mainly by the used car.

When first-car buyers returned to the market for the second
round, with the old car as a first payment on the new car, they
were selling basic transportation and demanding something more
than that in the new car. Middle-income buyers, assisted by the
trade-in and installment financing, created the demand, not for
basic transportation, but for progress in new cars, for comfort, convenience, power, and style. This was the actual trend of American
life and those who adapted to it prospered.

It was thus that the four elements with which I began the discussion in this chapter, installment selling, the used-car trade-in,
the closed-car body, and the annual model, interacted in the 1920s
to transform the market. But I have not completed the picture.
What of the annual model?

The annual model was not a declared policy of General Motors,
or of anyone, I believe, in the 1920s. It was, however, inherent in
the policy of creating a bigger and better package each year. With
this concept necessarily went the need for salesmanship.

At a General Sales Committee meeting on July 29, 1925, I stated
our commercial policy as follows:

We have elected, as a large Corporation, to build quality products
sold at fair prices and while there are others in the industry who do not
follow quite this policy, I am sure that we are in pretty general agree-

ment that it is the correct policy. At the same time, however, we must admit that such a policy throws the added responsibility upon our sales departments to get the cost of quality plus a profit on quality.

In justice to our sales departments, it is a fact that we have been handicapped by past reputation in connection with certain of our products, but as we pass into our new manufacturing year we have a line of cars that we can be proud of, without exception. I believe that we will all agree that these new products are thoroughly dependable and priced in the proper levels, both competitively and from the standpoint of costs. Some of the reductions in sales prices have come out of savings in cost, particularly in closed bodies, as a result of Fisher's increased volume; other savings have been effected through changes in design which have not affected quality. At the same time, however, it must be recognized that we have reduced our profits.

To give some idea of what this means, I might say that if we take our earnings for the past six months of 1925 and re-figure these earnings on the basis of the new list prices and the new costs—in other words, the new spread between cost and selling price—and assume the volume to be the same, we would have reduced our profits by about twenty-five percent.

As we are now running, General Motors hasn't increased its volume of business very much. Our success during the first half of the year results from a favorable margin between costs and selling prices. Our sales to consumers so far this year are just about the same as last year and while our prices have not been out of line, except in a few instances, our price line-up as of August first should certainly place us in a position to expand our sales in relation to competition. In fact, the only justification for our new prices, as I see it, is on the assumption that we are going to get added volume, and this added volume will mean a greater responsibility on our sales departments. With our present line-up as regards prices and quality, we must agree that it is a question of selling, directly up to our sales organizations.

I then gave a pep talk on avoiding inertia in large-scale operations and concluded my remarks on commercial policy with the observation that the industry had at that time entered a new period:

There are many things in connection with marketing concerning which we should be more progressive and aggressive. In my judgment, General Motors as a whole is relatively weak in sales endeavor. As a matter of fact, the entire automobile industry has been built up by and around people of mechanical and technical characteristics, rather than commercial, and I think we are just beginning to realize the great importance of the commercial side of the business.

As events proved, I was mistaken in worrying about the inertia of General Motors—like a football coach roasting a championship team. The words "quality products sold at fair prices" described the basic policy of selling the bigger and better car—a policy consistent with the product plan of 1921. Along with this went a policy of building strong dealer organizations in each of the divisions. We believed it was essential to have a prosperous, energetic, strategically located body of dealers to do the selling and the trading. There is a chapter on that subject later on.

So it was all of a piece. You started on a course with a policy and things not foreseen fell into place. When it came to the product, the policy meant continuous, eternal change. I have described some of the changes we made in the K Model Chevrolet in 1925. In that same year we began work on a new six-cylinder Chevrolet engine. In 1926, in the Cadillac Division, we introduced styling as a separate concept and, for the first time, as a specialization in the industry. In 1927 and 1928 we made styling changes in Chevrolet. In 1928 we put four-wheel brakes on the Chevrolet and lengthened its wheel base by four inches for the new six-cylinder engine. But we held off the new engine until 1929, after Mr. Ford had come out with his four-cylinder Model A.

At the General Sales Committee meeting on July 29, 1925, mentioned above, we called our new cars "annual models" but did our best to avoid a formal commitment to the concept. The record of this discussion is entitled, "Annual Models Versus Constant Improvement." The colloquy that took place under this heading, the only one I have a record of in the 1920s, may be of some interest:

MR. SLOAN: While the bringing out of yearly models results in many disadvantages and, for that reason, we are all against yearly models, I don't see just what can be done about it.

MR. [Richard H.] GRANT [general sales manager of Chevrolet]: I am against the yearly model idea and I think that instead of holding up our improvements until some given date of the year, we should work them in gradually and say nothing about them.

MR. SLOAN: Of course, that might be best in connection with some changes, but in the case of a different body it presents serious difficulties.

MR. GRANT: The question is "Shall we have Yearly Models?" I say "No", we should not have ["]yearly models." We ought to make all invisible changes without announcement. Now when we change the lines or change the bodies, then I think we have to have a new model, but I don't think there should be anything yearly about it. It might be a year and seven months or two years between the introduction of models. I don't feel we should concentrate everything on the first of August. On the other hand, I don't think we ought to follow the Dodge policy and say we will never have any new models.

MR. SLOAN: When you adopt their policy you are just saying that industry does not develop. Although you can make a few minor changes, the time certainly comes when you are forced to bring out a new model. You can say you are not going to do it, but you will have to do it sooner or later. The [o]nly two concerns who have successfully followed that policy are Dodge and Ford. Now Ford is bringing out a new model for the very reasons we are talking about. He has been driven to it. Dodge was driven to it in the beginning of 1923. The 31-State Report [on new-car registrations] showed how they had been slipping. Now we are all in the same fix and I think General Motors as a policy has been too easily influenced to make changes, but I think that was due to the fact that our products were not sufficiently stabilized.

MR. GRANT: Maybe the way this was put up here was a little confusing. If this means that if we had a bang-up new model to bring out and weren't going to capitalize on it, then I am not in harmony with it, but I do believe that the thought of the yearly model ought to be gotten away from and we should only bring out a model when we have a necessity of bringing it out and then we should handle it to our best advantage and advertise it. I think the people who are advertising this policy of not eve[r] bringing out a new model are storing up a lot of grief for themselves. Lines are going to change and bodies are going to change.

MR. [Lynn] McNAUGHTON [general sales manager of Cadillac]: We have felt in getting away from the name of a model we might get the attention of the public on the name "CADILLAC", instead of the designation of the model, and we are not going to call the new car by any model name, but it is just a new line of Cadillac cars. For the past three or four months people have asked us when we were going to bring out the new V-65 but we are not going to have anything else except, so far as the public is concerned, a new line of Cadillac cars without model designation. We are going to advertise the Cadillac instead of the model.

MR. SLOAN: Of course, there is one thing about it from the Fisher Body standpoint. The strain on their organization in bringing out all these dies at one time is something terrific and well nigh impossible.

MR. GRANT: I think what we ought to do is change our method of handling our policy and I think we ought to get a new model out when we have an advantage in getting a new model out, but I don't think we ought to set a date of August first, and I don't think if we are going to have changes in two different divisions they should necessarily come out on August 1st. It might serve one division better to come out January 1st like we did last year.

MR. SLOAN: You are really forced to change on August 1st, because any other date runs into your selling season. It must be done between August 1st and November 1st. You certainly wouldn't want to come out January 1st, as a matter of policy, unless you were driven to it as Chevrolet was last year.

MR. GRANT: It looks this year, from the way we are heading, January 1st might be a good time, yet you take the year after that it might be the poorest time, because I don't think we are going to have much stock on hand January 1st.

MR. [Dan S.] EDDINS [general sales manager of Olds]: If we could throw a new model in production the first of December we would build up the stock by spring to meet the spring demand but from January 1st to February 1st your plants can't get underway. On the other hand, other manufacturers bringing in their lines on August 1st would beat us to it and get a lot of our business.

MR. SLOAN: Between August 1st and September 1st is about the only logical time because if you move it back from August 1st you will minimize your spring business and if you attempt to change on November 1st there will be thousands of cars on the hands of your dealers which will be very hard to sell. You would have to liquidate your merchandise in an off season.

MR. GRANT: I think we ought to keep our policy just as it is but work to the end of avoiding as many drastic model changes as we can. In other words, we should change our method of manipulating the present policy.

General Motors in fact had annual models in the twenties, every year after 1923, and has had them ever since, but as the discussion above shows, we had not in 1925 formulated the concept in the way it is known today. When we did formulate it I cannot say. It was a matter of evolution. Eventually the fact that we made yearly changes, and the recognition of the necessity of change, forced us into regularizing change. When change became regularized, some time in the 1930s, we began to speak of annual models. I do not believe the elder Mr. Ford ever really cared for the idea. Anyway his Model A, which he brought out in 1928, as fine a little car as it was in its time, it seems to me was another expression of his concept of a static-model utility car.

At the time when Ford's plants were shut down for lack of a new model design, I thought that both his and our policies would survive—Ford's in the form of the new car, which would express the old policy adapted to the then higher state of the art. In other words, I had no idea in 1927 that the old Ford policy was washed out and that the General Motors policy of upgraded cars had won in a much larger sense than was reflected in the rise in sales of Chevrolet.

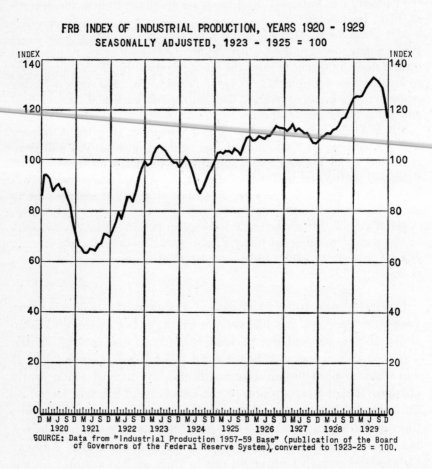

FRB INDEX OF INDUSTRIAL PRODUCTION, YEARS 1920 - 1929
SEASONALLY ADJUSTED, 1923 - 1925 = 100

SOURCE: Data from "Industrial Production 1957-59 Base" (publication of the Board of Governors of the Federal Reserve System), converted to 1923-25 = 100.

Chapter 10

POLICY CREATION

THE transformation of the automobile market was essentially complete in 1929. If Mr. Ford, in that pivotal year in the modern economy, still held stubbornly to his old concept in his new Model A, he was counterbalanced by Mr. Chrysler, who had come up from nowhere with tremendous vitality and with a market policy similar to General Motors'. The fact that Mr. Ford built nearly two million of the five million U.S.-produced cars and trucks sold that year was only incidental from the long-term point of view—it was a splurge, not the sign of a trend.

And General Motors itself had been transformed from the formless aggregation of 1920 into an integrated, effective enterprise. Its management philosophy of decentralization with co-ordinated control was working adequately for its time. Its financial method had become a kind of second nature, and a constantly evolving creative process. Its line of cars expressed the variety that Mr. Durant had originated and, in principle, the price classes set forth in the product plan of 1921. And perhaps I should add in passing that, although we had reached an all-time peak in the export of cars, we had started on a new course overseas with our own manufacturing operations in England (1925) and Germany (1929). In all of these matters the corporation reflected the trend of affairs in the economy. Doubtless it influenced some of those trends. Our progress in the automobile industry influenced other large-scale American enterprises to study and adopt our methods, particularly decentralization and financial control.

Not being a historian, I pass over much in this period that is of general interest to continue the story I set out to tell about the progress of General Motors.

The great depression of the early 1930s, despite its contracting effect, did not alter qualitatively the general characteristics of the enterprise except in one particular. Contraction required increasing co-ordination. That is, we had to find ways to react swiftly to this most difficult kind of change and to economize. These needs were to lead to the last basic modifications in the General Motors scheme of organization. In fact, the changes began before the stock-market crash in October 1929 in anticipation of a new situation, but before we had any real idea of what was coming.

For one thing, because of the tremendous success of Chevrolet, I wanted to spread the benefits of its management to the corporation as a whole by placing Chevrolet men in strategic positions. Mr. Grant and Mr. Hunt of Chevrolet were elected vice presidents of the corporation on May 9, 1929, with staff responsibility for sales and engineering, respectively. At the same time, C. E. Wilson, formerly of Delco-Remy, was elected vice president for manufacturing. A few years later Mr. Knudsen, who had been general manager of Chevrolet, was elected an executive vice president and put in charge of all car, truck, and body manufacturing operations. Thus it might be said that in this period a new executive group moved up in rank and into the general corporate area where their influence would affect the entire corporation.

We had at that time, however, only a modest staff organization outside of finance, Mr. Kettering's laboratories, and the work associated with the interdivisional committees. When we had occasion for an advanced engineering project we created a special "product-study group" and placed it in a manufacturing division. The election of these men therefore was a new beginning in staff activity, which would eventually displace the old interdivisional committees and develop into the great staff organization we have today. The stories of these staffs belong to later chapters in this book. I shall discuss here only how they bear upon certain general developments in co-ordination.

The national economy reached its peak, up to that time, in the late spring and early summer of 1929, after which industrial production decreased sharply, while the stock market continued on and up to its debacle in October.[1] On July 18 I made a statement to the Operations Committee expressing anxiety as to whether the corporation was capable of reacting to change, and declaring myself for new forms of co-ordination to that end as follows:

. . . I feel that we have been weak in that we have not been in a position or have not perhaps from the standpoint of policy, followed through on the many constructive suggestions involving programs and policies that have been developed. The usual reaction in the minds of all of us is, against any change, and I feel that our administration has been subject to criticism for not insisting upon changes and losing too much time in selling an idea and in not dealing promptly and effectively with weaknesses that are known to exist. It is for that reason that I have felt for some time past that we must have a more effective and definite form of coordination. Expressed otherwise, the resistance against progress has been greater than the man power to effect progress; therefore, progress has been slow. This now I feel has got to be changed if the Corporation is going to maintain its position, let alone improve it. We can not wait so long to do things as we have because competition is becoming keener and the problem is daily becoming harder. The remarks I am making are not directed so much to the ordinary business routine as they are to the recognition of new necessities in the form of better general principles and policies to carry out those principles, also better and more effective forms of detail organizations . . .

On October 4, 1929, shortly before the stock-market crash, I addressed a general letter to the organization noting the end of expansion and promulgating a new policy of economy for the corporation:

It appears to me that it would be most appropriate at this time to ask the earnest attention of all concerned to what I believe to be a very important problem, and which I will outline herewith.

For quite a number of years past the demands on our schedules have taxed our facilities to the utmost. This applies to practically all operations, both at home and abroad. In addition to this, the characters of our products have materially changed, and such changes necessitated a revision of some of our production facilities and modified, more or less, practically all of them. This has thrown on management, in addition to the ordinary problems, the responsibility of providing plant and facilities for expansion and the organization to effectively operate same.

[1] The Index of Industrial Production for 1920–29 is at the end of Chapter 9.

In connection with the above program, large amounts of capital have been expended. Still more has been invested in creating facilities for doing things that had not been previously done—in other words, developing plant for manufacturing a greater part of the various products we are selling. All this has been constructive and amply justified by the results that have been obtained. I am sure our position in the past and present has been and in the future will be greatly enhanced and strengthened by what we have accomplished in this general direction.

The purpose of the above is to make the point that in my opinion a different type of treatment is now essential, at least for the present and for the more or less immediate future. It seems to me that management should now direct its energies toward INCREASING EARNING POWER through IMPROVED EFFECTIVENESS and REDUCED EXPENSE. In other words, the drive during the past few years has been for more and better cars of constantly increasing value. From now on we should drive just as hard toward still better cars, but we must give more detailed consideration to values in respect to price and as a part of this program the efforts that have been so lavishly expended on expansion and development should now be directed toward economy in operation.

The above does not mean to convey the thought that our trend over a period of years will be other than of such a nature that still further demands on our production facilities will be required. I believe that, given a quality product at the right price, at the same time keeping abreast of the advances in engineering thought, there is no end to what we can accomplish. On the other hand, it is impossible to assume that the percentage increase from year to year will equal what we have enjoyed during the recent past. Further, it is reasonable to suppose that we must follow more closely the general trend of industry as a whole. I do not intend to convey the thought in anything that is said above, that the expense factor has not been watched, for I know it has. What I am trying to convey is the thought that in the future it should be the prime consideration of every division and subsidiary to put the energy previously directed toward expansion and development into the hardest kind of a drive in the direction of economy. In other words, economy in operation must now be the key-note rather than expansion of plant and equipment. By "expense" I mean not only manufacturing expense but every item of expense incident to cost of sales.

The responsibility of carrying through this program rests, of course, on every division and subsidiary. In order that I may be kept in touch with the general trend, I am asking Messrs. Bradley, Grant, Hunt and Wilson to study the situation from the Staff standpoint in collaboration with the corresponding functions in the various divisions and subsidiaries in various ways that will be outlined in due course. In that way we will all work together toward a better general result.

In harmony with the thought behind the above, it follows that new projects should be more carefully scrutinized than ever before and the burden of proof of their propriety should be more evident. According to the present form of organization, C. E. Wilson, Vice President, deals in a preliminary way with new projects as presented. It might be desirable for every division and subsidiary contemplating or feeling the necessity of further expansion, to consult Mr. Wilson before proceeding in the development of the necessary project. Naturally, the above remarks do not in any sense refer to changes definitely approved in which additional or different production facilities are essential for their proper execution.

As it turned out, I was not, of course, pessimistic enough; indeed it would soon be a question whether we were able to cope with the unbelievable course of events. Although the depression did not occur all at once, the downward steps were gigantic. General Motors' sales of $1.5 billion in 1929 fell about one third, to $983 million, in 1930.

After the close of 1930, I said in the annual report—which I used to write myself—the following: "The economic situation of practically all important consuming countries of the world during the year was materially out of adjustment. Involved as the corporation is in an important way in the business activities of nearly every country in the world, its operations were adversely affected by such a situation. There arose, as a result, unusual problems of administration and policy which had to be dealt with effectively and aggressively, if the interests of the stockholders were to be protected. The future position of the institution, not only from the standpoint of the confidence with which it is regarded by the public, which is a measure of its goodwill, but likewise from the standpoint of its future economic development, called for the most searching analysis of all problems . . ."

The analysis began.

As a matter of atmosphere, it may be of some interest to indicate how the management of a corporation like General Motors talks to itself when confronted by catastrophic events. On January 9, 1931, I addressed the following letter to the members of the Operations Committee:

For the benefit of those who were absent from the Operations Committee meeting on Thursday and to remind those who attended the meeting, I want to say that one of the principal points of business at the next meeting will be a contribution from each member as to what in his opinion have constituted weaknesses in procedure, policy or thought in the year just closed that should be eliminated and what new points can be developed that will be helpful in the year 1931.

The close of one year and the advent of a new forms a psychological and practical opportunity of dealing with a matter of this kind. Naturally, we must deal with broad principles of policy and type of thinking more than detailed problems of administration.

To illustrate what I have in mind I will give the following thoughts from some notes which I have already made on the subject:—

First:— I think we have lacked and perhaps still lack courage in dealing with weaknesses in personnel. We know weaknesses exist, we tolerate them and finally after tolerating them an abnormal length of time we make the change and then regret that we have not acted before.

Second. I think, notwithstanding that we have the reputation of a fact-finding organization, that we do not get the facts, even now, as completely as we should. We sit around and discuss things without the facts. I think we should break ourselves of that and not permit any member of the Committee to have an important problem determined upon without all members of the Committee have the facts before them and are placed in a position to exercise their own individual judgment, otherwise the Committee is not fair to itself and to the Corporation because it is not discharging its full responsibility to same.

Third. I think that we become too superficial and that we should correct this tendency. Problems are crowding in on us; time is limited; the meetings are some times long and we naturally get tired. These circumstances and many others lead us to make mistakes without adequate consideration and mistakes are bound to occur. It is easier not to do it at all than to do it haphazardly or without due consideration and even if we lose an opportunity it will come up again sooner or later and in the long run we will gain by more thoroughly dealing with our problems.

The above are just some thoughts that occur to me in order to give you the type of matters that I would appreciate your thinking over. Each member of the Committee will be expected to make a real contribution.

A pretty mild statement in the circumstances. But every business, profession, and group of people has its own way and often its own jargon. The top management understood that the above letter was a call to them to think everything over. For six months a deluge of memoranda came over my desk dealing with the broadest kinds of questions; and there was a divergence of opinion. Mr. Pratt, Mr. Mooney, and Mr. Knudsen felt we had become overcentralized.

Mr. Pratt wrote on January 12, 1931, as follows:

In my judgment the greatest weakness in the procedure and policy of General Motors Corporation is the tendency of the Operations Committee to originate and discuss detailed problems of the Divisions, instead of insisting that the Divisions initiate their respective policies and problems and refer their solutions to the Operations Committee for check and approval.

Consciously or unconsciously, the way in which we have operated General Motors in the past year there has been an alarming tendency towards centralization of all initiative and action in the Operations Committee. I think the reverse is necessary. The initiative must be in the Divisions and our job is to see that we have General Managers who will take the initiative rather than attempt to supply all of the initiative from the central organization.

I would also like to suggest where weaknesses are thought to be that they be placed on the table and frankly discussed, regardless of personalities.

There can be no doubt that, under the impact of severe contraction, some overcentralization took place, and it was wrong.

On the other side, however, Messrs. Wilson, Grant, Hunt, and Bradley, all staff men, thought the contrary. Each of them recommended some specific form of increased co-ordination. Mr. Wilson wanted to bring all the divisions up to the standard of the most progressive divisions in manufacturing organization, equipment, and processing method. Mr. Grant made a similar proposition for sales and general management. But he confessed he was unsure how to do it in a way consistent with decentralization. "For the time being, at least," he said, "I know only one answer to this problem and it is to have lots of will power, patience, and selling ability in making our divisional contacts . . ." Mr. Hunt, with the concreteness of the engineer, proposed to extend the interchangeable body program as far as possible through the car lines, and to make a new application of engineering research to car features that had immediate possibilities. Mr. Bradley, noting inadequate preparation for discussions in the Operations Committee, proposed the appointment of subcommittees to expedite the routine work of the top committee.

The truth is, I believe, that both sides were right. The horns of the old dilemma had reappeared. We had to have more co-ordination to meet the new conditions, and at the same time we had to keep the top management from falling into the hopeless position of trying to administer the affairs of the decentralized divisions.

On June 19, 1931, I took the first step toward a new setup, with the appointment of a number of advisory groups. I stated this proposal as follows: "That Advisory Groups be formed as advisory to the Group Executive for the purpose of establishing the broadest possible foundation of fact and opinion in order that the recommendations submitted to the [Operations] Committee and the decisions of operating policy, even when not submitted to the Committee, be as constructive as the best thought in the Corporation permits."

The significance of this proposal lay in its effort to achieve broader, more active, and more regularized contact between the general officers, the staff, and the divisions, without giving the staff any authority over the divisions. Some men feared that this move would encourage the staff executives to give orders to the division managers, but that was not a necessary consequence, as I shall indicate presently.

The advisory groups were adopted in 1931, but by the end of that year further discussions of broad problems of organization gave way to drastic emergency measures aimed at sheer survival as the nation and the world went to the bottom of the great depression. The automobile industry in the United States and Canada dropped from a production of about 5.6 million cars and trucks, worth about $5.1 billion at retail, in 1929, to about 1.4 million units, worth about $1.1 billion, in 1932. That was lower than any year since the war year 1918.

Thanks to the financial and operating controls, the development of which I have described in earlier chapters, General Motors did not approach disaster as it had in the 1920–21 slump. We made an orderly step-by-step retreat in all matters, including wage and salary reductions. Sales by our United States and Canadian plants dropped to 526,000 cars and trucks in 1932 as compared with about 1.9 million in 1929, a tremendous drop (72 per cent) when you consider the many expenses that are fixed. That we fared relatively better than the industry is shown by the fact that our share of the market increased from 34 per cent in 1929 to 38 per cent in 1932, the trough year of the depression. Our profits dropped from about $248 million in 1929 to $165,000 in 1932, still in the black, thanks

mainly to our financial-control procedures. In 1932 we were operating at less than 30 per cent of capacity.

To economize we co-ordinated to a greater extent our work in
purchasing, design, production, and selling, and some of these
changes were of lasting value. In purchasing and production, for
example, we achieved a finer classification of parts and increased
interchangeability of parts among the divisions, the most important single interchangeability being in a reduction of bodies to
three basic standard types. The most difficult economies to get were
in commercial or selling expense and here we took the most drastic
measures of reorganization. In March 1932 the Operations Committee, after a three-day session, adopted a radical revision of the product policy of 1921. The decision was taken to consolidate the manufacturing of Chevrolet and Pontiac, both thereby coming under Mr.
Knudsen's jurisdiction. A similar consolidation was ordered between Buick and Oldsmobile. On the sales end the activities of
Buick, Oldsmobile, and Pontiac were consolidated in a single new
sales company, B.O.P., and dealers were given more than one car
to sell. In effect, from a management point of view, General Motors
for a year and a half was reduced from five to three car divisions.

The severity of the contraction and the pressure of events attend-
ing it in and around the corporation caused me to reflect on
whether our scheme of management could respond properly to
such an era. Were we set up to contract and expand at will? To
co-ordinate and still keep clear the distinction between policy and
administration? If we restored the traditional five car divisions,
how would we relate the cars in the new situation? Inevitably when
an industrial enterprise is shaken with such a force as we met at
the onset of the great depression, there has to be confusion. In November 1933 I began to write again on the subject of new policies,
beginning at the beginning, on the subject of policy itself. I said:

I feel that this phase of the general organization problem is of particular importance to General Motors, not because of its size particularly,
but on account of the nature of its business, subject, as it is, to what I
might term "rapid changes". In other words, I contend a unit of the
automotive industry has far less "coasting ability", I might term it, than
units in most any other industry that might be selected for comparison.
As I analyze our picture, looking forward into the future, our success or,
let me say, the maintenance of our position, absolutely depends upon the

ability of our organization to lay down a strategy as will enable us to forecast the rapid changes that are taking place and will continue to take place in the various activities in which we are interested, involving all the functional divisions within such activities, and to provide for those changes with sufficient rapidity.

In making this statement I am not minimizing in any sense, the importance of effectively and economically carrying out such policies as may be adopted—I am simply trying to emphasize the point that the policy phase is of vital concern because, unless we can, with reasonable intelligence, meet this issue—no matter how able an administrative set-up we may have, it is limited in its opportunity to function. I might add further, that looking forward I feel that we have got to more aggressively deal with that phase of our problems than we have in the past. It is going to be harder to maintain both our competitive position and our profit position. We can not afford to take the time in the future that we have in the past, to make up our minds what we should do with respect to changes in trends which are having an influence on our position . . .

My main purpose in the memorandum from which the above passages are taken was to reassert the purely policy-making role of the Executive Committee. I also said that the committee should be "in a position to deal frankly and aggressively with any division, or the relationship of one division with another." To do this best I thought the committee should contain only general executives, not divisional executives. How then would the policy-making executives get and use their information? I wrote, ". . . we must develop ways and means to keep the members of the Executive Committee in contact with the problem so that they can exercise not only intelligent judgment on the question, but intelligent independent judgment . . ."

Of course the Executive Committee had always been legally, and in fact, the top operating committee, but because it met jointly with the Operations Committee, and because decisions were made with the participation of both policy and operating people, the line between policy and administration was not sharply enough drawn. The first thing was to limit the Executive Committee to policy decisions made independently of the administrative, operating people.

It was particularly important that independent policy-making be re-established because of the new conditions in the car market and the management problem that would arise if we restored the traditional five divisions, a move which I proposed.

The situation was this: In the automobile market of 1933 the low-price group grew relatively to encompass 73 per cent of the industry's unit car sales, as compared with 52 per cent in 1926. This meant, for the old car line, that we would have four lines in 27 per cent of the market and one line in 73 per cent of the market. Mr. Brown, for reasons of economy, preferred three divisions. I preferred five despite the extra cost, which I thought we could recover through increased volume. I stated, and in part restated, my long-standing views on commercial policy in a report to the Finance Committee on January 4, 1934, and, since they became the corporation's policy, I quote them here:

THE FUNDAMENTAL CONCEPTION OF GENERAL MOTORS CAR PRODUCT PROGRAM

Certain members of the Committee may recall that at the time Mr. P. S. duPont became President of the Corporation, one of his first acts was to appoint a group to study the very important problem of car products. Up to that time there had been no fundamental conception or plan —there was no definite relationship between the products of one car division and another, or, in other words, no coordination. It was generally recognized that there should be a definite relationship and a certain amount of coordination, and the purpose of the study was to establish what that should be. This study was authorized by a resolution of the then Executive Committee, under date of April 6, 1921—now approaching thirteen years ago . . . [The study referred to here was that concerning product policy discussed earlier.]

I took note of the general evolution of the automobile in those thirteen years under the pressure of intensified competition, and observed that the value of a car had come to be centered around certain considerations—appearance or style, technical qualities, price, and reputation. It was my impression at that time that differences in these matters were narrower than they had been in earlier years, and that because the state of the art was available to all, automobile technology would not in the future result in effective differences from a selling point of view. I was mistaken about that, although my general point, I believe, was valid, namely that selling had begun to focus on personal preferences of the consumer, especially in matters of style. I said:

People like different things. Many people do not want to have exactly the same thing that the neighborhood has. The design of any car is an artistic and engineering compromise. No car can embrace all the desirable features. Relatively inconsequential features will often influence a sale[,] adversely to the customer's interests with respect to other far more consequential features. No prospect is intelligent enough to definitely determine the weighted value of all the elements that enter into any particular car. The consumer is also greatly influenced by the personal relationship with the dealer and some times rightly, other times, wrongly, becomes antagonistic to one particular dealer. General Motors in selling 45% of all the units in the industry, which is practically one out of every two, assumes a tremendous responsibility with respect to all these questions. Under those circumstances, new customers are hard to get and an old customer lost is hard to replace. It is quite different selling 45% than in selling 5%.

It is perfectly possible, from the engineering and manufacturing standpoints, to make two cars at not a great difference in price and weight, but considerably different in appearance and, to some extent, different in technical features, both, in degree, built with the same fundamental tool equipment.

In view of the concentration of volume within a narrow price range, is it desirable for the Corporation to place all its eggs in one basket in view of the above and many other considerations, or is it better to capitalize the recognized fact that different things appeal to different people; that not all the sound engineering ideas can be incorporated in one unit; that the influence of the dealer is an important consideration? . . .

I answered these questions with a statement of my commercial policy as follows:

. . . I believe that in the low price field where from 80% to 90% plus of the volume is concentrating, we should have more than one appeal, and that our representation, whatever it may be, should contemplate the incorporation of sufficient differences in essential elements of design, as to make the broadest possible appeal to the largest number of people. I accept, as a corollary of this principle, the fact that manufacture and distribution is complicated. I regret that we can not make one thing that everybody will buy, but I do not think, under present circumstances, that is possible.

In communities of high potential where there must necessarily be many dealers competing against each other, with the same product in the same market, I believe that it is better policy to limit the number of dealers competing for one line and obtain the increased number of contacts through a different appeal than it is to go the other route.

To illustrate, let us take a community in which we might maintain "x" dealers. Rather than have those "x" dealers competing with each other on the basis of exactly the same merchandise, which is very de-moralizing competition, I believe it is better to have a part of same, and a major part of course, competing against each other with the Chevrolet line and additional dealers competing with lines diversified from Chevrolet.

For all the above reasons, I personally feel that the policy as outlined many years ago [1921] by the Executive Committee, should be modified substantially as follows:—

> THAT giving recognition to the concentration of volume in the low price field, it shall be the policy of the Corporation to increase its representation within that field, but in doing so the utmost consideration must be given to the importance of the greatest possible diversity in all elements of consumer appeal in such additional offerings so as to build the strongest foundation of acceptability to the consumer.

This proposal to maintain diversity in cars and separate divisional selling efforts in a crowded price class required new forms of co-ordination. And the more you co-ordinate, the more questions you draw up into the policy area, and therefore the finer must be the distinctions between policy and administration. For example, when two or more divisions use common components, the independence of each division is limited to the extent that there must be a common program between them. Someone therefore must co-ordinate such a program. As this process is elaborated, more questions come into the policy area which were formerly in the administrative area. I have always believed it is imperative to maintain the distinction between policy and administration. Without that distinction a decentralized organization would be in constant confusion as to what was decentralized and what was not. So the big question was the policy one. And it demanded a general solution. The solution we worked out at that time remains today the basic decision-making process in General Motors. It was contained in the following recommendation which I made to the Executive Committee in October 1934:

> It has already been developed that the creation of a policy might emanate either from the Central Authority or from within the Operating Division or Subsidiary. The finalization or authorization of a policy is exclusively within the province of the Central Authority as presented by a Governing Committee. From whatever source the policy may originate, it is essential that those involved in authorization should be qualified to

pass on the proposal with a full knowledge of its implications as affecting the present and future position of the business. Where a policy involves important consequences, as in the case of the operations of General Motors Corporation, it is essential that the broadest possible foundation of thought and fact and the approach of the proposal from as many different angles as possible, be established. To the degree that authorization becomes superficial, to that degree does the position of the business become jeopardized, or its progress adversely affected.

The above more or less philosophical discussion is for the purpose of establishing the reasons for and the desirability of formulating a broader conception of the policy creation phase of administration than has heretofore existed in the General Motors scheme of things.

This Procedure establishes, for the first time, the following principle:—

1—THAT the development, or creation of constructive and advanced policies, as defined, is of vital influence in the progress and stability of the business.

2—THAT in the organization of General Motors Corporation, the fact just recited, should be recognized through a specialization of policy creation, independent of policy execution, so far as that is reasonably practical.

The concept of policy creation described above was embodied in a set of new organs in General Motors, called policy groups. These groups, generally speaking, had functional titles, such as Engineering Policy Group, Distribution Policy Group, and the like, with later some line groups such as the Overseas Policy Group. They combined the top executive officers, including the president, with functional staff men, and each group was charged with making policy recommendations in its functional area to the top operating policy committee of the corporation. The divisional managers, being charged with administration, were specifically excluded from these groups. The groups themselves, as groups, were not given authority over the divisions, or any authority to finalize policies, but since the groups contained the principal officers of the corporation, policy-group recommendations were normally adopted by the governing committee in the area of operations. We tried out policy groups in the engineering and distribution areas between 1934 and 1937, and in the latter year expanded their use to other functions and some operations and adopted them officially for the corporation.[2] They

2 General Motors Corporation organization charts for 1937 and 1963 are at the end of this chapter.

express in more sophisticated form the management policy I first formulated in the "Organization Study" of 1919–20, that is, of decentralized operations with co-ordinated control.

There are now nine policy groups in the corporation, divided into two categories. First, there are those that deal with functions —namely, Engineering, Distribution, Research, Personnel, and Public Relations—all largely related, though not exclusively, to the car operations. And then there are those that deal with certain group operations—namely, Overseas, Canadian, General Engine, and Household Appliance. In the case of each functional activity, these policy groups work under the auspices of the section of the general staff to which they are related; the Engineering Policy Group, for example, is related to the Engineering Staff through the Engineering Staff vice president. In the case of operations, each group is under the auspices of the group executive for that set of operations.

Members of these various groups carry great influence at the highest level in the corporation. The chairman of the board and chief executive officer, for example, is a member of all but three of the policy groups, and the president a member of all but two. In the case of the Distribution, Engineering, Research, Personnel, and Public Relations policy groups, the members of the Executive Committee as well as others of the operating management are members. Their full membership comprises a cross-section of the whole of the corporation's executive talent. Hence their great weight in uniting staff and line operations, preparing policy recommendations, and developing the basis for executive decisions.

The activity of the policy groups varies with the changing needs for policy determination. The Engineering Policy Group, for example, meets regularly to work on new product programs.[3] In this activity the general managers individually and collectively, in person and through their functional departments, are in intimate con-

[3] The Engineering Policy Group consists of the chairman of the group, who is vice president for engineering; the chairman and chief executive officer of the corporation; the president of the corporation; the executive vice president for staff; the executive vice president for financial affairs; the executive vice president for the automotive and parts divisions; the executive vice president for the other operating divisions; the vice presidents for styling, distribution, research, and manufacturing; and the vice presidents who are group executives for the car and truck group, the body and assembly divisions group, the accessory group, and the Dayton, household appliance, and engine group. Of the fifteen members of the Engineering Policy Group, eight are members of the Executive Committee and constitute that entire committee, and four are also members of the Finance Committee.

tact with the work of the policy groups. They are not members of the policy groups, as I have said, because those groups are charged with policy development and the general managers are charged with administration.

The function of the Engineering Policy Group in the development of a new model in General Motors is a good example of the work of a policy group. The initiation of a product program in any division lies within the responsibility of the general manager of that division in collaboration with its engineering department, influenced of course by the market as reflected by its sales department and importantly co-ordinated with the needs of the other operating divisions. If we were to go back twenty-five or thirty years, we would find little co-ordination between a program proposed by one division and one that might be put forward by any of the other car divisions. But over the course of time a very great amount of co-ordination has become necessary. In other words, a divisional product program, instead of being integral in itself, is deeply involved with the product programs of many of the other divisions; therefore it must be developed from the corporate point of view. The time between the conception of any new program and its final execution is presently about two years. In the case of an advanced engineering concept, it is very likely to be more than two years. And during that time it is subject to an untold amount of change. Therefore, during the development period, detailed contact must be continually maintained between the engineering departments of all the car divisions, the Styling Staff, the Fisher Body Division, and more or less the accessory divisions—because they are all commonly concerned with and working together on a single problem. Here the corporation's Engineering Staff comes into the picture and collaborates with the other divisions in order to effect the necessary co-ordination. The co-ordination agency—if I may call it such—that passes on the problems involved in this process is the Engineering Policy Group. Its decisions are normally adopted by the Executive Committee, whose members are present through the whole process.

It was the depression, and the economies it forced in co-ordination of the product, as I have shown, that led to this new type of co-ordination in management. With the establishment of policy groups in 1937, the scheme of management which originated in the Organization Study of 1919–20 was complete.

Long reflection on the distinction to be made between policy and administration led me in 1937 also to consider the application of this concept more precisely to the organization of the governing committees of the corporation. Early that year I proposed that in place of the Finance and Executive committees we should have a single policy committee to concentrate on making over-all policy for the corporation and an administration committee to concentrate on the carrying out of policy. After considerable discussion we adopted this change in May of that year. The Finance Committee and the Executive Committee were discontinued. A new Policy Committee was formed. It was composed, of course, entirely of members of the board, and brought operating officers, financial officers, and outside directors into one senior group. The new Administration Committee was composed entirely of operating officers.

The Policy Committee took over all the responsibilities of the former Finance Committee and additional responsibilities for operating policy. From 1937 through 1941 the Policy Committee made policy for operations in a number of important areas. For example, it established the broad outlines of labor policies and programs and also decided a number of distribution policies, particularly those concerning dealer relations. As international conditions became increasingly unsettled, more and more of its time was given to determining policies for the overseas subsidiaries. As war approached, the Policy Committee had to deal with increasing shortages of raw materials, relations with the government, and the impact on our civilian operations of government requests for the production of airplane engines, tanks, and other military items.

The entrance of the United States into the war in December 1941 required a special change in our committee organization. To make the rapid shift to all-out war production, we set up on January 5, 1942, a War Emergency Committee composed of six top executives, mostly from the Policy Committee. This committee met once a week and sometimes more often. From January through April 1942 it ran General Motors. Temporarily the Policy and Administration committees did little more than ratify the War Emergency Committee's work. But in May 1942, as we settled into war production, we abolished the War Emergency Committee. We then transformed the Administration Committee, consisting of all the general executives and group vice presidents, into the War Administration Committee. For the next two to three years the War Administration Committee practically ran the organization. This was because our wartime policy was set and nearly all the corporation's work was war production. Aside from the technical problems of production, our policy decisions were concerned primarily with our relationships with various government departments.

By 1945 the Policy Committee once more had come into its own as we were developing our broad postwar planning. Since the problems of reconversion and postwar business were so enormously important, nearly all major questions, even some concerned with the running of the business, came to the Policy Committee. As a result of this overburdening of the Policy Committee, we began to reconsider the structure and function of the committees of the board.

A single policy committee was an ideal solution to the problem of separating policy from administration. But two factors promised to make it impractical in the new circumstances that were developing. First, it was apparent that the growth in the volume and complexity of the corporation's activities would require a greatly enlarged responsibility both in finance and operations at the board level. Second, it was going to be difficult to obtain the services of experienced outside directors with adequate time to serve on a committee dealing with operations as well as financial policy. Therefore, in 1946, we dissolved the Policy Committee and replaced it with the two traditional committees representing the primary functions of finance and operations, now renamed the Financial Policy Committee and the Operations Policy Committee. In 1958 we restored their old names, Finance Committee and Executive Committee, and in a further refinement, expanded their membership to obtain more overlapping of the individuals on the two committees.

So much for the evolution of the forms of policy making in General Motors. I want to say something now on my philosophy of the role of the board of directors, the supreme body of the corporation. The board, of course, functions as boards of large corporations usually do, in good part through its committees. There are four such committees in General Motors, each of which is composed exclusively of directors, authorized to exercise the powers of the board in the management of the business and affairs of the corporation. These are the Finance, Executive, Bonus and Salary, and Audit committees. I shall comment here only on the two that are the central authority for policy determination—the Finance Committee and the Executive Committee. The majority of the members of the Finance Committee are "outside" directors, that is, directors who are not active in the management of the business. They include former operations officers, like myself, and directors who have never been associated with the corporation except on its board. All of the members of the Executive Committee are directors who are active in management. Both committees deal with problems of policy as distinct from administration. The actions of both committees are subject to revision by the board.

The central responsibility of the Finance Committee is the corporation's purse. This committee has authority under the by-laws to determine the financial policies of the corporation and direct its financial affairs. It has authority over all capital appropriations and over entrance into any new line of business. It reviews and approves pricing policies and procedures as formulated by the Executive Committee. It has the responsibility to see that the corporation has adequate capital for its needs, and that it earns a satisfactory return on its investment. And this committee makes the dividend recommendation to the board.

The Executive Committee is responsible for operating policy. I have described earlier how policies have been developed in the policy groups, whose function is to channel the work of the operating staffs and other authorities in the corporation. However, the actual adoption of operating policy is the responsibility of the Executive Committee. Appropriation requests for capital expenditures are prepared under the supervision of this committee, for submission to the Finance Committee. In practice the Finance Committee has delegated to the Executive Committee the authority to approve capital expenditures up to $1 million.

The General Motors board as a whole meets regularly once a month and at times on special occasions. From time to time it elects from its members those who are to serve on the committees I have described. It also elects those who are to administer the business —that is, the officers of the corporation—and acts on legal and general corporate matters requiring board action, such as the declaration of dividends or the issuance of additional securities.

Furthermore, to my way of thinking, based on my experience, the General Motors board of directors has still another and, I believe, unique function of great significance. That is what I call an "audit" function. I do not mean audit in the usual financial sense but one that contemplates a continuous review and appraisal of what is going on throughout the enterprise. General Motors is, of course, both large and highly technical in all its ramifications. It is therefore impossible to conceive of every member of the corporation's board of directors having intimate knowledge of and business experience in every one of the technical matters which require top-level consideration or action. Also, those of its members with outside responsibilities would not have the time to examine and decide upon all such matters. The problems are too many, too diversified, and too complex. Nevertheless, although the board may not be equipped to deal with technical operating problems, it can and should be responsible for the end result. The General Motors board deals with the corporation's affairs before the fact through projections of what we hope to accomplish and after the fact through evaluation of reports and other data; and it is prepared to take proper action where needed.

For this purpose the General Motors board receives a comprehensive picture of the enterprise and its operations. Reports from its Executive and Finance committees are presented monthly, and those from other standing committees periodically, covering their actions. A visual presentation on a screen sets forth for examination every material aspect of the corporation's position, financial, statistical, and competitive, and a forecast of the immediate future. This is supported by explanatory comments and also by a summary of the general business outlook. In addition, operating officers make oral reports on the corporation's business in various areas. Also, formal presentations are made to the board regularly by various staff vice presidents and top operating executives covering developments in their fields of responsibility. Board members then ask questions and seek explanations. This audit function, as the General Motors board exercises it, is of the highest value to the enterprise and its shareholders. I cannot conceive of any board of directors being better informed and thus able to act intelligently on all the changing facts and circumstances than is the board of General Motors.

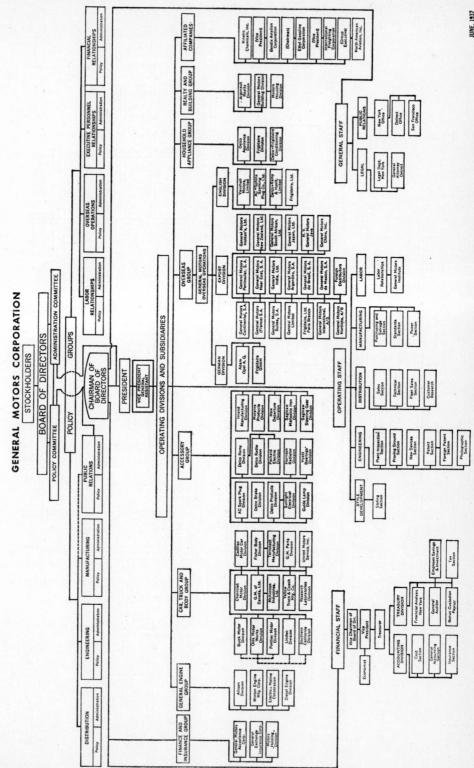

GENERAL MOTORS CORPORATION

JUNE, 1937

GENERAL MOTORS CORPORATION

STOCKHOLDERS

BOARD OF DIRECTORS

AUDIT COMMITTEE

BONUS AND SALARY COMMITTEE

EXECUTIVE COMMITTEE

FINANCE COMMITTEE

CHAIRMAN OF BOARD OF DIRECTORS

PRESIDENT

POLICY GROUPS
- CANADIAN
- GENERAL ENGINE
- HOUSEHOLD APPLIANCE
- OVERSEAS

DISTRIBUTION
ENGINEERING
PERSONNEL
PUBLIC RELATIONS
RESEARCH

EXECUTIVE VICE PRESIDENT

EXECUTIVE VICE PRESIDENT

EXECUTIVE VICE PRESIDENT

EXECUTIVE VICE PRESIDENT

EXECUTIVE VICE PRESIDENT

ADMINISTRATION COMMITTEE

LEGAL STAFF
Vice President
General Counsel

FINANCIAL STAFF
Vice President

Vice President

Comptroller

Business Research

Treasurer

General Auditor

OPERATIONS STAFF

Engineering
Vice President

Research
Vice President

Personnel
Vice President

Manufacturing
Vice President

Public Relations
Vice President

Styling
Vice President

Distribution
Vice President

Motors Holding Div
General Manager

AUTOMOTIVE AND PARTS DIVISIONS

CAR AND TRUCK GROUP
Vice President

- Buick Motor Division — General Manager
- Cadillac Motor Car Division — General Manager
- Chevrolet Motor Division — General Manager
- Oldsmobile Division — General Manager
- Pontiac Motor Division — General Manager
- GMC Truck & Coach Division — General Manager

BODY AND ASSEMBLY DIVISIONS GROUP
Vice President

- Fisher Body Division — General Manager
- Ternstedt Division — General Manager
- Buick-Oldsmobile-Pontiac Assembly Division — General Manager

ACCESSORY GROUP
Vice President

- AC Spark Plug Division — General Manager
- Central Foundry Division — General Manager
- Delco Radio Division — General Manager
- Delco-Remy Division — General Manager
- Guide Lamp Division — General Manager
- Harrison Radiator Division — General Manager
- Hyatt Bearings Division — General Manager
- Hydra-Matic Division — General Manager
- New Departure Division — General Manager
- Rochester Products Division — General Manager
- Saginaw Steering Gear Division — General Manager
- United Motors Service Division — General Manager

Allison Division — General Manager

OTHER OPERATING DIVISIONS

DAYTON, HOUSEHOLD APPLIANCE AND ENGINE GROUP
Vice President

- Delco Appliance Division — General Manager
- Delco Moraine Division — General Manager
- Delco Products Division — General Manager
- Detroit Diesel Engine Division — General Manager
- Diesel Equipment Division — General Manager
- Electro-Motive Division — General Manager
- Euclid Division — General Manager
- Frigidaire Division — General Manager
- Frigidaire Products of Canada Limited — Pres. & Gen. Mgr.
- General Motors Diesel Limited — Pres. & Gen. Mgr.
- Inland Manufacturing Division — General Manager
- Packard Electric Division — General Manager

OVERSEAS AND CANADIAN GROUP

- G.M. Overseas Operations Division — General Manager
- General Motors of Canada Limited — Chairman President & Gen. Mgr.
- McKinnon Industries Limited — Pres. & Gen. Mgr.

FINANCE AND INSURANCE GROUP

- General Motors Acceptance Corp. — President
- Motors Insurance Corporation — Chairman & Pres.
- Yellow Motors Credit Corp. — President

OCTOBER, 1963

Chapter 11

FINANCIAL GROWTH

GENERAL Motors is a growth company, and the sum of all I have said is expressed in this fact. For most of the early period of General Motors' existence, it did not grow as fast as the automobile industry as a whole. But after 1918, and more particularly because of the measures taken by the modern administration, the corporation grew faster than the industry and became its number-one producer. We like to believe that we have made a contribution as an industrial leader. Employees, shareholders, dealers, consumers, suppliers—and the government to a large degree—have shared in the success of General Motors. Although progress has been achieved for all of these interests, the story of financial growth in this chapter reflects mainly the point of view of the shareholder.

How has the corporation served its owners? I believe this can best be seen by looking at the financial record of the business—how the funds were supplied or secured, and how they were used from the beginning to the present.

Our shareholders have derived a substantial monetary benefit from the success of the business through the distribution of about two thirds of the income realized since inception—a proportion which is larger than that distributed by most businesses. In order to secure these benefits, the shareholders have underwritten the growth of the enterprise by their willingness to reinvest the substantial sums required to meet the needs of the business as it grew. Of necessity, during periods of expansion of facilities and of peak working-capital needs, this has meant that dividends have been something less than average. The shareholders thus assumed the risk of building for the future with no certainty of a return, and in the early periods the return was slow in coming. The financial community in general at that time was bearish on the automobile industry and its prospects, including General Motors. Many companies then in the automobile industry—all with a desire for success —are no longer in existence, with consequent loss of their shareholders' investment. Thus, it seems only proper to measure the monetary return of General Motors' shareholders against the risks they assumed when investing in an enterprise with an uncertain future.

Broadly speaking, from the financial standpoint three periods have characterized the corporation's existence. The first was the long-term period of expansion from 1908 through 1929; the second, the depression and World War II years from 1930 through 1945; and the third, the post-World War II years, which brought a renewal of expansion.

Within these periods, however, there were subperiods of expansion, contraction, and stabilization. I have related how Mr. Durant in the years 1908 and 1909 created the corporation by combining a number of enterprises, most importantly Buick and Cadillac and a few makers of car components, and how the tremendous problems of financing this endeavor cost Mr. Durant his position in the corporation in 1910. Then, this initial period of rapid expansion was followed by contraction and stabilization between 1910 and 1915 while the bankers pruned and righted the enterprise. The corporation grew slightly, but less than the industry. Again, between 1916 and 1920, particularly in the period 1918–20, Mr. Durant— now working in collaboration with Mr. Raskob and the du Pont interests—expanded the corporation by various financial means, including debt and stock issues.

The Early Expansion Period—1918 through 1920

In the three years 1918 through 1920 the corporation's expenditures for plant and equipment totaled some $215 million. In addition, between January 1, 1918, and December 31, 1920, more than $65 million was invested in subsidiary companies not consolidated, bringing the total outlay to over $280 million. This was a truly staggering sum for that period when you realize that at the start of the program on January 1, 1918, General Motors' total assets were about $135 million and its entire gross plant amounted to only $40 million. By the end of 1920 total assets had reached about $575 million, more than four times the amount at the end of 1917, and gross plant of almost $250 million was more than six times as great as the December 31, 1917, balance.

Despite some unfortunate investments—Samson Tractor, for example—this expansion program established principles which were to guide the corporation's investments in the period after Durant lost control. As the annual report for 1920 stated it:

The officers and directors of the corporation have thought it unwise to undertake the production of materials that do not relate largely to the automobile [that is, the bulk of the production of which does not go into car production]. Thus: a comparatively small portion of the total tires produced are consumed by the automobile manufacturer, the larger percentage being sold directly to users of cars for replacement purposes; the greater part of the production of sheets and other forms of steel is consumed by trades other than the automotive industry; therefore investment in these fields has not been made. By the pursuit of this policy, General Motors Corporation has become firmly entrenched in lines that relate directly to the construction of the car, truck or tractor, but has not invested in general industries of which a comparatively small part of the product is consumed in the manufacture of cars.

The capital expenditures of the 1918–20 period were responsible for General Motors' great growth—of a different kind—in the 1920s. At the beginning of 1918 General Motors had just four passenger-car manufacturing divisions—Buick, Cadillac, Oakland, and Olds— and one truck division. It had no capacity to manufacture a smaller car for the low-price field. It had no allied source of supply for many components and accessories—such as lighting, starting and ignition sets, roller and ball bearings—and no research facilities. Sales of General Motors cars and trucks in 1920 (393,000) were almost twice those of 1918 (205,000). Our productive capacity increased from 223,000 car and truck units a year at the beginning of 1918 to 750,000 units in 1922, a large part of the increase represented by facilities to make the popular-priced Chevrolet. In addition, the corporation had sufficient capacity to manufacture its own electrical equipment, radiators, antifriction bearings, wheel rims, steering gears, transmissions, engines, axles, and open bodies, and it had a source of supply of closed bodies, which were just becoming popular, through its interest in the Fisher Body Corporation. And General Motors had its own research facilities.

Needless to say, so rapid a growth could not have been financed entirely out of earnings. The industry was still getting started and in General Motors it was a case of laying a base for the years of high production ahead. To acquire the assets of Chevrolet and United Motors and to purchase a 60 per cent interest in the Fisher Body Corporation, General Motors paid with its own securities. But most of the expenditures were made in cash, and so the corporation had to go to the capital markets. On December 31, 1918, the board of directors authorized the sale of 240,000 shares of common stock to du Pont in order to provide additional capital for the expansion program. This netted the corporation close to $29 million. In May 1919 the corporation authorized Dominick and Dominick of New York and Laird and Company of Wilmington to form a syndicate to sell publicly an issue of 6 per cent debenture (preferred) stock. As Mr. Durant wrote the underwriters:

This corporation requires a large amount of additional money to avail [itself] of the opportunities . . . to extend its business profitably and has decided that the most provident way to obtain this money is through the issue of additional debenture stock . . . Furthermore, it is greatly to the interest of a corporation carrying on such a business as ours to have as many persons as possible interested in its prosperity. Accordingly, it desires to issue and to have distributed as broadly as possible, within three months after the closing of the present Liberty Loan Campaign, $50,000,-000 in par value of its debenture stock . . .

If you will proceed forthwith to form a syndicate for the purpose of distributing this proposed issue of debenture stock and . . . will definitely agree to take for such syndicate, $30,000,000 in par value thereof . . . we agree that such $30,000,000 par value of debenture stock, together with the whole or any part of an additional $20,000,000 thereof, shall be available to you . . .

When the syndicate was closed on July 2, 1919, only $30 million par value of the stock had been issued, with proceeds of $25 million to the corporation; none of the additional $20 million had been sold.

These issues were not enough to meet both the plant-expenditure and working-capital demands, particularly for inventories, which rose even more than expenditures for new plant and equipment. Early in 1920, therefore, in another major financing, holders of outstanding shares of 6 per cent preferred and debenture stock were given the right to subscribe to two shares of new 7 per cent debenture stock—to be paid for either wholly in cash or one half in cash and the balance with one share of the old 6 per cent preferred or debenture stock. Mr. Durant told the shareholders:

A careful forecast, looking far into the future, indicates that, for your corporation to continue occupying its leading position in the automobile industry, large capital investments will be required, which requirements can likely be better met by financing that portion of our growth which is not supplied from earnings, through the sale of a seven per cent. (7%) rather than a six per cent. (6%) senior security. This at once gives us an opportunity and a privilege; an opportunity to issue our senior securities at or above par, instead of at the substantial discount necessary in the sale of our present securities, and the privilege of extending to our senior security holders the right to subscribe to this new seven per cent. (7%) debenture stock on a most attractive basis.

The new issue was a failure. It revealed the concern with which the financial community regarded General Motors' growing inability to control its internal affairs. Mr. Durant and Mr. Raskob had hoped to raise about $85 million through the new debenture issue. They were able to raise only $11 million. Hence the du Ponts had to intervene, and with their aid General Motors sold more than $60 million worth of new common stock in the summer of 1920, and a little later borrowed over $80 million from a group of banks.

Altogether, General Motors increased its capital employed[1] by some $316 million during the expansion period from January 1, 1918, to December 31, 1920. Of this increase, $54 million came from earnings reinvested in the business after payment of dividends totaling $58 million. The rest of the increase resulted largely from the sale of new securities for cash and the issue of new securities in payment for properties acquired.

This increase of $316 million in the corporation's capital em-

---

[1] *Capital employed* consists of funds invested in the business by security holders. These are derived from equity issues (common and preferred stocks), debt issues, additional capital paid in (capital surplus), and net income retained for use in the business (earned surplus). The capital employed is invested in two broad categories—working capital and fixed capital.

ployed from the beginning of 1918 to the end of 1920 compares with: expenditures of some $280 million for plant and equipment and for investment in subsidiary companies not consolidated; and vastly enlarged working-capital[2] items, of which the major one, inventories, increased $118 million, or from $47 million to $165 million.

A Short Period of Contraction— 1921 and 1922

The expansion of 1918, 1919, and 1920 was followed by contraction in the pruning of 1921 and 1922. By the end of 1922 bank debt had been liquidated and inventories and plant were conservatively valued, and when the dust settled we were ready with a capacity to produce 750,000 cars and trucks a year, although we sold only 457,000 in 1922.

A Period of Firming Up— 1923 through 1925

Although the year 1923 marked the start of a great new era of expanded production in the automobile industry, the three years 1923 through 1925 involved no important expansion of productive facilities in General Motors, for the Durant-Raskob program had provided a sufficient base to meet a considerable growth in the car market. Our sales of 836,000 cars and trucks in 1925 were 83 per cent greater than the 457,000 sold in 1922. However, in the three years 1923 through 1925 the corporation spent less than $60 million for plant and equipment while providing nearly $50 million for depreciation. The new controls operated so well that this increase in sales volume was accompanied by a decrease of $5 million in inventories, from $117 million at the beginning of 1923 to $112 million at the end of 1925. In the same period net working capital increased $55 million, or 44 per cent, while dollar sales went from $698 million in 1923 to $735 million in 1925 and net income increased from $72 million in 1923 to $116 million in 1925. All told,

2 *Net working capital* represents the excess of current assets (cash, short-term securities, receivables, and inventories) over current liabilities (accounts payable, taxes, payrolls, and sundry accrued items).

as a result of our producing more cars more economically, our net income totaled $240 million in the years 1923 through 1925. Of this sum we paid out $112 million to the holders of common stock and $22 million to preferred shareholders, a total of $134 million, or 56 per cent of the total net income for the period.

A New Period of Expansion— 1926 through 1929

The rapid growth in our sales through 1925 indicated the need for additional investment in plant and equipment, and in 1926 we began a new period of expansion which extended through 1929. This move was quickly justified, for in 1926 we sold a total of 1,235,000 cars and trucks, an increase of almost 50 per cent over the previous peak volume of 1925. Now, however, unlike the earlier periods, the needed funds were provided out of earnings, provisions for depreciation, and newly issued stock. Altogether, in these four years our investment in nonconsolidated subsidiaries and miscellaneous units increased by $121 million and we added some $325 million to our investment in plant and equipment, including the plant and equipment acquired through the purchase of Fisher Body Corporation in 1926.

This program of expansion enlarged our facilities in several directions. We expanded our car-making capacity, especially for the Chevrolet Division, whose unit sales almost doubled in these four years, and for the new Pontiac. We expanded the capacity of our accessory-manufacturing divisions because of the growth in car-assembly capacity. We made more components. We expanded our merchandising operations, including overseas assembly plants and warehouses, and so brought our products closer to the ultimate consumers. We had acquired a small manufacturing base, Vauxhall, in England in 1925, and we acquired an 80 per cent interest in a larger one, Adam Opel, in Germany in 1929. And we expanded a number of other activities such as the Frigidaire Division, and made investments in the aviation and diesel fields.

In sum, we more than doubled our gross plant during the period January 1, 1926, to December 31, 1929—from $287 million to $610 million—and our investment in nonconsolidated subsidiaries and miscellaneous units rose almost two and one-half times, from $86 million to $207 million. Total assets were increased from $704 million to $1.3 billion. Our unit car and truck sales went from 1.2 million in 1926 to 1.9 million in 1929, while total dollar sales went from $1.1 billion to $1.5 billion.

Thanks to the financial and operating controls, we were able to finance virtually this entire expansion program out of earnings and depreciation and still pay out almost two thirds of net earnings to the shareholders. The only outside financing in this period was an issue of $25 million of 7 per cent preferred stock in 1927. The rest came from retained earnings. In 1926, however, the balance of the assets of Fisher Body Corporation was acquired for 664,720 shares of common stock, of which 638,401 shares were newly issued. Net income rose from $186 million in 1926 to $276 million in 1928— a record high—and $248 million in 1929. All told, we earned $946 million in the four years 1926 through 1929, of which $596 million (63 per cent) was paid to shareholders and the balance of $350 million reinvested in the corporation. Provision for depreciation totaled $115 million in this period.

Taking these two stages together, that is, 1923 through 1925 and 1926 through 1929, this is the record, using the year 1922 for comparison:

General Motors car and truck sales in the United States and Canada quadrupled, from 457,000 in 1922 to 1,899,000 in 1929, and dollar sales more than tripled, from $464 million to $1504 million. Instead of the runaway inventories of the preceding period, we achieved this phenomenal growth in production and sales volume with only a 60 per cent rise in inventories. (Net working capital rose from $125 million on December 31, 1922, to $248 million at the end of 1929, including cash and short-term securities, which rose from $28 million to $127 million.) Gross plant increased from $255 million to $610 million, and capital employed more than doubled, from $405 million to $954 million. Over the seven-year stretch we earned a total of $1186 million, of which $730 million (62 per cent) was paid out to shareholders, and $456 million was retained in the business.

Depression and Recovery—the 1930s

The early 1930s began with the depression, followed by stabilization and expansion in the middle of the decade. It ended with the industry under the influence of the preparation for World War II.

With the big depression—from 1930 to 1934—there was contraction in General Motors. But this time, unlike 1920–21, and despite its greater severity, the contraction was orderly. Of necessity, dividend payments were lower in some of these years than in others, but in no year did the corporation fail to earn a profit or pay a dividend. In the years 1931 and 1932 the corporation paid shareholders more than its earnings, which reduced some of the capital accumulated in more prosperous periods.

For the 1930s as a whole, dividend payments totaled 91 per cent of net income, for we found that we had more funds than we could profitably invest under the generally depressed economic conditions of this period.

The most difficult years, of course, were the three following the stock-market crash. I have mentioned earlier that between 1929 and 1932 car and truck production in the United States and Canada fell 75 per cent, from 5.6 million units to only 1.4 million, and that in dollar sales the decline in the industry was even more precipitous—from $5.1 billion at retail to $1.1 billion, or 78 per cent. And yet General Motors was able to earn $248 million in this three-year period and to pay shareholders a total of $343 million—$95 million more than the corporation earned. Despite the fact that dividends exceeded earnings, net working capital fell only $26 million, and the corporation's holdings of cash and short-term securities actually increased by $45 million, or by 36 per cent, a case you might say of pure liquidation.

What accounts for this exceptional record in a period in which many durable-goods producers failed or came close to bankruptcy? It would be unfair to claim any particular prescience on our part; no more than anyone else did we see the depression coming. I think the story I have told shows that we had simply learned how to react quickly. This was perhaps the greatest payoff of our system of financial and operating controls.

As a result of the speed with which we acted when sales began to fall, we were able to reduce our inventories in line with the sales decline and to control costs so that operations remained profitable. Our sales declined 71 per cent, from $1504 million in 1929 to only $432 million in 1932, but our inventories were reduced 60 per cent, or by $113 million. With this decline of more than $1 billion in sales, net income fell $248 million but we managed to earn $165,000 in 1932 while paying out $63 million in dividends.

In the early thirties, as noted above, we did not feel the need to spend very much for new plant and equipment. In the five years 1930–34, such expenditures totaled $81 million; in 1932 we spent only $5 million. Moreover, during these years we retired some of our surplus plant and equipment. In later years as the plant was needed, we restored some of it to the active account.

By 1935 sales from our United States and Canadian plants had recovered to more than 1.5 million cars and trucks—about 80 per cent of the 1929 peak and a nearly threefold increase in three years. The next year our United States and Canadian car and truck sales approached the 1929 mark and in 1937 they set a record of 1,928,-000 units. Net income, however, was $196 million in 1937, which was not up to the $248 million earned in 1929 or the $238 million in 1936. Earnings in 1937 were adversely affected by a six-week strike early in the year and by increasing costs. For example, the average straight-time wage rate for the corporation's U.S. hourly-rate employees in 1937 was 20 per cent higher than in 1936 and 28 per cent above the 1929 rate. But since our investment needs were relatively slight, dividend payments totaled $202 million in 1936—the highest on record—and $170 million in 1937; for the two years, dividends were 85 per cent of net income.

This rapid recovery in sales and output meant that our production facilities were again under strain. As noted above, we began to reactivate that part of the idle plant that had not been made obsolete by product or technological change. And we began to need new facilities, too. As output grew rapidly during 1935, we undertook a comprehensive survey of the corporation's manufacturing properties at home and abroad to assess our productive capacity in the light of what appeared to be the future sales possibilities. In the annual report for 1935 I wrote:

The rapid evolution of processing which is constantly going on in the automotive industry, due to the yearly turnover of models, produces a very rapid obsolescence of productive facilities. Naturally, specific tools and machine equipment, when changed, are provided, so far as volume is concerned, in harmony with the sales outlook of the following year. For these reasons, during the years of the depression, the actual capacity of the Corporation's plants for the production of current products had been reduced. In addition, further limitations have been placed on capacity due to the increased number of models apparently necessary to provide the essential coverage of the various markets in which the Corporation is competing. Increased complications of manufacture incident to changed style and added technical features have also had an important influence.

Equally important is the fact that, while the number of hours worked per week by productive workers of industry has been going through a process of reduction, through evolution, the depression period brought about a further demand for the reduction of weekly operating schedules for the workers . . . With the reduction of hours, irrespective of circumstances that might justify such hours, the impossibility of maintaining the annual averages of previous years has tended to reduce the capacity of plant and equipment, as compared with previous years.

The corporation, therefore, in 1935 authorized expenditures to reorganize, readjust, and expand the manufacturing facilities. They eventually exceeded $50 million.

Production and sales continued to expand rapidly, and so we made another survey of General Motors' operating facilities in relation to current and expected demand for its products. We gave consideration to three special factors affecting capacity: the trend toward a shorter work week, the probability of a reduction in operating efficiency, and the likelihood of some interruption of production due to labor difficulties. The latter two expectations proved correct for 1937.

Because of these factors, capacity of the Chevrolet Division was inadequate. The division had been unable to meet the demand for its products during each of the preceding three years. (In both 1935 and 1936 Chevrolet car and truck production topped one million.) Several other divisions had suffered from inadequate capacity, although to a lesser degree, and the development of new products in the General Engine Group and Household Appliance Group had placed these operations in a position where expansion was essential to exploit the new products properly. The capacity shortages, moreover, were not due to bottlenecks in localized areas; the corporation's productive facilities were very well balanced in that respect. But this meant that any fundamental increase in capacity would require expenditures on a broad front. We authorized a program, therefore, calling for an expenditure of more than $60 million for new capacity, in addition to substantial expenditures for modernization and replacement. This expansion program was completed in 1938.

The economy turned sharply downward during the latter part of

1937 and the first half of 1938, and then reversed itself to move upward at a rather rapid rate. Consumer sales of automobiles in the United States generally followed this economic trend. The economy paused during the first half of 1939 and then swung upward in the last half of the year, accelerated by the influence of the outbreak of war in Europe.

Over the decade of the 1930s as a whole, the corporation spent $346 million for new plant and equipment. This was a large capital expenditure in view of the generally liquidationist character of the 1930s, but quite small in comparison with our outlays during the preceding decade. Total capital expenditures, however, were $46 million less than our provision for depreciation. We were able to pay shareholders $1191 million in dividends, 91 per cent of our earnings, between 1930 and 1939, as compared with $797 million in the 1920s. This was done without reducing the corporation's liquidity. On the contrary, net working capital rose from $248 million on January 1, 1930, to $434 million on December 31, 1939. Cash and short-term securities went from $127 million to $290 million. And capital employed rose slightly, from $954 million to $1066 million.

World War II—1940 through 1945

Very large demands were made on General Motors during the next six years, and the corporation, I think I can say, like most of American industry, responded with distinction. When World War II began, General Motors rapidly converted itself from the nation's largest manufacturer of automobiles to the nation's largest producer of war materials. And when the war ended, General Motors rapidly reconverted to peacetime production, a capability, in both instances, that derived from our scheme of management and a great deal of planning.

Car and truck production, however, actually advanced 32 per cent during 1940, as the defense program stimulated purchasing power in the economy at large. General Motors' defense production totaled only $75 million during the year (compared to $1.7 billion of commercial sales), but orders mounted rapidly toward the end of the year and by the end of January 1941 defense contracts with our own and allied governments totaled $683 million. In 1941 defense production came to over $400 million (compared to commercial sales of $2 billion), and by the time of Pearl Harbor defense products were being delivered at the rate of $2 million a day.

Once the United States became a belligerent, of course, all our efforts were given to converting to volume production for all-out war. Total defense production for 1942 came to $1.9 billion, with $352 million of commercial production. By 1943 we had our engineering and production capabilities in full swing and defense production rose to $3.7 billion. In 1944 it rose slightly to a war peak of $3.8 billion; physical production was up even more, that is, by 15 per cent as against 3 per cent in dollar volume, since we reduced our prices as production expanded. After V-E Day, of course, partial reconversion began as war contracts were canceled, and full reconversion got under way after V-J Day. During 1945, therefore, war production dropped off to $2.5 billion and commercial production rose slightly, to $579 million. All told, General Motors produced nearly $12.5 billion of defense products. In producing this immense flow of war material, we made all possible use of our existing facilities, converting and in many instances expanding them, at a cost of over $130 million in the years 1940–44. We also operated some $650 million of plants owned by government agencies.

The war years were not years of high earnings and dividends. Although our sales volume expanded from $1377 million in 1939 to $4262 million in 1944, earnings did not grow. At the beginning of the war, and well before the profit-renegotiation law was passed, we adopted the policy of limiting our profit margin before taxes, on military business, to one half of that realized on civilian business in 1941, when the conditions of a competitive market still prevailed. Wherever possible, we took war-production contracts on a fixed-price basis, and we made it a practice to reduce prices as we were able to cut costs. Between 1940 and 1945, therefore, we earned a total of $1070 million on a sales volume of $17,669 million. Of these earnings we paid shareholders a total of $818 million in dividends. Our dividend payments, which had gone to $3.75 per share of the then outstanding $10 par value common stock in 1940 and 1941, were down to $2 per share in 1942 and 1943 and $3 per share in 1944 and 1945.

Although shareholders received 77 per cent of net income during the years 1940–44, our liquidity increased very substantially, owing to the fact that war shortages and priorities made it impossible to replace equipment on a normal schedule. Our capital expenditures of $222 million were less than our provision for depreciation in these five years. Between January 1, 1940, and December 31, 1944, therefore, we increased our net working capital from $434 million to $903 million, and our cash and short-term securities rose from $290 million to $597 million. In 1945 we increased our capital expenditures to a record $114 million; our net working capital declined to $775 million and our cash and short-term securities to $378 million.

The old epochs in our financial history, which reflected both the business cycle and our investment decisions, sometimes separately, more often together, came to an end, and we moved into the great cycle of expansion which we have known since World War II. A few things should be noted before proceeding.

The strategic question in industrial finance, assuming you have something to work with in the way of a going business, is how to optimize its elements. The latitude for opinion, or subjective judgment, here is wide. But I think it would be generally agreed that, in principle, debt enhances the return on the stockholders' investment, while at the same time increasing the risk involved. It would be agreed, I think, that both Mr. Durant and Mr. Raskob had a strong desire to spend and had little inhibition about debt. Mr. Durant carried this attitude far enough into practice in General Motors to create a situation between 1918 and 1920 that would more than serve the expansion needs of the corporation for the following six years. Even so, the expansion of 1918–20 might have worked without crisis if it had been assisted by management and financial controls. In his personal affairs it was obviously debt that brought disaster to Mr. Durant in the economic slump of 1920. So much for that.

It is equally evident that from 1921 to 1946 the corporation avoided long-term debt. I myself had feelings against debt, perhaps because of what I had seen of it in my experience. And yet I cannot really say that we had an antidebt policy in that period. The facts show that we were in general able to do without it. We needed little expenditure up to 1926; and from 1926 through 1929 it was not difficult to expand within the framework of earnings while paying dividends at what we considered a reasonable rate. In other words, we paid off and grew, without debt, except for bank loans during short periods in the 1920s. The 1930s being a time of contraction, the question of debt did not arise. During the war years we arranged for a bank credit of $1 billion, through the government, to finance receivables and inventories, but borrowings under these arrangements were limited. The maximum borrowings were $100 million and were outstanding for less than a year.

When we came to the postwar period, however, despite our liquidity, we were to meet all the financial questions again, including the necessity of providing for large capital expenditures and obtaining additional capital funds through debt as well as stock issues.

The Postwar Era—1946 to 1963

Over the seventeen years 1946 to 1963, our plant expenditures came to more than $7 billion. This amount was nearly seven times the value of the plant at the start of the period. Since increased costs, due to inflation, of equipment and construction accounted for a sizable portion of the postwar expenditures, this ratio does not indicate the increase in physical volume. Net working capital during the seventeen years increased $2753 million (from $775 million to $3528 million). Of total plant expenditures, $4.3 billion, or 61 per cent, was covered by provision for depreciation. The rest necessarily had to come from either reinvested earnings or new capital, or some combination of both. During these seventeen years, General Motors earned about $12.5 billion, and retained over $4.5 billion, or about 36 per cent—a larger proportion of earnings than had been our practice in the past, owing to the needs of the business. Even so, to meet the planned expansion we had to go to the capital markets—for the first time, with the minor exceptions noted, since the early twenties—for a total of $846.5 million during the seventeen-year period, of which by the end of 1962 we had made provision for repayment of $225 million. In addition, about $350 million of common stock was issued, principally for purposes of employee programs during the period 1955 through 1962. Hence between reinvestment of earnings and the sale of new securities, the capital employed in the business in this period rose from $1351 million to $6851 million.

We began our broad planning for this postwar growth long before the war ended. I presented a concept of a postwar program in 1943 in a speech called "The Challenge," which I made to the

National Association of Manufacturers. I argued in this speech that, in the postwar period, industry would meet an enormous pent-up demand for its products and we should boldly plan on this assumption. In doing so I argued against that body of opinion among economists which prophesied economic doom after the war, and, I might add, it was for me not only a matter of argument but also of laying the money on the line. In other words, we recognized that an urgent need would exist, when the war ended, to convert plants from war to peace production as quickly as possible in order to satisfy consumer demand, provide peacetime jobs, and fulfill our obligations to our shareholders, and that all this represented opportunity. Accordingly we had our staff begin to make long-term studies of demand, projecting our position for five to ten years ahead on the basis of the over-all economic outlook, probable consumer demand, and our productive and financial capacity to meet the demand.

On the basis of these studies I announced a postwar program calling for the expenditure of $500 million. This was considered a tremendous sum, and the announcement caused considerable comment. It was considerably more than the corporation had spent on new facilities in either the 1920s or 1930s, and was three fourths larger than the value of our net plant at the end of 1944.

The program, as our 1944 annual report summarized it, involved:

. . . the rearrangement and reorganization of plants, machines and other facilities to be used in producing the cars, trucks and other items that make up General Motors' peacetime products. It calls for the replacement of equipment sold to others during the war. It provides for the modernization of equipment and for replacement of worn tools of all kinds that have been subjected to severe wartime usage. It includes expansion of facilities to meet postwar needs, all in proper balance between short term and long term prospects . . .

So, two years before the war ended, we in General Motors were preparing for the day when we could return to mass production of cars and trucks. Detailed expansion plans were developed for each division, and we also made plans to renew peacetime relationships with the thousands of suppliers and subcontractors with whom General Motors had done business before the war, many of whom were associated with us in war production. Wherever practicable, for example, we advised our prewar suppliers that they could plan on orders for certain peacetime goods as soon as war conditions permitted. We thereby made it possible for them to make their own postwar plans and reduce the time they needed for reconversion.

At the time the postwar plan was formulated, we expected that General Motors would be able to finance the full costs out of earnings and depreciation and other reserves. As we converted facilities to war production in 1941, 1942, and 1943, for example, we had set aside reserves of $76 million to cover what we estimated would be the cost of reconverting them back to commercial output. And we had been accumulating very substantial liquid assets against the day when we could again buy new plant and equipment. Thus, at the end of 1944, we had a net working capital of $903 million, including cash and short-term securities totaling $597 million.

Our wartime estimate of the cost of the postwar expansion program was remarkably accurate, considering the degree of inflation that occurred in the cost of construction and new capital goods. Reconversion costs were $83 million, as compared with our reserve of $76 million. And total plant expenditures from 1945 through 1947, when the first big expansion program was substantially completed, came to $588 million, as compared with our estimate of $500 million.

Our estimates of our postwar working-capital needs, however, were on the low side. These needs were increased greatly, not only by the expanded volume of business we were to do in the postwar period, but also by the tremendous inflation which occurred. In the prewar period, 1935–39, our year-end net working capital averaged $366 million and our inventories $227 million. For the five postwar years, 1946–50, net working capital had increased to an average of $1099 million and inventories to $728 million.

By the end of 1945 most of the corporation's plants were closed by the United Automobile Workers strike, and our cash and investment in short-term securities had dropped $219 million, to $378 million. By the time the strike was settled, on March 13, 1946, liquidity was even lower. Labor troubles continued in some of the plants for another sixty days, and strikes in other industries created shortages of materials which held back the rise in production after our own labor troubles had been solved. As a result, the corporation was unable to earn a satisfactory profit during the initial reconversion period, despite the abnormally high level of demand. In

1946 we earned only $87.5 million, which was $21.4 million less than our dividend payments.

Even before the strike had been settled, the corporation had determined that additional capital might be needed and had requested a study and report on possible financing. By mid-1946 arrangements were completed to borrow $125 million on 2½ per cent twenty- and thirty-year notes from a group of eight insurance companies. Other alternatives had been explored, but the private placement of promissory notes with these institutional investors who had a surplus of long-term funds seemed the most expeditious and the cheapest method of financing. The private-placement negotiations were settled quickly and did not entail the waiting period and filing of documents necessary under a public offering.

The proceeds of this borrowing were received on August 1, 1946, and gave the corporation a good deal more flexibility in meeting its increased capital needs. But the Financial Policy Committee felt that the corporation needed still more capital of a permanent nature, and on August 5, 1946, it authorized Mr. Bradley to negotiate with underwriters "with a view to determining the basis upon which it might be possible to sell a new issue of $125,000,000 preferred stock." The committee had considered other methods of obtaining permanent capital. One factor in our decision was that we could market a preferred-stock issue which we could retire at will, under specified conditions, but which did not have any mandatory provisions requiring retirement by a certain date. As things worked out, however, the public market would not absorb as much preferred stock as we had hoped, except under terms we thought to be too stringent. As a result the issue had to be cut down to $100 million, that is, one million shares of $3.75 preferred offered at par. The stock was offered on November 27, 1946, and yielded the corporation $98 million after underwriting discounts and commissions. This was the first public sale of securities by the corporation in almost twenty years and was a very successful offering.

Some measure of the drain on our resources during the reconversion period is provided by the fact that our net working capital declined $7 million during 1946, and our cash and short-term securities dropped $42 million, even though we raised $223 million of new capital during the year. Had we not gone to the capital market, our net working capital would have dropped by $230 million during 1946.

With these new funds, and with the expansion program that had already been prepared, the corporation was ready to move. By 1948 unit sales from our United States and Canadian plants had risen to 2,146,000 cars and trucks—or almost equal to the prewar high established in 1941—and net income rose to $440 million, up from $288 million in 1947 and only $88 million in 1946. Unit sales established an all-time high in 1949, although general business declined, and our profit margin improved, too, so that net income went up to $656 million. We also were able to raise our inventory turnover ratio very substantially: Inventories declined $65 million on a $1 billion rise in sales. And because our expansion program had been completed, our plant expenditures were relatively modest —$273 million in 1948 and 1949, only $64 million more than our provision for depreciation. Our capital position improved so rapidly, in fact, that we decided to prepay the $125-million note issue in December of 1949, thereby eliminating our debt. We were also able to increase our liquidity and to pay substantial dividends.

Our next major expansion was an outgrowth of the Korean War. We had learned from experience that wars create a backlog of unsatisfied demand. After a good deal of thought we concluded that the long-run potential of the car market required a large expansion of our productive facilities and justified spending corporation money on new plant facilities for defense production that ultimately could be used for commercial operations. I outlined my views in a letter dated November 17, 1950, to the members of the Financial Policy Committee, with the following recommendations:

1. We should make a survey, which is under way, to determine the quantitative measurements of the trend of demand over the next ten years, with particular reference to that after five years. Consideration should be given to such peaks as may develop due to deferred demand resulting from the curtailment of production incidental to the rearmament program.

2. We should develop a broad outline of a master plan to meet such prospective increase in production, if any, as our judgment may determine. This should include ways and means to best carry out such expansion. It should embrace the various categories of production involved in the Corporation's present scheme of things—each category following its own potential. This broad outline should be [filled] in as more facts become available . . .

3. We shall be called upon to provide facilities for the rearmament

program. Such needs should be integrated with the proposed master plans in broad outline so that we shall be able to move more rapidly and efficiently when, and if, the circumstances justify. We should use corporation funds for such new plants needed for armament if that gives us better control over same from the long term position in relation to the master plan. Accelerated depreciation and high taxes make the use of corporation funds all the more feasible. We should avoid conversion. The policy should be, expansion.

And the policy *was* expansion indeed. In the four years 1950 through 1953 we spent $1279 million on new plant and equipment —about one third of it for defense facilities. During this period, however, our earnings were restricted by the excess-profits tax and by the fact that the margin on defense business under our policy was lower than on commercial sales. All told, we were able to reinvest $871 million in the business after paying dividends of $1.6 billion, or 65 per cent of net income. These retained earnings, together with $563 million in depreciation accruals, were only $155 million more than plant expenditures of $1279 million. Only the $155 million was available, therefore, to meet other requirements—for example, advances to steel suppliers and the costs of tooling up for defense production. Inflationary costs had left their mark on the corporation's capital structure. Our net working capital had declined slightly between December 31, 1949, and December 31, 1953, despite the need of added capital due to a 76 per cent rise in dollar sales.

At the beginning of 1954, with our financial resources already under strain, we announced a forward program of plant expenditures calling for an outlay of $1 billion in two years. This program was designed to provide additional capacity for our automotive divisions to meet the needs of an expanding market, and to modernize the existing facilities. We also had to add very substantially to our facilities for the production of automatic transmissions, power steering, power brakes, and V-8 engines.

With a plant-expenditure program of this magnitude, and the inflationary pressures on costs, it was clear that we would have to raise new capital if we were to continue to pay out a substantial part of each year's earnings in the form of dividends. Toward the end of 1953 the Financial Policy Committee reviewed the problem and determined that a debt issue could be sold to advantage. In contrast to the situation in 1946, however, the insurance companies and other institutional investors did not have any excess funds available; they were, instead, committed for some time ahead. Hence we turned to the public market and in December 1953 sold an issue of $300 million of twenty-five-year 3¼ per cent debentures, netting (after deducting underwriters' fees and commissions) $298.5 million. This, too, was an outstanding success.

But it was still not enough. In January of 1955 our plant-expenditure program was expanded from $1 billion to $1.5 billion (and later to $2 billion). In analyzing our future capital requirements, therefore, we decided that we would need to raise more outside capital. As Mr. Curtice, then president of the corporation, stated before the United States Senate Committee on Banking and Currency in March of that year:

Our recent decision to seek further outside capital resulted from our analysis of our forward capital requirements. This analysis was based upon our projections of economic trends and the outlook for the highly competitive automobile market. It led us to the conclusion that additional permanent equity capital in the area of 300 to 350 million dollars is needed if we are to be ready to share in the country's growth and meet expanding needs for the goods we make and at the same time maintain a reasonable dividend policy.

And so in February 1955 we offered holders of common stock the right to subscribe to 4,380,683 shares of new stock (five-dollar par value) at the rate of one share for each twenty shares held. The subscription price for each new share was $75; at the closing date of the offering, the stock was selling at 96⅝. The stock offer was underwritten by a group of 330 underwriters, but the underwriters had to subscribe to only 12.8 per cent of the issue. The net proceeds to the corporation approximated $325 million after payment of underwriting fees and commissions. This was the largest industrial common-stock issue in the United States up to that time and was a remarkable success, attesting to the correct evaluation of the market at a time when many experts considered an issue of this size to be a great risk.

Our stock and debenture issues made it possible for us to carry out our expansion program and at the same time continue our policy of paying liberal dividends. In the three years of expansion 1954 through 1956, we spent $2253 million on new plant and equipment, increasing our gross plant 74 per cent (from $2912 million to $5073 million). Provisions for depreciation totaled $874 million, and after paying out $1620 million or 57 per cent of earnings in dividends, we reinvested $1222 million. As a result, our net working capital increased by $510 million during this period of extraordinary capital expenditures, and our holdings of cash and short-term securities (exclusive of securities earmarked for payment of tax liabilities) almost doubled, from $367 million to $672 million. Our liquidity increased still more in 1957, since capital expenditures declined fairly rapidly with the completion of the big expansion program, while depreciation accruals continued to rise.

We had come through a critical expansion and our financial condition was stronger than ever. The period 1957 through 1962 was to include two recession years (1958 and 1961) and also the best year for dollar sales and earnings in the corporation's history (1962). In reviewing the events of this period, I feel that they offer indisputable evidence of our financial maturity. The recession year 1958 saw General Motors' sales of U.S.-produced cars and trucks decline 22 per cent from the previous year, yet the accelerated impact that declining unit sales have on earnings was effectively moderated. Earnings in 1958 of $2.22 per share were only 25 per cent less than the $2.99 per share in 1957. These results were due in no small part to the effective and timely financial controls which we had built into our organization over the years.

Plant expenditures in the 1958–62 period, including the cost of overseas expansion projects, totaled $2.3 billion, or about as much as was spent in the major expansion years of 1954–56. Nevertheless, depreciation accruals were sufficient to finance these expenditures in the United States, while local borrowings were used to finance a portion of the expansion in Germany. As a result, the corporation was able to pay out $3.3 billion in dividends over the period, or 69 per cent of earnings. In addition, net working capital was increased $1.7 billion.

Taking the postwar period as a whole, therefore, the shareholders fared rather well. Notwithstanding a better than six-fold increase in the stated dollar value of our gross plant—from $1012 million on January 1, 1946, to $7187 million on December 31, 1962—which was financed out of earnings and depreciation reserves, we nevertheless paid shareholders a total of $7951 million or 64 per cent of net income in dividends. Over the period, dividends per share, after adjusting for stock splits, rose from 50 cents per share in 1945 to $3 per share in 1962, and the market price of a share of stock rose from $12.58 to $58.13.

The financial story of General Motors is a story of growth—in goods and services, in the number of people involved, in physical facilities, and in financial resources. Between August 1, 1917, when the old General Motors Company became the General Motors Corporation, and December 31, 1962, the number of employees increased from 25,000 to over 600,000 and the number of shareholders from less than 3000 to more than one million. The corporation expanded its sales of cars and trucks produced in the United States and Canada from 205,000 units in 1918 to 4,491,000 in 1962, and, in addition, sales of cars and trucks manufactured in General Motors' plants overseas totaled 747,000 units. Dollar sales rose even faster, from $270 million in 1918 to $14.6 billion in 1962, and total assets grew from $134 million to $9.2 billion. This is a measure of the significance of General Motors as an institution in American economic life.

The measure of the worth of a business enterprise as a *business*, however, is not merely growth in sales or assets but return on the shareholders' investment, since it is their capital that is being risked and it is in their interests first of all that the corporation is supposed to be run in the private-enterprise scheme of things. The record shows, I believe, that we have done a very creditable job for the shareholders, without neglecting our responsibilities to our employees, customers, dealers, suppliers, and the community.

I described my philosophy of financial growth in the annual report for 1938, as follows:

Due to the force of economic necessity and through a process of evolution, the units of industry have become larger and larger. This is because of the continuously broadening market for industry's products and services resulting from the production of more useful things at continually lowered prices. There is superimposed upon this evolutionary process the additional influence of an increasing integration of manufacturing processes involved in mass production. The effect of such an evolution on the capital structure is to require ever increasing amounts of capital.

GENERAL MOTORS CORPORATION
Historical Summary of Sales, Net Income Before and After Taxes, and Dividends

Year	Unit Sales of Cars and Trucks — U.S. and Canada	Net Sales $	Net Income Before Taxes		U.S. and Foreign Income Taxes* $	Net Income After Taxes	
			Amount $	As % of Sales %		Amount $	As % of Sales %
1917#	86,921	96,295,741	17,143,056	17.80	2,848,574	14,294,482	14.84
1918	205,326	269,796,829	34,939,078	12.95	20,113,548	14,825,530	5.50
1919	391,738	509,676,694	90,005,484	17.66	30,000,000	60,005,484	11.77
1920	393,075	567,320,603	41,644,375	7.34	3,894,000	37,750,375	6.65
1921	214,799	304,487,243	(38,680,770)	(12.70)	-	(38,680,770)	(12.70)
1922	456,763	463,706,733	60,724,493	13.10	6,250,000	54,474,493	11.75
1923	798,555	698,038,947	80,143,955	11.48	8,135,000	72,008,955	10.32
1924	587,341	568,007,459	57,350,490	10.10	5,727,000	51,623,490	9.09
1925	835,902	734,592,592	129,928,277	17.69	13,912,000	116,016,277	15.79
1926	1,234,850	1,058,153,338	212,066,121	20.04	25,834,939	186,231,182	17.60
1927	1,562,748	1,269,519,673	269,573,585	21.23	34,468,759	235,104,826	18.52
1928	1,810,806	1,459,762,906	309,817,468	21.22	33,349,360	276,468,108	18.94
1929	1,899,267	1,504,404,472	276,403,176	18.37	28,120,908	248,282,268	16.50
1930	1,158,293	983,375,137	167,227,693	17.01	16,128,701	151,098,992	15.37
1931	1,033,518	808,840,723	111,219,791	13.75	14,342,684	96,877,107	11.98
1932	525,727	432,311,868	449,690	0.10	284,711	164,979	0.04
1933	802,104	569,010,542	95,431,456	16.77	12,217,780	83,213,676	14.62
1934	1,128,326	862,672,670	110,181,088	12.77	15,411,957	94,769,131	10.99
1935	1,564,252	1,155,641,511	196,692,407	17.02	29,465,897	167,226,510	14.47
1936	1,866,589	1,439,289,940	282,090,052	19.60	43,607,627	238,482,425	16.57
1937	1,927,833	1,606,789,841	245,543,733	15.28	49,107,135	196,436,598	12.23
1938	1,108,901	1,066,973,000	130,190,341	12.20	28,000,334	102,190,007	9.58
1939	1,542,545	1,376,828,337	228,142,412	16.57	44,852,190	183,290,222	13.31
1940	2,025,213	1,794,936,642	320,649,462	17.86	125,027,741	195,621,721	10.90
1941	2,257,018	2,436,800,977	489,644,851	20.09	287,992,343	201,652,508	8.28
1942	301,490	2,250,548,859	260,727,633	11.59	97,076,045	163,651,588	7.27
1943	152,546	3,796,115,800	398,700,782	10.50	248,920,694	149,780,088	3.95
1944	278,539	4,262,249,472	435,409,021	10.22	264,413,156	170,995,865	4.01
1945	275,573	3,127,934,888	212,535,893	6.79	24,267,778	188,268,115	6.02
1946	1,175,448	1,962,502,289	43,300,083	2.21	(44,226,228)	87,526,311	4.46
1947	1,930,918	3,815,159,163	554,005,405	14.52	266,014,032	287,991,373	7.55
1948	2,146,305	4,701,770,340	801,417,975	17.05	360,970,251	440,447,724	9.37
1949	2,764,397	5,700,835,141	1,124,834,936	19.73	468,400,704	656,434,232	11.51
1950	3,812,163	7,531,086,846	1,811,660,763	24.06	977,616,724	834,044,039	11.07
1951	3,016,486	7,465,554,851	1,488,717,641	19.94	982,518,081	506,199,560	6.78
1952	2,434,160	7,549,154,419	1,502,178,604	19.90	943,457,425	558,721,179	7.40
1953	3,495,999	10,027,985,482	1,652,647,924	16.48	1,054,528,446	598,119,478	5.96
1954	3,449,764	9,823,526,291	1,644,959,366	16.75	838,985,469	805,973,897	8.20
1955	4,638,046	12,443,277,420	2,542,827,439	20.44	1,353,350,357	1,189,477,082	9.56
1956	3,692,722	10,796,442,575	1,741,414,610	16.13	894,018,508	847,396,102	7.85
1957	3,418,500	10,989,813,178	1,648,712,588	15.00	805,120,153	843,592,435	7.68
1958	2,712,870	9,521,965,629	1,115,428,076	11.71	481,800,000	633,628,076	6.65
1959	3,140,233	11,233,057,200	1,792,200,149	15.95	919,100,000	873,100,149	7.77
1960	3,889,734	12,735,999,681	2,037,542,489	16.00	1,078,500,000	959,042,489	7.53
1961	3,346,719	11,395,916,826	1,768,021,444	15.51	875,200,000	892,821,444	7.83
1962	4,491,447	14,640,240,799	2,934,477,450	20.04	1,475,400,000	1,459,077,450	9.97

Five months ended December 31, 1917.
* For period 1917 through 1920, includes provision for extraordinary expenditures.
( ) Indicates red figure.

GENERAL MOTORS CORPORATION
Historical Summary of Sales, Net Income Before and After Taxes, and Dividends
(continued)

Year	Dividends on Preferred Stocks $	Net Income Available for Common Stock $	Dividends on Common Stock Amount $	Dividends on Common Stock As % of Income Available %	Income Retained for Use in the Business $	Per Share of $1 2/3 Par Val. Com. Stock Earn. $	Per Share of $1 2/3 Par Val. Com. Stock Divid. $
1917#	491,890	13,802,592	2,294,199	16.6	11,508,393	.15	.02
1918	1,920,467	12,905,063	11,237,310	87.1	1,667,753	.07	.10
1919	4,212,513	55,792,971	17,324,541	31.1	38,468,430	.30	.10
1920	5,620,426	32,129,949	17,893,289	55.7	14,236,660	.14	.09
1921	6,310,010	(44,990,780)	20,468,276	-	(65,459,056)	(.19)	.09
1922	6,429,228	48,045,265	10,177,117	21.2	37,868,148	.21	.04
1923	6,887,371	65,121,584	24,772,026	38.0	40,349,558	.28	.11
1924	7,272,637	44,350,853	25,030,632	56.4	19,320,221	.19	.11
1925	7,639,991	108,376,286	61,935,221	57.1	46,441,065	.47	.27
1926	7,645,287	178,585,895	103,930,993	58.2	74,654,902	.73	.42
1927	9,109,330	225,995,496	134,836,081	59.7	91,159,415	.87	.52
1928	9,404,756	267,063,352	165,300,002	61.9	101,763,350	1.02	.63
1929	9,478,681	238,803,587	156,600,007	65.6	82,203,580	.91	.60
1930	9,538,660	141,560,332	130,500,002	92.2	11,060,330	.54	.50
1931	9,375,899	87,501,208	130,500,001	149.1	(42,998,793)	.34	.50
1932	9,206,387	(9,041,408)	53,993,330	-	(63,034,738)	(.03)	.21
1933	9,178,845	74,034,831	53,826,355	72.7	20,208,476	.29	.21
1934	9,178,220	85,590,911	64,443,490	75.3	21,147,421	.33	.25
1935	9,178,220	158,048,290	96,476,748	61.0	61,571,542	.61	.38
1936	9,178,220	229,304,205	192,903,299	84.1	36,400,906	.89	.75
1937	9,178,220	187,258,378	160,549,861	85.7	26,708,517	.73	.63
1938	9,178,220	93,011,787	64,386,421	69.2	28,625,366	.36	.25
1939	9,943,072	173,347,150	150,319,682	86.7	23,027,468	.67	.58
1940	9,178,220	186,443,501	161,864,924	86.8	24,578,577	.72	.63
1941	9,178,220	192,474,288	162,608,296	84.5	29,865,992	.74	.63
1942	9,178,220	154,473,368	86,992,295	56.3	67,481,073	.59	.33
1943	9,178,220	140,601,868	87,106,758	62.0	53,495,110	.54	.33
1944	9,178,220	161,817,645	132,063,371	81.6	29,754,274	.61	.50
1945	9,178,220	179,089,895	132,066,520	73.7	47,023,375	.68	.50
1946	9,782,407	77,743,904	99,158,674	127.5	(21,414,770)	.29	.38
1947	12,928,310	275,063,063	132,167,487	48.0	142,895,576	1.04	.50
1948	12,928,315	427,519,409	197,845,688	46.3	229,673,721	1.62	.75
1949	12,928,316	643,505,916	351,380,264	54.6	292,125,652	2.44	1.33
1950	12,928,315	821,115,724	526,111,783	64.1	295,003,941	3.12	2.00
1951	12,928,313	493,271,247	350,249,851	71.0	143,021,396	1.88	1.33
1952	12,928,313	545,792,866	349,041,039	64.0	196,751,827	2.08	1.33
1953	12,928,312	585,191,166	348,760,514	59.6	236,430,652	2.24	1.33
1954	12,928,309	793,045,588	436,507,196	55.0	356,538,392	3.03	1.67
1955	12,928,305	1,176,548,777	592,245,497	50.3	584,303,280	4.30	2.17
1956	12,928,302	834,467,800	552,853,282	66.3	281,614,518	3.02	2.00
1957	12,928,300	830,664,135	555,453,812	66.9	275,210,323	2.99	2.00
1958	12,928,298	620,699,778	558,940,800	90.1	61,758,978	2.22	2.00
1959	12,928,296	860,171,853	561,838,126	65.3	298,333,727	3.06	2.00
1960	12,928,293	946,114,196	564,190,599	59.6	381,923,597	3.35	2.00
1961	12,928,292	879,893,152	707,383,013	80.4	172,510,139	3.11	2.50
1962	12,928,290	1,446,149,160	850,465,125	58.8	595,684,035	5.10	3.00

Five months ended December 31, 1917.
( ) Indicates red figure.

The financial growth of General Motors has followed that course. The total capital employed in the business has grown from about $100 million in 1917 to about $6.9 billion today without unduly burdening the corporation or its shareholders with debt, primarily by plowing back earnings. Of the $6.8-billion growth in capital, about $800 million, after subsequent repayments, was raised by resorting to the capital market. An additional $600 million was raised through the issuance of new stock, of which $250 million was for the acquisition of existing companies and $350 million for employee programs. All the rest of the growth in capital—a total of nearly $5.4 billion—came from reinvestment of earnings. And yet, unlike the situation in some rapidly growing companies, the reinvestment of earnings was not at the expense of dividend payments to the shareholders. Over this forty-five-year period, dividend payments totaled nearly $10.8 billion, or 67 per cent of total earnings.

This growth in the capital employed in General Motors reflects the progress of the corporation. In an economy based on competition, we have operated as rational businessmen, a fact I have tried to demonstrate with a close description of the development of our approach to management. The result has been an efficient enterprise. It should be noted that a rising successful economy like that of the United States is not only an opportunity, it is also very demanding on those whose ambition is to excel in it. Our performance has been demonstrated day by day in our production and distribution of goods useful to the community. I shall be glad for General Motors to be judged by this performance.

Part Two

Chapter 12

EVOLUTION OF THE AUTOMOBILE

URING the early years of the automobile industry, the immediate goal of the engineers and inventors was simply reliability—to get a car to go somewhere and come back under its own power. Many bright automotive ideas ended with a horse, a towline, and laughter. Although progress was expensive, American motorists cheerfully paid the bills for it. In their enthusiasm for individual transportation, they bought the cars, reliable or unreliable, and thus provided the source of a substantial portion of the risk capital for experiment and production. Not many industries have been so well favored by their customers. In twenty years the reliability of the motorcar in relation to the street and road conditions of the time was pretty well established. Individual mechanized transportation, one of the great achievements in the progress of mankind, was a commonplace fact of life, and everyone could enjoy it.

Great as have been the engineering advances since 1920, we have today basically the same kind of machine that was created in the first twenty years of the industry. We still deal with a vehicle moved by a gasoline engine. The heart of the engine is still a piston in a cylinder, moved by the burning of a mixture of gasoline and air, which is fired at regular intervals by an electrical spark from a spark plug. The resultant power of the thrust of the piston turns a crankshaft, which, by way of a transmission mechanism, turns the rear wheels. Springs and rubber tires cushion the driver and passengers

from the effects of bumps, and brakes stop the car by applying re-
tarding force at the wheels.

But since 1920 enormous improvements have been made at every
point: Engines are far more efficient, delivering more power more
smoothly from the same amount of fuel—and the fuel has also
been enormously improved. The transmission has undergone a complex evolution until it is now fully automatic. The suspension system
has gone through an equivalent evolution, as have the tires, and
together they provide a ride that was unimaginable forty years ago.
The driver can call upon extra power sources for braking and steering and to operate windows, seats, and radio antennas. The body
shines in a variety of hues, is usually entirely made of steel, and
has safety glass. With the development of the automobile, its importance in everyday use has enormously increased and also the
demand for better roads and highways has come. It is hard to
imagine what effect roads such as those of today might have had
on the development of the automobile of the early 1920s.

Today's driver, of course, would find the typical car of 1920 completely unsatisfactory. It had a four-cylinder engine whose crankshaft and associated connecting rods and pistons were inherently unbalanced. Ordinarily this car had two-wheel brakes with braking
confined to the rear wheels; it had no independent springing of the
front wheels; it had a sliding-gear transmission, and an engine of
low power. It vibrated and often shimmied; it veered and sometimes skidded when the brakes were applied; it rode hard and
rough; the clutch grabbed; the gears often clashed in the shifting,
and, owing to the low power available, they always had to be
shifted on hills of substantial gradient. But the car usually got
somewhere and back; fortunately it was unable to go fast or far
enough for many of its deficiencies to become serious drawbacks. It
was roughly adapted to its environment—and its major parts were
reasonably adapted to each other, at however low a level of integration and efficiency.

The problem of development of the automobile was to raise its
level of efficiency, and this often meant raising the level of its integration. The automobile today, instead of the loose assemblage
of parts and mechanisms of fifty-odd years ago, is a very complex
and closely integrated piece of machinery. It is only in recent
years that the mechanical arts have made possible the combined

effect of high performance, operating convenience, and comfort that characterizes the modern motorcar.

General Motors' research laboratories and the engineering staffs have played a major role in the development of the automobile during the past fifty years, and continue to be in the forefront of engineering development. It would be impossible to describe everything of importance General Motors and the industry have done: that would require another book. Only a few important and interrelated advances in this development are discussed here.

Ethyl Gasoline and High-Compression Engines

The central problem in automotive engineering has been to develop a more satisfactory relationship between the fuel and the engine. The efficiency of a piston engine—its ability to make an effective use of fuel, and thus to get the greatest power from a given quantity of fuel—depends on its compression. The concept of compression is a simple one, but the general reader will need a few words about it. The piston has one position in which it is as far down in the engine's cylinder as it can go, and another in which it is as far up in the cylinder as it can go. When it is at the bottom of its stroke, the cylinder is filled with fuel—a mixture of atomized gasoline and air. When it is at the top of its stroke, the fuel charge is compressed. The fuel begins to burn as a result of the spark, and the hot gases produced will expand and push the piston down. The down movement then turns the crankshaft, which transmits power to the wheels. The compression ratio is the ratio between the volume of the cylinder when the piston is as far *down* as it can go and the volume that remains when it is as far *up* as it can go. This ratio merely compares the volume of the fuel charge in its uncompressed state with that in its compressed state. In the early twenties, the average compression ratio was about four to one.

As I have said, to design a more efficient and powerful engine of a given size means to increase the compression ratio. But here a serious problem stood in the way—engine knock. The gasoline-and-air mixture should burn relatively slowly in order to push the piston down. If it detonated—burned too fast—the piston could not move rapidly enough to take advantage of the force generated. Indeed, not only was energy lost in engine knock, but the sudden force introduced severe strains on the engine parts, which could, and did, damage the engine.

The key to higher compression was to find some way of reducing engine knock. But what was the cause of engine knock? In the early days of motorcar use, it was discovered that one could reduce engine knock by adjusting the time of the spark jump. Most cars, for many years, had a hand-operated spark-adjustment lever convenient to the driver for choosing the best spark setting for different driving conditions. People learned to retard the spark setting by hand when driving uphill, to prevent engine knock as the engine labored under the strain.

The man who began General Motors' important studies in engine knock and who was largely responsible for our breakthrough to a solution of the problem was Charles F. Kettering, who had long been interested in the whole question of ignition, fuels, and the like. No automobile runs and no airplane with a reciprocating engine flies today without benefit of the antiknock fuel developments pioneered by Mr. Kettering. He brought his early knowledge of this problem to General Motors, and he was research chief of General Motors when the solution was found. The solution, in the main, was Ethyl gasoline, made with the additive tetraethyl lead.

Up to the time of World War I, knock was thought to be caused by too early ignition when the spark was too far advanced. Soon after World War I it was discovered that there was another kind of knock which was called "fuel knock," for by changing only the fuel and fuel setting without adjusting the spark, this knock could be lessened or eliminated. One of the people working on this problem was the late Thomas Midgley, Jr. He had come up through the Dayton Engineering Laboratories, where he was an assistant to Mr. Kettering, to become in the early 1920s the chief of the fuel section of the General Motors Research Corporation. In the words of Dr. Robert E. Wilson, formerly chairman of Standard Oil of Indiana, and a close friend of Mr. Midgley:

. . . [Mr. Midgley] had definitely proven that, contrary to general belief, knocking and preignition were different things, and that knocking was a chemical characteristic of the fuel. He pointed out that benzol and cyclohexane, which latter he had succeeded in making in his Dayton laboratory, knocked much less than gasoline, and gasoline much less than kerosene.

Almost every time I saw Tom he had some new theory regarding the mechanism of detonation or of antiknock action, on which I was the professional skeptic. While successive theories were usually discredited by further experimental work, they were always stimulating and frequently led to discoveries of importance. The most striking example of this was in his early work when he was trying to theorize as to why kerosene knocked worse than gasoline. He seized upon the obvious difference in volatility, and postulated that possibly most of the kerosene remained in droplets until after combustion started and then vaporized very suddenly with a resultant too-rapid explosion. If this explanation were correct, he reasoned that by dyeing the kerosene it might be possible to make the droplets absorb radiant heat from the combustion chamber and hence vaporize sooner.

Had Tom been a good physicist he could have doubtless found by calculation that this theory was untenable, but being a mechanical engineer he fortunately decided that it was much easier to try it out than to do the calculations. He accordingly went to the stockroom in search of some oil-soluble dye, and as usual the stockroom was just out of the desired product. However, Fred Chase suggested that iodine was oil-soluble and would color the kerosene, so Tom promptly dissolved a substantial quantity of iodine in the kerosene, tested it in a moderately high-compression engine, and found to his delight that the knocking was eliminated.

Tom immediately sent out to scour Dayton for all available samples of oil-soluble dyes and that afternoon tested out several different ones in rapid succession without getting the slightest result from any of them. To clinch the matter, he added a colorless iodine compound to the gasoline and found that this stopped the knock. Thus, the first theory of detonation went to start the graveyard, which is now fairly well filled, but along with its demise came the real birth of Tom as a chemist, and for the next few years he was an insatiable student of every branch of chemistry to aid him in endeavoring to explain his observations and to make new compounds for trial as antiknock agents . . .

Tom was then particularly enthusiastic about the possibilities of aniline though, as always seemed to be the case when he discovered a new antiknock agent, he had to go to work to improve the methods of manufacture and lower the cost before the agent would be economically feasible. He also had some hopes then for his first ethyl compound, ethyl iodide, if he could just locate a plentiful source of iodine . . .

It was at the annual meeting of the Society of Automotive Engineers in New York in January 1922 that Tom, with an air of great excitement and secrecy, showed me a little tetraethyl lead in a test tube and told me that that was really the answer to the whole problem. Its efficiency, he said, was very much higher than that of any previously discovered compound, and it appeared to be free from every one of the difficulties which had plagued earlier attempts to solve the problem. Of course, he did not yet appreciate either the toxicity or the deposit problems.

So, after all the years of experiments by Mr. Kettering, Mr. Midgley, and General Motors Research Corporation, we had the invention. But having an invention is one thing and getting to market with it is another. To make a long story short, in August of 1924 a corporation was formed called the Ethyl Gasoline Corporation, for the purpose of marketing tetraethyl lead as an antiknock compound. This company was a fifty-fifty partnership between General Motors and Standard Oil of New Jersey. Initially the Ethyl fluid was manufactured by du Pont under a contract and it was not until 1948 that Ethyl began producing all of its own requirements.

Tetraethyl lead was only one of the necessary steps in the development of high-compression engines. Despite its effects in improving the quality of the fuel, the fuel itself, in the early twenties, varied enormously in quality. Indeed, there was no known way of measuring one fuel against another to determine its relative value for use in a gasoline engine.

General Motors made a study of that situation and developed a method for measuring the antiknock qualities of fuels, or the ability of the engine to accept a given fuel in terms of the higher compression of the engine. This measurement scaled fuels according to their "octane number." Octane is a fuel with almost no knock; in the engineering of that day a rating of 100 in octane therefore was considered, practically speaking, a perfect fuel. Dr. Graham Edgar of Ethyl conceived the octane scale in 1926 and Mr. Kettering and the research engineers developed the first single-cylinder, variable-compression test engine by which fuel quality could be measured in terms of these octane numbers. A test engine utilizing the variable-compression principle was later adopted as standard by the automotive and petroleum industries.

Of course, one way to increase octane ratings was to add tetraethyl lead, but another was through better processes for refining crude oil. Tremendous progress has been made in cracking and in "re-forming" the hydrocarbons found in crude oil both to increase the yield of gasoline from a barrel of crude and to improve its octane rating before the addition of tetraethyl lead. This is another dramatic research story in itself and one in which Mr. Kettering and his associates played a very important part in pioneering. The octane rating of commercial gasolines available at filling stations was increased from 50 to 55 in the early twenties, to 95 to somewhat over 100 at the present time. (In aviation gasolines, octane ratings are even higher.) This has had a dramatic effect on fuel economy as measured in car miles per gallon for a given standard of performance and consequently on the efficiency with which we are today using our petroleum resources.[1]

Another factor in the reduction of knock was the design of the engine itself. We know today that in the engine combustion chamber a very complex shock-wave condition is produced by the explosion of the fuel. These shock waves can increase the temperature of the fuel very rapidly and contribute to detonation and knock. The study of various combustion-head shapes and contours has suggested special shapes for the least knock effect with the highest compression ratio.

Parenthetically, I will mention here one problem of engine design, quite independent of the fuel, which had a serious limiting effect on the development of more powerful engines. General Motors engineers made an important contribution to its solution. Vibration, which was always unpleasant, became a more critical engineering problem as speed and power started to go up. Then the unbalanced rotating and reciprocating parts in the engine became the source of destructive vibration and a limiting factor on the whole progress of the automobile.

One of the principal sources of vibration is the crankshaft, the "backbone of the engine," where any imbalance is felt throughout the engine and the car. General Motors Research Corporation began working in the early twenties on the problem of balancing engines, and a crankshaft-balancing machine was developed and first used in the production of the 1924 Cadillac engines. This machine, hundreds of which are now in use throughout the world, was exclusively a General Motors development and gave us a long lead in engine balancing in the industry. As in the case of many of our

[1] General Motors' role in the Ethyl Corporation came to a close in 1962, when both General Motors and Standard Oil sold their interests in Ethyl to the Albemarle Paper Manufacturing Company of Richmond, Virginia. With this sale General Motors, in line with its policy, disposed of the last of its investments in partially-owned companies, and now carries on all of its operations through divisions or wholly owned subsidiaries.

advances, we arranged to sell this equipment to other engine producers. Better balancing was a very important step in the reduction of wear and tear on the whole automobile structure and in permitting faster progress toward the satisfactory utilization of greater power and speed in practically all the engines we build.

As we learned more and more about knock, progress toward higher-compression engines became possible. From the four to one compression ratios of the early twenties, we have now come to ten to one and higher compression ratios. The development of fuels and engines proceeds in leap-frog fashion: an engine with higher compression demands a better fuel, and the availability of a better fuel encourages the production of more efficient engines. Under the urging of the automobile engineers, the petroleum industry has developed fuels of higher and higher octane ratings for general use. General Motors has supplied many high-compression test engines to the oil industry to help it develop higher octane fuels.

In this way the developments of tetraethyl lead and high-octane fuels have made possible the long-range improvement of the internal-combustion engine.

Transmission Development

I suppose almost everybody knows that the purpose of the transmission is to transfer power from the engine to the wheels of a car, and that this involves a change in the speed relationship between the automobile engine and wheels. The power developed by an engine depends on several things, but is closely related primarily to the rotational speed of the engine's crankshaft. With the old lower-powered cars, everyone became aware of this upon climbing a hill. This usually required a vigorous speeding up of the engine and a shift to a lower gear to get the power needed. Back in the 1920s shifting gears by hand through the normal three speeds usually resulted in considerable clashing unless the driver had a high degree of skill.

From the time the General Motors Research Corporation was set up in 1920, transmissions were an important subject of study and discussion. At first we concentrated on electrical transmissions of various types, for a large percentage of the original staff of engineers were of electrical background. An electrical drive was developed, and one of this type was used for a time on General Motors buses. The electrical transmission, which was tried out very early in the history of the automobile (in the Columbia and Owen-Magnetic passenger cars), eventually received its major commercial use in the large-vehicle field. This special form of transmission is used today in our diesel locomotives.

From 1923 on, the interest of our research organization in electrical transmissions for passenger cars declined. We began to study a wide variety of automatic transmissions, including the "infinitely-variable" type—in which a large number of speeds were available in uninterrupted sequence, rather than a lesser number in fixed steps, as in the standard transmission—and the step-ratio type in which a fixed number of speeds could be selected automatically. And as early as the middle twenties a hydraulic type of transmission having bladed turbine wheels was investigated. Most of the general principles that went into the making of the fully-automatic transmissions were thus known to us, and were being carefully investigated, at least fifteen years before automatic transmissions became available in production cars.

In the late twenties General Motors developed the synchromesh gearshift, with which almost any driver could shift from one speed to another without clashing the gears.

This significant development was put into production by Cadillac in 1928. The principle was taken up by other General Motors car-division engineers and was further developed for large-volume production by our old Muncie Products Division. By 1932 we were able to extend synchromesh all the way down through the whole General Motors line to the Chevrolet passenger car.

By 1928 the Research Laboratories had reached a consensus on an automatic-transmission form that might be satisfactory. This was an infinitely-variable type using a steel-on-steel friction drive employing a mechanical principle like that of a ball bearing. The Buick Division was assigned the job of developing this transmission since we had no general engineering staff at that time. Many units were built and tests conducted, and it was finally determined to produce this type of transmission in 1932. However, despite our best efforts, we never managed to solve all the problems involved, and this transmission was never put in any General Motors car sold to the public, although many experimental units were tried out in our test cars. A good deal, of course, had been learned about the problems of infinitely-variable transmissions, but it turned out that this specific steel-on-steel type was not the answer to the problem. I was convinced that it would always cost too much and I turned it down for our cars.

Our research and engineering staffs continued to work on the various types of automatic transmissions. By 1934 a group of engineers in the Cadillac Division were finally on the road that was to lead to the first mass-production automatic transmission for passenger cars, the Hydra-Matic, a modern form of automatic transmission. This special design group was transferred to the corporation's Engineering Staff at the end of 1934 to become the Transmission Development Group. The transmission they were working on was of a step-ratio type rather than the infinitely-variable type; however, it shifted automatically under torque, as do all of today's automatic drives. (Torque is the turning effect transmitted by the engine to the drive shaft.) This group also prepared production plans for different sizes of such units to meet a range of different power and load demands for the different General Motors cars.

A set of pilot models was built, tested, and turned over to the Oldsmobile engineers. During 1935 and 1936 thousands of test miles were run on different experimental units from one end of the United States to the other. In 1937 both Oldsmobile and Buick (1938 models) came out with these semiautomatic transmissions. (A semiautomatic transmission is one which provides a range of step-ratio shifts with one or more being hand selected, and one or more automatically selected.) These were manufactured by the Buick Division and still required the use of a main clutch pedal for starting and stopping. Our engineers now discovered that the main clutch and its pedal could be eliminated by the use of a fluid coupling built within the transmission assembly. This feature, together with the development of full-range automatic controls, resulted in the Hydra-Matic transmission, produced by the newly organized Detroit Transmission Division. It was announced in October 1939 and first appeared on the 1940 Oldsmobile. The Cadillac Division was the next to accept the new transmission, for its 1941 model.

Meanwhile a different kind of automatic transmission was under development by the GMC Truck & Coach engineering staff. This was known as a torque converter of the closed-circuit, fluid-turbine type. Such devices contain a set of bladed wheels, the blades being set at angles so that one bladed wheel, driven directly by the spinning of the engine, can pump the body of contained fluid into a second bladed wheel connected to the drive shaft, and so cause turning force on that shaft. There may be additional bladed wheels for changing the fluid-flow characteristics and in this way affecting the difference in speeds between the engine and the drive shaft—in other words, their speed ratio. This ratio, in a fluid torque converter, changes imperceptibly and gradually, rather than by a series of steps. The net drive effect is therefore very smooth.

The fluid torque-converter design with which General Motors engineers first worked had been developed in Europe. They eventually designed one which conformed better to American bus-operating standards. We first used such a transmission in 1937 in our own buses and it was soon widely accepted. On the eve of the war, in October 1941, our Engineering Staff Transmission Development Group was at work on the problem of adapting the fluid torque converter to passenger cars.

With America's entry into the war, our advanced work on automatic transmissions for passenger cars was suspended, but an enormous new field for automatic transmissions opened. For the passenger-car driver, the automatic transmission is of value because of its convenience and simplicity in operation—there is one less thing about driving a car he has to think about. When it comes to buses, trucks, tanks, tractors, and the huge vehicles of modern warfare, automatic transmissions are needed for smooth functioning. As early as 1938 we had been urged by the military engineers to think about the problem of designing transmissions for large vehicles such as the M-3 and M-4 tanks. At this time these were steered by levers, and in some cases the operator had to let go of one of the steering levers in order to shift gears. In doing this he temporarily abandoned steering control. Furthermore, the speed of the vehicle during the gear-change interval would fall off rapidly and perhaps cause a stall, thus presenting a stationary target.

The Engineering Staff Transmission Development Group designed heavy-duty Hydra-Matics for these tanks. But there were heavier tanks being planned to carry bigger guns and more armor, and for these we explored the possibility of applying the fluid torque converter. Shortly after our entry into the war, the Engineering Staff built a pilot model of a fluid torque converter which solved the problem of maintaining vehicle motion while the ratio between the speed of the engine and the speed of the vehicle was being changed. Large numbers of these transmissions were built during World War II by General Motors' divisions.

Our Transmission Development Group also designed a specialized tank transmission and steering system known as the cross drive. This made it possible for a driver to control accurately, with a relatively small effort, the steering, braking, and automatic drive of big vehicles of more than fifty tons. These cross drives went into gun carriers, amphibious and regular cargo carriers, and other vehicles of tremendous weight, and our development work in this field continued after the war.

With the war's end the Engineering Staff began an intensive research program designed to adapt the fluid torque converter to passenger cars. This program was successful, and led to the Buick Dynaflow of 1948 and the Chevrolet Powerglide of the 1950 line. The Dynaflow was the first fluid torque converter produced in volume for passenger cars.

Thus, by 1948, after many years of research and engineering development, General Motors offered to the public two different fully-automatic transmissions—Hydra-Matic and the fluid torque converter—which could be produced economically and efficiently even for low-priced cars. From the beginning, the car-buying public showed its approval of automatic transmissions—available on all of our cars—by its willingness to pay extra for them. Other automobile manufacturers used them in their cars as soon as they could—and in some cases the automatic transmissions used in their cars were built for them by General Motors. In the model year 1962 about 74 per cent of all the passenger cars sold in the United States—including General Motors' cars—were equipped with automatic transmissions. Among General Motors' passenger cars, 67 per cent of the Chevrolets, 91 per cent of the Pontiacs, 95 per cent of the Buicks, 97 per cent of the Oldsmobiles, and 100 per cent of the Cadillacs had automatic transmissions. During the 1962 model year about five million automatic transmissions were marketed by the industry, of which about 2.7 million were on General Motors cars. Thus this optional device has become an established feature of the American automobile.

Balloon Tires and Front-Wheel Suspension

From the beginning the problem of supplying a smoother and softer ride has been one of the most complex in automotive engineering. Since a car went much faster than a horse-drawn vehicle, it communicated the irregularities in the road surface to the passengers with greater intensity. The internal-combustion engine added its own source of discomfort in the form of vibration. Consequently, improvements in the cushioning of the driver and passengers were necessary, and this need increased as cars became speedier.

One basic approach to this problem was through the tires. Early motorcars had used solid-rubber or vented solid-rubber tires. These were soon replaced by inflated tires, but in this early stage neither the rubber nor the construction was good enough, and interminable tire-changing was a sad necessity on any extended trip.

By the early twenties the rubber companies had learned a good deal about construction methods, chemistry, rubber curing, and selection of materials. Tires were much better, and engineers began to consider the possibility of low-pressure tires, which would create a softer and more resilient air cushion under the wheels. Many problems had to be met, particularly in connection with steering and ride. The engineers had to deal with front-end instability, scuffing of the treads, squeals on turns, driving under fast braking conditions, and a peculiar condition known as wheel tramp, caused by a slight imbalance of the rotating mass of tire and wheel. These phenomena did not show up as major problems until car owners began to take long road trips at high speeds.

During this development of modern, low-pressure tires, General Motors engineers made important contributions because of our many miles of test road work under varying conditions. The General Technical Committee from the first maintained close contact with the tire industry, co-operating in standardization of sizes, and in the establishment of the best types, treads, and sections. Our recommendations, based on our research, have been incorporated year after year in better and safer tires.

The second basic approach to the improvement of the ride, and one of greater engineering complexity, was by way of the suspension—the attachment of the wheels to the chassis.

In one of my early trips abroad, my attention was called to an engineering development used in the production of European cars —the independent springing of the front wheels. Up to that time, independent springing had not been used in production cars in the United States. The use of this principle, of course, would add considerably to the comfort of the ride.

In France I came in contact with an engineer named André

Dubonnet, who had given considerable study to the matter and had taken out a patent on one form of independent springing. I brought him back to this country and put him in contact with our engineers.

Quite independently, Lawrence P. Fisher, then general manager of our Cadillac Division, had engaged a former Rolls-Royce engineer, Maurice Olley, who also was interested in working on the problem of ride. Mr. Olley recorded his recollections of the development of independent suspension in a letter he has written for me. I will continue the story in his words:

You have asked for my recollections of independent suspension on General Motors cars . . . You'll have to excuse the very personal atmosphere of the following notes, which may give the impression that independent suspension was a one man show. It was very far from that, and owes a great deal to Henry Crane, Ernest Seaholm [chief engineer of Cadillac], Charles Kettering and a number of Cadillac and Buick engineers. Also to the tolerance and constant support of L. P. Fisher, who accused the writer at that time of being the first man in GM to spend a quarter of a million dollars in building two experimental cars!

You will recall that I came from Rolls Royce to Cadillac in November of 1930. Frankly I was surprised to find Rolls Royce so popular. A Rolls Royce car had just completed a phenomenal test at the new GM Proving Grounds, and had been torn down for inspection . . .

At Rolls Royce, for the past several years, we had been engaged in a concentrated drive on riding quality. The British factory had become intrigued by this work because of the fact that cars which were considered acceptable on British roads, were far from acceptable when exported, even to the improved roads of the United States. And we were beginning to realize that this was not because . . . American roads were worse, but because the waves in them were a different shape.

A great deal of work had been done at Rolls Royce along the lines of swinging cars from overhead pivots to measure their moments of inertia . . . measuring the stiffness of chassis frames and coachwork . . . and measuring the suspension rates of the springs as installed on the actual car. The British factory had also developed one of the first practical ride meters, which consisted simply in measuring how much water was lost from an open-topped container in a measured mile at various speeds.

Some of this practice had been carried over to Cadillac in 1930, and soon we also were swinging cars, measuring installed spring rates, etc. We also built ourselves a "bump rig", along the Rolls Royce lines (the first in Detroit) and used it to produce a synthetic ride on a stationary car.

Early in 1932 we built the "K² Rig" . . . consisting of a complete seven passenger limousine, on which it was possible, by moving weights, to produce any desired changes in relative deflection of front and rear springs and in the moment of inertia of the vehicle. No instrumentation was used on this to measure ride. With the assistance of Henry Crane, to check up on our efforts, we simply asked ourselves under which conditions we got the best ride.

This was the best method because we did not know then, and do not know today, what a good ride is, but we could make so many fundamental changes in ride on this vehicle in a single day's running, that our impressions remained fresh, and direct comparison was possible.

It was at this stage, early in 1932, that we began to feel the urge towards independent suspension. The K² Rig was telling us, in no uncertain terms, that a flat ride which was an entirely new experience, was possible if we used front springs which were softer than the rear. But you will recall that all attempts to use extremely soft front springs with the conventional front axle fell down badly, because of shimmy . . . and a general lack of stability in handling . . .

The next step after the K² Rig therefore consisted in building two experimental Cadillac cars . . . These had two different independent front suspensions . . . [One of these was that developed by Mr. Dubonnet; the other, the "wishbone" type, we had developed.] An independent rear suspension was also used, as we had in mind that, as soon as possible, we should also get rid of the conventional rear axle (a change which in my own opinion is now several years overdue).

On these cars which were ridden by many of the Corporation engineers, it was evident that we had something very special in the way of improved ride and handling. We also ran into our usual share of troubles. The chief of these was the steering, which, especially on the wishbone suspension, was not free from shimmy.

We had to redesign the steering mechanism several times . . .

Finally, by March of 1933, we were ready for a full-dress demonstration. Early in March the General Technical Committee met at the Cadillac Engineering Building to ride our two experimental cars, and a Buick car without independent front suspension, but with an I.V. [infinitely variable] transmission . . .

I recall that [you] and Mr. Grant were riding one of the [wishbone-type] cars, when Ernest Seaholm and I, in one of the accompanying cars, pulled up alongside [you] at the traffic light in River Rouge. We could see [you] smiling widely at Dick Grant [vice president of sales] in the rear seat, and moving the flat of [your] hand up and down

[and] horizontally. Within two miles from the Cadillac plant the flat ride had sold itself!

After the run to Monroe and back on the three cars, the Committee sat at the Cadillac plant, and Seaholm and I, in the background, awaited the verdict, with the pious hope that Cadillac would be granted a clear year's run on the new suspension, ahead of the other divisions.

O. E. Hunt [vice president of engineering], I recall, led off by asking Mr. Grant what he thought of the new automatic transmission.

You will recall that in March of 1933 there was not a bank open in the United States, and anyone who owned a farm was thankful that at least he could eat. Under these circumstances Dick Grant's reaction was not surprising. He turned down the [automatic] transmission, and the hundred dollar cost that went with it, as something that a Buick buyer could very well do without. "But", said he, "if I could have a ride like you've shown us, for a matter of fifteen bucks, I'd find the money somehow."

Dutch Bower [chief engineer] at Buick had already put in his claim for the new front suspension, and the Oldsmobile and Pontiac engineers also seemed determined that they would show it in New York next November.

Then finally Bill Knudsen [the general manager of Chevrolet] declared in words of one syllable that Chevrolet [was] not going to be left out. O. E. Hunt tried to persuade him that there were not enough centerless grinding machines available in the United States to grind the wire for the coil springs for Chevrolet. But Knudsen was adamant, saying that the machine tool industry had been in a bad way for years, but they were going to be —— busy for the next year at least. And Chevrolet actually made the New York Show in November with their 1934 model on the Dubonnet suspension. Pontiac also inherited this suspension from Chevrolet, while the three other divisions adopted the wishbone suspension.

This meeting stays in my mind because it was such a tremendous demonstration of American enterprise in action. In the face of the conditions then existing, the millions of expenditure to which the Corporation was committing itself argued a type of courage which was new in my experience. I still remember Ket's statement, "It seems to me we can't afford *not* to do it."

We thus introduced simultaneously two different types of independent front-wheel suspension. However, after some further improvements on the wishbone type, it became apparent that it was cheaper and easier to manufacture and more trouble-free in operation, and soon all our lines of cars adopted it.

Duco

One of the striking scenes of America today viewed from the air in the daytime is the splash of jewel-like color presented by every parking lot. The colors are of an enormous variety, and the finishes are nearly indestructible.

All this is in contrast to the appearance of automobiles in the early twenties, when Ford, Dodge, Overland, and General Motors were using only black enamel on high-volume jobs. The external finish was then a subject of general complaint. The practices of the carriage industry had been carried over into automobile manufacturing without much change; automobiles for the first twenty-five years of their existence wore carriage paint and varnish. The customer could not understand why the finish of a carriage lasted for a long time, while when he bought a car the paint would sometimes soon peel off. The fact, of course, was that the carriage and the motorcar were very different mechanisms. The automobile was subject to much harder service; it was used in more kinds of weather, and the heat of the engine produced temperature changes in parts of the car—with a resultant disastrous effect on the finish.

We dreamed of what a wonderful thing it would be if a finish could be developed which would last even if the car stood out in all kinds of weather. We also began to realize that a good, fast-drying finish could revolutionize our time schedules and the consequent cost of production.

The finishing process at that time, using paint and varnish, was slow and cumbersome. Between the time a car was ready to be finished and the time the job was completed, something like two to four weeks went by, depending among other things on the temperature and humidity. It can readily be seen that this created a terrible inventory problem.

For a while many automobile manufacturers shifted from paint and varnish to oven-dried enamels, in an effort to deal with some of these problems. The Dodge Brothers' open car, for example, was wholly oven finished with no paint or varnish. This was a black Gilsonite enamel which was very durable. However, oven finishing was only a transition—there was a better and cheaper answer to the problem.

On July 4, 1920, more by accident, I think, than by intention, a chemical reaction was noted in one of the du Pont laboratories which led to the development of a nitrocellulose lacquer eventually called Duco. It was observed that a lacquer base could be created which would carry more color pigment in suspension, and produce more brilliant colors. Three years of experiment and development were required to get the bugs out of the new product. This was a co-operative project of the General Motors Research Corporation under the direction of Mr. Kettering and the du Pont laboratories. A Paint and Enamel Committee was organized in General Motors in 1921 (ironically both paint and enamel were soon to be superseded), and the first body finished in the new lacquer came off the production line in 1923. It was the "True Blue" Oakland of the 1924 line.

The new lacquer product, under the trade name Duco, was made available to the entire motorcar industry in 1925. There were still many problems to be solved, and research continued in the du Pont and General Motors research laboratories. A very important part of this work was the development of undercoats, for Duco as first developed was not very adhesive and sometimes stripped from the metal. Duco also required the use of natural resins, which were limited in quantity and of variable quality. In time, the invention of synthetics relieved us of dependence on these variable natural products.

Color had always been available in automobile finishes, both in the paint-and-varnish period and in the enamel period that followed it, but it was expensive and the range was limited. Duco, by reducing the cost of color finishes and increasing enormously the range of color that could be economically applied to cars, made possible the modern era of color and styling. Furthermore, its quick drying removed the most important remaining bottleneck in mass production, and made possible an enormously accelerated rate of production of car bodies. Today a car can be finished in an eight-hour shift, compared to the two-to-four-week period of the paint-and-varnish age.

Consider the saving in space alone: a production of 1000 cars a day once required space for 18,000 cars in process, since three weeks on the average were needed for the finishing work—that is, twenty acres of covered indoor space. Think of what this would mean at today's production rates of 15,000 or more cars per day.

Since the introduction of nitrocellulose lacquers in the twenties, there has been continuous study to improve them and to reduce the cost of application. In 1958 General Motors introduced a new line of finishes based on the acrylic resins. These again were the product of over eight years of research in our laboratories in co-operation with resin manufacturers. The acrylics are even more durable than the nitrocellulose lacquers and are capable of producing even more pleasing colors.

There were many other important improvements in which General Motors played a key role. Crankcase ventilation in the 1920s eliminated one of the main causes of deterioration of the engine. "Internal" crankcase ventilation, which reduced air pollution, was pioneered by General Motors in 1959 and made available to the industry in 1962. The development of four-wheel and hydraulic brakes contributed greatly to the safer and more effective use of the motorcar. Four-wheel brakes were not an exclusive General Motors development, but we participated in improving them, helped develop volume production, and created a special division to manufacture them for our cars. The corporation also took a leading role in the development of power brakes, power steering, car air-conditioning, and innumerable other refinements of the automobile. These are only a few important selections from the results of the ingenious and untiring labor of many thousands of research workers, engineers, and others who have given their professional interest to the development of efficient and comfortable individual transportation.

Chapter 13

THE ANNUAL MODEL CHANGE

Annual car models are now such a natural and accepted part of American life that few persons, I would imagine, have thought about the vast effort of management that lies behind them. The procedure we follow in designing a typical American passenger car differs significantly from that followed for foreign cars and specially designed domestic cars.

Each year we must produce a line of cars which embodies advanced engineering and styling features, and which will be competitive in price and meet the demands of the retail customer. The cars in this line must have some common styling features, giving them all a "General Motors look," but at the same time they must be clearly distinct from one another. They must also complement one another in price, which means that their own cost elements as well as the trend of competitive prices must be estimated well in advance of production.

In General Motors there are thousands of persons—in addition to production workers—involved in the creation of the new models: they include style artists and engineers; scientists; financial and marketing experts; members of the technical staffs of the various divisions; and the general executives and staff technicians of the corporation, not to mention our outside suppliers. The problem of co-ordinating their varied activities is extremely complex.

On the average about two years elapse between the time we make the first decisions on the new models and the time the cars appear in dealers' showrooms. Ordinarily, the sequence of events during these two years is determined principally by the requirements of body production. Body changes, of course, are usually substantial from one year to the next, and the body work takes the most time. There are continual changes in chassis components, too, of course, but only occasionally in any one year do we introduce changes in all the chassis units—the frame, engine, transmission, front and rear suspensions.

To generalize broadly, the first year of the model development is devoted to laying out the basic engineering and styling character-istics of the new model; and the second year is devoted mainly to the engineering problems entailed in bringing the cars into full pro-duction. It is extremely difficult to get either of these jobs done in much less than a year's time. If we compress the time given to set-ting the basic style concepts we increase the danger of "locking ourselves in" with a product which will not meet the approval of the retail customer. And if we compress the engineering-produc-tion time we pay extraordinary overtime charges, create inventory problems, and possibly delay the time when we can start produc-tion—which in turn might mean delays in a car's announcement date and loss of sales.

On the other hand it would be unwise to lengthen the time taken to produce the new models. There is, of course, no reason in prin-ciple why we could not begin to plan our model changes three or even five years in advance—and, in fact, we do some thinking that far ahead—but there is the practical difficulty that the planners are then remote from the realities of the market place in which their work will be tested. Even the two-year period usually required now imposes a severe strain on the corporation's ability to gauge the market correctly. The problem may be viewed this way: General Motors, like other automobile companies, is obliged to invest mil-lions of dollars to devise new products, which cannot, however, be sold until a long period of time has elapsed. Meanwhile the con-sumers' taste, income, and spending habits may all have changed radically. For that matter, we cannot even be certain that the new model is "right" at the time it is first conceived. Responses to sketches, and to survey questions, are often undependable. It is an axiom of marketing research that automobile customers never know whether they like the product well enough to buy it until they can actually see the real thing. But by the time we have a product to show them, we are necessarily committed to selling that product be-cause of the tremendous investment involved in bringing it to market. Every automobile manufacturer has on occasion been caught off base by the consumer. Nevertheless, in the nature of things, we must plan and co-ordinate our efforts in order to get to market with a new model.

This very special kind of co-ordination has evolved out of the planning experience of many years. I have described the near disaster that General Motors experienced in 1921–22 because there was no established co-ordination procedure which would enable the several distinct management groups to work together on a new-model program. After that experience we gradually put system and method into the introduction of the corporation's models. In 1935, we set down on paper for the first time, I believe, a procedure governing the production of new models. It was a manual designed "to provide a definite and orderly method for submitting the essential data required, in order that the economic, financial, engineering and commercial position of proposed new products may be evaluated; and, second, that their progress, from the time of approval to production, may be established, for the information of all concerned." The product-approval procedure was substantially revised in 1946, and to some extent is continually changing. It should be emphasized that these written procedures are not an exact "timetable" to which our model runs must conform.

In stating that the model-development periods average perhaps two years, I do not mean to imply that we start each model from scratch at the beginning of this period. The Styling Staff, for example, is continually experimenting with new designs for distant-future models, and at any point in time there is sure to be a sizable backlog of new styling ideas at our disposal, some of them quite conventional, some revolutionary. And each car division is continually engineering a variety of new features, mainly for the chassis. Some of these features may have been taken over from the Research Laboratories and the Engineering Staff or perhaps from the accessory divisions and refined in the car divisions to the point at which it seems feasible to introduce them into production models; others may have been developed entirely within the car divisions' own engineering shops and laboratories.

Usually, the first formal meeting on a new model is preceded by many informal discussions. For example, the car-division management and the Styling Staff review the advantages and disadvantages of past production programs, they examine customer-research reports and market analyses, and discuss the general package size and styling concepts for the new cars to be designed. Some of these issues may be taken up with the central-office Engineering Staff and with Fisher Body Division, as well as with the chief officers of the corporation.

Even though some important work on future models is always going on in the corporation, most of us have come to think of each new model program as "beginning" with a meeting called by the Engineering Policy Group. The reader will recall that this group reports directly to the Executive Committee and includes the corporation's chairman, president, and the principal central-office executives. The group's chairman is the vice president in charge of the Engineering Staff. Since the group concerns itself with broad corporate policy, the membership does not include the general managers of the car divisions or Fisher Body, although these men and the chief engineers of those operations are often invited to attend the group's meetings for a review of the programs in which they are involved.

The main business of this first meeting is to determine the outline of our styling and engineering programs, that is, to determine the cars' general appearance and size characteristics, and to indicate the direction of further styling and divisional development. The desired seat widths, head and leg room, as well as exterior height, width, and length are all considered. The Styling Staff displays full-size styling drawings, so that those present can get a feeling about the appearance, size, and roominess characteristics. Along with the drawings, we generally show full-size, dummy seating arrangements, commonly referred to as "seating bucks," which are constructed to simulate the proposed car interior. This "buck" allows us to check entrance-room conditions, vision, roominess, and seating position. The members of the group look over, you might say, what the stylists have to offer.

In line with the ideas developed at this "kickoff" meeting, the Styling Staff progressively develops several series of full-size styling drawings, as well as full-size clay models and seating bucks for each kind of car in our line. In order to achieve the desired objectives of the program, and to keep abreast of tooling and manufacturing requirements, the Styling Staff must work closely with the car divisions and Fisher Body for many months following this first meeting. In general, it is the Styling Staff's responsibility to set the basic appearance of each kind of car. That is, the staff works out the basic appearance of the General Motors sedan, coupe, hardtop, station wagon, and convertible—and usually the work is done in that order. Each division has its own studio within the Styling Staff, and these studios are responsible for giving each car line its own distinctive features—for example, the features which distinguish the Chevrolet and the Pontiac lines.

During these first few months of the program, the various clay models are changed and refined continually; and at each stage the seating arrangements are modified in line with the styling suggested by the clay model. Many of these changes are worked out with the help of sketches and small-scale clay models which are developed by Styling in an attempt to experiment with newer and more attractive concepts.

Meanwhile, the engineering departments of the car divisions and of Fisher Body have been working continually with the Styling Staff in order to reach an agreement on the chassis dimensions—that is, on the wheel base, ground clearance, tread, and the space required for the engine and drive mechanisms. An agreement on these fundamentals is necessary to permit the Styling Staff to "firm up" its concept of the new models.

About two months after the first meeting the Styling Staff offers the Engineering Policy Group a fairly advanced styling proposal, presented with a full-size clay model and seating bucks, for the sedan. (This proposal will have already been approved by the interested car divisions and by Fisher Body.) At subsequent Engineering Policy Group meetings, which are held at least once a month, proposals for the other body types are shown. This does not result in a prescribed order of approval, however. In the ensuing period of review and change, which may last for four or five months, it is quite possible that the coupe style, for example, may receive general acceptance ahead of the sedan style. However, at least eighteen months before the start of production the Engineering Policy Group should approve the sedan clay model in order that Styling can begin to release drawings to Fisher Body.

When the clay model is approved, Styling builds an inexpensive plastic model of the exterior. The plastic model is useful in checking the styling concept. Inevitably, the clay model looks bulkier than the car would actually be, but the plastic model can be painted to give the same light reflections as a finished car, and, indeed, with glass and simulated chrome trim, its exterior is almost identical with the finished product.

About eighteen months before production begins it is possible to make some calculations about the cost of the models. The size and estimated weight of the cars are known by then, and Fisher Body has begun to develop information on production-engineering costs —that is, the cost of the dies, jigs, fixtures, and so forth. It is generally Fisher's practice to begin estimating these costs even before the clay model is approved by the Engineering Policy Group. At this stage it becomes possible to weigh the sales appeal of certain features against their cost, and to modify the design if necessary. In recent years tooling costs have been lowered somewhat by General Motors' ability, in some cases, to utilize certain structural features and inner panels that are common to several different bodies.

When the Engineering Policy Group, Fisher Body, and the car divisions approve the clay and initial plastic models—often with some modification—the Styling Staff sets to work building new, much more elaborate plastic models, which are identical, inside and out, with the models that will come off the production lines. These reinforced plastic models were first used in an effort to build Motorama Show cars and other experimental cars quickly and economically. Later we began to use these plastic models just to give ourselves a "last look" at the cars we were putting into production. Until reinforced plastic was developed we had to make wood-and-metal styling models for this purpose, and it took as much as twelve to fourteen weeks to make one of them. The reinforced plastic models can be built in four or five weeks, which gives us more time to make tools and dies.

In the next six months or so the problem of co-ordinating work in the new models becomes very complex. While the final plastic model is being built, the Styling Staff sends drawings of major sheet-metal surfaces, and of such details as door handles and molding sections, to the car divisions and Fisher Body. As it gets this information Fisher Body moves ahead as rapidly as possible on the design of production tooling, beginning with the large and complex components—for example, the cowl, door panels, floors, roofs—and going on from there to the smaller and simpler parts.

About twelve months before production begins, the Engineering Policy Group must give its final approval to the design shown on the final, reinforced plastic model. Fisher Body can then finalize designs for the tools and prepare for their manufacture.

This Engineering Policy Group approval constitutes a general acceptance of the complete line of cars. From this point on, the car divisions work directly with Styling on the approval of specific details—for example, body moldings, trim, instrument panels, and, of course, on the front, side, and rear treatments developed by the individual styling studios. These details are also presented to the Engineering Policy Group for approval. At the same time, the car divisions will be building handmade experimental chassis for testing and giving Fisher detailed drawings of the chassis.

In other words, about one year in advance of the appearance of the cars in the dealers' showrooms, the major decisions of policy have been made—at least they have been if all has gone well. The Engineering Policy Group and representatives of Fisher Body, the Styling Staff, and the car divisions have reviewed the completed plastic models. Presumably, the models will have been approved. From here on, any substantial changes in the models will involve expensive reworking of dies and a variety of additional tooling costs, and also a serious loss of time, which could mean excessive preparation and production expense. Sometimes, however, these changes are unavoidable, because reviews after the first year may still uncover serious weaknesses in the proposed models. The divisional management and the chief officers of the corporation are now viewing the complete line of cars as they will appear in the showrooms and comparing them with the current line of General Motors and current competitive lines. It is entirely possible that some of the body types which looked good in drawings, and continued to look good in the clay or first plastic models, may now require correction. And while changes at this stage are expensive, they may be less expensive than the lost sales resulting from an unappealing model. On more than one occasion we have had to choose one of these drastic alternatives.

Where in sum do we stand at this point, one year after work on the model has begun, one year before the public announcement date? Styling has completed its work on the fundamentals of the model. There are now in existence a number of reinforced plastic bodies which look exactly like the final cars. Styling is still completing work on new seats, instrument panels, interior trim, and new materials. However, the Styling Staff can defer for a while the decisions on upholstery materials, colors, and so forth so that it will be closer to the trend of taste at the time the new model goes on the market. Fisher Body is progressing rapidly on engineering drawings and on the design of dies and other production tools. Divisional engineering work on the new chassis is nearing completion, and the prototype chassis are ready for test. From this point on, Fisher Body and the car divisions must work closely together to assure proper co-ordination on the body and chassis work.

The production tooling phase is now ready to begin. The general managers of the car divisions submit their final "product programs" through the Engineering Policy Group to the president of the corporation. These programs describe the features of the new models—their performance characteristics; their dimensions; their estimated weights; their estimated costs, including the expenditures required for plant rearrangement, and tooling and equipment. The Engineering Policy Group further compares car specifications with those of the current models of competitors and again it weighs the attractiveness of the product against the costs involved in its production. The president, the chairman of the corporation, and the other members of the Engineering Policy Group review the new-model program in its entirety. When they approve the program, each division submits an appropriation request for the approval of the group executive in charge of the division, for review by the vice president of manufacturing and then for the approval of an executive vice president, the president, and the Administration, Executive, and Finance committees. Then the manufacture of production tools gets under way.

The engineering departments of the car divisions now begin to release a vast number of drawings of the parts for the new cars. These drawings are forwarded to the master mechanics' departments for decisions on whether the parts are to be made or purchased (in some divisions this is determined by a "buy or make" committee); to the processing departments for preparation of routing sheets which detail the sequence of operations by which the part will be made; to the standards department for determining the direct-labor time allowances for each operation, and to the cost department, which sets up cost sheets on all items of labor and material cost. The manufacturing departments, along with the master mechanics' and plant-engineering departments, determine how the production lines are to be set up—what new machinery and equipment will be required and where it will be placed—and what plant rearrangement will be necessary.

By this time, too, the actual production engineering is well under way—among our outside suppliers as well as inside the corporation. As soon as we have finally approved the new models we consult with our many suppliers—of wheels, frames, rubber products, and so forth—in order to facilitate their engineering and development work and to help them plan their production.

Some seven to eight months before the new models are to go on sale Fisher Body will have completed the first prototype bodies, incorporating many hand-built parts. We can now put complete prototype cars together for test. We generally build a number of bodies for each model on a pilot line at Fisher Body about three months before production. These bodies are built from production dies, so the pilot line provides a test of body-production dies and tools and an opportunity to train production supervisors. Many of these pilot-line bodies are mounted on the prototype chassis and used for additional testing at the Proving Ground and in the engineering departments of the divisions. Finally, the cars that come off the pilot lines can be used by the Sales and Advertising sections for promotional purposes—for example, for advance showings to our dealers.

The production run itself is not started until about six weeks before the new cars go on sale. On the day the cars are formally introduced to the public our plants are, of course, rapidly attaining full production and many thousands of cars are already in the hands of dealers. The new-model program is over—and we are ready to concentrate more fully on the models that will reach the dealers one and two years hence.

The entire new-model program thus has three phases. *Styling* dominates the first year of the program; *engineering design* is continuous almost throughout the entire two-year period, with work ending just before mass production begins; *equipment and tooling* begin before Styling completes its work, and cover the multifarious and elaborate procedures required actually to make a car. The key point, perhaps, is the period halfway through the process, at the end of the first year, when the new design is approved and we "lock ourselves in" by beginning the production phase.

This is the way our procedure calls for new models to be produced, and this is the way, in large measure, they are in fact produced. However, no sooner do we "blueprint" reality than we begin to change it. In recent years the competitive situation has at times required us to produce a new model in somewhat less than two years. At the same time the increasing pace of competition has forced General Motors and other producers to speed up the rate of development of new design and engineering features. Naturally, when a larger part of a new car is "new," greater pressure is exerted on the process of design and the preparation for production.

We are continuously involved in this process of making a new and better car. Although the many complex steps over the long period between the conception of a new-model program and its execution are costly, they are worthwhile. For the annual model change is part of the very nature of the development of the industry. Since its earliest days, long before the expression "annual model" was used, the process of creating new models has generated the progress of the automobile.

Chapter 14

THE TECHNICAL STAFFS

ENERAL MOTORS is an engineering organization. Our operation is to cut metal and in so doing to add value to it. About 19,000 engineers and scientists work in the corporation, of whom 17,000 are in the divisions and 2000 in the general technical staffs. Many of our leading executives, myself among them, have an engineering background. It is natural, therefore, that we should always have understood that our progress is linked to technological progress, and that our effort to achieve it is necessarily never-ending. I expressed a policy on this subject at the time I set up the General Technical Committee in 1923: research and engineering in General Motors were to be on the same organizational plane as operations.

The permanent drive of research and engineering in industry is to accelerate technological progress, to incorporate in products and in manufacturing the advances made in science and technology, and to shorten the time between development and production. To achieve these ends we long ago differentiated a staff function from the operation function. We gathered together a research staff in the early 1920s and an engineering staff about ten years later. Today we have in General Motors, outside of operations, four technical staffs: the Research Laboratories, Engineering, Manufacturing, and Styling.[1] They are grouped in physical proximity to each other in a modern university atmosphere at the $125-million General Motors Technical Center near Detroit.

[1] Charts of the staff organizations discussed here and elsewhere appear at the end of the book.

There are logical reasons for grouping these staffs geographically. Certain similarities exist among them in the creative nature of their work and its broader scientific and technical aspects, and there are overlapping areas of interest and activity which require co-ordination.

Research

The present approach to research in General Motors is the result of evolution. Research of one kind or another in the corporation goes back almost fifty years. A laboratory was organized for General Motors by Arthur D. Little, Inc., in 1911 to conduct, mainly, materials analysis and testing. The main stream of General Motors' research, however, comes down from the Dayton Engineering Laboratories Company, organized independently by Charles F. Kettering (with E. A. Deeds) in 1909—before he came to General Motors—for the purpose of working on developments in the automotive field.

Mr. Kettering was, of course, the outstanding individual in the evolution of General Motors' research. For many years, paralleling my own, he was head of this technical activity in the corporation. In 1912, before he was associated with General Motors, he made automobile history when he brought out the first practical electric self-starter. One of his companies, the Dayton Engineering Laboratories, bought components for the starter and began assembly operations, and so became a successful manufacturer as well as a research laboratory. Three years later there were eighteen companies offering electric starting equipment. The first letters of the name of Mr. Kettering's company were taken to form the now famous trademark Delco. When Delco was brought into the United Motors Corporation in 1916, along with my company, Hyatt, I came to know Mr. Kettering intimately.

Mr. Kettering, an engineer and a world-famous inventor, a social philosopher, and a super-salesman I might say as well, gave a great deal of time and effort to conducting research in various fields that captured his interest and imagination. Before he came into General Motors in 1919, his laboratory had begun its great work on combustion. His organization was purchased by General Motors and combined with other research activities to become, in 1920, the General Motors Research Corporation at Moraine, Ohio, with Mr. Kettering as president. In 1925 we moved the Research Corporation to Detroit, and brought all General Motors' general research activities together under Mr. Kettering. Mr. Kettering retired in 1947 and was succeeded by Charles L. McCuen, an outstanding engineer who came up through the Oldsmobile organization. Mr. McCuen followed an advanced engineering approach, and produced very good results in a number of important areas in General Motors until he retired in the 1950s.

In 1955 a new phase in General Motors' research was begun with the appointment of the eminent nuclear scientist Lawrence R. Hafstad as vice president of research. Dr. Hafstad's training, of course, was not as an automotive engineer; he had never been associated with an automobile company. His appointment reflected the fact that the emphasis in the work of the Research Laboratories was moving steadily in the direction of investigation of new, broad research problems.

The activity of the Research Laboratories today lies mainly in three kinds of work. First, it does trouble-shooting around the corporation and it may be called in to help wherever its specialized knowledge is needed, for example, in the elimination of gear noise, in the testing of castings for material defects, or in the reduction of vibration. Second, it makes engineering improvements of a creative nature, growing out of problem-solving. These problems range from improvements in transmission fluids, paints, bearings, fuels, and the like, to high-level applied research, such as the work on combustion, high-compression engines, refrigerants, diesel engines, gas turbines, free-piston engines, aluminum engines, metals and alloy steels, air pollution, and the like. And third, it encourages some intensified basic research.

The dramatic accomplishments of science in recent years have captured the imagination of everyone, and have caused industry as a whole to move into a "research era." The word "research" is used in industry in a number of different ways: to denote scientific discovery, or advanced engineering, or even traditional and routine product improvements, the last being clearly an abuse of the term. Research has always been difficult to define in a way that distinguishes the more basic or fundamental type from applied research. There is no commonly agreed hard-and-fast line as to how "basic" a thing has to be, objectively, to be called "basic research."

The definition upon which there seems to be wide agreement is that basic research is the pursuit of knowledge for its own sake. In this sense, we in this country are not doing nearly enough.

The solution to this problem lies mainly in the universities and in government activity, but in recent years the question has arisen of the role of private industry. Obviously the major portion of the work must be undertaken in the universities. They have the academic viewpoint, the purpose, the tradition, the atmosphere, and the talent for seeking knowledge for its own sake. My personal viewpoint is expressed in the Alfred P. Sloan Foundation, which supports a program of basic research in the physical sciences in the universities. That this research is basic is indicated by the fact that the foundation bets not on the project but on the talent of the individual, who selects his own research in accordance with his individual interests, desires, and ability.

Obviously, too, basic research that requires unique and expensive facilities beyond the resources of universities is properly the province of government establishments such as the Bureau of Standards and the more recent Atomic Energy Commission and the National Aeronautics and Space Administration.

As to the participation of industry in basic research, the question has two parts: research inside the industrial organization and that done outside the organization but financed by it. I think, first of all, that since the outcome of basic research is the foundation of the knowledge used in industry, it is appropriate and an expression of enlightened self-interest for industry to make outside grants to universities for basic research. In other words, industry should do this because in the long run it will help industry. I think that shareholders and management will agree in principle with my position on this.

The extent to which industry should engage in basic research *inside* its own borders is a complex and somewhat unsettled problem. I cannot see how industry in its own work can properly distract its attention, in a large way, from its own practical projects. From the standpoint that basic research is the seeking of knowledge for its own sake, it is apparent that it does not belong, in a primary sense, in industry.

It does not follow, however, that industry should not engage at all in basic research. To a certain extent I think it should. A compromise is necessary. The scientists seek knowledge primarily for its own sake; industry seeks knowledge for eventual application. It is, however, reasonable for industry to engage in basic research in specified areas where any advance in knowledge, however speculative, is likely to be of eventual use to the industry: a kind of scientific reconnaissance. In other words, industry might legitimately employ scientists to work on basic research within the industry in areas where the scientists' fields of interest coincide with those of the industry, even though the motivations of each are different.

For example, a scientist might say: "My chief interest is the relation of the properties of individual metals to the properties of alloys. I don't care of what use this is. I want to know *why* it is." A producer of alloys could hardly help but be interested in the results of the research. So long as the motives of the scientist and the industry are not prejudiced, it is reasonable for them to establish a working relationship. The compromise lies not in motivation, but in the overlapping objective fields of interest. The scientist's "basic research" may be the industry's "exploratory research." This is the kind of basic research I think industry is justified in engaging in, since there is a reasonable expectation of an application regardless of the scientist's disinterested motive. To avoid any possible limitation on research activities, we need side by side both the industrial and the academic approaches.

In sum, therefore, my argument is this: that basic research, defined as the search for knowledge for its own sake, belongs primarily in the universities; that industry should give support to basic research in universities; and that industry has a special interest in engaging in several types of basic research inside of industry where there is a common broad area of subject matter. Useful results come more quickly from basic research than heretofore and so a basic-research group inside industry becomes a valuable intelligence group in the physical sciences. And the presence of scientists, well known for their work in basic science, helps morale and the prestige of the industrial laboratory and of the enterprise itself.

The Engineering Staff

The Engineering Staff provides an intermediate, medium-range link between the Research Laboratories and divisional engineering activities. It chiefly develops new engineering concepts and designs, and appraises them for commercial application.

We did not have a department or section of the corporation under the title "Engineering Staff" until 1931. But the various persons and functions that were brought together to make up this staff already existed. Some of them went back to the early twenties. When, for example, Mr. Hunt and Mr. Crane worked up the new Pontiac car in the Chevrolet Division in 1924 and 1925, that was a species of improvised staff operation for a special purpose. The General Technical Committee, formed in 1923, was another step toward an engineering-staff concept. Our divisions then differed greatly in their engineering practices, and in the quality of their engineering work. Some of our products were well designed; others were not. I have described the lack then of any extensive interchange of information among the divisions, or any means which insured that this would take place, and how the General Technical Committee, uniting research, divisional engineers, and general executives, was made to serve this purpose. The General Technical Committee, growing as it did out of our experience with the copper-cooled engine, was the beginning of all engineering co-ordination in General Motors. From this committee came the corporation's first regular testing program. Cars then were being tested on public roads, and there was no easy way of telling whether the test driver had pulled up at the side of a road, taken a nap, and then driven faster than the test schedule called for to make up the necessary mileage. Once one of our engineers discovered a test car jacked up outside a dance hall with the engine running up the required mileage on the odometer.

The most important step we took to standardize and improve test procedures was the establishment in 1924 of the General Motors Proving Ground, the first of its kind in the automobile industry. The thought was that we would have a large area, properly protected, and entirely closed to the public. It would be provided with roads of various types representing all the various demands on the motorcar from the standpoints of high speed, hills of various grades, smooth roads, rough roads, ability of a car to move through water—which is frequently required in severe storms—and the like. There we would be able to prove out our cars under controlled conditions both before and after production, and we could also make comprehensive tests on competitive cars.

The idea was approved and the necessary capital made available. The next problem was to find out where such a proving ground could be located. What we wanted was a varied terrain centrally situated with relation to our manufacturing operations in Lansing, Flint, Pontiac, and Detroit. Michigan is rather flat, and at first we had difficulty locating an area of sufficient size that would give us all the various grades we needed. However, almost every foot of the United States has been measured topographically, and the record was available in Washington. We went to Washington and from the Geological Survey maps available there we determined a location that appeared to fulfill our needs. Then the general executives and engineers of the various divisions and myself spent a day at the prospective site. We walked all over the place, ate a picnic lunch under the trees, and finally came to the conclusion that that particular area of 1125 acres—now 4010 acres—at Milford, Michigan, would meet the requirements we had in mind.

I delegated one of my executive assistants, W. J. Davidson, to take responsibility for developing the Proving Ground, and he appointed F. M. Holden as the first resident manager. Not long afterward Mr. Holden went to Oakland at his own request and was succeeded at the Proving Ground by O. T. ("Pop") Kreusser. All three of these men contributed greatly to the success of this project.

The land was surveyed; the straightaways were laid out so that we could check the effects of different winds on speed; a track was built and banked so that it was reasonably safe to operate cars at speeds up to 100 miles an hour or more. Engineering buildings were erected, so that indoor tests could be made in correlation with outdoor tests. Headquarters and facilities were provided for the corporation's engineers. Separate engineering headquarters and garage facilities were eventually provided for the staffs of the engineering departments of the various divisions, so that they could preserve their divisional autonomy in testing. Chevrolet, for example, could do its own testing if desired, in addition to that being done by the corporation. A clubhouse was erected that provided sleeping quarters, dining facilities, and the like for those attached to the Proving Ground operations, since the Proving Ground itself was a considerable number of miles from any town where commissary facilities were available.

In those days I used to spend a day and a night, sometimes longer, at the Proving Ground every other week. I would go over the engineering of General Motors' cars and competitive cars. I would examine what was being done in the way of testing future products. The Proving Ground thus afforded my associates and my-self a wonderful opportunity to find out what was going on in the automobile industry from the engineering point of view. To the orig-inal Proving Ground we have since added a special, desert proving ground at Mesa, Arizona, and a station to test cars in mountain driving and a garage and shop facility to service our test cars at Manitou Springs (Pike's Peak), Colorado.

The General Technical Committee, it will be recalled, acted in the 1920s as a kind of board of directors for the Proving Ground as a part of its work in co-ordinating and standardizing engineering procedures throughout the corporation. It also administered certain other central staff activities, such as the Patent Section, the New Devices Section, which evaluated technical devices submitted to the corporation by outside persons, and a foreign engineering liaison section.

But the General Technical Committee had no engineering staff of its own. Advanced engineering of corporation-wide interest was conducted in the 1920s either by the Research Laboratories or by the engineering departments in the individual operating divisions. We made a practice after a few years of having each operating division undertake some problem of long-range significance. These divisional engineering departments of the 1920s were the ancestors of the modern corporate Engineering Staff. They were not the best arrangements in the world, for the divisional responsibility is to the product the division is sponsoring. The division, charged with bring-ing out a new model every year, constantly encounters new prob-lems which are its primary responsibility. When you inject a piece of long-range research and development into this situation you are superimposing on an already loaded organization something to which it cannot properly give its attention. Recognition of this led to the formation of the Engineering Staff which was responsible to the central office.

This great advance in the engineering area was begun in 1929 when O. E. Hunt of Chevrolet was made the corporation vice presi-dent for engineering. Mr. Hunt then succeeded me as chairman of the General Technical Committee and took on the task of co-ordinating the advanced engineering work of the whole corpora-tion. Under Mr. Hunt's guidance, the advanced engineering in the divisions became a corporation staff responsibility. The functions of the old General Technical Committee were gradually absorbed into other parts of the corporation. Special product-study groups, for example, were developed for certain major problems. The product-study group was a "task force" of engineers assigned to a specific mission. Although in most cases situated physically within a specific division, a product-study group was a corporation activity, financed by its own corporation budget. The top operating group would try to identify the major directions in which car development was moving. We would then locate a capable engineer and set up a group under him to work on a selected problem. We set up the first product-study group in 1929 to adapt the Chevrolet for the use of Vauxhall in England; this group also designed cars for Opel in Germany, and other small cars. Afterward we set up the Suspension Product Study Group and the Transmission Product Study Group in the Cadillac Division (subsequently involving the Oldsmobile Division and the GMC Truck & Coach Division), and the Engine Product Study Group in the Buick Division. The first was responsible for developing independent front-wheel suspension; the second developed the fully automatic Hydra-Matic transmission for passenger cars and related units for larger commercial vehicles; the third was responsible for many improvements in the car engine. As time passed we changed the product-study groups from corporation task forces situated physically within the operating divisions into permanent separate organizations engaged in the continual process of research and testing in four vital areas—power development, transmission development, structure and suspension development, and the design of new types of cars. Eventually we took them out of the divisions and brought them together in the Engineering Staff, and called them development groups. They form the heart of the Engineering Staff today.

The Engineering Staff is closely linked to the Engineering Policy Group through the vice president of engineering, who directs the Engineering Staff and is chairman of the Engineering Policy Group. Since this group reviews the major steps in the development of new models and major departures from current engineering practice, it is in close touch with the engineering work of the operating divisions. The best thought of the Engineering Staff thereby makes a direct impact on the work of the divisions, and they make a direct impact on the development work of the Engineering Staff. The present organization, I believe, ensures the most rapid discovery of new concepts of engineering and their translation into current operating motorcars.

The Manufacturing Staff

Our over-all engineering work may logically be viewed as falling into two areas: one centers on the product and the other on the process of making it. The Manufacturing Staff works with conjectural, experimental, and pilot-model concepts; when these concepts prove successful in solving problems, they are adopted and used in our regular manufacturing operations in the form of improved manufacturing tools, equipment, and methods. This staff deals principally with the various aspects of manufacturing from the time the materials enter a plant until the finished product is shipped. These include machine and tool design, plant layout, materials handling, plant maintenance, equipment maintenance, work standards, methods engineering, materials utilization, and process and equipment development for the fabrication, final assembly, and test of the product.[2] This staff's general aims are to improve product quality, increase productivity, and reduce the cost of manufacture.

Centering these activities in a single corporate staff was the idea of one of our executives, B. D. Kunkle, who in 1945 felt that there was need for the same kind of function in the manufacturing area that the product-study group fulfilled in the product-development area. The manufacture of automobiles had rapidly become a more and more involved process requiring a constant study of new materials, new machinery, and new methods. Hence the idea of specialists to develop ideas for use in the manufacturing process. Logically, this was a staff function, and as such could be better fulfilled by a corporation group than by the individual divisions.

The technical work of the Manufacturing Staff is largely centered in the process-engineering activities of its Manufacturing Development Section, where the problem of automation arises. Process engineering necessarily includes automatic operations. Beyond the semiautomatic and automatic machine looms the image of the semiautomatic and automatic factory—the whole vague area summed

[2] This staff also has certain other responsibilities relating to real estate, industrial photography, production control, and procurement.

up under the term "automation," in which it is often difficult to distinguish science fiction from practical manufacturing possibilities. The Manufacturing Staff will play a large role in this field in General Motors. How far automation should go is a difficult question which will have to be decided on the highest policy levels of the corporation. General Motors and the Manufacturing Staff have tended to be somewhat more cautious in this area than some other manufacturers. There exists a widespread belief that "if it's automatic, it must be good," but our experience shows that this is not always the case.

A good, balanced view on this subject was given in a paper presented before General Motors' 1958 Conference for Engineering and Science Educators, by Robert M. Critchfield, who was then in charge of process development. He said:

In recent years we've all heard a lot of talk about automation. It seems to me that most of this talk has done little more than confuse a great many people, including a few in the engineering profession, as to the true implications of the word. As you know, automation is nothing new; it's merely a relatively recent word for a process that has been going on in manufacturing for more than half a century, perhaps even as far back as the time of Eli Whitney's successful attempts to mass produce muskets for the continental armies. I can recall that we had some types of transfer machines and other automatic production devices 35 years ago in General Motors, which was long before the word "automation" was coined. Our misconceptions seem to stem from the fact [that] the literature overflows with too many notions that automation is the obvious solution to the mass production of a particular part or product involving a number of highly repetitive hand operations. Nothing could be further from the truth. The decision to mechanize or not to mechanize a production process or operation involves much more than the number of repetitive operations; it involves a good many fundamentals of economics . . .

By economic solution we mean the solution to the problem which will provide the best return on our capital investment. And, of course, produce the product according to specifications and of the desired quality. And the expression, the most effective use of the manual and mechanical elements, is meant to convey that hand operations do not necessarily disappear entirely when a process or an operation is mechanized.

While the completely automatic factory is an interesting possibility, there continues to be a good deal of immediate practical work to be done in reducing production costs, building better machines, improving factory layouts, and designing better factories—and in all these areas the Manufacturing Staff is making major contributions.

The Technical Center

The General Motors Technical Center, which was completed in 1956, is noted for its architectural elegance and breathtaking vistas; and there is no doubt that Eliel and Eero Saarinen, who designed it, created something unique. It is located on a 900-acre site northeast of Detroit, about twelve miles from the General Motors Building. At the center of the site is a twenty-two acre artificial lake surrounded on three sides by clusters of buildings. On the north side are the Research Laboratories. To the east are the Manufacturing Staff and the Engineering Staff buildings. To the south are the Styling Staff buildings, including a distinctive domed auditorium in which fairly sizable groups can gather for showings of the staff's work. Altogether, the Technical Center now has twenty-seven buildings, which house some 5000 scientists, engineers, designers, and other specialists. Wooded areas to the south and west help to seal the center from other real-estate developments and preserve its distinctive, rather "campus-like" atmosphere.

But of course the primary function of the Technical Center, as of all General Motors' facilities, is to get work done; and perhaps its real greatness resides in the fact that it is wonderfully functional as well as elegant. To understand why it has been a valuable investment for the corporation, easily worth the $125 million that has been put into it, the reader should know something of its origin.

The inadequacy of our previous facilities was obvious even before the end of World War II. Our different staff operations were then scattered all over the Detroit area, in a wide variety of rather makeshift quarters. I was especially struck by the unhappy situation of the Styling Staff, whose fabricating shops were located in an old Fisher Body building several miles from the staff headquarters. This building was adjacent to some heavy engineering work we were doing, especially on diesel engines, and Mr. Earl's men were oppressed by the noise. In any case, they did not have enough room.

During the war, the different staffs began to formulate plans for their facilities in the postwar era. From a consideration of this problem in relation to research and engineering, there began to emerge the idea of setting aside and developing one area for all the technical staffs. This implied some organizational changes, of course. I discussed these changes, and first proposed something like a new staff center, in a letter to Mr. Kettering, dated March 29, 1944:

My dear Ket:
   I have been thinking about certain Corporation problems as affecting the long term position of our affairs and I would like to ask your point of view, if I may, on one of these problems as I see it.
   I am not going to present an argument to you as to the importance of technological progress. We both recognize that as the keystone of our future position. In our Research activities down through the years, we had a marvelous balance between the scientific side and the engineering side . . . what I'm wondering about is, whether this marvelous balance that we have, can and will be maintained . . . if I were to venture an opinion, I would be inclined to think that ten to twenty years from now, General Motors Research would be much more in the scientific area than it is now . . . By the "scientific area" I . . . [mean] problems that were related directly [to our areas of interest], or perhaps indirectly, but not in any sense of the word what we normally term engineering in character.
   Now I have in mind the point that you have always raised with me, in which I have agreed; viz., the difficulty involved and the importance of shortening the time when Research developments are incorporated in an engineering sense, in our products . . .
   In an attempt to accelerate engineering progress in our products, down through the years I have tried several different approaches; first, to charge the Engineering Department of the Division with the development of a certain forward device, like the synchro-mesh transmission, for instance . . . Subsequent to that, we have, as you know, set up Product [Study] Groups under the direction of the general head of the Engineering Staff . . . In that way we can carry our engineering development to the point of its practicability, after which it can be dealt with in an engineering or production way, as circumstances may justify . . .
   I believe we should set up in the Corporation in the staff of the Vice President in charge of Engineering . . . a properly accredited central engineering activity to deal with the car as a whole . . .
   I would visualize the physical development of this activity to consist of a set-up close to, but outside, the City of Detroit. The Proving Ground[3]

[3] Located at Milford, Michigan, forty-two miles northwest of Detroit.

. . . is probably too far away for contact . . . I believe that such a set-up . . . would serve to reduce the time element in bringing into our products, advanced research work . . .

. . . Nothing need be done here to in any way change the combined engineering and scientific areas in which the Research . . . is now dealing . . . and if in future years the trend of our research work should be more in the scientific area, then we would have a set-up that would make up for the delinquency . . .

Mr. Kettering responded to this suggestion with a plan for expanding the research facilities and moving all of them except the machine-tool and model shop to a new location. He sent this proposal to O. E. Hunt, who forwarded it to me. On April 13, 1944, I sent Mr. Hunt a letter making these points, among others:

First: I think we all agree . . . that . . . [w]hatever it might cost would be inconsequential compared with what we will get out of it . . . after all, the necessity of additional facilities is what I might refer to as an end necessity . . . we can only sell . . . a product that is sound, desirable and advanced, technically.

Second: I am convinced that we need additional facilities for Research [and] . . . that the present facilities are not only inadequate but poorly located for the result that we must have. I am absolutely against spending more money for the same type of thing, where we are . . . Therefore, I believe that the project is sound and desirable so far as establishing an entirely new location where the operating conditions will be more in line . . . as we look forward into tomorrow.

I concluded the letter by proposing an amendment to Mr. Kettering's plan, and suggested:

Let's set up what we would call—

GENERAL MOTORS TECHNICAL CENTER

. . . The center to which I have referred would comprise an expanded Research activity as defined by Mr. Kettering; and Engineering activity which would comprise Harley Earl's body design, cor[r]elated with the broadened product activity such as we are now conducting in Detroit . . .

By the end of 1944 this proposal had advanced to the point where I felt able to take it to the Administration Committee for discussion and approval. I quote from the minutes of the meeting of that committee for December 13, 1944:

Mr. Sloan advised the group that plans are being formulated to establish, in the vicinity of Detroit, a technical center in line with the corporation's policy of improving its technological position. He stated that the plans are in a tentative stage and complete data will be submitted at a later date. It is proposed that the center shall house the present activities carried on by the research division and the art and color section; and also provide facilities for engineering research of a character comparable to present product studies carried on by the central office engineering staff that are neither research activities presently carried on by the research division nor the individual engineering work carried on by the various divisional engineering groups.

In response to an inquiry from the chairman, those present expressed themselves as being enthusiastically in favor of the proposed technical center.

There remained the sizable question of where the center should be situated. After some discussion it was agreed that the center should be outside of highly congested areas, near a railroad, twenty-five to thirty minutes from the General Motors Building, and adjacent to residential areas. It was also agreed that each activity should retain its individual identity. By the middle of December 1944 a suitable section of land meeting the various requirements had been located at the present site and we proceeded to option most of the West Half of Section 9, Warren Township, northeast of Detroit. All concerned agreed on the desirability of this location.

There also remained a question about the architectural and aesthetic standards we should aim at. Harley Earl had contended from the beginning that we should engage an architect of stature, and aim for a center that would be distinctive. Several others felt that any emphasis on high aesthetic standards might be detrimental to the practical operations of the center, and so they wanted General Motors itself to design and plan the project. At about the time this argument was in progress, I happened to visit the Ethyl Corporation laboratories in Detroit, which had just been completed. These handsome facilities made an excellent impression on me, and so I inclined to Mr. Earl's point of view more than I might have otherwise.

Among those who expressed some concern about the effects of

an aesthetically oriented center was Mr. Lammot du Pont. He felt, quite properly, that he would not be fulfilling his responsibilities as a director unless he was satisfied on certain points. I wrote to him on May 8, 1945, arguing the advantages of retaining an outside architect, and on May 17 he replied that he was satisfied on the point. His letter said, in part:

The whole layout and the description of its preparation gave me the impression that the matter of esthetic treatment, or as I would style it, "dressing up the place," had been an important factor from the beginning. I questioned whether the matter of appearance was of any importance in a project of this kind, the sole object being to get technical results. It was with this thought in mind that, in offering my remarks, I started out with the layout, which had been made by an architectural firm, whereas according to my line of thought, it would have been more appropriate to have had the layout made by an engineering firm or General Motors engineers.

I gather from your letter that it is not the intention to allow the appearances to interfere with the technical possibilities or to add substantially to the cost of the project. With those two assurances, my only remaining question with respect to the project would be answered.

We asked Mr. Earl himself to find the right architect for the center. He visited a number of leading architectural schools, and sought out the opinions of others who were knowledgeable in the field; and he found, in the end, that virtually everyone made the same recommendation. The selection of the Saarinens was not a difficult choice.

By July 1945 we had the architects' preliminary plans, an elaborate scale model, and artists' renderings of various buildings. On July 24 we announced the project publicly, and it received wide and favorable comment in the press. By October the property had been rough-graded and entirely fenced in. The project was then delayed by the great postwar strike, running from the fall of 1945 through March 1946, and by the fact that, in the booming postwar market, we found we needed expanded production facilities more than any other kind of building—even the Technical Center. Construction was resumed in 1949 and the Technical Center opened formally in 1956. I am satisfied that the decision to provide this aesthetically distinctive and functional center for our technical talents was a sound and desirable one.

Chapter 15

STYLING

T HE prominence of styling in the automobile market in recent
years is the outcome of the evolution of the annual model
and the high state of the art of automotive engineering. Styling, as an organized staff activity, was first undertaken in the automobile industry by General Motors in the late 1920s. Since 1928
styling and engineering in the corporation have evolved together
in a continuous interaction that brought about the modern General
Motors style.

Throughout the first three decades of the industry, until the late
twenties, the engineer dominated the whole design of the car. O. E.
Hunt in a letter to me summed up this early background:

Even comfort, initially, was a secondary matter, and appearance,
economy, etc., got scant, if any, attention . . . Engineering was the all-
absorbing activity and the engineer was usually the dominant personality, often to the point of unreasonable insistence on having his ideas as
to the design followed to the letter regardless of manufacturing feasibility
or ease of maintenance in point of time or money. Even advertising and
the sales effort voiced largely the engineer's convictions as to desirable
motor car features and characteristics . . .

We came into the 1920s with two kinds of engineers—one in
product and the other in production—in a certain relation of tension, which necessarily affected the design of the automobile. The
production engineer's problems in creating techniques for mass
production often caused him to want to hold up design changes in

the product. They were headaches to him. But by the mid-twenties, the product engineer had begun to feel the influence of the sales people. He then began to yield to market considerations, though still largely in terms of purely engineering design. In the course of time the product engineer raised the state of his art so high that he produced not only a superb creation but also a mature one, so far as the present type of gasoline-powered car is concerned. Now he devotes much of his skill to solving the problems created by the stylist. The consumer recognizes this today by taking for granted the varied engineering excellence of all competitive makes of cars, and so his shopping is strongly influenced by variations in style. Automobile design is not, of course, pure fashion, but it is not too much to say that the "laws" of the Paris dressmakers have come to be a factor in the automobile industry—and woe to the company which ignores them.

As a producer, General Motors is in harmony with this trend of the industry and of consumer desire. At the close of World War II we made the projection that for an indefinite period the principal attractions of the product would be appearance, automatic transmissions, and high-compression engines, in that order; and that has been the case.

The degree to which styling changes should be made in any one model run presents a particularly delicate problem. The changes in the new model should be so novel and attractive as to create demand for the new value and, so to speak, create a certain amount of dissatisfaction with past models as compared with the new one, and yet the current and old models must still be capable of giving satisfaction to the vast used-car market. Each line of General Motors cars produced should preserve a distinction of appearance, so that one knows on sight a Chevrolet, a Pontiac, an Oldsmobile, a Buick, or a Cadillac. The design must be competitive in its market. Great skill and artistry are needed to fulfill these complex styling requirements. General Motors has a Styling Staff of over 1400 employees engaged in this function. They have a very large responsibility for the success of the product.

Mass production necessarily imposes certain limitations on styling. The enormous cost of bringing new models to market—in some years it has amounted to more than $600 million—makes it imperative to weigh the cost of each suggested change. General Motors reduces the cost of retooling for new designs to some extent through the common use of major structural parts of a basic body concept. Tooling costs also are reduced by trying to limit major design changes to two- or three-year intervals.

The stylists' control of design is qualified by several factors. They interact with the car divisions, the Fisher Body Division, and the staff engineers; and their work must be co-ordinated with the over-all decisions of the Engineering Policy Group. Although in the past, new designs were subordinated to engineering limitations set by the car-producing divisions, today they are evaluated more from the standpoint of their potential eye appeal. Engineering and production have adapted to the requirements of styling as styling adapted to mass production.

In the early automobile in the United States there was a certain relationship between the various parts that was adhered to by almost every car maker for many years. The radiator, for example, had to be in line with the front axle and the rear seat had to be directly above the rear axle, a relationship which was responsible for the height of the cars of the period. Inevitably, these fixed relationships between the axles and the body of the old car meant that the car had to be high. However, this did not matter much during the period when the industry principally was building open cars—that is, until the mid-twenties.

A fairly satisfactory design had been evolved for the motorcar when it was an open car. In 1919, when 90 per cent of the cars manufactured were touring cars or roadsters, the touring car had a clean, uncluttered look. Body surfaces were smooth; doors were flush, and the hood had been raised and lengthened until it was the most prominent feature. It was a product of the period of motorcar history when the car was used mostly for sport and pleasure rather than for everyday travel and business. The main problem was, of course, the weather. For twenty years we protected ourselves with a variety of rubber coats, hats, lap robes, and other makeshift things. For some reason or other, it took us a long time to realize that the way to keep dry in a motorcar was to keep the weather out of the car. With the closed car came styling as we know it today.

The General Motors product-policy program of 1921 emphasized "the very great importance of style in selling." But it was not until 1926, when closed bodies were becoming dominant, that I first turned to the problem of styling in a practical way. The appearance of the closed car at that time left much to be desired. The period of automobile elegance during the early days of the motor-car, when cars were, in effect, handmade and reflected the design of the carriage, was already far past and almost forgotten. The mature open car was all but obsolete. The new closed car was a high, ungainly contraption, with narrow doors and a belt line (that is, the line between the windows and the lower part of the body) high above the already high hoods. General Motors' closed cars of 1926, for example, were 70 to 75 inches or more high, as compared with 51 to 57 inches in 1963, and since the bodies did not overlap the frame, they were very narrow—65 to 71 inches in 1926 compared with over-all widths of about 80 inches in the 1964 models. They were well made but their height was not attractive. And as cars were driven more rapidly by more efficient motors, it became dangerous to have vehicles with their center of gravity so far above the ground.

The awkwardness of these cars came in part from the nature of the design process. There were then generally two completely separate operations, one for the production of the car body, and the other for the production of the chassis, including some of the parts of the car that contributed to its appearance. In General Motors at that time the car divisions designed and built the chassis as a separate unit complete with cowl, fenders, running boards, and hood. Fisher Body then designed and built a body with doors, windows, seats, and roof, which also was assembled separately. Then the body was installed on the chassis. The final appearance of the cars reflected the independence of the two operations.

I expressed my general views about the need to develop a styling program on July 8, 1926, in a letter to H. H. Bassett, general manager of Buick:

My dear Harry:—
    . . . [For] The first Cadillac car that I ever had . . . I purchased small wire wheels in order to get the car down nearer the ground and I never could see why, as motor car people, we have apparently been so loath to do a thing which contributed probably more to the appearance of the car from the attractive standpoint than any other single thing. Chrysler, in bringing out his original car, certainly capitalized that idea to the fullest possible extent and I think a great deal of his success . . . was due to that single thing. Slowly but surely we are . . . getting our cars down nearer the ground . . . This, of course, is to a certain extent a

mechanical feature but nevertheless it involves the appearance as well.

I am sure we all realize . . . how much appearance has to do with sales; with all cars fairly good mechanically it is a dominating proposition and in a product such as ours where the individual appeal is so great, it means a tremendous influence on our future prosperity. When it comes to our body design, I am sure we all recognize the quality, the wonderful workmanship and the constructiveness from every standpoint of Fisher bodies. They speak for themselves . . .

Irrespective of all this, however, the question arises—Are we as advanced from the standpoint of beauty of design, harmony of lines, attractiveness of color schemes and general contour of the whole piece of apparatus as we are in the soundness of workmanship and the other elements of a more mechanical nature? That is the point I am raising and I believe it is a very fundamental one . . .

At the present time one of our very important lines is being revamped from the appearance standpoint . . .

The action I mentioned in the last line of this letter was to make styling history. Lawrence P. Fisher, who was then general manager of Cadillac, shared with me a belief in the importance of appearance. He had been visiting some of the dealers and distributors around the country, among them Don Lee of Los Angeles, California. Don Lee owned, in conjunction with his sales operation, a custom body shop in which he built special bodies on both foreign and American chassis for Hollywood movie stars and wealthy people of California. Mr. Fisher was impressed with the styling of these California cars and paid a visit to the shop where custom bodies were built. There he met their young chief designer and the director of the custom body shop, Harley J. Earl.

Harley Earl, the son of a carriage maker, had studied at Stanford; he had received training in his father's carriage shop, which Don Lee subsequently purchased. He was doing things in a way that Mr. Fisher had never seen before. For one thing he was using modeling clay to develop the forms of various automobile components, instead of the then conventional wood models and hand-hammered metal parts used in development work. Also he was designing the complete automobile, shaping the body, hood, fenders, headlights, and running boards and blending them together into a good-looking whole. This, too, was a novel technique. Mr. Fisher saw Mr. Earl lengthen the wheel base by cutting the frame and inserting an extra piece. The result was a long, low custom body that pleased many famous screen personalities.

It was an important meeting, for Mr. Fisher's interest in this young man's talent was to result in actively influencing the appearance of more than fifty million automobiles from the late 1920s to 1960. Mr. Fisher invited Mr. Earl to come east to Detroit and work for him at the Cadillac Division. Mr. Fisher had a particular project in mind: that of designing a quality car of the same family as Cadillac but somewhat lower priced. We felt that there was a growing market for a car of this type. The idea was to approach the design with a new concept in mind: that of unifying the various parts of the car from the standpoint of appearance, of rounding off sharp corners, and of lowering the silhouette. We wanted a production automobile that was as beautiful as the custom cars of the period.

Harley Earl came to Detroit under special contract as a consultant to Mr. Fisher and the Cadillac Division in early 1926. He worked with Cadillac body engineers on the design of the new car. This was the car, then in the design stage, that I referred to in my letter to Mr. Bassett. The car, named the La Salle, made a sensational debut in March 1927, and it was a significant car in American automotive history. The La Salle was the first stylist's car to achieve success in mass production. The effectiveness of the new design can be seen by comparing it with the 1926 Buick sedan. The La Salle looked longer and lower; the "Flying Wing" fenders were drawn deeper than their predecessors; side windows had been reproportioned; the belt line had a new type of molding; sharp corners had been rounded off, and other design details were added giving it the unified appearance that we were looking for.

I was so impressed with Mr. Earl's work that I decided to obtain the advantages of his talent for other General Motors car divisions. On June 23, 1927, I took up with the Executive Committee a plan to establish a special department to study the question of art and color combinations in General Motors products. Fifty, persons would make up the department, ten of them designers, and the rest shopworkers and clerical and administrative assistants. I invited Mr. Earl to head this new staff department, which we called the Art and Color Section. Mr. Earl's duties were to direct general production body design and to conduct research-and-development programs in special car designs. The section was made a part of the corporation's general staff organization, even though it received its funds through the Fisher Body Division. I was concerned about how the divisions would take to the new department, and felt that Mr. Earl needed all the support and prestige that Mr. Fisher, the Cadillac Division manager, could give him. Furthermore, as chief executive officer of the corporation, I lent Mr. Earl my personal support. He has recalled to me that, when he started his staff work for the corporation at large, I said to him, "Harley, I think you had better work just for me for a while till I see how they take you." With the support of Mr. Fisher and myself, the new section, I hoped, would be accepted by the car divisions.

One of the first problems Mr. Earl had to deal with was to find the staff of designers called for in the plan. There were automotive stylists in the business in 1927; for example, Ray Dietrich and Ralph Roberts of Le Baron, Inc., of New York City, who in the late twenties were engaged respectively by the Murray Corporation of America and the Briggs Manufacturing Company. There were also R. P. Williams and Richard Burke of the Locomobile Company, of Bridgeport, Connecticut, and others. But there was no going profession from which to draw young men adept in advanced automobile design.

Shortly after the Art and Color Section was established, Mr. Fisher and Mr. Earl went on a tour of Europe to study European car design. A good many European cars then were better, mechanically and in appearance, than American cars; but of course they were made in relatively small numbers. It struck me that our new section might be improved by the addition of foreign designers. I wrote Mr. Fisher on September 9, 1927, suggesting he consider that possibility:

In view of the fact that you and Harley Earl are going abroad, would it not be a constructive thing to try to get in touch with men on the other side who could contribute ideas that would be helpful in our art and color work. This may, at the first consideration, seem impractical because I recognize the different viewpoints and all that sort of thing. On the other hand, as I see it, the great problem of the future is to have our cars different from each other and different from year to year. Recognizing the extraordinary talent that Harley Earl has along these lines, it must be recognized [also] that even with that fact before us, all the additional talent that we can get will be needed in view of the tremendous possibilities and the magnitude of our operations . . .

From time to time Mr. Earl brought car designers from Europe to his studio in Detroit. At the same time he developed over the years a school of American car designers. The problems of designing a foreign car and an American family car are quite different. The European car usually has little or no trunk space and has seats for two or four people. The economics are different too. Horsepower taxes and high gasoline taxes have caused European car design to go toward smaller engines and greater gas economy. The big market in America wants a larger and more powerful engine, and room for several passengers and enough luggage for a long-mileage motor trip. These basic differences in utility cause the difference in appearance between the European and American car designs.

Despite the public acceptance of the La Salle in 1927, acceptance of the new Art and Color Section within the corporation was slow. An automobile stylist is an advocate of change to a degree that was at first somewhat startling to production and engineering executives. The Sales Section also had its fears. Wouldn't the cars begin to look alike? On December 5, 1927, B. G. Koether, director of the Sales Section, wrote: "Several people have expressed the fear that if the art and color end of our business would be dominated by one personality, it might possibly be that in the future all General Motors cars would more or less resemble each other . . ." I replied to Mr. Koether as follows:

. . . The exact working out of the new set up [Art and Color Section] is not yet completed, but if I have my way and I shall influence a program so far as I can that provides an organization having artistic ability and while it may be dominated from the operating standpoint by one individual, it will have in its organization a sufficient number of individuals to develop a diversity of ideas. Formerly, the one indivdual had no appreciation of the importance of having things different. Mr. Earl has a very keen appreciation of that phase of his problem and recognizes that it will be impossible for him to revise eight or nine lines of cars every year and have them continually better, more artistic and yet different— at least he cannot do that by himself. It is also our idea to include in the activities of this Section, color and upholstery. Much has been left undone . . . in the past.

Still, in addition to the above, it is my idea to have the divisions set up more or less of a duplicate organization on a smaller scale, of course, in order that a competitive situation may at all times be maintained . . .

This divisional approach was tried but did not prove practical. But we maintained the divisional separateness by setting up a different studio in the Styling Staff for each of the divisions.

Sales, however, were in the end the decisive factor in the acceptance of the Art and Color Section. The market made it clear that appearance was selling cars. Chrysler was getting good results with color, and so were we wherever we used it. Furthermore the year we started the Art and Color Section, 1927, was the year in which the Model T Ford came to the end of its career. This was the car that, according to legend, Mr. Ford said one could have in any color so long as it was black. Thus styling came into the picture as one era ended and another began.

On September 26, 1927, I wrote to William A. Fisher, then president of Fisher Body Corporation:

To sum up, I think that the future of General Motors will be measured by the attractiveness that we put in the bodies from the standpoint of luxury of appointment, the degree to which they please the eye, both in contour and in color scheme, also the degree to which we are able to make them different from competition.

The hesitation within the corporation to make use of the "beauty parlor," as the Art and Color Section was sometimes called, was gradually overcome. Its first job outside the Cadillac organization was a "face lift" on the 1928 Chevrolet for O. E. Hunt, who assisted in establishing the authority of the Art and Color Section within the corporation.

The first car to be styled completely by the Art and Color Section was a tremendous flop from the public standpoint. This was the 1929 Buick, introduced in July 1928 and soon dubbed by the public "the pregnant Buick." Into that car went some of the most advanced engineering seen in any production car of the day. Low sales figures for the year 1929 indicate that this particular design was not accepted, and the car was taken out of production as soon as a suitable replacement design could be developed. The controversial feature of the design was a slight bulge or roll just below the belt line, which started at the hood and continued around the entire car. By actual measurement, this curvature extended one and a quarter inches from the side of the belt line. The failure of its appeal indicates that taste is related to a particular period. In modern cars we tolerate a bulge of three to five and a half inches. The "pregnant Buick" of 1929 is a classic example of how the public generally prefers gradual rather than drastic changes of design.

Mr. Earl had an artist's explanation of this event. He said in 1954:

. . . I designed the 1929 Buick with a slight roundness both ways from the beltline highlight, and it went into production. Unfortunately the factory, for operational reasons, pulled the side panels in at the bottom more than the design called for. In addition, five inches were added in vertical height, with the result that the arc I had plotted was pulled out of shape in two directions, the highlight line was unpleasantly located, and the effect was bulgy.

The Styling Section then had not been as well integrated into other company operations as it is now, and I was unaware of what had happened until I later saw the completed cars. Of course, I roared like a Ventura sea lion, but it was too late to keep car buyers from having a lot of fun naming the poor *enceinte* Buick.

For a long while the Art and Color Section occupied quarters in the General Motors Building Annex in Detroit. The focal point of the work area was the blackboard room. To this room came executives from Fisher Body and every car division. Executives mingled with designers, engineers, woodworkers, clay modelers; they were an active, talkative crowd, always comparing and pointing to the designs on the blackboards, which, surrounded by black velvet curtains, made the white body lines stand out sharply.

In this stimulating atmosphere in the early 1930s you might see gathered together Mr. Knudsen of Chevrolet, Alfred R. Glancy or Irving J. Reuter of Oakland (now Pontiac), Dan S. Eddins of Oldsmobile, or Edward T. Strong of Buick, Mr. Fisher of Cadillac, and perhaps one or two of his brothers from Fisher Body.

We were all window-shoppers in the Art and Color "sales" rooms. Art and Color was proposing new designs, presenting new idea sketches, selling progress. And as time went by more and more of these ideas appeared to be feasible. New divisional customers materialized as more and more people in the corporation bought the ideas. Furthermore, we employed women as automobile designers, to express the woman's point of view. We were the first to do so, I believe, and today we have the largest number of them in the industry.

One of the main problems of Harley Earl and his section was to fix upon certain lines of development for car styling. If one had a conception of how automobile styling would or should evolve, small successive changes could be made year after year, as the annual model program demanded; consumers could be prepared, by measured steps, for more radical changes in styling, and it would be possible to avoid such mistakes as the 1929 Buick, or the error of Chrysler in 1934, when it came out with a car (the Airflow design) that was overly streamlined.

Harley Earl had no doubts as to what the main line of development in car styling should be. He said in 1954: "My primary purpose for twenty-eight years has been to lengthen and lower the American automobile, at times in reality and always at least in appearance. Why? Because my sense of proportion tells me that oblongs are more attractive than squares . . ."

Contributing to this main line of styling development was a secondary line—to integrate projections from the car into the body. Almost all the major achievements of Mr. Earl and his Styling Section in the thirty-five years since it was established have contributed to this styling evolution. In the 1930s I renamed the Art and Color Section the Styling Section. In the terminology of the automobile business, model appearance is now generally called "styling," and the designers are "stylists."

The 1933 models presented the first of the so-called A-bodies for Chevrolet, and introduced some significant developments. The body was extended in all directions in an attempt to cover some of the ugly projections and exposed parts of the chassis which were still in evidence. The gas tank was covered with what the stylists called a "beaver tail." The radiator was hidden behind a grille. The traditional exterior visor had been removed in the 1932 models and replaced by a curved windshield header, and in the 1933 models the height of the apron—the panel between the bottom of the doors and the running board—which was nothing more than a cover-up for the frame, was reduced. The final touch was to add fender skirts, which helped hide the encrustations under the fender.

Mr. Earl's effort to reduce the height of the car ran into engineering problems. The car body of the late twenties, as I have pointed out, did not drop down between the front and rear wheels, as it does today, but rested upon the axles and was therefore so high that a running board or step was needed to enter the car. Mr. Earl wanted to lengthen the wheel base and move the engine forward of the front wheels, from its position behind them, so that the frame and body could be lowered and the passengers could sit ahead of the rear wheels, instead of above them. But if the body were lowered to this extent, it created the problem of where to put the transmission. The engineers also objected that lengthening the body added weight, and shifting the position of the motor changed the standard weight distribution, all of which created new and difficult problems.

There were various ways of overcoming these problems. One was the "drop frame," in which the frame took a dip between the axles. The Art and Color Section put on a dramatic demonstration in the interest of showing how a "drop frame" could reduce the over-all height of a car. On one occasion a Cadillac chassis and a separate body were shown assembled in the conventional manner on a stage before us. A number of workmen lifted the body from the chassis and proceeded to cut the chassis frame apart with acetylene torches. Proceeding very quickly, they welded the frame back together in such a way as to lower its height by a good three inches. When they replaced the body on the makeshift frame they had proved a point—not only could the body be lowered but in its new position it looked 100 per cent better.

The roofs, too, got the stylists' attention. General Motors body construction was still wood framing in the main with sheet metal used on all exterior surfaces, except the roof. The center portion of the roof was covered with a synthetic rubber material joined to the steel side panels. But water, dirt, and so forth collected in this juncture, causing a gradual deterioration of the roof. In a salt atmosphere the process was accelerated. Fisher Body was hard pressed to keep up with warranty replacements. Furthermore the stylists had a profound dislike for the appearance of the "half-and-half" roof.

When the steel industry perfected the modern high-speed strip mill and came up for the first time with sheet steel in eighty-inch widths, we were able to make a one-piece steel roof. There were many people in the corporation who were dead set against this innovation. Some of the old-timers, remembering how early versions of the all-steel roof made a drumming noise, objected. But the old roofs were square and boxy while the new design had a generous crown and curved sides which helped to reduce the "drumming."

The new silhouette also fitted into the main line of development of automobile styling.

But the new roof led to some heated discussions among the responsible executives of the corporation. When a division chief engineer would condemn the design for noise-making characteristics, another executive would claim that the trouble was caused not by the design but by the vibrations within the engine. But the advanced ideas won out and in 1934 the corporation's 1935 models appeared with all-steel tops, the now famous "Turret Tops." This was a constructive move, one of the big advances in car design, in car safety, and in manufacturing technique. It made it possible to stamp out whole tops on a monster press.

In the early thirties the Art and Color Section proposed making the trunk an integral part of the body, an idea that was quite a departure from the then accepted practice of using a separate trunk strapped to a rack. The idea was tried out on the 1932 Cadillac and on other luxury cars, and, after this tryout, was adopted on the high-volume Chevrolet in 1933. The built-in trunk and its partner, the extended deck on which it sits, were significant, however, because they altered the over-all shape of the car and helped make it longer and apparently lower. And by providing storage space for the spare tire, the built-in trunk helped eliminate one more projection from the car. Here was another case where styling changes made some people unhappy, for these developments meant an apparent loss of accessory business in trunk racks, tire covers, and the like, at a time when accessories were very profitable items. But such is the price of progress.

The first sedan to use an extended deck was the 1938 Cadillac 60-Special. This car holds an important place in styling history. It was the first "special" car, designed to introduce new features and to be sold at a higher price, and was followed later by the Ford's Lincoln Continental and other special cars. It was the first General Motors car and the first modern mass-production car without a running board. In addition to disposing of another projection, the elimination of the running board made it possible to widen the basic body pattern to the full tread of the wheels, so that the standard car became one that could hold six passengers. It was the first car that, though a sedan, was styled like a convertible, and was thus a forerunner of the very successful "hardtop," introduced by Buick, Oldsmobile, and Cadillac in 1949. It was well received in the market, and demonstrated the dollars-and-cents value of styling, for consumers were ready to take smaller trade-ins on old cars to acquire it.

The growing importance of styling was symbolized by the appointment of Harley Earl as a vice president of the corporation on September 3, 1940. He was the first stylist to be given such a position, and indeed, I believe, the first designer in any major industry to become a vice president.

During World War II automobile styling ceased, for no new models were produced, and the Styling Staff engaged for a time in military camouflage design. It was at the end of the war, as I have said, that we concluded that the consumer would rank styling first, automatic transmissions second, and high-compression engines third. But in the years immediately following World War II there were few extensive changes in automobile design, for the first aim of all manufacturers was simply to supply the great backlog of demand. However, in these years the long lead built up by General Motors in styling before the war paid off. General Motors had had the first styling staff and for a long time the only one. After the war Ford and Chrysler set up systems of styling, and of integrating styling into production, similar to those first developed at General Motors, and staffed their new departments in part with men who had learned styling under Harley Earl. The sequence of sketches, full-scale drawings, miniature scale models in various sizes, full-scale clay models, and fiberglass reinforced plastic models, which Mr. Earl and the Styling Section had pioneered, now became standard throughout the industry.

The role of styling became dominant in the industry as competitive conditions returned. Until the late 1940s it had been customary to change bodies on a four-year or even five-year cycle, with "face-lifting" changes in between. But as the desirability of new body styles became apparent, a shorter cycle of varying lengths became common.

One of the factors contributing to the increased tempo of change in styling was the experimental car. The first of these, the "Y-job," was built by the Styling Staff and the Buick Division in 1937. The idea of the experimental car was to test new styling and engineering ideas in a complete, new car. After the war we built new experimental cars and exhibited them to the public to test the reaction to the advanced ideas they incorporated. The reactions of the hundreds of thousands of viewers to these so-called "dream cars" showed that the public wanted and was ready to accept more daring steps in styling and engineering.

The Styling Staff also built experimental cars of such advanced design that they were not expected to influence production cars for years to come. Such was the XP-21 Firebird I, the first gas-turbine passenger automobile in the United States, built in co-operation with the Research Laboratories in 1954.

Indeed, the rapid movement in styling in the late forties and fifties sometimes seemed to many people to have become too extreme. New styling features were introduced that were far removed from utility, yet they seemed demonstrably effective in capturing public taste. One of the most striking of these features of the postwar car was the "tail fin," which first appeared on the Cadillac in 1948 and which, though at first it was not easy to sell, has since appeared on almost every major line of cars, in one exaggerated form or another. The story of the tail fin began during the war when an air force friend of Harley Earl invited him to see some new fighter planes. One of them was the P-38, which had twin Allison engines, twin fuselages, and twin tail fins. When Mr. Earl saw it, he asked if he could have some of his designers look at it, and after they received clearance, they were allowed to view the plane. They were just as impressed as Mr. Earl, and a few months later their sketches began to show signs of fins.

One important new development has been a growing emphasis on special types of cars—sports cars, station wagons, hardtops, and other special cars at higher prices. Years of prosperity have made it possible for many families to own two or even three cars, and it is reasonable for the second or third car not to be a standard sedan. For this and other reasons the demand rose also for the small car—thus widening the range of the market at the bottom as well as the top. The growing emphasis on leisure-time activities has led to a greater interest in pleasure cars, as was the case in the early days. As Harley Earl has said: "You can design a car so that every time you get in it, it's a relief—you have a little vacation for a while." Today the Styling Staff designs a variety of "vacations." At the same time the automobile is more than ever the dominant form of basic ground transportation in the United States.

Chapter 16

DISTRIBUTION
AND THE DEALERS

WHENEVER the automobile market shifts from a buyers' to a sellers' or a sellers' to a buyers' market, a turbulence takes place in the industry, which disturbs both producers and dealers, and certain adjustments have to be made to meet the changing conditions. Some of these adjustments are commonplace, but since history never exactly repeats itself, there is always some element of novelty to be met. So it is in the present and so it has been throughout the development of the dealer system of distribution.

When I was chief executive officer of General Motors, I gave a large part of my attention to dealer relations, amounting at times, you might say, almost to a specialization. I did so because the experience of the 1920s, when the modern problems of automobile distribution took shape, taught me that a stable dealer organization is a necessary condition for the progress and stability of an enterprise in this industry.

Contrary to this, the prevailing attitude of the industry in the early twenties was rather that the manufacturer should attend to the product, the prices, the advertising and promotion, and leave the rest of the elements of distribution to the dealer to work out. There were some who minimized the role of the dealer. They assumed that the customer was for the most part sold before he entered a dealer's salesroom, and so neglected to develop a stable dealer organization. The soundness of the individual dealer's position and the complexity of the internal problems of his organization and market were not considered to be the concern of the manufacturer.

From my point of view, the welfare of the more than 13,700 General Motors passenger-car dealers in the United States, with their $2 billion or so of invested capital, must be a major concern of the corporation. The franchise system of distribution makes sense only if you have a group of sound, prosperous dealers as business associates. I have never been interested in business relationships that are not of benefit to all concerned. It is my belief that everyone should hold up his end of the relationship and be rewarded accordingly.

The significance of the dealer in automobile distribution is twofold. First, as in many industries, the dealer makes the direct personal contact with the customer; he makes and closes the deal that sells the car. The producer's contact, on the other hand, is with the dealer, not the customer, except to the extent that the producer speaks to the public as a whole through advertising, automobile shows, and other instrumentalities—and I might add that the product on the streets and highways is a persuasive message to the consumer.

Second, in the automobile industry, the dealer is franchised. What is a franchised dealer? If you imagined a spectrum of the types of retail distribution in the United States, you would find typically at one end the merchant, such as the corner grocer, who sells numerous and often competing products made by various manufacturers, and whose only relationship with any manufacturer is that of a conventional buyer. At the other end of the spectrum is a merchant—for example, a gas-station owner—who is the agent of a single manufacturer, even sometimes a branch or subsidiary of a manufacturer. In this spectrum, the franchised automobile dealer, in his relation to the manufacturer, lies somewhere between the above extremes. Legally he is not the agent of the manufacturer. Yet in his community he is identified with the manufacturer's product. Generally speaking he is assigned an area of sales responsibility for cultivation. However, he is not restricted from selling elsewhere, and the other dealers are free to sell in his area.

The individual franchised dealer, usually a substantial businessman in his local community, meets the customer, often as a neighbor, trades with him, and services the product sold. The personality, acquaintance, and standing of the dealer as a local merchant are basic to the type of franchise distribution which has become the custom in the automobile industry. Our entire sales approach is based upon this system of individually financed merchants, to whom we offer a potential profit opportunity based upon the General Motors franchise.

Both the dealer and the manufacturer in their relationship have special rights and undertake special obligations. They sign a selling agreement that involves conditions; in other words, the relationship of dealer and producer is governed by the franchise. The dealer agrees to provide capital, a place of business, an adequate number of salesmen, mechanics for service, and the like. He is expected to cultivate his area of responsibility, and to stock and sell spare parts, and so on. In return for such franchise obligations, the manufacturer sells almost entirely through the franchised dealer. Dealers as a group obtain the privilege of selling the manufactured, trademarked products and are supported in their sales effort by the general merchandising activities of the manufacturer. The manufacturer makes large investments in tooling for the annual model change and in research and engineering development to ensure that his product is desirable. A special feature of the franchise system is the amount and type of assistance that the manufacturer renders to the automoile dealer. This includes technical help and programs in all phases of the dealer's business, such as sales and service, advertising, business management, and specialized factory-conducted training programs designed to assist in every phase of the dealer's operation.

The automobile is not like the usual product that customers buy "off the shelf" every day. It is a highly complex mechanical product. It represents a large investment for the average purchaser. He expects to operate it, perhaps daily, yet the chances are he possesses little or no mechanical knowledge. He depends on his dealer to service and maintain the product for him.

Therefore the dealer must not only make a substantial investment in facilities and organization for the display and sale of his product —which is practically the sole function of the average retail establishment—but he must also provide facilities and an organization to service the product after it is sold and throughout its useful life. Beyond this, he must be prepared to take in trade, recondition, and sell one or two used cars on the average for each new car sold, since he may need to resell the used car on a trading basis.

Both the manufacturer and the franchised dealer undertake normal and related business risks, the dealer in his investment in selling and service facilities, the manufacturer in his investment in producing facilities, including engineering development and high annual tooling costs. Both depend upon the appeal the manufacturer gives to the product and the ability of the franchised dealer efficiently to sell and service the product.

The achievement of our two goals in distribution—namely, the economic movement of the product, and a stable network of franchised dealers who move the product—has taken much thought and work over many years, for the problems are complicated, they change to some extent with changing circumstances, and the solutions have not always immediately presented themselves. Policies and practices that were satisfactory at one time may not be best suited to later conditions. A "new model," so to speak, in dealer relations may be needed from time to time.

Before 1920 automobile distribution was based in the main upon distributor-wholesalers who subcontracted to dealers in their jurisdiction. But in the course of time, manufacturers, generally speaking, took over the wholesale function for more intensive cultivation, and the franchised dealers maintained the retail function.

The question might arise why the automobile industry adopted this form of distribution. The answer, I think, in part is that automobile manufacturers could not without great difficulty have undertaken to merchandise their own product. When the used car came into the picture in a big way in the 1920s as a trade-in on a new car, the merchandising of automobiles became more a trading proposition than an ordinary selling proposition. Organizing and supervising the necessary thousands of complex trading institutions would have been difficult for the manufacturer; trading is a knack not easy to fit into the conventional type of a managerially controlled scheme of organization. So the retail automobile business grew up with the franchised-dealer type of organization.

Between 1923 and 1929 the leveling of demand for new cars logically resulted in a change of emphasis in the industry from production to distribution. On the sales end that meant a change from easy selling to hard selling. Dealer problems of an entirely new nature began to arise.

To meet this situation I made it a practice throughout the 1920s and early thirties to make personal visits to dealers. I fitted up a private railroad car as an office and in the company of several associates went into almost every city in the United States, visiting from five to ten dealers a day. I would meet them in their own places of business, talk with them across their own desks in their "closing rooms" and ask them for suggestions and criticism concerning their relations with the corporation, the character of the product, the corporation's policies, the trend of consumer demand, their view of the future, and many other things of interest in the business. I made careful notes of all the points that came up, and when I got back home I studied them. I did this because I realized that, irrespective of how efficient our regular organization might be, there is a special value in personal contact, and furthermore, as chief executive officer of the corporation, my interest was primarily in general policies. This time- and effort-consuming approach to the problem was particularly effective under the circumstances existing at that time, when we knew so little about the facts of distribution in the field. Many things that we learned were subsequently reflected in our dealer selling agreements, and communications in particular were put on an established basis through councils and in other ways which at least in part served to meet the same need.

From the field studies that we made, I was able to see the historic change that was under way during the middle and late twenties, that the economic position of the dealers was becoming less satisfactory than it had been, and that our franchises were less in demand. It was clear that something had to be done not only in the interest of our dealers whose businesses were at stake, but in the interest of the enterprise as a whole. We had to distribute cars on a sound and economic basis for all concerned.

I noted the dealers' predicament in the changing conditions in an address I made to the Automobile Editors of American Newspapers on September 28, 1927, in connection with a meeting at our Proving Ground at Milford, Michigan. Speaking of past practices in the industry as a whole, I made this observation:

The sole idea was to make as many cars as the factory could possibly turn out and then the sales department would force the dealers to take and pay for those cars irrespective of the economic justification of so doing—I mean, irrespective of the dealers' ability to properly merchandise such cars. That certainly was wrong and it is just as wrong in other industries as it was in our industry. The quicker merchandise can be moved from the raw material to the ultimate consumer and the minimum amount of merchandise, of whatever it may consist, involved in the "float," so to speak, the more efficient and more stable industry becomes . . . It is absolutely against the policy of General Motors to require dealers to take cars in excess of what they properly should take. Naturally, once in a while in the closing out of a model, our dealers must necessarily help us. They appreciate their responsibility and never object to doing so . . .

This statement of policy in 1927 started a new approach to producer-dealer relations in General Motors, based upon the recognition of the community of interest between the corporation and its dealers and of the interdependence of our interests.

The central and continuing problems of automobile distribution, which first arose in the twenties and thirties, are inherent in the nature of the business. These are, broadly, the penetration of markets, the liquidation of inventories at the end of a model run, dealer economics, and the general difficulty of two-way communication between the manufacturer and its dealers on all of their mutual business affairs.

Our intention, naturally, was to penetrate the market as effectively as possible, and since in the end this had to be carried out by our dealers, it was necessary to have the appropriate number of dealers, each of the appropriate size and in the appropriate location. The difficulty was to determine these locations. In the 1920s we did not know as much as we do now about the automobile market. We began then to make economic studies of the market and its potential in terms of population, income, past performance, business cycle, and the like.

With this kind of information we were able to take up the problem of placing dealers in relation to the market potential. In a community of a few thousand inhabitants, for example, the problem was simple. A single dealer could do everything necessary to penetrate the market, and we and the dealer could judge on the basis of our studies what his goals should be and how well he performed in relation to those goals. But in the larger urban communities, those with a million inhabitants or more, the problem was complicated.

Hence we studied a larger community, first as a whole, to determine its likely potential for any particular line of cars. Then we broke it down on a neighborhood basis to determine the potential of its constituent parts. With that information we were able to place dealers through the territory largely on the basis of neighborhood potential. It was, of course, necessary for the dealers to have the individual capital, plant, overhead, and organization appropriate to the size of the area served.

This strikes me as a rational approach to the problem of distribution. It provides basic advantages for both the dealer and the manufacturer. The dealer, as I have said, is a specialist in his area, and knows its character and inhabitants better than anyone else could. Also, it is often more convenient for a customer to deal with a local merchant from many standpoints, including service. And it provides the manufacturer with a microscopic understanding of his distribution problems. Naturally we expected a dealer to give his first attention to his immediate market and to perform well in it.

The problem of liquidating an old model to make way for a new one—and to keep inventory losses at a minimum—is a permanent feature of the business except in periods when there is a strong sellers' market. This problem first appeared in an important way in the late 1920s. It occurs because the dealers must establish estimates of their requirements three months in advance, based on prospective demand. The corporation takes these estimates into account in establishing its final production schedules. These must be determined months in advance, and if the expected demand is upset by changing conditions, the problem of liquidation of the current model may become abnormal. But normal or abnormal, it is a problem to be met.

In the early twenties the cars the dealers had on hand at the time the new model was announced, had to be liquidated at their own expense. After a good deal of study, we came to the conclusion that it would be only fair for the corporation to share the responsibility for liquidation of the old model. My recollection is that we provided allowances for liquidation at the end of the model year as early as the second half of the 1920s. In 1930 we made it a matter of policy to help the dealer dispose of his excess stock at the end of the model year. For the dealer who had "taken his contract," we granted an allowance on the unsold, new vehicles in stock when new models were announced. The allowance was limited to those cars in excess of 3 per cent of the estimated quantity of new vehicles to be handled by the dealer, as provided for in the selling agreement. The amount of such allowance was determined by General Motors. At times the amount and basis of computation has differed. At present the rebate is 5 per cent of the list price on every new unused car of the model being discontinued in dealers' stock and unsold at the time of the new model announcement.

This policy, I believe, was new in the industry when we began it. It reflected our desire to protect dealers against unreasonable product-depreciation losses and to place the responsibility for reasonable production schedules in the later months of the model year on the management of the divisions. It imposed a penalty on the factory in the form of an automatic assessment if for any reason there was an excess supply of cars in the model year.

A theoretical solution of the annual production and sales cycle, one might think, would be to have no stock in dealers' hands when the new car is announced. But that is neither possible nor desirable for a number of reasons, from both the manufacturer's and the dealer's standpoint. Competitively we must do as much business as can be done in each month of the year. And at the end of the model year the pipelines of distribution must be emptied as the new cars come through. Furthermore, it is often desirable to have some stocks of old cars on hand to do business during the early period of the new model run when the new models are first coming through. For these reasons the problem is a permanent one and all in the day's work.

Although in the 1920s we had made great advances in getting the facts about General Motors' economic position, we did not then have the facts regarding the economic position of our dealers, and so were handicapped in thinking through dealer problems. When a dealer's profit position was failing, we had no way of knowing whether this was due to a new-car problem, a used-car problem, a service problem, a parts problem, or some other problem. Without such facts it was impossible to put any sound distribution policy into effect.

In the Proving Ground address which I mentioned earlier, I made the following observations on this subject:

. . . I want to outline to you what I believe to be a great weakness in the automotive industry today and what General Motors is trying to do to correct that weakness.

I have stated frankly to General Motors dealers, in almost every city in the United States, that I was deeply concerned with the fact that many of them, even those who were carrying on in a reasonably efficient manner, were not making the return on their capital that they should. Right here let me say that so far as General Motors dealers are concerned, from what facts I have—I realize there has been much improvement during the past two or three years, but interested as the management of General Motors must be in every step, from the raw material to the ultimate consumer, and recognizing that this chain of circumstances is no stronger than its weakest link, I feel a great deal of uncertainty as to the operating position of our dealer organization as a whole. I hope that this feeling of uncertainty is unwarranted. I am sure that with a responsibility so great, all elements of uncertainty must be eliminated and that our dealers should know the facts about their operating position as clearly and as scientifically as I have outlined to you we feel that we know the facts about General Motors operating position.

This brings us back to . . . two words—*proper accounting*. Many of our dealers, and the same thing applies to dealers of other organizations, have good accounting systems. Many of them have indifferent ones and I regret to say that too large a percentage of them have practically no accounting system at all. Many of those who have accounting systems, through lack of their being properly developed, are not able to effectively use them. In other words, they are not so developed that they give the dealer the facts about his business; where the leaks are; what he should do to improve his position. As I said before, uncertainty must be eliminated. Uncertainty and efficiency are as far apart as the North Pole is from the South. If I could wave a magic wand over our dealer organization, with the result that every dealer could have a proper accounting system, could know the facts about his business and could intelligently deal with the many details incident to his business in an intelligent manner as a result thereof, I would be willing to pay for that accomplishment an enormous sum and I would be fully justified in doing so. It would be the best investment General Motors ever made.

Accordingly, in 1927 we set up an organization called Motors Accounting Company. We developed a standardized accounting system applicable to all dealers and sent a staff into the field to help install it and to establish an audit system. Later, as dealers became more experienced in the financial end of their business, and under the pressure of depression economies, we modified the reviewing procedure. We developed a sampling system for auditing by which we were able to get a cross-section analysis applicable to the whole setup. To this end the accounting records of a group of approximately 1300 automobile dealers (representing about 10 per cent of dealers or 30 per cent of General Motors unit sales) are still reviewed regularly at General Motors' own expense. In addition, General Motors gets monthly financial statements from 83 per cent of its dealers or 96 per cent of General Motors unit sales. This was a big and expensive effort but it enabled each division of General Motors and the central office to look through the whole distribution system, dealer by dealer and group by group, and determine just where the weaknesses were and what should be done about them. Furthermore, the dealer himself could not only judge his own complicated business intelligently but also compare his operations, item by item, with group averages. Often the soft spots would be discovered in time to make corrections before harm was done.

Soft spots, of course, on occasion had a way of making themselves known. In the late twenties General Motors put up considerable capital to save a couple of strategic dealerships from bankruptcy and suffered a loss of $200,000. One thought leads to another, however, and when we got this one generalized, we realized that our broad purpose should be not only to reduce dealer turnover by stabilizing dealerships but furthermore to assist capable individuals who lacked capital to become the owners of profitable General Motors dealerships. Albert L. Deane, then a vice president of GMAC, and Donaldson Brown worked these thoughts into a practical program. We took action on the idea in June 1929 by setting up Motors Holding Corporation with Mr. Deane as its first president. In 1936 this subsidiary became the Motors Holding Division. The function of this division was to furnish capital to dealerships, and in doing so to assume temporarily the rights and duties of a shareholder in those dealerships. We put $2,500,000 into it to start. When we got past the experimental stage, we realized that this was one of the best ideas we ever had in the distribution field. We also realized that its real value was not in the first idea of salvaging bankruptcies but in the second idea of grubstaking capable men—not only with capital but with management advice and training in sound dealer operations.

Motors Holding developed management techniques for dealers which increased the profit possibilities of dealerships. It found qualified operators, backed them with adequate capital, and enabled them to produce profits sufficient to retire Motors Holding's interest and become independent.

In my time it worked this way, and with some alterations in

financial details it still does: The prospective dealer invested his available funds in the dealership. Motors Holding put up the balance of the capital needed. (At present the dealer usually puts up a minimum of 25 per cent of the total required capital.) When the arrangement was established, the dealer got in addition to his salary a bonus, which was provided by Motors Holding through its relinquishment of a portion of the profit which would otherwise accrue to its investment. This bonus was equivalent to 50 per cent of Motors Holding's earnings above 8 per cent on its investment. Motors Holding retained the voting control of the dealership until all of the Motors Holding investment had been bought out.

Several changes in the bonus arrangements were made in later years. At present the bonus is paid directly by the dealership to the operator and is therefore a direct expense of the dealership corporation. It amounts to 33⅓ per cent of the profits in excess of 15 per cent a year on total invested capital including notes. Originally the dealer was required to apply his entire bonus to buy out Motors Holding's share of the capital stock. Subsequently, it was found that the dealer's personal income taxes did not enable him to carry out this provision and now the dealer need apply only 50 per cent of his bonus to purchase Motors Holding's stock, although he may, of course, apply the entire amount. The result has been that as earnings accumulate the dealer becomes the owner of all the stock in the dealership. As it turned out, the assistance provided by Motors Holding was so highly valued that dealers often resisted purchasing the last shares of Motors Holding's investment.

From its inception through December 31, 1962, Motors Holding in the United States and Canada invested more than $150 million in a total of 1850 dealerships, most of them in the automobile field. Of these dealerships, 1393 have retired Motors Holding's investment, and at the end of 1962, current investments in 457 dealerships totaled nearly $32 million. Of our approximately 565 alumni dealers still operating through 1962, many rank among the outstanding dealers of the United States and Canada. In some instances operators who were qualified in all other respects but lacked the established minimum investment were enabled through the Motors Holding plan to become sole owners of their businesses. Some, starting with very modest investments, became millionaires. And the plan has been profitable to General Motors too.

Motors Holding dealers produce approximately the same results as other General Motors dealers with like potentials. This applies from both a standpoint of sales and of net profits, thus fulfilling one of the original objectives in the conception of the activity.

Of the 1850 investments in dealerships made by Motors Holding in the United States and Canada, it has been necessary to liquidate only 198 because of subnormal operations, 62 during the depression period 1929 through 1935, and 136 since then.

Although Motors Holding dealers' new-car sales have never attained 6 per cent of the total General Motors Corporation sales, they have nevertheless sold since 1929—during the period of Motors Holding's investment—more than three million new cars with a total profit to these dealerships, before bonus, of more than $150 million.

The corporation has authorized successive increases in the funds available for investment in Motors Holding dealerships in the United States and Canada, and in May 1957 the authorized maximum investment was increased to $47,000,000, of which $7,000,000 is now available for financing real estate.

Through its intimate association with dealers in the Motors Holding operation, General Motors has obtained a clearer and more sympathetic knowledge of dealers' problems. Motors Holding has also provided the corporation with a better knowledge of the retail market and consumer preferences. But more important than anything else, it has been useful in the development and maintenance of a strong, well-managed, adequately capitalized dealer body.

General Motors was, I believe, a pioneer among industrial companies in the United States and Canada in making such "character loans" of equity capital to small businessmen and in recognizing that one of the greatest needs of the economy was a source of risk capital for small businesses. Two of General Motors' competitors now operate similar plans, Ford since 1950 and Chrysler since 1954. As Herbert M. Gould, a former general manager of Motors Holding put it: "When your competitors follow you, that's the medal in business."

What the manufacturer and the dealers needed most at the end of the 1920s was a better means of communicating and a sound contractual relationship. We had, of course, zone and regional executives, who were in constant contact with the dealers on day-to-day matters of business. But there were many problems of broad, corporation-wide policy that required closer contact and information leading to some definite co-operative actions. As I have said, the other general officers and I made frequent field visits to the dealers. These visits made clear to us that the dealers appreciated having a direct contact with corporate as well as divisional executives. It was equally clear that something more substantial was needed than these occasional visits. Out of these early field trips, therefore, grew a related idea, that of bringing representative groups of dealers into the conference rooms of General Motors. This idea took shape in the creation in 1934 of an important and unique institution in General Motors, the General Motors Dealer Council.

The Dealer Council was originally a body of forty-eight dealers, divided into four panels of twelve each. It met with a group of corporate executives at the top level of corporation responsibility. We formed the council to hold a continuing series of round-table discussions on distribution policies. Each year for many years I chose a different panel of dealers, representing all car-manufacturing divisions, all sections of the country, and all types of territory and capital commitment. They brought to the council a broad diversification of dealer problems and thinking.

As president of the corporation I was chairman of the council. The vice president in charge of the Distribution Staff and other top officials of General Motors were also members. The first job of the council was the long process of working out the general policies for improved dealer relations. Our meetings dealt with policy and not the administration of policy.

The principal specific work done by the Dealer Council was to hold discussions aimed at the development of policies on which an equitable dealer selling agreement could be based. This selling agreement, when achieved, was to add value to the General Motors franchise, which in recent years has supported a retail business of as much as $18 billion a year.

In a talk on the Dealer Council on September 15, 1937, I reviewed my experience in the meetings of the council, as follows:

The meetings of the various Council Groups during the past three years have been bright spots in my operating experience. I value most highly the personal contacts and the friendships that have developed as a result of same. That alone would justify the plan, from my standpoint. And the opportunity to discuss such interesting problems. It has stimulated our thinking and I am sure has accelerated our progress. I have been particularly impressed with the broad approach to these problems by every member of the Council. I am encouraged by the practically unanimous desire to solve these problems from the standpoint of fundamental soundness rather than from the easier approach of expediency. This is particularly interesting in a period where expediency seems to be the keynote of our national thinking. This point of fundamental approach was particularly impressed upon me at the very first meeting. We were just coming out of the depression. Heavy losses had been sustained by almost every one engaged in business—the dealer body being no exception to the rule. Anxiety with respect to the possibility of future profits, was naturally the dominating subject before the Council. Many suggestions were made, analyzed and subsequently discussed. And it is gratifying that the unanimous opinion was that we should tackle the essential question of profit, not from the standpoint of inflation, but from the standpoint of getting our house in order, finding ways and means of eliminating deductions from the gross that we already had—better efficiency, in other words, rather than passing our inefficiency on to the public in the form of a higher retail price. Subsequent experience has justified that kind of a decision—and it always will, in the final analysis.

As Chairman of the Council, at all our meetings I have tried to impress upon the members, the sincere desire of the Corporation's executives to aggressively tackle any problem likely to result in a more satisfactory relationship, and as rapidly and consistently as possible. Naturally, in a business as large as General Motors, where there are many groups that must be consulted and viewpoints reconciled, progress must necessarily be slow. I have been concerned with the fact that perhaps some of our Council members, and many of our dealers who necessarily cannot be familiar with what we are doing, have felt that we should move more rapidly. It is natural that they should feel that way. It is comparatively easy to lay down a policy in a relatively small number of words, but the application of that policy, in an administrative way, in a country as large as the United States, with a scope of operations such as we conduct, must necessarily be a matter of evolution—it cannot be a matter of revolution—patience is essential. I cannot over-emphasize that point. And superimposed upon these practical difficulties is the still hardest problem of changing the viewpoint of a large organization with respect to any particular way of doing any particular thing. We all know how great is the inertia of the human mind.

The dealer selling agreement was a pioneer work in co-operative business relationships. Its technical details have evolved over the years, and some of them are complex. Some of the important features were designed to meet problems unique in the automobile industry.

The question of cancellation of a selling agreement naturally is a serious matter both for the dealer and for the manufacturer. If the dealer operating in a certain area is not doing the job he should, is not delivering a reasonable amount of the potential business of the area, or for some other reason is inefficient, how should a change be effected? It must be remembered that he usually has a substantial amount of his own capital tied up in the business. He owns used cars. He has parts. He has a showroom and product signs.

In the early days of the industry, the dealer's franchise was just canceled and a new dealer was appointed, and that was that. The problem of liquidating the dealership was left to the dealer. During the 1930s the agreement generally in use in the industry provided for an indefinite term which could be terminated without cause by the manufacturer on ninety days' notice and by the dealer on thirty days' notice. Provision also was made for cancellation by the manufacturer for cause, with, of course, the validity of such cause always subject to test in the courts.

In considering this problem, it must be recognized that the dealer, as I have said before, can sell the assets of the business, but he cannot sell the franchise since he does not own it. Therefore, it seemed desirable to have a definite, liberal policy to protect the dealer from capital losses in case of cancellation, even if the cancellation was due to his inefficiency. We adopted a policy which included the following arrangements: The corporation would take back from the dealer, at the price he had paid, any new cars that he had on hand. The corporation would take back certain product signs and special tools. The corporation would take back the parts that he had on hand, provided they were not for models beyond a certain age. If the dealer had a lease which could not be transferred to another dealer, and so incurred a loss on liquidation, the corporation would participate in the loss. The corporation in effect gave the dealer a check for his unencumbered assets and for a certain amount of liability on the lease.

In 1940 we recognized complaints that on occasion selling agreements of dealers had been canceled just as the best selling season was about to commence. The result was that the outgoing dealer operated his business at low profit or no profit for a substantial period prior to termination of the selling agreement, while the newly appointed dealer undertook his operation at the beginning of the profitable selling season. Therefore we incorporated in our selling agreement a provision to the effect that termination without cause on three months' written notice could be accomplished only by giving the notice in the month of April, May, or June, to be effective in the month of July, August, or September. In 1944 General Motors introduced a selling agreement for a specific period, which provided for expiration at the end of two years following the resumption of production after the war (actually a term of more than three years). Later the term was set at one year. At present each dealer is offered the option of an agreement for one year, five years, or for an indefinite period. All of these agreements permit termination only for cause, although upon expiration of the term there is no obligation to renew.

Another unusual General Motors dealer institution, set up in January 1938, was a Dealer Relations Board. It acted as a review body, and enabled the dealer who had a complaint to appeal directly to the top executives of the corporation. I was the first chairman of this board, which consisted also of three other top executives. Sometimes we would listen to a case all day. After getting a complete report from the dealer and the division, we rendered a decision binding on General Motors. The chief benefit of the board was a preventive one. Divisions made very sure they had a sound case and were observing all the equities in taking action against any dealer, for it was the division itself, as well as the dealer, that came up for executive review.

I would like to indulge in a sentiment and in a certain amount of pride, and tell this story. In 1948, after I had retired as chief executive officer, three General Motors dealers came into my office and said that the dealers as a body wanted to show their appreciation of what I had done in advancing the opportunities of the dealer organization. They said they knew of my interest in cancer research and would like to create a fund to help me in that activity. A year later they came back and handed me a check in the amount of $1,525,000 for the Alfred P. Sloan Foundation, and since then dealers have sent in additional contributions to the fund. This became known as the General Motors Dealer Appreciation Fund for Cancer and Medical Research. I invested this fund mainly in General Motors common stock, and the original fund is now worth more than $8.75 million and earns more than a quarter of a million dollars a year.

Here I shall draw together a few strands of thought and carry them through to contemporary problems. Between 1939 and 1941 General Motors and its dealers enjoyed increasing prosperity. Then came the war and what amounted to a new way of life for us all. No cars were manufactured in the United States during the war period, and stocks of new cars on hand were sold under government regulation. Some dealers liquidated their businesses voluntarily, and many went into various branches of the armed forces. A few took on war-production subcontracts, but for most of those who remained active, the principal business was service and some trade in used cars. The service phase of their operations increased substantially as people came to realize the importance of keeping their cars in condition during the war. To the extent permitted under government regulations, we manufactured functional parts and made them available to dealers. This enabled dealers to render a constructive service in sustaining the automotive transportation system of the United States.

The declaration of war caused a wave of apprehension to pass over the dealer body. Shortly after our entrance into the war, I sent a special message to the dealers outlining certain policy decisions made with a view to maintaining dealer organization and dealer morale. These policies included:

(1) An offer to buy back new cars, parts, and accessories that the dealer elected to return (within certain limits). This was for the protection of a dealer who might be drafted or who for any reason wished to terminate his selling agreement.

(2) Preferential consideration after the war for reappointment if the dealer closed his business on conditions which were mutually agreeable to the dealer and the division.

(3) A special allotment plan for new cars, for two years following resumption of car production, to those dealers who remained in business during the war period.

During the war the number of General Motors dealers in the United States dropped from 17,360 in June 1941 to 13,791 in February 1944, a net reduction of 3569. Most of the decrease was concentrated in smaller communities. Some of the dealers who remained were no longer ideally located with respect to the postwar redistribution of population. There had been a movement from the cities to the suburbs and also a movement from the eastern and central states to the southeast, southwest, and Pacific Coast areas.

In accordance with our long-standing distribution policies, we re-surveyed individual areas. In some cases we found that an area could support more than one dealer. Our recruitment of new deal-ers continued as required until 1956, when a moratorium on addi-tional appointments was declared. This remained in effect until late in 1957. However, due to a decrease of dealerships in metro-politan areas, and to other causes, at the end of 1962 the General Motors passenger-car dealer body in the United States totaled about 13,700, about the same as 1944, despite the growth of the automobile market.

While the number of dealers had decreased, the number of Gen-eral Motors passenger cars in operation had increased from about 11.7 million in 1941 to about 24.6 million in 1958, an increase of 13 million, or 111 per cent. The number of General Motors passen-ger cars in operation continued to increase, and as of 1962 totaled 28.7 million, an increase of 17 million over 1941, or 145 per cent. The average individual dealer's business thereby increased as fol-lows:

In 1941, the peak prewar year, the average General Motors car dealer sold about 107 new vehicles. In 1955 he sold 222 new units, an increase of 107 per cent. In 1962 he sold 269 new units, an in-crease of 151 per cent over 1941.

In 1941 the average number of General Motors vehicles in opera-tion per car dealer was 710. This represented his total service po-tential. By 1958 this potential had grown to 1601 units, an increase of 125 per cent, and by 1962 this potential had increased to 2095, an increase of 195 per cent.[1] Since 1960 the average volume

[1] Today, General Motors passenger-car and truck dealers employ 275,000 mechanics, salesmen, and other personnel compared with 190,000 in 1941. Their facilities under roof, including salesrooms, office space, and parts and service areas, occupy 227 million square feet of space, compared to 117 million prewar. Not only have the facilities of many dealers been made larger but they have been modernized and otherwise improved to handle adequately the increasing mechanical complexity of our postwar cars and trucks.

The great increase in car ownership since the war and the technological advances made in our products—such as automatic transmissions, higher-compression engines, power steering, power brakes, and air-conditioning—put a renewed emphasis on the need for well-trained mechanics. In 1953 we put into operation an important new policy of practical co-operation with our dealers when we established thirty perma-nent Service Training Centers for dealer personnel in service and sales. The training centers, fully equipped and manned by specially trained instructors, have provided mechanics with the latest information on the repairing and servicing of our products. The maximum earning ability of mechanics has been increased and the quality of

of business of dealers has been 2.5 times the 1939–41 average in constant dollars. Their net worth of more than $2 billion is 2.7 times the 1941 figure, again in constant dollars, which shows how the individual General Motors dealer has been growing with the economy and with the corporation.

Immediately after the war, market conditions changed radically. We had to meet the tremendous pent-up demand for cars created by the stoppage of production during the war and the wearing out of existing cars. Material shortages were the limiting factor on production. General Motors recognized that serious problems were in store for the customer, the dealer, and the factory. The customer's problem was to get transportation. Usually he was willing to pay a premium for it, and in many cases he sought preferred delivery. The manufacturer was faced with the problem of allocations to the dealer. The dealer's problem was how to distribute his car allotments.

General Motors had a plan on March 2, 1942, for allocation of cars to dealers. It was known as "The Sloan Plan" because I had promulgated it. It was in operation from October 1945 to October 31, 1947, and proved to be both equitable and satisfactory. It ensured the dealer a fair allocation of cars based on his 1941 performance record, and it reduced to a minimum claims of favoritism in distribution. It gave us a rule for a situation which might otherwise have got out of hand.

During the period of shortages, competitive market conditions were practically nonexistent. Our recommended resale prices were substantially below what buyers were willing to pay, and our dealers always establish their own retail prices. But in the face of such urgent demand, the inevitable result was that a second or "gray" market came into existence. It frequently happened that, when a customer drove out of a dealer's place of business with a new car, he would not get beyond the first stop light before somebody, perhaps a used-car dealer, would drive up and offer to take the car off his hands at a substantial premium over the price he had paid for

---

service has been improved to meet the new conditions. The centers provide training facilities also for sales personnel, and they are used for meeting with dealers. During 1962 more than 187,000 persons were given nearly 2.5 million man-hours of training in various technical subjects at the centers, and approximately 260,000 persons attended meetings on sales and other nontechnical subjects.

it. This was the beginning of some new postwar distribution problems.

One of the most difficult problems was "bootlegging," or the wholesaling of new cars by franchised dealers to used-car lots. This phenomenon can exist both in periods of ample supply and in periods of shortage such as existed after World War II. As the situation actually developed, it was not until the latter part of 1953 that supply began to catch up with demand in some lines of cars. I would like to emphasize "began" because many lines continued in short supply into 1954 and, in the case of Cadillac, into 1957.

Beginning about 1950, certain abuses and bad merchandising practices had begun to flourish. Some had been in existence before the war but had been dormant during the forties. Others represented an outgrowth of the unusual conditions of the early postwar years. Bootlegging, for example, had existed before the war in scattered areas, but now, encouraged by an apparently new legal climate, it returned in epidemic and malignant form.

This new legal climate, as I call it, was established in the late 1940s as a result of interpretations of court decisions later expanded by opinions of the Department of Justice. These legal trends indicated to us that clauses in our selling agreement relating to bootlegging and territorial security might be considered unduly restrictive of the dealer's freedom of action. Both these clauses were reluctantly dropped from the selling agreement in 1949 upon the insistence of legal counsel. We foresaw serious consequences in the dealer setup even though at the time the effect was negligible because dealers were having difficulty getting enough cars to supply their own regular customers.

During the first half of the 1950s the "bootlegging" situation became serious. New models of General Motors cars were in the bootleg market even before there was sufficient production to supply dealers with necessary stocks for display and sales purposes. The corporation urged the dealers not to move cars into the bootleg market. It also submitted to the Department of Justice for consideration a proposed new clause for the selling agreement which would have required dealers to offer cars back to General Motors before disposing of them in bootleg channels. The Attorney General's opinion was to the effect that "the Department of Justice cannot undertake to waive the institution of criminal proceedings with respect to such contractual provisions should we decide to test their legality if they are incorporated in General Motors Corporation selling agreements, since they raise important questions under the anti-trust laws."

Thus blocked in its efforts to contract with dealers for the repurchase of cars which the dealer thought surplus, General Motors next advised dealers that for the balance of the 1955 model year it was "prepared to repurchase, or to arrange for the repurchase by other General Motors dealers in other areas, at the respective prices paid by the original purchasing authorized Distributors or Dealers, any such new and unused passenger cars that might be considered excess supply." The purpose of this was to allow dealers to liquidate through authorized channels any cars believed to be in excess. Only a few dealers took advantage of this offer, either because they had no surplus cars or they preferred to sell to a bootlegger at a small profit—contrary, in my opinion, to their own self-interest from the broad point of view. It was the franchised dealers who supplied and supported the bootlegger, for the latter could not obtain cars except through some franchised dealer. Our efforts continued to be limited to trying to adjust our production schedules to realistic appraisals of the market and the competitive situation.

Our various attempts over the years to curb the practice of bootlegging have been hampered by practical limitations beyond our control. However, there was a sharp decrease in the practice during the second half of the 1950s. We believe in the franchise system of distribution and have sought to provide opportunity that would be reflected in quality dealers, but the franchised dealers as well as the corporation must support the opportunity if it is to last and prosper. The concept of "The GM Quality Dealer Program," founded on the proper placement of dealers based on analysis of territories, goes back to the 1920s when Richard H. Grant, General Motors' great sales executive of a generation ago, and William Holler, another of our top sales executives, first established it. But policies based on this concept may be idealizations. Sound policies are often modified by the impact of outside forces over which one has no control.

Another recurrent practice which for a time adversely affected the dealer's ability to operate as a quality dealer, and which was obviously unfair to the customer, was "price packing." Price packing means adding something to the manufacturer's suggested retail price of the product. This enabled the dealer to offer an apparently excessive allowance for the used car trade-in. A dealer is able to make any allowance whatsoever on the car to be traded in, provided that he is also able to name the price on the new car to be sold. This practice was neither sound nor desirable, and I have often said so in addresses to dealers. However, to condemn the practice did not cause its disappearance, especially where the power to control did not exist. We tried to discourage the pack, but the forces approving the practice were too strong. Eventually we came to the conclusion that only by individual and voluntary action on the part of the dealers could this evil practice be wiped out.

In 1958 Congress enacted legislation requiring the manufacturer to affix a label on the window glass of each new car shipped to a dealer. This label contains detailed information on the various elements making up the manufacturer's suggested retail price. There is every evidence that through this law the evil of price packing of the type I have described has been practically eliminated.

The shift from a sellers' to a buyers' market, accompanied by "blitz" or high-pressure selling, further complicated the market from 1954 through 1958. Perhaps the transition could have been executed more smoothly by all concerned. It may be that the publicly raised hue and cry was of benefit in calling attention to needed adjustments to the new conditions. But in my opinion the responsibility for equitable co-operation between dealers and manufacturers is not for a legislative body to work out. It is a joint responsibility of manufacturers and dealers. We are in a competitive business, and a lost position is difficult and sometimes impossible to regain.

In 1955 General Motors made a study of the new developments, and worked out a new selling agreement, which became effective March 1, 1956. I mention only its highlights: a choice among a five-year, one-year, or continuing agreement (99.2 per cent of the dealers were operating under the five-year term in 1962); a liberalization of the policy of the dealer's right to nominate a qualified person to succeed him upon his death or incapacity; a spelling out of the basis for evaluating dealer sales performance, and a number of changes improving the dealer's economic position under prevailing conditions.

A long-term selling-agreement period, such as five years, even though subject to cancellation on ninety days' notice for nonperformance, must contemplate a freeze of many significant distribu-

tion factors—all normally subject to change—such as shifting population, product potentiality, dealer efficiency, economic trends, and
competition. The effect of such a policy on the efficiency and aggres-
siveness of the dealer organization can only be evaluated by time
and experience.

Among other important changes in General Motors' distribution
policy was the appointment of an outside impartial umpire, a retired United States district court judge in place of the Dealer Relations Board, to hear and determine appeals by dealers from
decisions of the divisions. Another was in the method of electing
the divisional dealers' councils. Dealers are first elected at the zone
level; these dealers then elect representatives who converge at the
regional level and elect a representative from the region, and the
dealers so elected constitute the national council.

The group of dealers comprising the General Motors Council,
now known as the President's Dealer Advisory Council, has always
been appointed by General Motors rather than elected. We have
felt that this method, because of the particular setup of General
Motors—made up as it is of five car divisions and one truck division
—would require quite a complicated arrangement if the council of
dealers was to be on an elected basis. Membership on the various
groups of this council reflects sizes of dealerships, sizes of dealers'
communities, and geographical location, as well as numbers in each
division.

Much has been done, and much remains to be done. Problems
exist which, if allowed to continue unsolved, could well mean the
end of the franchise system as we know it. But what are the alternatives? There are only two that I know of: either manufacturer-
owned, manager-operated dealerships, or the selling of cars by
anyone and everyone, as cigarettes are sold—with the manufacturer
maintaining a system of service agencies. I look askance at either
of these changes. I believe that the franchise system, which has
long prevailed in the automobile industry, is the best one for manufacturers, dealers, and consumers.

Chapter 17

GMAC

A STRANGER to the history of the automobile business might wonder how it happens that General Motors owns one of the most important financial institutions in the United States, through which the corporation is engaged in consumer financing.

First as to the fact. General Motors subsidiary, the General Motors Acceptance Corporation, in the past few years has extended 16 to 18 per cent of the estimated credit given in connection with car sales in the United States. GMAC seeks business only from General Motors dealers and is in competition with banks, other sales-finance companies, credit unions, and local lending institutions. I say "in competition" because it is not a closed business; the General Motors dealer is free to use any finance service that he chooses and his retail customers may do likewise. GMAC's total annual business currently comes to about $4 billion in retail credit and about $9 billion in wholesale credit extended to dealers to finance purchases from General Motors.

We got into this business over forty years ago when the need for financing the distribution of automobiles first arose. Mass production brought with it the need for a broad approach to consumer financing, which the banks did not then take kindly to. They neglected—I might say they declined—to meet the need; and so some other means had to be found if the auto industry was to sell cars in large numbers. When GMAC was formed in 1919, facilities for consumer credit on a national basis did not exist. Merchants as far back as I can remember—and before that, I am told—granted time-payment loans for houses, furniture, sewing machines, pianos, and other articles too expensive for most people to buy for cash; and I suppose that banks must have lent to selected individuals some money that went for that purpose.

The idea of consumer finance, therefore, was not new in principle. I understand that the Morris Plan banks began financing some automobile purchases around 1910 and that the practice grew from then on. But the application of consumer finance to the automobile in a routine way was still new in 1915 when my friend John N. Willys, then president of the Willys-Overland Company—one of the most successful motorcar manufacturers at that time—persuaded me to become a director of Guaranty Securities Company, which proposed to finance the sale of Willys and other cars. This was one of the first automobile financing institutions, if it was not actually the first, to be formed to fill the vacuum created by the absence of normal credit facilities. It was also my first experience with the installment plan of purchase. At the time I did not have a direct interest in it since I was then still with Hyatt and, of course, not making or selling motorcars. John J. Raskob, as chairman of General Motors' Finance Committee, was instrumental in starting GMAC. From where I was then on the Executive Committee, I supported the idea.

The public announcement of the formation of GMAC was made with the publication of a letter dated March 15, 1919, from Mr. Durant to J. Amory Haskell, GMAC's first president. Mr. Durant said in part:

The magnitude of the business has presented new problems in financing which the present banking facilities seem not to be elastic enough to overcome.

The constantly increasing demands for our products, particularly the passenger cars and commercial vehicles, has correspondingly increased the difficulty of our dealers in commanding at the seasons of the year when most needed the banking accommodation necessary properly to handle the volume of business which their ability as salesmen and the merit of our product as merchandise has developed.

This fact leads us to the conclusion that the General Motors Corporation should lend its help to solve these problems. Hence the creation of the General Motors Acceptance Corporation; and the function of that Company will be to supplement the local sources of accommodation to such extent as may be necessary to permit the fullest development of our dealers' business.

A few words about the difference between the banking and the manufacturing mentalities at that time. The bankers, I suppose, must have had their minds on Barney Oldfield and Sunday outings in landaus along the boulevards then in existence; that is, they thought of the automobile as a sport and a pleasure, and not as the greatest revolution in transportation since the railway. They believed that the extension of consumer credit to the average man was too great a risk. Furthermore, they had a moral objection to financing a luxury, believing apparently that whatever fostered consumption must discourage thrift. Consequently, automobiles were sold to consumers mainly for cash.

Distributors and dealers, too, had to develop their own sources of financing, largely out of their own capital supplemented with customers' cash deposits and bank credit. This phase of automobile credit worked all right in the early days when distributors had wide territorial contracts and were able to make their sales for cash. It was not too difficult for them to cope with their financial requirements. As the business grew, however, and manufacturers continued to require cash on delivery, dealers simply did not have the funds to finance inventories, not to mention retail installment sales.

Thus in 1915, about eight years before the automobile industry was to become the largest American business in volume of sales, its distribution system had no routine retail credit structure outside of normal banking channels, and those channels were pretty narrow. The automobile industry had to develop this credit structure itself.

Today a very high proportion of dealers' stocks are financed, and about two thirds of all new and used automobiles in the United States are bought at retail on the installment plan. The anxieties of those who doubted the soundness of consumer credit have proved groundless.

In the case of GMAC, the retail loss ratio on installment paper from 1919 to 1929 was approximately one third of 1 per cent of the retail volume purchased. I speak of the GMAC ratio and not of any losses by dealers after a car had been repossessed. In 1930 this ratio rose to one half of 1 per cent; in 1931 to six tenths of 1 per cent, and in 1932 to five sixths of 1 per cent. By 1933 the loss ratio was equivalent to approximately one fifth of 1 per cent. Thus, in the worst of the depression the rate of loss never reached 1 per cent of volume—a remarkable indication of the safety of the system and the integrity of the purchasers.

When we first undertook the systematic financing of the distribution and sale of General Motors' products, we had no notion that this system of credit would be subjected to a test as severe as the depression or that it could survive such a test so well. We were convinced, however, that if we exercised ordinary care in the risks assumed, financing wholesale and retail distribution and sale of our products would promote a sound demand for automobiles which lack of credit was restricting.

GMAC today operates directly or through subsidiaries in the United States and Canada and in a number of overseas countries. GMAC was started and still operates specifically to meet the credit needs of General Motors dealers and distributors, and it has always limited its activities to financing the distribution and sale of new and used products by those dealers.

GMAC provides financing plans for both wholesale and retail transactions. Its wholesale plans provide a service for General Motors dealers whereby they may stock General Motors products under trust receipts or other security documents. The dealer obtains title to the product upon payment of the corresponding obligation and the item may then be sold at retail. Should he fail to pay his obligation upon demand, or to comply with other agreed-upon terms and conditions, GMAC has the right to take back the product.

From 1919 to 1963 GMAC financed for distributors and dealers, as distinguished from consumers, over 43 million new cars, in addition to other products of the corporation. In the same period GMAC financed a total of over 46 million cars for consumers, 21 million new and 25 million used.

Its method in retail financing, known as "the GMAC Time Payment Plan," is to buy approved, retail time-sales contracts from General Motors dealers, after they have been concluded between the dealer and the retail purchaser. GMAC is not, however, obligated to buy every contract a dealer submits to it. Nor is the dealer required to offer the contract to GMAC for purchase. For both parties the transaction is voluntary. GMAC has the right to refuse risks it does not wish to assume. The dealer may place his paper elsewhere if he thinks that is to his advantage. If the dealer does submit the contract to GMAC, and all credit factors prove satisfactory, GMAC purchases the obligation. GMAC, and not the dealer, then undertakes collection of all payments from the customer.

Outside the United States, local laws and other circumstances may dictate that the technical forms of GMAC financing plans and operations differ somewhat from those in this country. With this exception, the U.S. pattern with respect to retail and wholesale plans is followed closely in other parts of the world. It is our experience that prudent financing of wholesale and retail sale and distribution of our products works as well abroad as it does in the United States. On the record, the average consumer at home and abroad is a remarkably good business risk in the field of automobile financing.

GMAC's basic policies were formulated and refined between 1919 and 1925. In the beginning we had two primary motives, to establish the validity of the system, and to crusade for reasonable rates for the customer. We were interested in making a paying business out of it, and we were also interested in the long-term good will of our customers, and in protecting them from high rates.

The risks in consumer financing centered around default, repossession, and the used-car market. Hence the importance of the down payment and the length of time over which repayment was to take place, the ability of the purchaser to make payment, and the need in the credit structure of the repossessed car's being worth the balance due. To the dealer, as an endorser of the purchaser's obligation, it was most important that there be collateral which, if necessary, could be repossessed and resold at a fair price. In the absence of such collateral, the financial burden on the dealer was very heavy.

We were encouraged by a study of consumer credit along these lines made over a period of years under our sponsorship by the eminent economist Professor E. R. A. Seligman. His two-volume work, *The Economics of Instalment Selling*, the culmination of this study, published in 1927, became a standard work in the field. It had a strong influence, I believe, in bringing about an acceptance of installment selling among bankers, businessmen, and the public.

Professor Seligman drew some conclusions that are accepted as axiomatic today but then were novel. Installment credit, he said, not only strengthens the motive to save but increases the individual's ability to do so. It not only advances the time of demand but by interaction with the economy actually increases purchasing power. It both stabilizes and increases production, so the cost of financing is outweighed by the advantages gained.

One early question we had to answer was how much of the financial burden the dealer should carry. We had little experience by which to gauge the magnitude of the risk which dealers would actually assume under their unrestricted endorsement of the purchaser's obligation. In addition to the risk of resale loss on repossessed collateral, there was also the hazard that the collateral, the car itself, might disappear through conversion by the purchaser or confiscation by the government, or become worthless through total or partial collision loss.

In 1925, as a result of a thorough study by A. L. Deane, then a vice president of GMAC, a modification was adopted which limited the risk on the part of the dealer. Under this revised plan, GMAC agreed to absorb any losses on retail transactions if the collateral could not be returned to the dealer in reasonable condition within ninety days after the first default of the customer. Further, it provided that a certain percentage of the GMAC finance charge would be placed to the credit of the dealer to establish a reserve fund against which any losses on the sale of repossessions could be offset. Thus, to a large extent, the profits of the dealer on all sales were freed from the hazard of being reduced by credit-sale losses.

Insurance protection against fire, theft, and collision hazards was made available at the same time by the organization of another General Motors subsidiary, General Exchange Insurance Corporation. This company offered insurance to customers who requested it, against physical damage to the car (not against such risks as public liability and property damage). This was important to the dealer since companies insuring automobiles were, in those days, highly selective and the purchaser could not always get the insurance that was often a prerequisite to financing. The idea of finance companies offering physical-damage insurance became broadly accepted, with some modifications, as a standard pattern for finance-company relations with dealers. Today the company that offers the physical-damage insurance to installment purchasers is Motors Insurance Corporation, a subsidiary of GMAC.

At that time some finance companies relieved the dealer from responsibility for the unpaid balance of the retail credit transaction when the customer defaulted. This "nonrecourse" system had the disadvantage of reducing the dealer's interest in checking the soundness of the original credit. Also, it was more expensive to operate for a number of obvious reasons. Not the least of these was the fact that the finance company was not in a position to sell repossessions at as good prices as a franchised dealer. The purchaser eventually paid for the additional cost involved through a higher finance charge.

At first GMAC chose not to follow the so-called nonrecourse route. There were a number of reasons for this. Among them was this matter of cost to the consumer. GMAC felt it undesirable to relieve the dealer of all obligation on retail installment transactions. It felt that its plan, with its guaranty of the return of the collateral, would provide the necessary protection to the dealer at the lowest cost to the purchaser. Experience has proved this to be correct. However, because of competitive pressure, GMAC added a nonrecourse plan to its service.

The finance charge itself is an important element of the cost of a car. Throughout the years, both General Motors and GMAC have emphasized this fact. GMAC has pointed out that additional and unnecessary costs are incurred by the purchaser if the repayment time is unnecessarily long and the down payment lower than is justified. GMAC has campaigned against excessive financing charges—I think it fair to say it took the leadership in this matter. The man whose name is associated with GMAC more than anyone else's is John J. Schumann, Jr., who joined GMAC in 1919 and was its president for twenty-five years, from 1929 to 1954. He was a strong leader for sound practices and he put the stamp of his personality on the organization. In uncompromising terms he advanced policies and practices that were guided by the time-tested formula of honesty and square dealing.

In General Motors' annual report for 1937, in support of Mr. Schumann's policies, I wrote:

. . . charges to consumers in excess of an equitable minimum are not consistent with the policy of the Corporation in providing services to the end that the public may be adequately served by its dealers, at the lowest sound price.

History took some interesting turns in this connection. In 1935 GMAC announced the so-called "6% Plan." This told the public that they could get financing for 6 per cent per annum on the initial unpaid balance—the conventional form of computing finance charges and therefore a comparative basis for measuring the charges of competing finance companies. The actual rate on the money advanced, calculated on a true interest basis, was of course higher; but GMAC followed the convention and advertised it. GMAC believed that the "6% Plan" gave the customer a convenient, publicly known yardstick for measuring his actual finance charges. Competition did not like the GMAC "6% Plan." There were complaints to the Federal Trade Commission that this was an "unfair trade practice" which misled the public into believing that the stated finance charge was a simple interest rate. I thought it was made perfectly clear when we said in the advertising that the "6%" was a multiplier (i.e., not an interest rate), but the commission ruled that GMAC must discontinue using the term "6%"—in my opinion, to the advantage of high-rate finance companies and to the disadvantage of the consumer.

In 1938 the government attacked General Motors and GMAC, charging that General Motors dealers were required to use GMAC's financing service. General Motors denied that it had made such a requirement, and urged that our interest was confined to protecting the customer and to persuading our dealers to follow our policy of low customer rates.

The government, however, commenced criminal proceedings in South Bend, Indiana, against General Motors Corporation, General Motors Acceptance Corporation, two subsidiary companies, and eighteen executives. The trial was held in the fall of 1939 and terminated in an unusual and apparently inconsistent verdict acquitting all the personal executive defendants and finding the four corporate defendants guilty. Thereafter, the government commenced a civil action against General Motors and GMAC and the same two subsidiary corporations, based on the same charge that General Motors dealers were required to accept GMAC's financing services. In 1952, after a long contest with the Antitrust Division of the Department of Justice, we entered into a consent decree which set ground rules for the relations of General Motors and GMAC with the dealers. We have operated satisfactorily under these rules. Under them GMAC still conducts its business independently in competition with other financing organizations.

Toward the end of 1955, with a number of General Motors executives, I was requested to appear in Washington at a hearing conducted by the Senate Subcommittee on Antitrust and Monopoly. During this hearing, which was largely related to the issue of "bigness," the position of GMAC was discussed at some length. Some felt that GMAC should be disposed of by General Motors. I was interested in the conclusions in the report of the staff of the subcommittee, which state that General Motors has had a competitive advantage over other manufacturers of cars because it has owned a sales-finance company, and that it should be forced to divest itself of this activity.

But why? Plenty of money is available to other sellers of cars. The advantage GMAC offers to General Motors is a sympathetic relationship, equitable to the consumer. And I am glad to say that, in providing an economical service to consumers and dealers, it has built a profitable business for General Motors.

Many others in more or less similar types of industry recognize the value of a sales-finance subsidiary—for example, General Electric Company with its General Electric Credit Corporation, and International Harvester Company with its International Harvester Credit Corporation. The suggestion that General Motors or any other company should be deprived of a sales and distribution tool operated in the interest of the consumer strikes me as very unusual in our scheme of things. To me it would seem that it can stem only from those elements which attacked, for their own gain, the earlier farsighted and public-minded activities of GMAC and the policy that the public should be treated fairly with respect to service and the cost of such service.

I subscribe to the simple truth expressed by Charles G. Stradella, then president of GMAC, to the subcommittee in 1955. He said:

In its association with General Motors Corp., GMAC may have advantages. In all probability, there are dealers who are influenced by the assurance of continuity of service, community of interest, fair treatment, et cetera, which go with the association. Lenders [to GMAC] are influenced by the assurance of adequate capitalization, sound management and conservative financial policies and practices. On the other hand, unless these advantages were supported by the record of GMAC and its aggressive pursuance of sound practices, the association would do it little good in the eyes of the parties concerned.

GMAC helped to bring consumer financing into being in the early days. It has had an influence on keeping the terms of down payments and time span on a reasonably conservative basis. Its disciplinary influence in the direction of reasonable rates to the customer is gradually being taken over by legislation; more than half the states now set maximum rates by state law. I believe the time is not far off when all the states will have rate legislation. In my personal opinion, this is the right procedure provided the states set reasonably low rate ceilings in the consumer's interest.

While legislation may be desirable to control effectively the maximum charge which the public must pay for the privilege of installment credit, I have never felt that other conditions of the transaction between the dealer and the purchaser, such as down payment and length of time, should be regulated, except in the case of national emergency. This does not mean that I have not been aware, along with others, of the dangers of overexpansion of consumer credit. The record is clear that GMAC has been continually interested in discouraging unduly small down payments and in keeping the length of term within reasonable limits. I think I might add that conservative financing is essential to the health of the automobile industry. The man who pays too little down and takes too long to pay will have no equity with which to come back soon for a new car.

In late 1955 considerable concern was expressed in many quarters that consumer credit might have been overexpanded and that down-payment and term control might have become too loose. In my opinion the facts did not warrant such conclusions. There was agitation for legislation to control consumer credit in order to check inflation. In his economic report of January 1956 the President of the United States raised the question whether permanent authority for standby control of consumer credit by some governmental agency would be a useful adjunct to other stabilizing measures. The study of this question was assigned by the President through the Council of Economic Advisers to the board of governors of the Federal Reserve System. We, with many others, responded to the questionnaires issued during the course of the study and stated the reasons for our belief that permanent standby controls, to be operated by a government agency, were unnecessary; that generally the control of consumer credit can safely be left in the hands of consumers and lenders until Congress identifies specific circumstances which dictate otherwise, or a national emergency calls for presidential action. A statement of the Federal Reserve Board released in 1957 found, among other things, that "fluctuations in consumer installment credit have been generally within limits that

could be tolerated in a rapidly growing and dynamic economy";
that "a special peacetime authority to regulate consumer instalment credit is not now advisable," and that "the broad public interest is better served if potentially unstabilizing credit developments
are restrained by the use of general monetary measures and the
application of sound public and private fiscal policies." I agree with
these ideas.

So far as GMAC is concerned, I would say in brief that it offers
a service related to the product and in the interest of the consumer.
The advantages to the customer, the dealer, and the corporation
seem obvious to me.

Chapter 18

THE CORPORATION OVERSEAS

OUTSIDE the United States and Canada, the free world absorbed more than seven and a half million cars and trucks in 1962 and over eight million in 1963. General Motors has a substantial position in this overseas market, totaling 855,000 vehicles in 1962, and an estimated 1,100,000 in 1963. Our Overseas Operations Division is a large international organization today with assets of over $1.3 billion and about 135,000 employees. This division is responsible for manufacturing, assembling, or warehousing activities in twenty-two foreign countries, for the export of our products from the United States and Canada, and for distributing and servicing General Motors' products in every country in the free world except the United States and Canada—about 150 countries. The 1963 sales of the division are an estimated $2.3 billion.

Looking back on the rapid growth of this division during the past four decades, one might regard our progress overseas as a kind of natural and inevitable extension of our progress in this country. In reality, there was nothing at all inevitable about it. I have reviewed a number of documents dealing with the formulation in past years of an overseas policy in General Motors. The documents have revived in my mind the long and complex history of that policy, and they have also reminded me of the difficult decisions on which our progress turned. For the overseas market is no mere extension of the United States market. In building up our Overseas Operations Division, we were obliged, almost at the outset, to confront some large, basic questions: We had to decide whether, and to what extent, there was a market abroad for the American car—and if so, which

American car offered the best growth prospects. We had to determine whether we wanted to be exporters or overseas producers. When it became clear that we had to engage in some production abroad, the next question was whether to build up our own companies or to buy and develop existing ones. We had to devise some means of living with restrictive regulations and duties. We had to work out a special form of organization that would be suitable overseas. All of these problems were considered fully within the corporation for a period of several years in the 1920s when the basic policies were established.

Today, General Motors participates in the overseas market in two ways: as an exporter of American cars and trucks, and as a producer abroad of smaller foreign vehicles. In 1962, for example, about 59,000 cars and trucks were exported from the United States and Canada in what are called SUP's, or Single-Unit Packs. This means that the vehicles were shipped fully assembled, and could be made ready for the road with only minor adjustments. Another 46,000 were sent abroad as CKD's, that is, Completely Knocked Down, and they had to be put together at one of ten General Motors assembly plants abroad. (Ordinarily, CKD shipments do not include certain parts—upholstery and tires, for example—which can be supplied locally.) Altogether, over 105,000 General Motors cars and trucks were exported from the United States and Canada; these were all of makes and models available in the United States, and they represented all of the corporation's automotive divisions.

In addition, in 1962 about 750,000 vehicles were designed and manufactured abroad, and an estimated one million in 1963. The gain in 1963 reflects the introduction of a new small car by Opel. The three principal General Motors overseas car-manufacturing subsidiaries are Adam Opel A.G., in Germany, Vauxhall Motors, Ltd., in England, and General Motors-Holden's Pty. Ltd., in Australia. Each of these companies manufactures relatively small (by American standards) cars, a type which predominates almost everywhere in the overseas market. The three companies are entirely owned by General Motors and all three now have a substantial export business of their own and ship vehicles to countries all over the world. In recent years manufacturing plants have been established in Brazil, where 19,000 trucks and commercial vehicles were produced in 1962, and in Argentina, where production of complete engines and stampings was recently started.

The corporation's overseas business hinges largely on our overseas production facilities. In 1962 about 88 per cent of all General Motors vehicles sold abroad were produced abroad. This proportion has been rising, and is likely to increase in the years immediately ahead, for major expansion programs have recently been completed by our overseas producers. The corporation's exports from the United States and Canada, on the other hand, are no larger than they were in the 1930s, and are actually smaller than they were in the late 1920s. (In 1928, the peak year for exports, the corporation shipped almost 290,000 vehicles abroad from the United States and Canada.)

It is easy for Americans to forget how undeveloped this market still is. Its potentialities appear to be almost limitless. In large areas of the world, the motor age is only now dawning. Vast areas are still not serviced by good roads. Even the industrial nations of Western Europe lag far behind the United States in their use of motor vehicles; the countries in the European Common Market, taken together, have about one vehicle for every nine persons, compared with one for every three persons in this country. General Motors now sells as many vehicles abroad as it sold in the United States as late as 1926.

In our early gropings toward the development of a policy for overseas business, we were soon made acutely aware of the problems engendered by economic nationalism abroad. From the earliest days of the automobile industry, dollar-poor nations abroad imposed high tariffs and severe quotas upon the import of American cars (and other American products). This nationalism has led many foreign nations to press for production at home, even when the home market appeared too small to sustain an efficient, integrated automobile industry.

In 1920 the entire overseas market absorbed about 420,000 cars and trucks. About half of these were sold in four industrial nations of Western Europe: Great Britain, France, Germany, and Italy. While this Western European market was the richest, it was also the most difficult to penetrate; for these four countries as a group produced about three quarters of the vehicles they absorbed, and they were determined to exclude effective American competition. The other half of the overseas market consisted of relatively undeveloped nations scattered over the face of the globe. In this "second market," American producers generally had free access.

Although we dealt with each country as a separate proposition, a pattern of sorts began to emerge in our overseas operations during the 1920s. We gradually perceived that two main kinds of marketing situations predominated abroad. The first of these situations was largely confined to Western Europe. Superficially, our export business to the Continent appeared to be thriving. But it became increasingly clear that, in the long run, our European export and distribution systems were threatened by economic nationalism. We continued to press our export business there as best we could, and we backed up this position by building assembly plants in several European countries. The assembly plants made it possible for us to identify ourselves more closely with the local economies by utilizing local management and labor. Moreover, as we gained experience with local supply conditions, we made increasing use of local sources for such items as tires, glass, upholstery, and the like. In other words, we could ship unassembled cars from the United States without these items, and purchase and install them locally if the economics justified. This had another advantage, compared with exporting complete cars, in that it resulted in lower duty payments. (Today, American automobiles are assembled by General Motors in Belgium, Denmark, and Switzerland.) But the conviction grew that our future in Europe lay in producing cars there. The case for European production was stated vigorously and insistently by James D. Mooney, who was head of our Export Companies. However, the Executive Committee of the corporation, of which I was chairman, remained doubtful about the wisdom of our becoming producers abroad until close to the end of the 1920s.

A different kind of marketing situation prevailed in large areas of the world outside of Europe—areas which were not heavily industrialized. No manufacturing operations would be feasible in these areas for many years. Accordingly, our efforts there had to be primarily in exports, with both SUP and CKD shipments playing a role. Our assembly operations outside of Europe today are in the Republic of South Africa, Peru, Mexico, Venezuela, Australia, New Zealand, and Uruguay.

Though our unit sales overseas have grown more than eight times since 1925, I think it is fair to state that the character of the operations and our basic overseas marketing strategy were both established in the twenties.

Our first thoughts about securing a European production base concerned the Citroën Company in France. Negotiations for the acquisition of a half-interest in Citroën consumed several weeks during the summer and early fall of 1919. In that year, as mentioned earlier, Mr. Durant sent a group of General Motors executives abroad to make a study of the European automobile industry, and it was this group, consisting of Mr. Haskell as chairman, Mr. Kettering, Mr. Mott, Mr. Chrysler, Mr. Champion, and myself, that did the actual negotiating. André Citroën was an aggressive, imaginative businessman, and as it happened he was interested in selling his company. At the end of our stay in France we were still uncertain about the wisdom of acquiring the property. I recall that, the night before we were due to sail back, we sat up until early in the morning in a room in the Hotel Crillon, arguing at great length about the issue. In a general way, we were for the acquisition, but there were some specific difficulties. For one thing, the French government did not like the idea of American interests taking over an enterprise that had contributed importantly to the war effort. For another, the production facilities did not appeal to us, and it was clear that if we undertook to run Citroën, an investment running far beyond the initial cost would be required. Furthermore, the company's management then was not entirely adequate. At one point that evening, we discussed a proposal that either Mr. Chrysler or myself move to France and run the company. I was personally not interested in this proposition, and I argued that, in general, our own management at home was not strong enough to supply the top men that would be needed to operate Citroën.

I sometimes wonder just how different the history of the industry would have been if either Mr. Chrysler or I had offered to operate Citroën for General Motors. In those days when the industry was new and expanding explosively, its future was shaped by a small number of individuals who took leading positions; as often as not, the capital went to these men rather than the men to the capital. At any rate, a few hours before we were due to sail, we decided not to buy Citroën. The company was later taken over by the Michelin Company, which did very well with it. General Motors never has established an automobile-producing company in France; somehow, the time and circumstances have never seemed quite right. However, we do have a large Frigidaire operation in France, and we are an important manufacturer there of spark plugs and some other components for the automobile industry.

Our next effort to secure a manufacturing position abroad was made in England. The future of American cars in the British market looked poor in the early 1920s. The so-called McKenna duties raised a formidable tariff barrier to all foreign vehicles. In addition, motor-car license fees were assessed per unit of horsepower. The formula for determining horsepower greatly favored a small-bore, long-stroke, high-speed engine, and penalized the American engine, the bore of which was nearly equal to the stroke. And since insurance costs were generally related to the license fees, the owner of an American car was doubly penalized. Altogether, the fees, insurance, and garage charges on a Chevrolet touring car in England in 1925 came to one pound sterling a week (about $250 a year)— all this before normal operating costs. By contrast, the owner of an English-made Austin had fixed charges of perhaps eleven shillings a week (about $138 a year), and his first cost was lower too.

While the export of American cars to England was inhibited by these circumstances, British manufacturers faced some difficulties of their own. By the mid-twenties, a large number of British producers had come into the automobile industry, but their combined volume amounted to only about 160,000 cars and trucks, split up into a large number of designs and price levels. The British producers therefore lacked many of the economies associated with American mass-production techniques, and their prices were chronically depressed. In gaining a manufacturing base, then, we had to think of the long-term prospects; there was no hope of large immediate gains.

Our first efforts were directed to acquiring the Austin Company. It produced nearly 12,000 cars in 1924, which in England at that time was fairly substantial production. Mr. Mooney, then vice president in charge of the General Motors Export Companies (now the Overseas Operations Division), discussed the prospects of acquiring Austin with me and with others in the corporation several times during 1924–25. We saw that Austin had managed to build up its volume and profits even when the protection of the McKenna duties was temporarily suspended. (They were removed on August 1, 1924, then re-established on July 1, 1925.) Mr. Mooney inspected the Austin properties in the spring of 1925, and wrote a report recommending that we buy them. In July a committee went to England to look into the question further. It included Fred Fisher, Donaldson Brown, John Pratt, and of course Mr. Mooney. In August the committee sent me the following cable:

Committee agrees unanimously English Company will be of advantage to General Motors Export Company. STOP. Think we can buy all certificates of common stock Austin million pounds sterling leaving outstanding million six hundred thousand pounds cumulative preferred stock requiring 130,000 pound[s] sterling 3,000 [or 133,000] pounds sterling dividend [total in dollars: $5,495,050]. Think we can earn at least 20% on our investment in addition to protection and increased earnings on our American Manufacturers. STOP. Conservative estimate net assets after deduction liability two million pounds sterling plus 600 thousand pounds sterling goodwill [total: $12,610,000]. STOP. Are we authorized to close in the event of unanimous agreement among ourselves.

On the same day I cabled this answer:

Finance Committee stated meeting June 18th would approve any recommendation Executive Committee. STOP. Assuming your Committee unanimously agree without reservation desirability purchase and fairness price we satisfied go ahead and authorize you do so. STOP. Impossible we here pass any judgment propriety of purchase or amount proposed pay. STOP. When deal actually made kindly cable so I can make suitable announcement. STOP. Conditions here continue very satisfactory, all well, regards.

The deal never was consummated. I will not recapitulate here all the obstacles which arose in the course of negotiations, except to say that the principal disagreement concerned the manner in which Austin valued its assets. On September 11 Mr. Mooney cabled me that our offer had been withdrawn.

As I recall the incident, I was actually relieved to hear this news. For it seemed to me that Austin had largely the same disadvantages that had bothered me about Citroën six years earlier; its physical plant then was in poor condition and its management was weak. And I still had some doubts whether our own management was strong enough to make up for Austin's deficiencies; indeed, the continued dilution of our management strength as we expanded overseas and at home was a problem all during the 1920s.

The reader may wonder why, in these circumstances, I had ever authorized our team in England to close the Austin deal in the first place. The answer, essentially, is that I always tried to run General Motors by a policy of conciliation rather than coercion; and when a majority was opposed to my thinking, I was often disposed to give way. I might add that the top officers of General Motors who were involved in this situation were men of unusual talents and strong convictions, and as president I felt I should respect their judgments. But notice, in my cable to our group in England, that I placed the responsibility for the deal squarely on their shoulders. They would have to validate it.

Soon after the Austin deal fell through, we entered into negotiations to purchase Vauxhall Motors, Ltd., a much smaller concern in England. This acquisition in the latter part of 1925 was a much less controversial matter in General Motors. Vauxhall manufactured a relatively high-priced car, roughly comparable in size to our Buick, and had an annual volume of only about 1500 units. It was in no sense a substitute for Austin; indeed, I looked on it only as a kind of experiment in overseas manufacturing. The experiment seemed appealing, however; and the investment required of us was only $2,575,291.

Vauxhall lost money in the first few years after we took it over, and it gradually became clear to us that we would have to develop a smaller car if we hoped to capture a much larger share of the British market. Mr. Mooney was eager to begin this development as rapidly as possible. He also saw Vauxhall as a precedent for expansion of our production operations in other countries. My own feelings about the future of our overseas operations were much less clear than his at this time, and in general I took the line in the next few years that we should move slowly and cautiously until we had worked out a clear policy for overseas operations.

The peculiar fact is that, although we had made the gestures I have described toward producing abroad, and had taken on Vauxhall, the Executive Committee had not yet crystallized an overseas policy. The decisive debate on this subject in the corporation began in 1928. In January 1928, while I was still concerned with keeping our position flexible, I offered to the Executive Committee a preliminary formulation as follows:

THAT recognizing the desirability of employing additional capital for the purpose of increasing the Corporation's profits and developing its business, the Executive Committee will consider favorably, as to principle, the employment of capital for manufacturing purposes in overseas manufacturing countries, either in the form of employment of such capital on its own account or through association with foreign manufacturers.

Thus I expressed my opinion as to the desirability of overseas manufacturing in principle. This view of mine was considered at length by the Executive Committee on January 26 and ordered filed without any concrete action. It was clear that we were still in search of a policy. By this time, the broad policy issues had come to center on several specific issues: Should we expand Vauxhall, or should we write it off as a bad investment? Was it really necessary to manufacture in Europe? Or could a modified Chevrolet, exported from the United States, compete with European cars in the European market? We were especially uncertain what to do in Germany. If we decided to produce there, should we expand our Berlin assembly plant into a manufacturing operation, or should we affiliate with some other producer? Our overseas operations men, especially Mr. Mooney, were inclined to favor expansion of existing facilities, while I rather preferred affiliation with a German producer. There were certainly substantial reasons for supporting either approach.

The question of manufacturing abroad was discussed in the Executive Committee again on March 29, and still again on April 12; at the latter meeting we discussed particularly the question whether we should manufacture a small car in England and Germany. As a matter of fact, that question was discussed by the Executive Committee through practically the entire year of 1928. There was a strong sentiment that our export organization should be limited to selling American products abroad and should not get into overseas manufacture. Meanwhile, I was interested in a suggestion that we create in the United States an organization to design a modified "small-bore" Chevrolet—a car that would escape the heavy horsepower tax in England and Germany. I felt that if this were done, it might prove unnecessary to develop a new small car at Vauxhall or to go into production in Germany; or, if it should become necessary to produce such a car abroad, we would at least have a design available. In any case, I wanted the facts established to everyone's satisfaction before proceeding further in either country.

At a meeting of the Executive Committee on June 4, 1928, I urged that each member talk to Mr. Mooney individually, in the hope that these discussions might clarify our thinking. In July Mr.

Mooney addressed a long memorandum to me, detailing his point of view on all the issues. A few weeks later I conveyed this memorandum to the Executive Committee, together with my own comments on the points raised by Mr. Mooney. Perhaps the simplest way of describing the contending views, and of re-creating some of the atmosphere of the discussion, is to quote some excerpts from his memorandum.

One of the first points made by Mr. Mooney concerned the desirability of continuing expansion by the Export Company. He pointed out that "over the past five years the Export Division has increased its dollar volume from $20,000,000. to $250,000,000. . . . Our general problem . . . is to raise our total dollar volume in Export from its present level of $250,000,000. to $500,000,000. in the shortest possible time, and to provide a means that will maintain a continuing increase into the future . . ."

Mr. Mooney pointed out further that ". . . the lowest price product that we can offer for sale in the world markets today, which is the Chevrolet, costs the user approximately 75% more than it does the user in the United States, and the user in the world markets has approximately only 60% of the money of the United States user to pay for it. Therefore, the Chevrolet when put down in world markets is not in the largest volume area, and is in a relatively high price class."

Mr. Mooney made his case for the expansion of Vauxhall along these lines:

(1) We had already started on a manufacturing program which we proposed to expand by adding another car model.

(2) We had a large and growing distribution system in England, and an investment in the Vauxhall plant that had to be safeguarded.

(3) The fact that the British Empire covered 38 per cent of the world markets outside of the United States and Canada was important in the consideration of England as a source for export markets.

The discussion then turned to the question of our future dealings in Germany, on which Mr. Mooney made his case with the following salient points:

(1) We already had an established organization in the form of the General Motors assembly plant in Berlin.

(2) We proposed to manufacture a car model at this plant, rather than acquire an interest in the Opel automobile company.

(3) Since the automobile industry in Germany was in its formative state, the time was right to establish a successful manufacturing operation.

(4) Our existing investment had to be safeguarded.

(5) Not only was the domestic German market potentially large, but Germany was also in a good position to export to neighboring countries.

I agreed with some of his main points, and on some others I was, as I have already suggested, frankly undecided. The one clear point of disagreement between myself and Mr. Mooney concerned an aspect of what our policy should be in Germany. I viewed the case there something like this: If the idea was to make a very small car, much smaller than the Chevrolet—assuming that was an economic thing to do—then we might be better off dealing directly with Opel. I felt that we would get off to a better start that way than we would by trying to compete on our own in a country with which we were largely unfamiliar.

During the following six months our policy in Germany was finally established. In October 1928 I made an inspection trip to Europe, accompanied by John Thomas Smith, who was general counsel of General Motors, and Charles T. Fisher. We visited our export and assembly operations throughout Europe and also visited Adam Opel A.G. My prior interest in acquiring Opel was stimulated by this visit, so much so that I negotiated an option for General Motors to buy Opel. The option was to expire on April 1, 1929, and we agreed, subject to further examination of the company, that we would pay about $30 million if we bought it.

I reported this arrangement to the Executive Committee on November 9, 1928. The committee was generally sympathetic to the idea of buying Opel, and it was agreed that we should look further into the property. At a committee meeting on November 22, 1928, we decided to appoint a study group to do just that. The group finally agreed upon consisted of Mr. Smith, who was to be in charge, together with Albert Bradley, general assistant treasurer, C. B. Durham, the head of manufacturing at Buick, and E. K. Wennerlund, who was an expert on factory arrangement and flow of material. Before the group sailed, I gave Mr. Smith a formal memorandum outlining the situation as I saw it. I asked him to bear these questions in mind:

1. Must we not look forward to the time when restrictions will be placed upon us and where exportation of American cars will be confined to the higher priced cars and that the real market from the standpoint of volume will, to a large extent, go to locally made cars and through evolution corresponding influence is bound to be felt on the higher priced cars?

2. Is there not a tremendous opportunity, both on the Continent, in England and overseas, for the production of a car having less of the elements of luxury than the present Chevrolet, providing it is so designed and developed that it can be sold at a price sufficiently lower than the present Chevrolet?

3. Is it not reasonable to suppose that assuming the second point above is correct, that even if not now . . . through the development of the German industry the point will soon be reached when the difference in cost of manufacture will be less than the tariff and importing charges, especially writing into the picture the handicap of the h.p. tax, in which event importation abroad will be more and more limited?

4. Is there not an opportunity for the Corporation to protect its large organization, large volume and substantially large profits accruing to it through its Continental and English operations and, to some extent, afford protection to its overseas business elsewhere by investing capital in manufacturing abroad and making a substantial return on that additional capital?

I concluded with these general admonitions:

. . . I want particularly to say to the members of the Committee individually and to you as Chairman that you should take nothing for granted—every point should be studied and approached with an "Open Mind", without prejudice and with the sole purpose of getting the facts wherever they may lead us. As a matter of fact, this is one of the most important steps from the standpoint of capital investment and expansion of the organization that the Corporation has made since the present management has been connected with its administrative side. The advent of General Motors into the manufacturing situation abroad is bound to stir up a great deal of discussion, both within industrial circles as well as within Government circles, therefore, our reputation for doing a constructive thing and doing it in a constructive way, is in the balance. The Committee has a tremendous responsibility not only to itself but to the whole Corporation in analyzing the problem.

The study group sailed about the 1st of January, 1929, and on the 18th I brought up the Opel issue—and, indeed, the entire issue of overseas production—before the Finance Committee. The committee was, in general, disposed sympathetically to the Opel deal, and adopted the following resolution unanimously:

RESOLVED, that to a sub-committee of the Executive Committee instructed to go abroad for the purpose of determining the advisability of purchasing a substantial interest, to close or extend an option held by General Motors Corporation to purchase the entire business of the Opel Automobile Company of Germany for 125,000,000 marks, there be lodged full authority to do in connection with this matter whatever in their opinion is for the best interest of General Motors Corporation; it being understood that, in the event part of the ownership is left in the hands of the Opel management, it is desirable to have such string attached to said interest as will enable General Motors Corporation to acquire same later on (should the future dictate the desirability of such a course in connection with any plans the corporation might have for extending its operations in Europe) on the basis of the original price plus accrued profits.

It is clear from the above record that the Executive and Finance committees were now in agreement. The subcommittee authorized to close the Opel deal consisted of Fred J. Fisher, a director of the corporation and a member of the Executive and Finance committees, and myself. Early in March we sailed for Europe and met the study group in Paris. The group handed us a report, dated March 8, 1929, which embodied their findings about Opel. The report was complete and the recommendations were crisp and specific. In the covering letter delivered to me, as president of the corporation, the study group said: "We strongly recommend the exercise of the option to purchase upon the terms as modified." The pertinent findings in the report may be summarized as follows:

(1) The German domestic automobile market was in about the same state of development as the United States market had been in 1911.

(2) Germany was naturally a manufacturing country, well supplied with coal and iron, with a large population of skilled labor. In order to develop its domestic economy, Germany had to produce and export a surplus of goods and to manufacture at low cost. It

followed that to be successful in the German automobile market you had to manufacture in Germany.

(3) The firm of Adam Opel A.G. was the largest motorcar manufacturer in Germany; it led the low-price field and manufactured 44 per cent of all the German-made cars sold in Germany in 1928 (and 26 per cent of all cars sold in Germany).

(4) The Adam Opel A.G. factory at Rüsselsheim was well equipped for the manufacture of automobiles. Buildings were well designed. Seventy per cent of the machinery had been purchased during the past four years and had been well selected. Practically all special tools had been written off. The plant was flexible and readily adaptable to new models. A good supply of high-class labor was available.

(5) Opel had 736 sales outlets, constituting the best dealer organization in Germany.

(6) The allowance for good will ($12 million) over and above the net tangible assets of the corporation ($18 million) was reasonable. For us to build or equip for manufacturing a new factory in Germany would require at least two or three years before operations could be put on an efficient and profitable basis. The amount paid Opel in excess of net assets would be returned within the time required to start from the ground up.

(7) The acquisition would give General Motors the Opel dealer organization, and we would acquire a "German background," instead of having to operate as foreigners.

It was clear to Mr. Fisher and myself that the recommendation of the study group was adequately supported by the comprehensive report. We therefore decided to approve the acquisition of the property, and proceeded to Rüsselsheim, the home base of Adam Opel A.G. In due course we concluded an agreement which was only slightly different from that contemplated at the time I had secured the option. The final agreement provided that we receive an 80 per cent interest in Opel at a cost of $25,967,000; in addition, we received an option to buy the remaining 20 per cent for $7,395,000, and the Opel family received a "put" which entitled it to sell the 20 per cent to us within five years, at a specified scale of prices. The family exercised that option in October 1931 and General Motors thus came into complete ownership of Adam Opel A.G. at an aggregate cost of $33,362,000.

Though Opel was a well-run company, it was not without management problems, especially at the top policy level. The company also had a problem, as we saw it, with its dealers. Many of them had set up rather elaborate machine shops of their own, in which spare parts could be produced. Adam Opel A.G. had not developed a system of interchangeable parts. When a customer needed a spare part, the distributor had to make the part to fit that particular car; or, if he got a part from the factory, he would have to refit it. That did not make sense to an American producer used to a system of mass production based on interchangeable parts, and we set out to correct this.

The purchase of Opel gave us a strong position in Germany. The company's 1928 output of about 43,000 cars and trucks was small by American standards, but we made no secret of our plans for a dramatic expansion. Soon after the deal had been completed, Geheimrat Wilhelm von Opel, the company president, brought all its dealers and distributors together at a big meeting in Frankfurt; altogether, some five or six hundred of them came, from Germany and from nearby countries to which Opel was exporting. I spoke to the group about the policies of General Motors. I observed to them that, while Germany was a highly industrialized country, its automobile production was very low by American standards, and that I anticipated Opel production might one day run as high as 150,-000 vehicles a year. When the statement was translated into German, it was received with a good deal of derision. I was viewed as another impractical, visionary American. Yet as I write this, the capacity has been brought up to 650,000 vehicles.

Soon after we took over Opel, we installed I. J. Reuter as managing director. Mr. Reuter had been general manager of our Olds Division. He was an operating executive who combined a good engineering background with production and sales experience. He was also of German extraction and spoke the language with a fair degree of fluency. It took a good deal of persuasion on my part to get Mr. Reuter to accept the assignment, but he finally yielded; and in September 1929 he and I and several men whom we had chosen to be his assistants made a trip to Rüsselsheim, and formally inaugurated his regime.

While my own point of view prevailed, in general, in our development of a policy for Germany, Mr. Mooney's recommendations were finally adopted in England. It was clear by 1929 that we either had to build up Vauxhall or else give up on the English market. Mr. Mooney was successful in advocating that Vauxhall should develop a smaller car. In 1930 a lower-priced six-cylinder model was added. The year was also notable for the fact that Vauxhall first entered the commercial-vehicle market. The company gained a strong position in the truck business, but its position in the passenger-car business remained disappointing. I therefore appointed a committee early in 1932 to proceed to England to make a report and submit recommendations for a product program. This committee, under the chairmanship of Albert Bradley, then vice president of finance, recommended that Vauxhall discontinue its current passenger-car lines and then manufacture and sell a smaller and lighter six-cylinder passenger car, to be followed at a later date by a four-cylinder line. The new "Light Six" was introduced in 1933 and the lower-horsepower four in 1937. The committee's recommendations were of lasting significance for Vauxhall. At present Vauxhall's capacity is being expanded to 395,000 passenger cars and trucks on an annual basis.

In acquiring Opel and building up Vauxhall, General Motors underwent an important change. It was transformed from a domestic to an international manufacturer, prepared to seek markets for its products wherever they existed, and to support these markets with manufacturing and assembly facilities and organizations where the circumstances justified such a course. A high-level determination of policy had been established.

We were fortunate in acquiring Vauxhall and Opel during the late twenties. For when the great world-wide depression began in 1929, our export business went into a sudden steep decline—as did that of other American producers. General Motors exports from the United States and Canada went from 290,000 vehicles in 1928 to only 40,000 in 1932. Thereafter, they began to grow again, but the growth in our overseas production was more rapid still. In 1933, for the first time, the Vauxhall and Opel sales were greater than the sales abroad of General Motors' American-made vehicles. The biggest prewar year for all overseas operations—domestic and foreign production—was 1937. In that year we exported 180,000 vehicles from the United States and Canada and sold 188,000 vehicles manufactured abroad.

The future of our entire overseas operations was, of course, very much in doubt after World War II broke out. Assuming the ultimate defeat of the Axis powers, it was still hard to say with any certainty just what political and economic conditions would prevail in much of the world. In 1942 at my suggestion we set up a Post War Planning Policy Group inside the corporation, and entrusted it with the heavy responsibility of making some estimates of the future political shape of the world, and also of recommending future General Motors' policies abroad. I was the chairman of this policy group. Edward Riley, General Motors vice president and the general manager of the Overseas Operations Division, undertook to provide for me and the policy group a detailed summary of the best available thinking on the political and economic situation in the postwar overseas world. Most of these findings are contained in a letter to me dated February 23, 1943. I shall quote at some length from this document, because during the war years it was the guideline of much of our thinking about future overseas operations.

. . . I should like to submit it as our belief [wrote Mr. Riley] . . . that the United States will assume and hold a stronger position and attitude in the world after this war than we did after World War I. By this I mean that regardless of the course of our domestic political developments . . . America, with the past quarter century of experience before it, will not again withdraw into a position of isolation from world problems and activities which, if permitted to run their course without benefit of American guidance, intervention and support, have turned, and can again turn, in directions wholly opposed to our interests . . .

In England . . . we believe certain indications of future events can already be identified.

Amongst these, as we see things today, is the English determination in important quarters, to compete as a world trading nation on the basis of low costs through efficient production as opposed to the prewar position of cartel-protected basic industries, with resultant high production costs and consequent need for protected markets.

Another discernible trend in England is the undoubted growing realization that the future well-being and safety of the British Commonwealth can best be protected by closer political collaboration with the United States.

. . . in the light of information available today, we feel that the dominant center-line of Russian political thought will continue to be expressed in terms of peaceful development rather than external conquest through aggressive warlike action . . .

Russian influence has been directed not only westward toward Europe, but to the south and east as well. Persia, India, China, Manchukuo and even Japan have felt this influence in the past . . . Russia will continue her efforts after the war to maintain this influence in all directions.

We feel . . . that the Russian social and political philosophy . . . will continue to spread beyond the borders of Russia into areas where conditions favor its acceptance and development . . . The most effective means of counteracting the spread of this Russian philosophy is to prevent or relieve the conditions favorable to its development and to demonstrate that the system of life which represents the American and British point of view can offer as much or more to the mass of the people . . .

The net result of the foregoing general viewpoints . . . is that there will probably be certain lines of demarcation or division to the west, south and east of the Soviet Union, within which the Russian idea will predominate, and outside of which the American and British viewpoint will prevail.

. . . Based on past experience, the areas under strong Russian influence after the war will probably not present a fertile field for our type of business.

Though these predictions were put forward only as tentative "educated guesses," they proved to be reasonably good on the whole. I think I might summarize our wartime perspective by saying that we anticipated something like the "cold war"; but at the same time we were confident that our overseas operations would be able to flourish in large areas of the world when the war ended.

After studying Mr. Riley's report and much other material, our Overseas Policy Group, under the chairmanship of Albert Bradley, adopted in June 1943 a statement dealing with the corporation's plans for expansion abroad. One large question confronting the policy group was whether we wanted to acquire any new manufacturing companies abroad after the war. The statement took note of the world-wide trend toward industrialization, and suggested that this would be continued and intensified. It went on to say that General Motors expected to participate in and support these trends wherever the corporation had overseas operating companies. "However," the statement said, "General Motors does not believe that the basic conditions required to support complete manufacture of cars and trucks exist or will be found to exist for some time in any countries abroad which did not already have such manufacture before the war. An exception to the above is Australia . . ." In other words, except for Australia, we anticipated that we would not want to acquire any more major manufacturing bases abroad when the war ended.

The largest immediate problem we faced after the war concerned the Opel properties. These had been seized by the German government soon after the war began. In 1942 our entire investment in Opel amounted to about $35 million, and under a ruling which the Treasury Department had made concerning assets in enemy hands, we were allowed to write off the investment against current taxable income. But this ruling did not end our interest in, or responsibility for, the Opel property. As the end of the war drew near, we were given to understand that we were still considered the owners of the Opel stock; and we were also given to understand that as the owners, we might be obliged to assume responsibility for the property.

At this point we were somewhat in the air about resuming control of Opel. We did not know the physical condition of the property, and our tax position was quite unclear. A committee appointed to study the question stated the case as follows in a report to the Overseas Product Group, on July 6, 1945:

1. Due to the lack of available information as to the condition of the property, no decision can be reached currently as to the advisability or inadvisability of disposing of the stock investment . . .

2. It would be incorrect to consider that the sale of the stock for a nominal amount at this time would eliminate any further tax liability arising from recovery of the Opel property . . .

3. The statutes which deal with War Loss recovery, as now written, are not at all clear as to rate of tax on recovery, limit of tax, date of recovery and method of evaluation . . .

To complicate matters still further, the Russians were demanding that the Opel properties be turned over to them as reparations, and it appeared for a while as though this might actually be done. But in the latter part of 1945, after the war had ended, the American government took a firm position against such a move. I should mention, perhaps, that General Motors played no role at all in any of the discussions concerning the possibility of using the Opel properties as reparations. Indeed, I felt at one point that we could not possibly regard Opel as a money-making operation. In a letter to Mr. Riley dated March 1, 1946, I wrote:

My personal conviction, be it right or wrong, is that under existing circumstances . . . so far as we can see, there is no justification whatsoever of General Motors taking any operating responsibility commensurate to what it was carrying before the war, from the standpoint of making a profit . . . It does not appear to me that a limited market such as indicated in your assumptions justif[ies] all that we would have to go through . . .

My pessimistic conclusion, I am afraid, reflected a good deal of the emotional impact of the war and its devastation, and of course the large number of unknowns in the Opel situation tended to intensify my feeling. This feeling changed as the future unfolded and facts evolved out of the area of unknowns. Negotiations between General Motors and the Allied Military Government in the American zone of Germany continued during the next two years. General Lucius D. Clay, the American military governor, made it clear to us that he was in favor of our taking the properties back as soon as possible. He emphasized that if we delayed indefinitely the properties must pass to a custodian appointed by the German State.

On November 20, 1947, the Operations Policy Committee recommended to the Financial Policy Committee that General Motors resume control of Adam Opel A.G. This recommendation was in line with the findings of the Overseas Policy Group, which had also recommended resumption of control.

On December 1, 1947, the Financial Policy Committee considered the matter and directed the appointment of a study group to review all the facts about Adam Opel A.G. as they then existed. This group was appointed by C. E. Wilson, then president of the corporation. Its chairman was B. D. Kunkle, an operating executive with experience and competence. Its other members included E. S. Hoglund of our overseas operations; Frederic G. Donner, then vice president in charge of finance; Henry M. Hogan, then general counsel, and R. K. Evans, vice president, an executive experienced in engineering and production who had had many years of overseas experience.

The group left New York on February 11 and returned on March 18. During that interval they closely examined Opel's financial situation and interviewed military-government representatives in Berlin, Frankfurt, and Wiesbaden, and also many Germans, including Opel executives, important German suppliers, local representatives of the German government, and officers of the Opel Works Council. Before they completed their observations the study group also contacted industrialists, bankers, and government officers in England, Holland, Belgium, and Switzerland, and representatives of the U. S. State Department and U. S. Army in Washington.

The study group's findings were submitted to the president of the corporation on March 26, 1948. The group presented its report in the form of a balance sheet showing the points in favor of resuming control as well as those against it. Its own recommendation was that we resume control of Adam Opel A.G. However, the Financial Policy Committee, at its meeting of April 5, 1948, questioned the justification for General Motors resuming the responsibility for operation of Adam Opel at the time. The minutes of that meeting show the following:

Report dated March 26, 1948 (❇580) was received from the special committee appointed by the President to examine the desirability of resuming operations in western Germany.

It was the conclusion of the [Financial Policy] Committee that, in view of the many uncertainties surrounding the operation of this property, the Corporation is not justified in resuming the responsibility for its operation at this time . . .

The Overseas Policy Group held a meeting on April 6, 1948, and discussed the conclusions reached at the April 5 meeting of the Financial Policy Committee. After further consideration of the report submitted by the special study committee, the opinion was expressed that the generally unfavorable attitude of the Financial Policy Committee toward resumption of operating control of Adam Opel A.G. arose largely from uncertainty in the minds of the various members of the committee with respect to certain important aspects of the situation. The group thought that these uncertainties might be boiled down to a few basic questions. In the discussion I urged that if a majority of the points of uncertainty were clearly set forth and clarified in a brief memorandum they might provide a basis for reopening the question of resuming control with the Financial Policy Committee. I suggested that Mr. Riley undertake the preparation of basic material for such a memorandum and stated that if upon completion it was agreed that the points thus dealt with possessed sufficient substance and effectiveness, I would be willing to submit a further report and to request the Financial Policy Committee to reconsider the entire matter.

Mr. Wilson, in a letter to me dated April 9, 1948, had pointed out that the Opel situation had been much in his mind since the Financial Policy Committee action. Excerpts from this letter are as follows:

. . . I was surprised Monday to find myself the only member of the [Financial Policy] Committee who was willing to resume operations in Germany, with the exception of Mr. Donner who concurred in and supported the unanimous recommendations of the special committee of which he was a member . . .

It is obvious to me, however, that the matter cannot long be left in its present status, and that it will again have to be considered by the FPC. I do not believe that such a review should be undertaken until after the election in Italy and until Walter Carpenter and Albert Bradley can join in the discussion and share in the responsibility for the final decision . . .

In reply to Mr. Wilson's letter to me I wrote him under date of April 14, 1948, in part as follows:

. . . You state you were surprised Monday to find yourself the only member of the Committee who was willing to resume operations in Germany, with the exception of Mr. Donner and perhaps Mr. Bradley. That is not correct. So far as I am concerned, I have been willing right along to resume operations in Germany. And still am willing to do so, providing I have a definite bill of particulars which I can consistently support . . .

I came into the meeting of the FPC with the hopes that we could lay down certain definite principles along the lines of your assumptions. I urged that this be considered. In their absence I was forced, against my fundamental convictions, to take the negative position . . .

I agree with you that the matter is in very unsatisfactory condition at the moment. I felt so at the close of the meeting on Monday, and even more so after the subsequent discussion on Tuesday. It was for that reason that I urged on Tuesday, the same as I tried to have considered on Monday, a concrete proposal setting forth the conditions under which we would resume. I am quite of the belief that if that can be done, it is not impossible that the FPC may reverse itself. Anyway, the effort is with them.

There followed a series of discussions between Mr. Riley and myself to clarify some of the uncertainties and establish realistic limitations that would be acceptable to the Overseas Operations Division from the operating point of view. As a result of this exchange of views I drafted a report and submitted it to the Financial Policy Committee under date of April 26, 1948, in which I stressed the following points:

1. It must be recognized that this is not the same question that came before the then Finance Committee in 1928. It is not a question of whether we will enter Germany in an operating way. We are already there. The original question involved in general a very important principle of major policy which I will expose later. Put more specifically, the problem in 1928 involved the export of a very considerable amount of capital, the uncertainty of our ability to organize a complete and highly technical manufacturing operation in a foreign country, the potentiality of the market for a somewhat different although related line of products, the profit possibilities and other considerations. The present question must contemplate no export of capital . . .

2. There is no doubt that the report reflects a situation existing close to economic stagnation so far as a foundation for constructive enterprise is concerned. But how could it be otherwise? The whole German economy since the close of the war, has been in status quo so far as a constructive and aggressive attack to rebuild it is concerned . . .

3. The question of whether General Motors was to remain a national enterprise, manufacturing in this country and exporting its products outside wherever markets exist, or whether it was destined to continue to expand as an international organization, manufacturing where constructive opportunities present themselves, in support of or independent of its American production, was determined in the latter part of the twenties . . . I am convinced that GM must—whether it likes it or not—aggressively follow that policy. I believe the sole consideration involving any particular question, is as to whether the opportunity for profit justifies the venture from the long term position of the business.

Specifically I made these recommendations:

1. That the Committee reconsider the decision reached at its meeting on April 5th and bring the report before it for further consideration.

2. That the Committee authorize the resumption of the management of Adam Opel A.G. for a probationary period of approximately two years and after the two year probationary period the situation be reviewed in light of the then existing circumstances.

3. That the conditions under which we resume the managerial responsibility shall be as hereafter defined. It is not intended that the conditions so defined will be underwritten by any authority or that any au-

thority will take any responsibility relative to same. It is intended that they shall be used solely as a pre-determined basis of withdrawing from the management responsibility any time during the two year period if in the opinion of our administration of the business, the operating conditions have become such that it is useless or impossible to continue further.

My fourth point spelled out the conditions referred to in the previous point: General Motors should risk no additional capital in Opel. Credit facilities should be available. We should have complete freedom in personnel policies and administration. The products produced by Adam Opel A.G. should be solely within the jurisdiction of management, and if prices had to be approved by government authority, a reasonable return on the capital employed should be allowed.

At its meeting on May 3, 1948, the Financial Policy Committee reviewed the Opel situation. The minutes of the meeting read as follows:

A report dated April 26, 1948 (⚹606) was received from Mr. Alfred P. Sloan, Jr., recommending that the Committee authorize resumption of the control of Adam Opel A.G. under certain conditions. It was the consensus of opinion that the Committee should base its conclusions on the following premises: (1) that General Motors Corporation will not advance or in any way guarantee the advance of any additional funds to Opel, and (2) that resumption of control does not alter the U. S. Federal income tax situation of General Motors Corporation.

A general discussion concerning the tax liability of General Motors Corporation followed. Messrs. Hogan and Donner gave their opinion that the U. S. Federal income tax position of General Motors Corporation would not be affected adversely by resumption of control at this time.

Upon motion duly seconded, the following preambles and resolutions were unanimously adopted:

WHEREAS it is the understanding of the Financial Policy Committee that the resumption of control of Adam Opel A.G. will not require or obligate General Motors Corporation to advance, or in any way guarantee the advance of, any additional funds to Adam Opel A.G., and

WHEREAS it is the understanding of this Committee that the U. S. Federal income tax position of General Motors Corporation would not be affected adversely by resuming control at this time;

NOW, THEREFORE, IT IS

RESOLVED that the Financial Policy Committee advise the Operations Policy Committee that on this basis it does not object to the resumption of control of Adam Opel A.G.; and further

RESOLVED that, in the light of the above, the resumption of control and management of Adam Opel A.G. be under such terms and conditions as are deemed advisable by the Operations Policy Committee; and further

RESOLVED that a copy of the report of Mr. Alfred P. Sloan, Jr., dated April 26, 1948 (¾606) entitled Adam Opel A.G., be forwarded to the Operations Policy Committee for its consideration.

The position of the corporation was now clearly established. Its purpose was to resume the control of Adam Opel A.G. consistent with the limitations laid down by the Financial Policy Committee and the clarification of innumerable important details covering the negotiations with the American Military Government for the release of the Opel properties, permitting the resumption of control and management of Adam Opel A.G. by General Motors Corporation. All this was finally accomplished and on November 1, 1948, a press release was issued by General Motors Corporation, as follows:

General Motors has announced that, effective today, it has resumed management control of Adam Opel A.G. located at Rüsselsheim, near Frankfurt am Main, Germany. Edward W. Zdunek, formerly regional manager for Europe of General Motors Overseas Operations Division, has been named managing director of the company. The Board of Directors, elected this week, is composed of nine American representatives of General Motors, with Elis S. Hoglund, assistant general manager of General Motors Overseas Operations, as chairman of the Board.

By 1949 sales of Opel cars and trucks were up to 40,000 vehicles; and expansion thereafter was rapid, as was the remarkable industrial recovery in other sectors of Western Germany's economy. In 1954 Opel sales had reached nearly 165,000 units, which was higher than the best prewar year.

While we were negotiating over Opel in the early postwar years, we were also acquiring a new manufacturing property in Australia. We had secured our first foothold in that country in the early twenties. Australia then favored the American automobile overwhelmingly, by over 90 per cent in some years. But the Australian government was making it difficult to import American car bodies. The duty was £60 on a touring-car body—nearly $300 at that time. This duty had its origins in World War I, when shipping space was at a premium, and it was afterward encouraged for a familiar-sounding reason—to encourage domestic industry. Because of the high duty, General Motors made an arrangement in 1923 to purchase car bodies from Holden's Motor Body Builders, Ltd., in Adelaide, a former leather-goods concern that had begun to produce bodies during World War I. We established close business relationships with this company, and obtained almost its entire output during the latter part of the twenties. In 1926 we formed General Motors (Australia) Pty. Ltd., and began to develop assembly plants in Australia and to build our own dealer organization. In 1931 we bought the Holden's company outright and merged it with General Motors (Australia) to form General Motors-Holden's, Ltd., which began manufacturing a number of components. Thus at the end of World War II we already had manufacturing experience in Australia as well as a dealer organization and familiarity with the local market.

Our decision to build Holden's into a full-fledged manufacturing operation was made while the war was still in progress. As I mentioned earlier in this chapter, the statement adopted by our Overseas Policy Group, of which Mr. Bradley was chairman, had concluded in June 1943 that Australia was probably the only country in which we would want to consider establishing a new major manufacturing base after the war. By September 1944 the Overseas Policy Group had further decided that it would be desirable to move in the direction of complete car manufacture in Australia. This proved to be a timely decision, for in October of that year the Australian government officially invited General Motors, as well as other interested parties, to submit proposals for the manufacture of a motorcar in Australia. As our thinking in this area had already largely crystallized, we were able to move quickly in accepting this invitation. In a report to the Administration Committee dated November 1, 1944, which had the approval of the Overseas Policy Group, the case for manufacturing in Australia was stated. It was pointed out that:

(1) We were already manufacturing there, to some extent, and a decision to go all the way was only a question of degree.

(2) Australia had the skilled labor, low-cost steel, and other economic foundations for an automobile producer, as well as a good climate.

(3) The alternative to manufacturing would doubtless be a declining share in a protected market.

The status of General Motors-Holden's was agreed on with the Australian government authorities by March 1945. During the remainder of that year, and on into 1946, General Motors assembled in Detroit a group of about thirty American engineers and production men and their Australian understudies, and briefed them on starting the new manufacturing operation. Three prototype cars were built before the group left this country. In the fall of 1946 these men and their families—some seventy-five persons—left Detroit on a specially chartered Canadian Pacific train to Vancouver. With them were test cars, all the required engineering data, several tons of drawings and prints, and a good deal of the spirit of Detroit. A chartered steamship took them from Vancouver to Australia in December 1946. Their first production for the Australian market was in 1948, when 112 cars were sold. By 1950 production was up to 20,000 cars, and by 1962 to 133,000 cars, and expansion to a capacity of 175,000 units is under way.

Chapter 19

NONAUTOMOTIVE: DIESEL ELECTRIC LOCOMOTIVES, APPLIANCES, AVIATION

G ENERAL MOTORS manufactures not only cars and trucks, but diesel electric locomotives, household appliances, aviation engines, earth-moving equipment, and a variety of other durable goods; altogether, our nonautomotive business accounts for roughly 10 per cent of our civilian sales. And yet there have always been limits to our product diversification. We have never made anything except "durable products," and they have always, with minor exceptions, been connected with motors. Not even Mr. Durant, for all his expansion and diversification, ever suggested that we should stray into any broad field clearly outside the boundary suggested by our corporate name, General Motors.

No attempt will be made here to present detailed individual histories of our products outside of the automobile. The stories of our pioneering in the diesel business, of our development of the Frigidaire line of products, and of our aviation business are the subjects of this chapter.

It would be nice to be able to trace a coherent pattern in General Motors' ventures outside the automobile business, but chance and other factors that entered the picture make it difficult to do so. We had, of course, some natural interest in diversification which might afford us a hedge against any decline in automobile sales. But we never had a master plan for nonautomotive ventures; we got into them for different reasons, and we were very lucky at some crucial points. We got into the diesel field, for example, because of Mr. Kettering's special interest in diesel engines, dating back as early as 1913, when he was experimenting with diesel power in an attempt to find a suitable engine for the generator in a farm-lighting set he wanted to manufacture. Mr. Durant put General Motors in the refrigerator business for reasons of his own; but it is clear, as I shall show, that we would have abandoned Frigidaire in its earliest years had it not been for an odd combination of events. And we got into aviation because we thought the small airplane would be an important competitor of the automobile.

It is worthy of note, I believe, that these were relatively new products at the time we first invested in them. There was no diesel locomotive capable of providing mainline service on American railroads; the electric refrigerator was only an impractical gadget, and the future of aviation was anybody's guess. In other words, we did not simply use our financial and engineering resources to "take over" new products outside the automobile business. We got in early—as long as forty-five years ago—and helped develop them. Our operations in these fields have been expanded, but we have gone into nothing entirely new in more recent years except for the purchase in 1953 of the Euclid Road Machinery Company (manufacturer of earth-moving equipment), and war and defense production.

Diesel Electric Locomotives

General Motors entered the locomotive industry in a small way in the early 1930s. At the time, railroads in the United States seemed to have very little interest in diesel locomotives except for special switch-engine use. Yet in less than a decade the diesel was outselling the steam locomotive, and General Motors was outselling all other locomotive manufacturers combined. Because we led the diesel revolution, with tremendous savings to the railroad industry, the Electro-Motive Division today enjoys a large part of the locomotive market.

There were, I think, two principal reasons for this rather spectacular progress. The first was simply that we were more tenacious in our efforts to produce lightweight, high-speed diesel engines suitable for over-the-road use on American railroads. The second reason was that we brought to the locomotive industry some of the manufacturing, engineering, and marketing concepts of the automobile industry. Until we began making diesels, locomotives had always been produced on a custom basis, with the railroads specifying their requirements to the manufacturers in considerable detail so that virtually no two locomotives on American railroads were alike. But almost from the beginning we offered the railroads a standard locomotive—one that we were able to produce in volume at a relatively low price. In addition we guaranteed performance at a lower net cost per ton mile than was possible with the use of steam engines, and we made good our guarantees by maintaining a service organization and providing standardized replacement parts. This program revolutionized the locomotive industry and secured our own place in it.

There was, of course, nothing new about the principle of the diesel engine at the time that General Motors first became interested in it. Rudolph Diesel, a German inventor, received the original patent for this kind of engine in 1892 and built a successful unit with one cylinder and twenty-five horsepower in 1897. As early as 1898 a sixty-horsepower, two-cylinder diesel unit was built in this country. These early devices embodied essentially the same compression-ignition principle as the engine in a modern diesel locomotive.

The four-cycle diesel engine works this way: On the first suction stroke of the piston, the engine draws in air and nothing else. The next stroke of the piston compresses the air to something like 500 pounds per square inch, creating a temperature of around 1000° Fahrenheit. Just before the end of the compression stroke, oil is injected as a fine spray into the combustion chamber under high pressure. The hot air ignites this fuel. The third and fourth strokes of the piston provide the power and exhaust—as in a gasoline engine. However, the diesel requires neither a carburetor nor an electric ignition, and thus has an edge in simplicity over the gasoline engine.

As this description indicates, the diesel converts its fuel directly into a source of energy. In this respect it is unlike the steam engine, whose fuel is used only to create steam, and unlike the gasoline engine, which vaporizes its fuel before it can be ignited. Both of these engines are less efficient than the diesel—which has in fact the highest thermal efficiency of any heat engine in everyday use. The modern diesel uses a distilled petroleum fuel oil, but other fuels have been used in the past. Rudolph Diesel himself had intended to run his engine on powdered coal, but his engineer associates persuaded him at the outset to use petroleum oil in order to avoid the problem of scoring. Powdered coal was used later experimentally by others attempting to follow Diesel's original intentions, and other fuels have been tried. But petroleum oil remains the standard diesel fuel.

Despite its great efficiency, the diesel engine was for many years quite limited in practical use. With few exceptions the engines were large, heavy, and slow running, and so found their greatest application in power stations, pumping, and marine use. They weighed 200 or 300 pounds per horsepower, and this, indeed, was the heart of the problem—to build a powerful, fast-running diesel of relatively small size.

I have said there was nothing new about the principle of the diesel engine. I might add that there were no unknown principles concerning any component part of the diesel-powered locomotive that General Motors created. What was lacking was the imagination, the initiative, and the talent to work out the problem to the point of practicability.

Europeans had been working on this development since the second decade of this century and had some diesel railcars and locomotives in operation by 1920. By 1933 a few U.S. diesel manufacturers had successfully built a number of diesel engines for switcher service. Since weight was an advantage in switchers, and since they showed economies over steam in operation, they met with some success. However, attempts to build diesel engines for mainline passenger and freight applications in this country were not successful, since in these cases weight, power, and size are critical. Bringing the diesel engine down to more manageable proportions, with a low weight-per-horsepower ratio, was the principal concern of our engineers.

In a large organization like General Motors it is seldom possible to assign to any one person the credit—or blame—for initiating some major undertaking. But in the case of the diesel, Charles F. Kettering comes very close to being the whole story. The General Motors Research Corporation, forerunner of our present Research

Laboratories, was testing diesel engines, under Mr. Kettering's close scrutiny, as early as 1921. After Mr. Kettering bought himself a diesel-powered yacht in April 1928 these engines became a major preoccupation of his. As anyone who knew him might have guessed, when on his yacht he was more often tinkering in the engine room than relaxing on deck. He was already convinced that the diesel did not have to be unreasonably large and heavy.

I became interested in the possible development of the diesel engine for General Motors at about the same time. If my memory serves me correctly, I remember dropping in one day at the Research Laboratories in Detroit and saying to Mr. Kettering: "Ket, why is it, recognizing the high efficiency of the diesel cycle, that it has never been more generally used?" In his characteristic way he said the reason was that the engine would not run in the way that the engineers wanted it to run. I then said to him: "Very well—we are now in the diesel engine business. You tell us how the engine should run and I will see that available manufacturing facilities are provided to capitalize the program." Of course, saying that we were in the diesel business was a manner of speaking. I meant I would support him in the organization.

In 1928 Mr. Kettering and an engineering group at the Research Laboratories began a series of comprehensive tests on the diesel engines then being offered by various manufacturers. An analysis of these tests, combined with a thorough study of current scientific literature on diesels, finally led Mr. Kettering to conclude that the solution to his problem was the so-called two-cycle diesel engine. The two-cycle engine was nothing new at that time. Indeed, the truly remarkable feature of Mr. Kettering's conclusion was his conviction that the two-cycle principle was ideally suited to the smaller diesel engines. Though it had been thoroughly explored before, it generally had been rejected as unworkable except in large, slow-speed engines.

In the two-cycle engine the intake of fresh air and the exhaust of burned gases take place at the same time. One stroke out of every two is a power stroke instead of one out of four, as in the four-cycle engine. The result is an engine that has less than one fifth the weight and one sixth the size of its predecessor four-cycle engine of equivalent power output. But this smaller device created some awesome engineering problems. For one thing, the two-cycle engine as developed by Mr. Kettering called for much greater precision in the fuel-injection system. Specifically, what the Research Laboratories were called upon to produce—and finally did produce —was a unit fuel injector whose parts fitted with a clearance of 30 to 60 millionths of an inch and an injector pump which built up pressures as high as 30,000 pounds per square inch as it forced fuel through holes 10 to 13 thousandths of an inch in diameter drilled in the injector tip. The two-cycle engine also has to have an external air pump. This became another major project, but finally Research delivered what was needed: a light, compact device able to pump large quantities of air at a pressure of about three to six pounds.

By the end of 1930 it was clear that the two-cycle engine was practical and that Mr. Kettering had achieved a major breakthrough in diesel technology. It was also clear that the time had come to provide the manufacturing facilities I had promised him. We looked around for the special facilities that were needed. Our buildup consisted principally of the purchase of two companies: the Winton Engine Company and the Electro-Motive Engineering Company, both of Cleveland, Ohio.

Winton was a manufacturer of diesel engines, primarily for marine uses (it had built Mr. Kettering's second set of yacht engines), and also of certain kinds of large gasoline engines. Electro-Motive was an engineering, design, and sales firm with no manufacturing facilities of its own. The two firms had had an intimate business relationship for almost a decade. During that time Electro-Motive and Winton had built a substantial business and reputation in the design and sale of gas-electric railcars, primarily for use on short-haul runs. Building the engines for these railcars was a major part of Winton's business during most of the 1920s. Relative to steam, however, the operating economies of gas cars kept diminishing, and toward the end of the decade Electro-Motive began to find itself in trouble trying to continue to sell the gas-electric car, which in turn had its effect on Winton.

Against this background Winton and Electro-Motive began, around 1928 and 1929, to look seriously into the possibility of using diesel power on the railroads. Harold Hamilton, then president of Electro-Motive, encountered the same problems of fuel injection that Mr. Kettering was then wrestling with. Mr. Hamilton was also trying to develop a small diesel engine. With the technology then available to him, the smallest diesel he could build was one weighing about sixty pounds per horsepower. A locomotive, he felt, required an engine weighing no more than twenty pounds per horsepower, with a crankshaft speed of about 800 revolutions per minute. Though there were a few available diesel engines which closely matched these specifications, Mr. Hamilton did not feel that they could stand up to the performance and reliability requirements which he felt were necessary for successful railroad application. Furthermore, Mr. Hamilton realized that the diesel he wanted would require metal tubes and joints able to last for long periods of time even when they had to carry fuel under pressures of 6000 and 7000 pounds to the square inch. Winton was not able to develop this kind of metallurgy and Mr. Hamilton knew of no place in the industry where it was available. He finally concluded that it would take about $10 million of venture capital to solve his and Winton's problems—perhaps $5 million to overcome the technological obstacles, and another $5 million or thereabouts to provide the plant and equipment needed for manufacturing facilities.

It was speedily made apparent to Mr. Hamilton, and also to George W. Codrington, the president of Winton, that they would not be able to raise the money at the banks and that there was certainly no such venture capital anywhere in the railroad industry. (Neither the carriers nor the locomotive manufacturers showed enough interest in the diesel to undertake the research necessary.) At about this time, however, Mr. Kettering became acquainted with Mr. Codrington as the result of ordering Winton engines for his second yacht. He bought these engines simply because Codrington agreed, though reluctantly, to put in a new kind of injector that one of the Winton engineers was developing at the time, and which Mr. Kettering felt held great promise. I don't know who first suggested the idea of Winton's coming into General Motors. In any event, we began to negotiate formally in the late summer of 1929. Agreement on the purchase of Winton had almost been reached in October when the great market crash temporarily confused the picture.

But there was never any serious question in our minds that Winton was a good buy for us. For one thing, we were not at this point certain about the future of the U.S. automobile market, which had not been expanding during the late 1920s. Consequently, we had a natural interest in any enterprise within our scope that offered us a reasonable opportunity to diversify.

The case for buying Winton was stated by John L. Pratt, vice president, in a memorandum which he addressed to the Operations and Finance committees, dated October 21, 1929, as follows:

We have had under consideration for some time past the possible purchase of the Winton Engine Company located at Cleveland, Ohio, which subject has been informally discussed at previous meetings.

It is believed that the Diesel Engine development in this country has arrived at a point where it has become commercial and is probably on the eve of considerable expansion. The Winton Engine Company is unquestionably the outstanding Diesel engine manufacturer in the United States . . .

The Winton Company has a capable management and would not require any additional personnel immediately. If the business continues to expand, as we believe it will, we may think it desirable to add to its personnel another good executive, perhaps as Assistant General Manager or Sales Manager . . .

. . . The purchase of this company will give us a vehicle for capitalizing the developments of our research organization along engine lines and will assist materially in keeping us abreast of Diesel engine developments. The business should also be reasonably profitable, and if expansion continues, as most of our engineers believe it will, we should ultimately make a good return on the investment required to purchase the Winton Company . . .

Finally, in June 1930 the Winton operations became a part of General Motors with Mr. Codrington continuing as president. Winton's principal market continued to be in large marine engines.[1] Five months after the Winton acquisition we also acquired Electro-Motive and again the old management of the company continued to run its affairs. During the negotiation to acquire Electro-Motive, Mr. Hamilton and Mr. Kettering continued to hold many lengthy discussions about the challenge of the lightweight diesel engine. In his 1955 testimony before a Senate subcommittee Mr. Hamilton described the tremendous enthusiasm of Mr. Kettering for the job of developing a diesel engine: ". . . it was just like ringing a bell to a fire horse," he recalled. Mr. Hamilton, in fact, made it

[1] In 1937 Winton's name was changed to Cleveland Diesel Engine Division and in 1962 its operations were consolidated with those of the Electro-Motive Division. In 1937, too, we set up the Detroit Diesel Engine Division to produce smaller diesel engines for marine and industrial use. Though there has been some overlapping in their products over the years, it has been generally true that the Detroit Diesel Engine Division has specialized in smaller engines.

clear that he was not attracted to General Motors merely by the corporation's great economic strength. ". . . we had more than that in General Motors," he commented. ". . . of the companies that I knew at that time, many of them with plenty of financial resources, none of them had the mental approach to this problem that was necessary to take it at that stage that it was in then, and the courage that went along with it to move it to its point of success. At least that was our opinion in the matter."

For a while Winton and Electro-Motive operated about as before. Mr. Hamilton and Mr. Kettering both had the impression that it would take a considerable length of time to build a commercially acceptable diesel engine for the railroads. Meanwhile, Mr. Kettering devoted his efforts, in large measure, to perfecting the two-cycle diesel engine. By 1932 Mr. Kettering decided he could build a two-cycle, eight-cylinder engine that would produce about 600 horsepower. Since Mr. Kettering's new engine would have a good edge over existing four-cycle engines in the 600-horsepower range, particularly in the weight-per-horsepower ratio, his engine seemed worth building.

At about this time we were planning our exhibit for the Century of Progress World's Fair, which was scheduled to open in Chicago in 1933. Our exhibit was to be a dramatic display—an automobile assembly line in actual operation, producing Chevrolet passenger cars. We needed a source of power for the assembly line and decided that two of Mr. Kettering's proposed 600-horsepower diesel engines would do the job.

When we first conceived the idea of powering our World's Fair display with the new diesel engine, what we had in mind was to get a good long look at the engine under actual operating conditions. We were primarily concerned with proving that Mr. Kettering's basic design was a good and practical one; we did not anticipate that the commercial applications would come as soon as they did. But before the engine for the display was even finished, our perspective on this matter was drastically altered.

What changed it, principally, was the sudden interest of one railroad president—Ralph Budd of the Burlington—in the diesel engine. Mr. Budd was then hoping to build a new, streamlined, lightweight passenger train that would be dramatic in appearance and economical in operation. One day in the fall of 1932 he stopped off in Cleveland to see Mr. Hamilton, who told him about General Motors' diesel experiments and put him in touch with Mr. Kettering. Mr. Budd was excited about the prospects.

He paid a visit to Detroit and to the General Motors Research Laboratories. Mr. Kettering showed him the experimental two-cycle engine but warned him that the eight-cylinder model was not yet built and certainly required a great deal more development work before it could be considered seriously as a source of locomotive power. Mr. Budd was told about General Motors' plans to test the engine at the World's Fair.

When the fair finally opened, our diesel engines were visible, through a plate-glass window, to anyone who cared to inspect them. However, we were still apprehensive about them, and the publicity man for our exhibit was under strict orders to say nothing about them—even though they were, in a sense, the most dramatic feature of our exhibit. The engines were unheralded, then, but Mr. Budd, at least, paid close attention to them during the entire fair. He was well aware of the difficulties we were having with the engines. He knew that every night one or two engineers had to work on them to ensure that they would still be functioning the next day. He knew the opinion of Mr. Kettering's son, Eugene, who was in charge of the maintenance operation, and who later commented that "the only part of that engine that worked well was the dip-stick."

Nevertheless, Mr. Budd continued to press us for a diesel engine that he could use on his Burlington Zephyr. He became more insistent than ever when, in 1933, the Union Pacific publicly announced its plans to build a streamlined train. The Union Pacific was planning only a small, three-car affair without any real locomotive—the power car was to be an integral part of the train itself. The power was derived from a twelve-cylinder, 600-horsepower gasoline engine, which was built by Winton. There were no major technological innovations in this Union Pacific train; but pictures of it were widely distributed, the public reception was quite favorable, and suddenly the nation was very much interested in streamliners. All of this served to fortify Mr. Budd's desire, which was intense anyway, to put his own streamliner in business. But he still wanted diesel power.

We would have preferred to spend another year or two taking the "bugs" out of Mr. Kettering's engine, but Mr. Budd's insistence finally won us over. In June 1933 we agreed to build an eight-cylinder, 600-horsepower diesel engine for his Pioneer Zephyr. When it was put in test operation in April 1934 it broke down continually, as we had feared. However, the defects were gradually ironed out of it, and in June 1934 Mr. Budd ordered two more 201A General Motors Diesels, as they were called, for his Twin Zephyrs. Meanwhile, the Union Pacific had not waited for the delivery of its streamliner. Before this, it had placed a new order with Winton in late June 1933, this time for a twelve-cylinder, 900-horsepower diesel for a six-car articulated sleeping-car train; and again in February 1934 the Union Pacific ordered six 1200-horsepower diesel passenger units for its "City" series.

These early diesel-powered streamliners were spectacular successes. In a memorable test run from Denver to Chicago, the Burlington Zephyr averaged 78 miles per hour for a total running time of only thirteen hours and ten minutes. The Union Pacific "City" trains cut the running time from the West Coast to Chicago from over sixty to less than forty hours. Operating costs to the railroads were lower and passenger patronage was considerably higher. Both of our customers immediately began calling upon us for more power so they could lengthen their trains. In May 1935 we began delivering the Union Pacific's 1200-horsepower diesels; we furnished the Burlington with two engines of 1200-horsepower apiece. These engines were able to pull twelve-car trains.

One day early in 1934 Mr. Kettering and Mr. Hamilton paid me a visit, and we got to talking about the diesel. Mr. Hamilton, who was always in close touch with the railroad people, told me that our engines were considered by them to be a vast success. However, he said, the railroads were beginning to ask General Motors to supply them with all-purpose diesel-powered locomotives instead of merely engines for power cars. Mr. Kettering indicated that he would like to undertake the development of an experimental diesel-powered locomotive. I inquired how much money he thought he would need. Mr. Kettering said that he thought it might take as much as $500,000. I told him that my own experience with new development projects suggested strongly that he could not give us a new locomotive on such a comparatively modest sum. "I know," he replied amiably, "but I figure if we spend that much, you'll come through with the rest." He got the money.

Actually, we were a long way from being in the locomotive business at that time. Our only production facilities were those for making engines in the Winton plant, and even these were somewhat outmoded; we had nothing at all for building electrical transmission equipment and locomotive bodies. Accordingly, we decided early in 1935 to build our own factory at La Grange, Illinois. This plant originally produced only the body of the locomotive—the cab and the truck—with the engines coming from Winton and the other components from outside suppliers, as before. But the La Grange plant was designed so that we could expand its operations to produce and assemble all the parts of a locomotive. We began this expansion soon after the plant was completed. By 1938 La Grange was a fully integrated locomotive plant.

Our early experience with the diesel was, as I have indicated, in the passenger-locomotive field. But in the mid-thirties Mr. Hamilton and his group decided that there was a great economic potential for diesel-powered switching locomotives. At that time one of our competitors was offering the railroads a diesel-powered switcher that weighed about one hundred tons and sold as high as $80,000. The locomotive was, in large measure, built to the customer's specifications. It was Mr. Hamilton's contention that if the customer was willing to accept a standard diesel switcher "right off the shelf," then we could market one for $72,000. Under his prodding we began to build these switchers. Indeed, we put fifty of them in production before we had one firm order.

The importance we attached to this new policy may be gauged by a memorandum written on December 12, 1935. It was from Mr. Pratt to me, and it said, at one point:

There is one fundamental policy which we believe will have to be maintained, namely, that the Electro-Motive Corporation will build a standardized product and not undertake to build to the many different standards and specifications on which each railroad demands to purchase; and our recommendation is that the policy of building a standard product be given at least a fair trial before we yield to obtaining business by letting each railroad write its own specifications as to what the locomotive should be.

As it turned out, the issue was settled very quickly. Our first batch of switchers was sold easily, deliveries beginning in May 1936. Although the margin of profit was small at first, it was enough to make a big difference in Electro-Motive's profit picture. Mr. Hamilton promised the railroads that, as our volume in switchers increased, we would pass along our operating economies to them in the form of price reductions. By 1943 when the War Production Board took General Motors out of the switcher field and directed us to concentrate entirely on freight locomotives, we had built 768 switchers; and the price to our customers on the 600-horsepower switchers was down to $59,750 by October 1940.

Meanwhile, our passenger-locomotive business expanded rapidly. By 1940 we had about 130 diesel-powered passenger locomotives in service on railroads all over the country. We began to build freight locomotives in 1939. There was an interruption during the early part of World War II when our plant was virtually out of the locomotive business while producing LST engines for the Navy.

At this point the reader may be wondering what the rest of the locomotive industry was doing while we were pushing ahead with our diesel program. With only a few exceptions and qualifications, the answer is that the rest of the industry was sticking with steam power. Though a few attempts were made, in this country and Canada, to build diesel passenger locomotives before 1940, production never advanced beyond the prototypes. (In 1940 a diesel-powered passenger locomotive built by a competitor finally went into service.) Outside of one attempt made by a group of builders in the late twenties, no manufacturer in this country, other than ourselves, brought out a diesel-powered freight locomotive until after World War II. Aside from switchers, it might be said, we were first everywhere on the railroads of this country with diesel power. To suggest, as a Senate subcommittee did in 1955, that we shoved ourselves into the locomotive market by main force, is to ignore the fact that other manufacturers failed to see the potential of the diesel. As Mr. Kettering once remarked during another congressional investigation, our biggest advantage in the locomotive industry was the fact that our competitors thought we were crazy.

Yet the superiority of diesel power over steam was apparent from the beginning. Rudolph Diesel first mentioned this superiority in railroad applications in 1894 and numerous times afterward. During the late 1920s engineering and railroad journals were carrying full reports and operating-cost data on diesel locomotives then in operation in Europe. To anyone who would listen, we could prove that the diesel offered smoother, faster, cleaner service, and an enormous saving in fuel and other operating costs. The railroads, which were eager to trim their operating costs in every way possible during the 1930s, listened eagerly; the other locomotive manufacturers continued to regard the diesel as a sort of passing fad. This explains why a group of long-established, economically strong locomotive manufacturers, with strong ties to their customers, were so easily outdistanced by one newcomer to the business.

It was not until the mid-1950s that the building of steam locomotives in this country stopped completely, with production in the closing years going largely to export. Less than a hundred steam locomotives remain in operation in the United States today. Diesel power alone is now being purchased by the railroads, except for electric locomotives used on electric-powered roads. This revolution in the railroad industry in the United States was made very largely by General Motors.

It is hard to make precise statements about the future of the diesel locomotive business, but it appears that the market in the United States will be somewhat smaller in the years ahead. Railroad passenger service is being discontinued in many areas of the country, and even freight carloadings have declined somewhat in recent years. There were about 60 per cent more steam locomotives in service during the mid-1930s than there are diesels today. This fact reflects the greater power and operating availability of the diesel, of course, but it also reflects the depressed condition of the railroads.

Overseas there still are some 100,000 steam locomotives in operation. These eventually will be replaced by diesel-electric, diesel-hydraulic, and electric locomotives. The potential market for diesel-electric locomotives overseas is approximately 40,000 units. The Electro-Motive Division has developed a wide range of lightweight, restricted-clearance locomotives to meet this export demand. Where applicable, standard domestic locomotives have been sold overseas. Over four thousand General Motors locomotives are now in service in thirty-seven countries outside the United States—nine countries, including Canada, in the Western Hemisphere and twenty-eight countries of the Eastern Hemisphere.

The U.S. market is now a replacement, reconditioning, and upgrading rather than a new-user market. The so-called upgrading market is, of course, an increasingly important one today, and I do not mean to minimize it. Still, the industry in the United States has been dieselized; the revolution is over. At the same time, it is just under way overseas.

Frigidaire

Despite a lack of enthusiam at the highest levels of the corporation in the early days, the Frigidaire Division has grown steadily for about forty-five years and has become a major factor in the appliance industry. The Frigidaire line today includes electric household refrigerators, food freezers, ice-cube makers, automatic clothes washers and dryers, electric ranges, water heaters, dishwashers, food-waste disposers, air-conditioning equipment, and commercial laundry and dry-cleaning equipment. Frigidaire now has about ten thousand outlets in the United States.

The curious story of how General Motors got into the refrigerator business begins in June 1918 when Mr. Durant, who was then president of the corporation, purchased the Guardian Frigerator Company of Detroit. Mr. Durant made the purchase in his own name and with his own funds; the precise amount was $56,366.50. The company passed from Mr. Durant to General Motors in May 1919 at the same price. It was a small enterprise of no great substance. He soon renamed the company the Frigidaire Corporation, and also gave the name Frigidaire to the rather crude, primitive device which was then its sole product. Mr. Durant's motives in this transaction are not within my knowledge. But he was, of course, a man of boundless enthusiasms and great curiosity; and it is easy to understand that an "iceless frigerator"—as the Guardian product was called—would excite both of these qualities. I can only admire his gift for being in touch with future developments in this as well as the automotive field.

While I had no personal knowledge of Mr. Durant's transaction at the time it took place, John L. Pratt has told me that in his opinion more than enthusiasm for a new appliance underlay the purchase. He says that Mr. Durant was concerned about the prospect of the automobile business being declared unessential to our World War I mobilization effort, and was looking for an "essential" business to take the place of civilian automobiles. Given the great national effort to conserve food during World War I, a refrigerator company might be considered essential. However, the government made no effort to end automobile production; and in November, five months after his purchase had been made, the war ended.

The original Guardian refrigerator had been built by a Dayton mechanical engineer named Alfred Mellowes in 1915. The following year he organized the Guardian Frigerator Company in Detroit to manufacture and sell his device. Between April 1, 1916, and February 28, 1918, Guardian built and sold only thirty-four refrigerators, all of which were installed in homes in the Detroit area. Guardian's manufacturing facilities in 1917 consisted of only two lathes, one drill press, one shaper, one power saw, and a hand vacuum pump. In addition to manufacturing the "frigerators," Mr. Mellowes personally serviced them; he kept in close touch with the purchasers, visiting each of them every two or three weeks. As we ascertained at the time we bought Frigidaire, most of these early Guardian customers were pleased with the product. Many of them had, in fact, despite the numerous service problems, invested in Mr. Mellowes' company. But as investors, it appeared, they were less happily situated than they were as consumers. During its first twenty-three months Guardian showed a loss of $19,582. In the three months just before Mr. Durant bought it the company lost another $14,580, bringing its total deficit to $34,162. Less than forty refrigerators had been built and sold in the entire period. It is not difficult to understand why the original shareholders were happy to sell out.

When Frigidaire passed into General Motors, we tooled up in our Northway plant in Detroit to manufacture Frigidaire Model A—a machine which was identical to the old Guardian except for minor mechanical changes. Our miscalculation about the product's suitability for mass consumption was speedily brought home to us. Model A, and its successors in the first few years, remained a luxury product. What was worse, we could not get the "bugs" out of the machine, which broke down repeatedly. Our efforts to introduce a sales and service organization into a number of cities outside of Detroit were largely unsuccessful. It appeared that the machine really needed the kind of steady personal service that Mr. Mellowes had provided his small group of customers; but this kind of service was obviously impossible in a product intended for a mass market. After about a year and a half we seriously considered whether the Frigidaire operation might not be jettisoned. Something of our frame of mind may be sensed from the minutes of a meeting which took place in my office on February 9, 1921. The summary of my remarks includes these comments:

Frigidaire Corporation: Located at Detroit, Mich. and makes Frigidaires which up to the present have been a failure. Models have been changed frequently in order to create demand, but without success. Branches were opened at various points which have since been discontinued . . . Loss to date about $1,520,000. Inventory is about $1,100,000 —total loss expected to run about $2,500,000.

In a year when General Motors was in serious need of operating capital, the continued losses and relatively high inventory could not long be tolerated. And it is possible that Frigidaire would somehow have been disposed of then except for one fortuitous circumstance, upon which hangs a story.

In an earlier chapter I told how General Motors in 1919 acquired the Dayton properties with which Mr. Kettering was associated. Among these properties were the Domestic Engineering Company and the Dayton Metal Products Company.

The Domestic Engineering Company—later renamed the Delco-Light Company—was a manufacturer of home-lighting plants, which were sold mostly to farmers.

The Dayton Metal Products Company, an armament manufacturing concern, had begun research in the refrigeration field early in 1918 as part of a program designed to obtain a product which might keep the company in operation when the war ended and the armament business ceased.

The two enterprises—Domestic Engineering and Dayton Metal Products—were in the appliance business in some items, and were preparing to expand into some other items. With these enterprises General Motors also acquired all of the refrigeration developments of Mr. Kettering's research group. This informal research organization continued operations at Dayton until June 12, 1920, when the subsidiary General Motors Research Corporation was organized. General Motors thus acquired some outstanding engineers in this field, as well as the management and sales ability of Richard H. Grant, who was to contribute importantly to the success of Frigidaire in the early and middle 1920s.

All of these factors came together in our decision during the slump of 1921 to continue with Frigidaire. It was clear that we had at Dayton the research background and an organization to back up the Frigidaire development. Delco-Light had available a fine sales force spread over large areas of the country, and some unused manufacturing capacity which could be made suitable for the production of refrigerators. So we moved Frigidaire to Dayton, combined its operations with those of Delco-Light, and started on a new course in the refrigerator industry on a larger scale than theretofore.

The decision proved to be a sound one. Frigidaire's heavy losses in 1921 were reduced steadily in the next two years, and in 1924 the operation showed a profit for the first time. Meanwhile, production rose rapidly. Only a few more than a thousand units had been produced in 1921 at the Northway plant; about 2100 were sold in 1922, the first full year of operations at Dayton. The figure rose to 4700 in 1923, 20,200 in 1924, and 63,500 in 1925. By the last year, Frigidaire was established as a leading factor in the new refrigerator industry; it represented, I believe, more than half of the market. By 1927 it was apparent that Frigidaire was becoming much too big to be operated within Delco-Light, and in January 1928 it was removed from that company. Part of its operations had already been moved to nearby Moraine, Ohio, where we had a plant available. Frigidaire became a division of General Motors in December 1933.

Once we had decided to build up Frigidaire we made a number of major ground-breaking advances in the design and manufacture of the machine. Without these contributions, it is safe to say, popular acceptance of the refrigerator would have been delayed for a considerable period of time.

As I have indicated, the Guardian organization originally had no real research staff outside of Mr. Mellowes himself. Even in 1921, when Frigidaire was moved into Delco-Light, there were only twenty-odd engineers, modelmakers, testers, and the like engaged in this work. We realized that the whole future of Frigidaire depended on our ability to crack several research problems, and to produce a machine that would operate safely, economically, and dependably; hence we placed great emphasis on research. We soon managed to get rid of the space-consuming brine tank and water-cooled compressor used on the original Guardian machine; these devices, which were major sources of refrigerator breakdowns, were replaced by a direct-expansion coil and a two-cylinder, air-cooled compressor. In the early machines, food was sometimes contaminated when moisture leaked into the refrigerator; we overcame this problem by introducing asphalt-and-cork sealing. We reduced the weight of the machine and considerably improved its appearance when we introduced the all-porcelain cabinet in 1927. All of these improvements were instrumental in the great expansion of the Frigidaire market during the 1920s. Another major cause of this expansion was our ability to get prices down. The 1922 B-9 wood refrigerator with brine tank and water-cooled compressors had a net weight of 834 pounds and sold for $714. In contrast, the M-9 Frigidaire model of 1926, a steel cabinet fitted with an air-cooled compressor and direct-cooling coils, had a net weight of 362 pounds and sold for $468.

During the 1919–26 period no other manufacturer or organization made any appreciable contribution to the refrigeration business in research, engineering development, mass-production methods, or distribution and servicing techniques. Our biggest research problem in Frigidaire, and the corporation's great ultimate contribution, concerned the refrigerant itself. The fact was, during the 1920s, that the refrigerants used by Frigidaire, and by all its leading competitors, had some health hazards; fumes from the refrigerating agents were toxic and in a few cases had actually caused the death of persons who breathed them. Because of the health hazard, these early refrigerators were sometimes kept on the back porch rather than in the kitchen; hospitals generally could not use them at all. We believed that sulphur dioxide, the agent first used in our refrigerators, was the least dangerous of the known refrigerants—principally because its distinctly irritating odor served as a warning to anyone breathing it. Nevertheless, it was clear that, ultimately, something better had to be found.

In 1928 Mr. Kettering, who was then director of General Motors Research Laboratories, initiated a major assault on the whole problem of the refrigerating agent. He commissioned one of his former associates in General Motors, Thomas Midgley, Jr.—the man who had developed tetraethyl lead—to find a new agent. After a series of conferences between Mr. Midgley, Mr. Kettering, and Frigidaire executives, they agreed that the refrigerant they were looking for should meet certain requirements. These were:

Of primary importance:

(1) To have a suitable boiling point.
(2) To be nonpoisonous.
(3) To be nonflammable.
(4) To have a distinct but not unpleasant odor.

Of secondary importance:

(5) To be immiscible with lubricating oils.
(6) To be relatively inexpensive.

These "secondary" requirements, it was understood, would be met so long as they did not conflict with the primary requirements. But there was agreement that all of the first four specifications *had* to be met before the electric refrigerator could be regarded as a complete success. A study of all existing literature was made at the Research Laboratories, under Mr. Kettering's direction, for compounds which might meet these specifications. This study pointed out the possibility of using fluorinated hydrocarbons. All through 1928 Mr. Midgley and some associates, especially Dr. A. L. Henne, worked in a private laboratory in Dayton in an effort to find a suitable refrigerant. They soon came to believe that some of the chlorofluoro derivatives of methane might do the job. By the end of the year Mr. Midgley had determined that dichloro-difluoro-methane, called Freon-12, would meet all four of the primary requirements agreed upon. It would not meet either of the two secondary requirements, but since it was clearly the best refrigerant available, Mr. Midgley and his associates began working on the development of processes for manufacturing the compound. A pilot plant was designed and put in operation at Dayton during the fall and winter of 1929–30.

In the fall of 1929 we knew as much about the Freon-12 refrigerant as we had to know. Frigidaire chemists had made exhaustive studies of the compound's physical properties. They had determined the corrosion effects of Freon-12 on high- and low-carbon steels, aluminum, copper, monel metal, tin, zinc, tin-lead solders, and other metals and alloys used in refrigerating systems. They had examined the effect of Freon-12 on different foods, and on flowers and furs. The tests were satisfactory to us. At the 1930 meeting of the American Chemical Society, Mr. Midgley read a paper on Freon-12 and publicly demonstrated that it was nonflammable; he proved that it was nontoxic by inhaling some of it himself.

As I have indicated, Freon-12 did not meet either of Mr. Midgley's two secondary requirements. It was quite expensive, in fact. Whereas sulphur dioxide had cost six cents a pound, the initial price of Freon-12 was sixty-one cents in 1931. Even now it costs more than sulphur dioxide did then—but health-department codes do not allow the use of the latter.

Since we regarded our new compound as the safest refrigerant available, we offered it to our competitors from the beginning, and by the mid-1930s Freon-12 was used almost universally in electric refrigerators. Even today, no better refrigerant has been found.

By 1932 or thereabouts it was unmistakably clear to us that in Frigidaire we had a property of vast growth potential. In 1929 we had manufactured our one-millionth Frigidaire, and three years later we had manufactured 2,250,000. Our success in developing Freon-12 removed the last roadblock standing in the way of the refrigerator industry. But while it was clear that Frigidaire and the industry would expand, it was also clear that Frigidaire's share of this great market must inevitably decline somewhat. Several companies would begin making refrigerators toward the end of the 1920s. Kelvinator was, of course, a pioneer. The original Kelvinator Corporation entered the electric-refrigerator field in 1914 and was the first enterprise to manufacture mechanical refrigerators for household use on a commercial scale. General Electric and Norge entered the field in 1927, Westinghouse in 1930. By 1940, the last prewar year of unregulated commercial production, Frigidaire's share of the refrigerator market—which had been above 50 per cent in the 1920s—was down to 20 to 25 per cent. But our smaller percentage represented a larger volume. Shipment of our refrigerators rose from some 300,000 in 1929 to 620,000 in 1940.

During the years 1926–36 a number of Frigidaire's competitors gained an advantage over us in the marketing area. They began to make and sell radios, electric ranges, washers, ironers, and dishwashers, while Frigidaire concentrated on refrigerators. In 1937 we added electric kitchen ranges to the Frigidaire line, and a few years later, window-type room air-conditioners. But these did little to overcome Frigidaire's competitive disadvantage. Obviously, families and home builders who wanted to purchase a full complement of household appliances would buy from one of the manufacturers who offered a complete line.

We failed to expand the Frigidaire line in the years before the war. As early as 1935, for example, Mr. Pratt had suggested that Frigidaire get more actively into air-conditioning; but his suggestion did not register on us, and the proposal was not then adopted.

During the war we made a review of Frigidaire's prospects and concluded that it would no longer be feasible to operate in the appliance field on a limited basis. A survey of Frigidaire dealers conducted prior to the end of the war served to fortify this conviction. In response to the survey question, "Should Frigidaire manufacture additional appliance products?" 99 per cent of the dealers who were polled replied, "Yes." The dealers indicated that, principally, they wanted automatic washing machines, refrigerator-freezer combinations, conventional washing machines, food freezers, gas ranges, and ironing machines—in that order.

Most of these appliances and several others were added by Frigidaire in the postwar years. The following list shows the years in which we introduced new household appliances:

Home food freezers	1947
Automatic washers	1947
Dryers	1947
Automatic ice-cube makers	1950
Dishwashers	1955
Wall ovens	1955
Fold-back cooking units	1955
Built-in cooking units	1956

Meanwhile, our original product—the refrigerator—has been enlarged and improved little by little to such an extent that it has become almost a new appliance. The typical refrigerator sold in the early 1930s was a five-cubic-foot model, styled rather drearily, and depressingly bulky in relation to its actual refrigeration space. Refrigerators sold today have, as a rule, from ten to nineteen cubic feet of storage space. They are beautifully styled, require no defrosting, and have considerable freezer space. There is no question that the modern refrigerator is a much better buy than its early counterpart. I am indebted to a study by Professor M. L. Burstein of Northwestern University for some detailed data bearing on this point. He has calculated that "the real price of refrigeration services in 1955 was but 23 per cent of that in 1931." That comes pretty close to the essential meaning of progress.

Aviation

General Motors has been involved in the aviation industry in several different ways. The bulk of our aviation business has been military, of course, and has consisted of work done under contract for the federal government—most of it during World War II and in the ensuing years of the cold war. But that is not the whole story.

It will, I suspect, come as a surprise to many readers that General Motors long ago made a major effort to enter the commercial aviation field. Bendix Corporation, North American Aviation, Trans World Airlines, and Eastern Air Lines, all owe something of their present identities to the activities of General Motors.

Our venture into commercial aviation was made in 1929. In that year we made two large investments and one small one in aviation. We purchased a 24 per cent interest in the newly formed Bendix Aviation Corporation and a 40 per cent interest in the Fokker Aircraft Corporation of America. Together, these investments cost us some $23 million. In addition, we purchased the entire capital stock of the Allison Engineering Company. This investment cost only $592,000, and did not play an important part in the plans we had then to enter the aviation industry.

Our 1929 decision to get into aviation has an interesting background. I should mention that General Motors was not entirely a stranger to the aviation industry at that time. During World War I, Buick and Cadillac had combined to manufacture the famous Liberty aircraft engine for the government, along with Ford, Packard, Lincoln, and Marmon. More than 2500 of these engines were actually produced by us, and orders for over 10,000 more were on our books at the time of the 1918 armistice. From an engineering standpoint, there was not a great deal of difference in those days between an airplane engine and an automobile engine, and we were able, in consequence, to make good use of our automotive experience in compiling an outstanding production record. In addition, General Motors acquired in 1919 the Dayton Wright Airplane Company, which had produced a total of 3300 airplanes during the war period. Fisher Body also—before its purchase by General Motors—was an important manufacturer of military airplanes.

During the 1920s it became steadily clearer that aviation was to be one of the great American growth industries; and especially after Lindbergh's dramatic flight in 1927 there was a vast public enthusiasm for aviation and a widespread conviction, which we shared, that it would soon accomplish many more "miracles." As automobile producers, we were especially concerned about one possible use of the airplane. There was in the late 1920s a great deal of talk about developing a "flivver" plane—that is, a small plane for everyday family use. We knew, of course, that any such plane would have to be much safer than existing models and also much cheaper. But as one aviation miracle succeeded another, our conviction grew that the flivver plane was at least a possibility. The development of such a plane would have large, unforeseeable consequences for the automobile industry, and we felt that we had to gain some protection by "declaring ourselves in" the aviation industry. In 1929 we did not plan to operate either Bendix or Fokker as a division of General Motors; our investments were made as a means of maintaining a direct and continuing contact with developments in aviation. Our 1929 annual report to shareholders summed up our thinking on the matter as follows:

. . . General Motors, in forming this association [with the aviation industry], felt that, in view of the more or less close relationship in an engineering way between the airplane and the motor car, its operating organization, technical and otherwise, should be placed in a position where it would have an opportunity to [come into] contact with the specific problems involved in transportation by air. What the future of the airplane may be no one can positively state at this time. Through this association General Motors will be able to evaluate the development of the industry and determine its future policies with a more definite knowledge of the facts.

As these words suggest, the engineering techniques of the automobile and aircraft industries were still quite similar in 1929—much more similar than they are today. Thus in acquiring our interests in the aviation companies we also gained access to some valuable technical information that was directly relevant to our own automobile operations. Bendix, especially, owned or controlled some important patents for devices applicable to the automobile industry. Indeed, its accessory lines included some automobile components— for example, brakes, carburetors, and starting drives for engines. The company had a superb technical staff—a fact which made our investment all the more attractive. Our principal contributions to both Bendix and Fokker, after we had made our investment in these companies, were in the realm of corporate organization and management.

Our 40 per cent interest in Fokker cost us $7,782,000. This company had two small, leased plants at the time we made our investment: one in Hasbrouck Heights, New Jersey, and one in Glendale, West Virginia. Anthony H. G. Fokker, a brilliant Dutch aircraft builder, had formed the company some time earlier to exploit the American manufacturing rights to his work. His aircraft had figured prominently in the pioneer days of aviation; they had been involved in such historic events as the first nonstop flight across the United States, Byrd's flight over the North Pole, and the first flight from the United States to Hawaii. When we bought into Fokker, the company was engaged primarily in aircraft manufacture for the United States government and, to a lesser extent, for commercial air-transport operators. Soon after our investment, the company incurred some serious operating losses. We felt that these losses reflected weakness in the company's management, and we conveyed our views to Mr. Fokker. He did not agree with us, but after a series of exchanges he withdrew from the company and returned to Holland. We then embarked upon a course of action which completely transformed the character of the organization.

The following interrelationships are complex, and I see no way to simplify the description of them. First of all, we changed the name of the Fokker Aircraft Corporation of America to General Aviation Manufacturing Corporation and consolidated the operations in a leased plant in Dundalk, Maryland. In April 1933 we took another important step. We combined General Aviation and North American Aviation; all of General Aviation's assets were exchanged for approximately 1,500,000 shares of North American common stock. General Aviation was subsequently liquidated, and its holdings in North American stock distributed to the shareholders. As a result of this distribution, and of open-market purchases for our own account, General Motors' equity in North American amounted to nearly 30 per cent of that company's outstanding stock by the end of 1933.

North American Aviation had been organized as a holding company in 1928. Although it had some substantial investments in aircraft manufacturing companies even before it was joined with General Aviation, its primary concern had been the airline business. It owned all of Eastern Air Transport (later called Eastern Air Lines), 26.7 per cent of Transcontinental Air Transport, and 5.3 per cent of Western Air Express Corporation. General Aviation had also owned 36.6 per cent of Western Air Express stock. Afterward, therefore, North American owned 41.9 per cent of Western Air Express stock. Furthermore, Western Air Express and Transcontinental Air Transport each owned 47.5 per cent of the stock of Transcontinental and Western Air, Inc. (now Trans World Airlines). The upshot of the arrangement, then, was that General Motors held a 30 per cent interest in North American, and North American held about a 33 per cent interest in TWA. North American was thereby enabled to co-ordinate the transcontinental operations of TWA with the East Coast system of its own Eastern Air Lines.

The Air Mail Act of 1934 prohibited the ownership of stock in an airline company by companies engaged either directly or through a subsidiary in aircraft manufacturing. North American therefore distributed its holdings in TWA to its shareholders. As a shareholder of North American, General Motors received some 13 per cent of TWA's stock, which we sold in 1935.

For a time North American operated Eastern Air Lines as a division, and then disposed of this airline in March 1938. As the largest single shareholder in North American, General Motors had several representatives on its board of directors. One day, during the period when North American was negotiating the sale of Eastern Air Lines to some Wall Street interests, I received a telephone call from Eddie Rickenbacker, the United States' great World War I flying ace. He had been active in the Eastern Air management and was now interested in bidding to buy control of the airline. He complained that he was not being given a chance, however, and asked if I would intervene in his behalf.

I had always considered Eddie to be a capable operator, and I naturally wanted him to have an equal opportunity to bid for Eastern; I felt that he could be counted on to develop an efficient operation. I told him I would see what I could do. The next morning I looked into the matter and found that the Eastern Air stock had not yet been sold. I made a plea in Eddie's behalf, and as a result he was given thirty days to get the backing which would enable him to bid.

He did not get his backing very easily, however, and as the dead-

line approached he became understandably nervous about the outcome. The next to the last day fell on a Saturday. Eddie called me
at my apartment as I was preparing for bed, and inquired if he
could come over for a few minutes. When he arrived he indicated
that his prospects for getting the money were still excellent, but
that he might need more time. He wondered if he could have a few
days' extension. I told him not to worry, and he left in good spirits.
But as it turned out, he did not need the extension. His backers
called him the next morning and told him that they were prepared
to go through with the deal. This disposal by North American of
its Eastern Air Lines operation was a transaction that gave us all
a great deal of satisfaction.

In the reorganization that followed the Air Mail Act of 1934,
North American became an operating company. Its manufacturing
operations were consolidated and moved to a new plant in Ingle-
wood, California. During the ensuing years, the company placed
emphasis on the development of military aircraft and made some
notable strides in that direction. In the late 1930s the company won
several military design competitions, and these successes established it as one of the nation's leading aircraft manufacturers.

A number of aircraft which evolved from this early development
work played a vital part in World War II. Among the more famous
of the North American planes were the P-51 Mustang fighter—perhaps the most highly regarded fighter plane employed by the Allied
forces during the war; the B-25 Mitchell bomber used by General
Doolittle in his historic raid on Tokyo; and the ubiquitous AT-6
Texan trainer, which became virtually standard equipment at Air
Corps and Navy training bases and was used extensively by other
Allied countries.

The AT-6, by the way, reflected the General Motors influence on
North American. As automobile men, we naturally thought in terms
of "standardized" production models which could realize the inherent economies of volume production. North American began looking for a plane that could be marketed this way and soon decided
that a good basic-training plane was the best bet. Even before the
war the AT-6 became its "bread and butter" model.

General Motors was continuously represented on North American's board of directors from 1933 until we finally disposed of our
interest in 1948. During that time—and especially in the earlier
years—we provided a considerable amount of policy and adminis-

trative guidance through our representatives on the board, and we were instrumental, I believe, in developing an efficient, systematic approach to management in the company. North American's corporate organization and its financial, production, and cost controls were our special contributions. It appears that in 1939 North American was the only aircraft-manufacturing company with production and cost-control systems like those used in the automobile industry.

A major share of the credit for introducing General Motors' management techniques at North American, and at Bendix, too, must go to Ernest R. Breech. Mr. Breech was originally a financial man in General Motors (he was general assistant treasurer from 1929 to 1933), but when he moved over to North American he soon showed a great talent for operations as well. He was chairman of the board of North American Aviation from 1933 to 1942—the years during which the holding company was converted into a large manufacturing operation. In addition, he became a director of Bendix in 1937. I had always considered Mr. Breech to be an excellent prospect for top management, and had tried for some time to bring him into a good operating position in General Motors. I was opposed in this effort by William S. Knudsen, executive vice president and later president of General Motors, who still regarded Mr. Breech as a financial man. But finally, in 1937, I found a spot for him as group executive in charge of General Motors' household-appliance operations. He filled this post with distinction while continuing to serve as chairman of North American and as a Bendix director.

In 1942 he became president of Bendix, relinquishing his other assignments. At Bendix again, he performed brilliantly all during the war years and more than justified my faith in him. But the story of his career has an ironic twist, as many persons know. In performing so well in all his General Motors assignments, he attracted the attention of Henry Ford II, who wanted someone to head the rebuilding program of the Ford Motor Company. Mr. Breech got that job in 1946, and introduced General Motors' management and financial techniques into the new modern Ford organization.

When Mr. Breech was chairman of North American, he induced J. H. ("Dutch") Kindelberger, who had been chief engineer for Douglas Aircraft, to head up operations. Mr. Kindelberger was elected president and chief executive officer of North American at the end of 1934. He was an extremely capable engineer and demonstrated great technical competence in aircraft design and manufacture. He developed into a fine administrator, and came to be recognized as a man who could produce outstanding military planes at low cost. But he had had very little general administrative experience before coming to North American, and, recognizing his own limitations, he relied at first on the General Motors directors for advice and counsel. Messrs. Breech and Kindelberger, together with Henry M. Hogan, then assistant general counsel of General Motors, constituted a sort of informal executive committee and regularly consulted each other on all the important company problems which arose between meetings of the board of directors. Messrs. Breech and Hogan in turn reported to Albert Bradley or C. E. Wilson, who, in addition to their regular duties as executive officers in General Motors, had group responsibility for our investments in associated companies.

Our relations with Bendix were much the same as with North American. We were represented on the Bendix board of directors from 1929 until 1937 by Messrs. Wilson and Bradley; the latter was also chairman of the Bendix Finance Committee throughout that period. In 1937 the press of other duties forced these two to give up their Bendix directorships, and they were succeeded on the board by Mr. Breech and by A. C. Anderson, the comptroller of General Motors. Our representatives on the Bendix board took a direct interest in the internal management of Bendix and were instrumental, I believe, in improving management effectiveness. They were responsible for some organizational changes and for a new and effective system of co-ordinating the semi-autonomous divisions. Our representatives also had a direct hand in the elevation of Malcolm Ferguson to the important post of general manager of the South Bend automotive parts plant of that company. He later became president of Bendix.

By the end of the 1930s our perspective on North American and Bendix had changed considerably. Our original motive for investing in the aviation industry—the feeling that the industry might somehow produce a flivver plane which could compete with the automobile—came to seem less relevant as the years passed. No plane suitable for "family use" was ever developed; indeed, the whole commercial-aviation field remained a small one during the years of the depression. North American and Bendix continued to grow, but both companies discovered that their greatest opportunities lay in the military field. By 1940 each company had annual sales running around $40 million, and the great bulk of this was defense work done under government contracts. In 1944 at the peak of wartime production, North American's sales were about $700 million, and Bendix's sales came to more than $800 million. These huge figures suggest the far-reaching consequences for us of our original concern about the flivver plane.

The Allison Engineering Company, which we also acquired in 1929, has had a growth history no less spectacular than North American and Bendix. As I have mentioned, we purchased Allison outright for only $592,000. By our standards, it was a small operation: the company had fewer than 200 employees in 1929, and its manufacturing facilities occupied only about 50,000 square feet of floor space. We considered it to be of only minor importance in our plans to enter the aviation industry. Yet as events turned out, we were to make Allison our principal link to the industry.

When we acquired Allison in 1929 the company had been in existence for fourteen years. In its early years it was not in the aviation field; it was primarily a supporting machine shop for racing cars at the Indianapolis Speedway. Its founder, James A. Allison, gradually shaped an organization of skilled mechanics, machinists, and engineers, and began to produce a few marine engines and reduction gears for boats and aircraft. In the early 1920s Allison was able to accept a contract for the modification of World War I Liberty aircraft engines. Chronic failures in the crankshaft and connecting-rod bearings had seriously limited the durability of these engines. But Allison was able to develop a steel-backed, lead-bronze, crankshaft main bearing that was capable of supporting higher horsepower loads without failure. The company also developed an ingenious method of casting lead-bronze on both the inner and outer surfaces of a steel shell, which could be used in making connecting-rod bearings of great durability. These developments were the basis for the highly regarded Allison bearing that came to be used extensively in high-horsepower engines throughout the world. The production of this bearing, and the contracts to modify Liberty engines, accounted for the principal business of the company during the 1920s.

When Mr. Allison died in 1928 the company was put up for

sale, on the condition that operations must continue in Indianapolis. Several prospective buyers were approached, but none was willing to accept this stipulation. Fortunately, C. E. Wilson had become well acquainted with the Allison organization while he was general manager of the Delco-Remy Division in Anderson, Indiana. He knew that the organization possessed valuable mechanical skills that we could use. We had no objection to continuing operations in Indianapolis, and on Mr. Wilson's recommendation we approved the purchase in early 1929. Norman H. Gilman, who had been president and chief engineer under Mr. Allison, continued in charge as general manager after our acquisition.

Early in the 1930s Allison embarked upon a project which proved to be of great military significance. This was the V-1710 engine project, and it was initiated by Mr. Gilman. After a careful survey of all the military aircraft engines then in existence, Mr. Gilman concluded that the armed services would one day require a reciprocating engine of 1000 horsepower; he also concluded that the engine should be liquid cooled (which would give it a slimmer shape than an air-cooled engine).

Only very meager funds for such projects were available from the military in the early 1930s, but Mr. Gilman did win a small contract, and Allison set to work designing the engine. A partial success was achieved in 1935 with a 1000-horsepower engine that functioned well for about fifty hours. However, the engineers could not get the engine to function for 150 hours—which army specifications required. To speed up development work on the engine we assigned Ronald M. Hazen, an outstanding engineer with the General Motors Research Laboratories, to work at Allison. Mr. Hazen's efforts were successful, and on April 23, 1937, the V-1710 passed all the tests required by the Army Air Corps. It was the first airplane engine in the United States to qualify at 1000 horsepower and the nation's first really successful high-temperature, liquid-cooled engine.

Until the V-1710 engine was developed the Air Corps had taken for granted the superiority of the air-cooled engine. But the Allison engine quickly proved its worth: In March 1939 a Curtiss P-40, powered by a V-1710 engine, won the Air Corps fighter aircraft race with a clear speed advantage of forty miles per hour over the previous winner. There was, naturally, a sudden great surge of interest in the Allison engine after that event. Not only the U. S. Air

Corps, but the armed forces of Britain and France began to look closely at our product.

Allison now had a serious problem. Though we had built it up somewhat since 1929, the year of our acquisition, it was still essentially a small engineering firm, geared mainly to experimental work with no facilities at all for quantity production. And quantity production at the end of the 1930s was being desperately demanded by the government.

The Assistant Secretary of War, Louis Johnson, personally visited Mr. Knudsen, who was then president of General Motors, to see what could be done about producing Allison engines. At that time there were firm orders for only 836 engines; and, as Mr. Johnson conceded, he was in no position to assure us that more orders would be forthcoming. Viewed simply as a business proposition, building a factory to make 836 engines seemed to be a bad risk; indeed, there was the risk that some new turn in the international situation or some new technological breakthrough might wipe out even this small demand before our factory was built. Nevertheless, we decided, after weighing the matter closely, to establish a new Allison plant in Indianapolis. This decision was based on a feeling that the V-1710 engine would probably be in great demand. Moreover, one does not lightly turn down any government request having to do with national security.

And so, on May 30, 1939, we broke ground in the shadow of the Indianapolis Speedway for a new plant to build the Allison engine. As it happened, more orders for the V-1710 did follow: the French government ordered 700 of the engines in February 1940, and the British ordered another 3500 a few months later. By December 1941 Allison was producing engines at the rate of 1100 a month. During the war we forced this rate still higher—even though the engine was being continually redesigned and repowered until it finally attained a combat rating of some 2250 horsepower. By December 1947, when we stopped making the V-1710 engine, total production was up to 70,000 engines. They had performed brilliantly all during the war and were used on such famous fighter planes as the Curtiss P-40 Warhawk, the Bell P-39 Aircobra, the Bell P-63 King Cobra, and the Lockheed P-38 Lightning.

Early in the war it became apparent that our involvement in aviation was so large as to raise a question about our permanent place in the industry. Accordingly, we made an effort to redefine our thinking about aviation and the part we should play in it. The principal statement on this important matter is a report which I made in 1942 to the Postwar Planning Group in General Motors. The recommendations in this report were eventually adopted by the corporation's Policy Committee, and they became the basis for our postwar aviation program.

In the report I indicated that there would be three major markets in the postwar aircraft industry—military, commercial air transport, and private civilian flying. I then raised the question whether we wanted to participate in any or all of these markets as producers of complete aircraft. I pointed out that the manufacture of military aircraft would involve a large amount of engineering and development work with continuous modification of low-volume models. Moreover, there would undoubtedly be excess capacity in the industry, resulting in severe competition for whatever business did exist, with little prospect for anything more than a small margin of profit.

In the commercial transport field I foresaw a rapid acceleration of transportation by air, not only for passengers but for freight as well. Even in this expanded market, however, the potential sales volume available to a manufacturer would be limited. I assumed that there would be something on the order of a tenfold increase in the number of transport planes in use—roughly 4000 planes altogether. But with an average life span of perhaps five years for each plane, the potential volume available to a single producer in any one year would not be great.

I was also dubious about the advisability of our manufacturing small private planes. While I believed that there would be some postwar expansion in the market for these planes—for both business and personal use—I felt that growth in this area would be limited until technology had advanced to a point where a far greater degree of safety could be attained. I stated that, unless there was some revolutionary breakthrough on safety, the private plane would not become a serious competitor of the motorcar in the foreseeable future.

In short, none of the three aircraft markets seemed inviting to General Motors. Furthermore, I said, if General Motors got into the business of manufacturing complete aircraft, we might jeopardize the other aviation business of the corporation. Our Allison Division was, and would continue to be, a major producer of air-

plane engines and certain aircraft accessories. In general, these accessories, with comparatively minor variations of an engineering
and production character, would be applicable to many kinds of
planes and might normally account for some 40 to 45 per cent of the
cost of a complete airplane. The sales potential in this area of the
market was substantial. But in order to realize this potential, an
accessory manufacturer would need the engineering co-operation
and confidence of the aircraft manufacturers who were his customers. If we were producing complete aircraft ourselves, we would
have difficulty establishing such a relationship with our customers.
How could we expect an airframe manufacturer engaged in developing a new plane to disclose its forward designs to an accessories producer who had the opportunity to make use of these
designs as a competitor? In short, it seemed incomprehensible to me
that we could expect to sell our accessories successfully and at the
same time compete with those to whom we must sell them by producing one or more types of airframes ourselves.

Discussion of this subject continued for some time and on August 17, 1943, our postwar aviation policy was formally defined in
the following resolution of the corporation's Policy Committee:

First: The corporation should not contemplate the production of complete airplanes in either the military or transport areas.
Second: The corporation should develop as complete a position in
the manufacture of accessories as its capacity and circumstances make
possible.

The reader will observe that we did not, at this time, specifically
exclude the possibility of our manufacturing a small plane for private business and personal use. We still doubted that volume production of such a plane would be possible on a basis attractive to
General Motors; however, we felt we could not ignore the possibility completely. In my report I recommended that we establish a
program to keep abreast of technological developments in the
small-plane business, but we later discarded the idea as impracti-
cable. However, North American Aviation did go on to design and
manufacture a plane for individual transportation, the Navion.

The formulation of our postwar aviation policy naturally had
considerable bearing on our attitude toward our investments in
North American and Bendix. During the war North American

became one of the nation's leading airframe manufacturers, and we concluded that a continued investment in the company would be no less damaging to General Motors' accessory business than direct manufacturing of airframes ourselves. Furthermore, it became increasingly clear that General Motors could not employ its mass-production techniques effectively in the airframe industry. We decided, therefore, that it would be in the best interests of both General Motors and North American to dispose of our holdings in the company at some appropriate time.

Bendix was a somewhat different proposition. This company already held a strong position in the aviation accessories field, and its activities fitted in very nicely with our own scheme of operations and postwar policy objectives. At one point we gave very serious study to acquiring Bendix outright and operating it as a consolidated division or subsidiary of General Motors, but decided against it. We gradually arrived at a general policy of disposing of minority interests, and in 1948 sold our interests in North American and Bendix. The capital thus released was employed in our rapidly expanding automotive operations.

Our contributions to Bendix and North American during the period of our association were not in the engineering and technological fields. They were in the more intangible area of business management. To the extent that our management philosophy was imparted to these companies and to the aviation industry in general, General Motors, I think, made a tangible contribution to that industry.

Chapter 20

CONTRIBUTIONS TO
NATIONAL DEFENSE

THE problem of defending the United States against aggression has come to seem a permanent one; and as each year passes, it grows increasingly hard to envisage a time in which we would not have to maintain our vast military establishment. For General Motors—and for hundreds of other corporations—defense work appears to be one of the inevitable facts of modern corporate life. In the years 1959 through 1962 General Motors' defense business amounted to between $350 million and $500 million a year, or about 3 per cent of sales—important, but relatively not large, and not comparable to what General Motors has done in time of war. The history of our defense work has several episodes —each largely unrelated to its predecessor.

Four distinct periods are involved. The first was World War I, during which we were one of the important manufacturers of aircraft engines for the army. Our total military production during this period was only $35 million, an insignificant amount by modern military standards. No serious effort was made to "mobilize" the corporation during the war; we produced automobiles without interruption, and it was possible to regard our military work as a kind of temporary sideline. When World War I ended, so did our military activities. For more than a decade, we had very little defense work and certainly no awareness that we would one day be the world's largest private producer of military "hardware."

This unexpected distinction was achieved during the second

period—the years just before and during World War II. In this period we produced an incredible $12 billion of military goods. Most of this production was compressed into a few years, during which we were fully mobilized for war. Between February 1942 and September 1945 we did not make a single passenger car in the United States. Our earlier experience in World War I was largely irrelevant to the problems we faced in World War II, and, in fact, I can think of only a few lessons learned during the first war that we were able to apply during the second. One of these, for example, concerned the rigid control of inventories and commitments in line with definite contractual agreements.

The third period, 1950–53, covered roughly the Korean War. Here again we faced a new situation. At the end of World War II virtually all our military business had ceased, and we had looked forward to a time in which we could devote ourselves substantially to making automobiles and other commercial products. However, we proposed to continue close liaison with the armed services, and we in fact continued to produce a few military items. This work was concentrated largely at Allison, which, in addition to its aircraft engines, began development and production of powershift transmissions for military tactical tracklaying vehicles. Thus in June 1950, when the Korean crisis brought new demands for defense production, Allison already had delivered substantial quantities of jet engines for fighter aircraft and was producing tank transmissions. In addition, several divisions were also at work on special engineering and development assignments. This time, the proposition we faced was a sort of "partial mobilization": the government reimposed controls on wages and prices, and it restricted the use of some materials (for example, rubber and copper), but we were allowed to continue most of our commercial business. As it turned out, our military products accounted for no more than 19 per cent of our business during the Korean War. However, we were kept alert to the possibility that full mobilization might be reimposed, and we had to plan accordingly.

The fourth period, the present one, is quite unlike all the previous periods, and it has required still another adjustment on our part. For one thing, military technology has become so advanced as to require new modes of production and new kinds of research. Meanwhile, the concept of total mobilization has become almost archaic. We know now that we will never again be fully organized for war. It is generally conceded that if there is another major war, it will be over in a relatively short period of time.

Our World War II experience with full mobilization is nevertheless of some interest, I think. Few people realize the dimensions of the task imposed on us then, or the manner in which we performed it.

To begin with a rather obvious point, General Motors turns out a different product during a war. In this respect we are unlike other military contractors, whose conversion to war production involves relatively minor changes. Clothing manufacturers, for example, can make uniforms for the armed forces; builders can make barracks or set up housing for defense workers; airframe manufacturers make more bombers and fewer passenger planes. But only a small proportion of General Motors products have wartime applications. When we were mobilized during World War II, we were obliged to transform the great bulk of our operations almost completely, to learn rapidly and under great pressure how to produce tanks, machine guns, aircraft propellers, and many other kinds of equipment with which we had no experience at all. We had to refit many large plants and retrain hundreds of thousands of workers. One statistic is perhaps worth citing: of the $12 billion of military equipment turned out by General Motors during World War II, more than $8 billion was represented by products that were entirely new to us. We were able to do this because we were decentralized: each division sought its own contracts; the yearly model change gave them know-how and flexibility.

In another way, too, perhaps a more fundamental way, our business was transformed by war. When we were mobilized for war, we operated under a new set of economic and other rules. General Motors at war became an entirely different organization from the one that sells automobiles in peacetime. Even the people who comprised the organization were different. More than 113,000 of our employees left us to go in the armed forces during World War II, and several of our highest executives served as administrators in Washington, prominently Mr. Knudsen, who was made one of the heads of war production. This change in the character of General Motors took place quite suddenly, for the most part; the bulk of the change was compressed within a few months of the year 1942.

Our assignment for that year, stated briefly, was to transform the world's largest automobile company into the world's largest manufacturer of materials for war. The dimensions of this task became clear immediately after Pearl Harbor. In the one month of January 1942 we received orders for some $2 billion of military goods—a figure which approximately equaled the total of all the orders we had got during the entire defense program until then. During the rest of 1942 the government placed $4 billion more of military orders with General Motors. Thus by the end of that year we had received military orders totaling more than $8 billion—an immense figure even for a corporation like General Motors, whose record prewar total output, achieved in 1941, was $2.4 billion. In other words, we had not only to alter the character of our product, but to increase our total output substantially.

Fortunately, we had done some advance planning which enabled us to take on this vast problem systematically. In June 1940 our Policy Committee, of which I was chairman, had begun to study the problems that would arise in General Motors if the corporation were converted to war production on a large scale; and in the ensuing months the committee made some basic policy decisions. One of these decisions concerned the size of our wartime operations. We concluded that, since General Motors then had about 10 per cent of the nation's facilities for manufacturing metal products, the corporation should endeavor to produce about this proportion of the nation's armaments in wartime. In retrospect, it is hard to say whether we ever did achieve this goal. Altogether, the United States government spent some $150 billion on military hardware during World War II. General Motors sales of war materials came to $12 billion, which would represent only 8 per cent of the total. However, I believe that our costs were lower than those of the average war contractor for similar products.

Another basic decision reached by the Policy Committee concerned our form of organization during wartime. Three members of the Policy Committee—Mr. Wilson, president of the corporation, and Mr. Bradley and Mr. Hunt, executive vice presidents—were made a "triumvirate" to handle all operations policies. Then in 1942 we formally set up the War Administration Committee to take charge of all war operations for the duration. The committee had twelve members, later increased to fourteen, including the triumvirate who remained as its senior operating members.

At the same time we concluded that our basic organizational policy—the policy of "decentralized responsibility with co-ordinated control"—should stand in war as in peace; for flexibility was as important in the one as in the other. This decision meant that in war the primary responsibility for contracting, pricing, and production rested with each individual division of the corporation, subject, of course, to our over-all policies. The decision also meant that our system of corporate integration, under which the various divisions "subcontract" work to one another, should be preserved. This system of internal subcontracting worked very effectively under wartime conditions, even though it required a great effort of co-ordination. For example, the M-24 tank, which Cadillac began to produce in 1944, had parts supplied by seventeen other divisions.

We also decided that we would continue to rely heavily on outside subcontractors. We had business relations with some 13,500 peacetime suppliers. During the war, this figure grew steadily, and at the peak of our wartime production, in 1944, we were using the facilities of some 19,000 subcontractors.

Another policy decision, designed to increase the efficiency of our production effort still further, called for the transfer of plant and equipment within the corporation, and to some extent outside it. During the war years, almost 5000 machines belonging to General Motors, and almost 2000 belonging to the government, were transferred from one division to another. We leased several of our plants to other corporations that were able to make better use of them; and we in turn acquired the use of many other plants for varying periods. (At the beginning of 1945, eighteen of the 120 plants we were operating in the United States were leased from the government, and another six were leased from others.)

I should mention one other very important decision reached in 1940. We decided that General Motors should seek to perform the most complicated and difficult production assignments.

As I have already indicated, most of the military products we made were entirely new to us. But the problem was not merely one of production; the military sciences were then advancing so rapidly that we were also obliged to design, and redesign, much of the equipment we produced. Toward the end of the war, we prepared a list of all General Motors military products, broken down by design origin. The breakdown based on net orders received through 1944 was as follows:

Twenty per cent were war products designed by General Motors in co-operation with the armed services. These products included light, medium, and heavy tanks, tank destroyers, armored cars, aircraft engines and propellers, and the amphibious "Ducks."

Thirty-five per cent were designed by others but incorporated some major design or production-engineering improvements by General Motors. These included the .30- and .50-caliber Browning machine guns, the M-1 carbine, and the Wildcat fighter and Avenger torpedo-bomber planes.

Seventeen per cent were peacetime General Motors products which we were able to redesign for military use; for example, trucks, diesel engines, and electrical equipment.

Thirteen per cent were peacetime General Motors products which could be put to war use with no major design changes; for example, commercial trucks, certain gasoline and diesel engines, ball bearings, and spark plugs.

Fifteen per cent were military products designed by others and produced by General Motors with no major design changes; for example, the Pratt & Whitney aircraft engine, B-29 and B-25 subassemblies, and ammunition items.

The upshot of these figures is that of all the military products which General Motors manufactured during the war, it designed, at least in part, 72 per cent. The table on page 381, based on deliveries through 1945, shows the great diversity of our military output.

This tabulation suggests yet another of our big problems: the continuous change in our "product mix" all during the war. In part, the change was caused by the rapid rate of obsolescence of all weapons. In 1944 the War Department reported that it was "not now using a single weapon in the same form or design as before Pearl Harbor." In part, the steady change in our output was caused by the changing tactical requirements of our fighting forces. Scheduling production under these circumstances was a hair-raising problem. Consider a typical situation: In January 1945 our Delco Products Division, which produced, among other things, landing-gear struts for the B-24, was told that production of the struts for the month of April should be 95 sets. In February the April target was suddenly raised to 285 sets. In March the April target was cut back to 60 sets. On April 1 the target was raised again to 120 sets. Actual production for the month of April was 85 sets—a remarkably close approximation of the final target, considering the scheduling problems Delco Products had been confronted with.

Despite these difficulties, our record of meeting contract delivery schedules was exceptionally good, on the whole. To enable the top officers of the corporation to check continually on this record, we

GENERAL MOTORS DELIVERIES OF WAR MATERIALS

PRODUCT CLASS	TOTAL THROUGH DECEMBER 31, 1942 %	PER CENT DISTRIBUTION			TOTAL THROUGH DECEMBER 31, 1945 %	TOTAL THROUGH DECEMBER 31, 1945*
		YEAR 1943 %	YEAR 1944 %	YEAR 1945 %		
Military trucks, amphibious trucks, parts & accessories	22.3	11.3	18.0	18.2	17.0	$2,090,620
Aviation:						
Allison engines	16.5	8.3	7.1	3.2	8.4	1,038,964
Pratt & Whitney engines	8.2	13.7	11.0	9.8	11.0	1,356,640
Jet-propulsion engines	- -	- -	- -	1.2	0.3	32,565
Complete aircraft and subassemblies	2.4	9.4	14.6	13.9	10.6	1,305,088
Aircraft parts, propellers, etc.	5.6	9.8	9.3	11.3	9.1	1,128,452
Total Aviation	32.7	41.2	42.0	39.4	39.4	4,861,709
Tanks, armored cars, gun motor carriages	11.8	17.9	15.6	19.0	16.2	1,999,365
Marine diesel engines	14.1	10.7	10.9	8.5	11.0	1,351,849
Guns, gun mounts & controls	12.2	12.6	7.5	4.8	9.3	1,148,369
Shells, shot, cartridge cases, etc.	4.2	3.8	3.0	4.7	3.8	468,135
Other	2.7	2.5	3.0	5.4	3.3	406,011
Total	100.0	100.0	100.0	100.0	100.0	
Dollar Total (in billions)	$2.4	$3.5	$3.8	$2.6	$12.3	

* In dollars, ooo omitted.

devised two kinds of production progress reports, to be sent to us regularly by each division. The first progress report, which was prepared monthly, had this information in it: total production to date on all major war contracts; anticipated production on these contracts for each of the following four months; expected total production at the end of these four months, compared with contract requirements; termination date of each contract; peak contract requirements; peak capacity of present facilities. In addition, detailed explanations had to be given for any recent or expected contract delinquencies.

The other report covered the short-term prospects. This report was submitted semimonthly, and it compared the actual production through the fifteenth or the end of the month with the schedules set up by the armed forces at the beginning of the month. Again, the division had to report and explain every contract delinquency, however minor, for every product, however unimportant. I may add that our delinquencies were relatively few; furthermore, the large majority of them were caused by circumstances over which we had no effective control—labor or material shortages, lack of shipping instructions, changes in government requirements, and so forth.

Our over-all record of success in meeting production schedules, and in maintaining a high quality of production, was attained in the face of severe manpower problems. During the war we had to hire and train in the United States a staggering number of new workers: 244,000 in 1942, 332,000 in 1943, and 156,000 in 1944. During the war period more than 750,000 new workers were hired. The sheer numbers involved were distressing enough; but in addition, the workers we got were generally at a very low level of industrial skill. Many of them were not physically fit; many, especially the women, had no prior industrial experience at all. Between the end of 1941 and the end of 1943 the proportion of women hourly employees working for General Motors rose from about 10 per cent to about 30 per cent of total hourly employees.

To work with this volatile and largely unskilled labor force, we were obliged to rationalize our production techniques as much as possible. For example, when the M-24 tank went into production at Cadillac, the division developed a "merry-go-round" type of conveyer which made it possible for each of the welders to perform one specialized, relatively simple task, instead of a difficult series of welding operations. By 1944 skilled manpower was in such short supply that its availability at a particular plant often became a controlling reason for performing certain jobs there—even when other plants had superior machinery for the jobs.

The basic financial policies which underlay our operations during the war had much to do with our performance. Early in 1942 the Policy Committee of the corporation adopted a new policy on wartime prices and profits. As we described this policy to the War Department's Price Adjustment Board, it was designed "to limit the over-all rate of profits from manufacturing operations, before provision for income and excess profits taxes but after all other charges including reserve provisions, to 10% or approximately one-half the profit margin, expressed as a percentage of sales, secured in the year 1941 largely under the conditions of a competitive market." In other words, we voluntarily halved our pre-tax profit margin—even though it was clear that taxes would be substantially higher than they had been in 1941.

Related to this policy of profit limitation was another policy of taking war-production contracts on a fixed-price basis, wherever possible. We preferred the fixed-price contract because of the greater incentive which it provided for efficient operation (as compared with the cost-plus-fixed-fee type of contract). We realized, of course, that in undertaking the production of many war materials which were new to us—which had not, in fact, been manufactured by anyone on a mass-production basis—there was always a possibility that our cost estimates might turn out to be higher than actual costs. We therefore stipulated to the War Department's Price Adjustment Board that we would reduce prices as we got the cost down.

As we foresaw, our costs did go down significantly on most contracts after we had some production experience and achieved high volume. The example below, which shows the pricing history of Frigidaire's .50-caliber aircraft machine gun, suggests the close relationship between high volume and low sales price. Early in 1945, due to a decrease in schedule, it was necessary to raise the price of the gun slightly.

	Effective Date	No. of Units	Sales Price (per unit)
Original Price	7/41 – 1/42	5,674	$689.85
1st Revision	2/42 – 3/42	4,043	515.80
2nd "	4/42 – 7/42	10,281	462.29
3rd "	7/42 – 10/42	15,922	310.21
4th "	11/42 – 12/42	14,744	283.75
5th "	1/43	6,000	386.93
6th "	1/43 – 4/43	32,938	252.50
7th "	5/43 – 8/43	40,723	231.00
8th "	9/43 – 1/44	40,000	222.00
9th "	1/44	10,257	207.00
10th "	2/44 – 3/44	21,579	197.00
11th "	4/44 – 6/44	34,126	186.50
12th "	7/44 – 8/44	21,031	180.30
13th "	9/44 – 1/45	43,824	169.00
14th "	1/45 – 4/45	12,819	176.00
15th "	4/45 – 6/45	13,306	174.50

By making price reductions of this character on most of our military production, by voluntary refunds, and through renegotiation, our pre-tax operating profits were held to about 10 per cent of sales subject to renegotiation in 1942–44. In 1945 pre-tax profits on sales related to the war were less than 10 per cent, due in part to heavy cancellations after the war ended, and the added costs of reconverting to peacetime operations.

It is an unshakable article of left-wing doctrine that wars are immensely profitable to "big business." So far as General Motors is concerned, this notion is wildly erroneous. Our limitation on pretax profits, combined with heavy corporate taxes, reduced our net income substantially during the war. Our income was lower in every one of the war years than it had been in 1940 or 1941. Our average net income for the years 1942–45 was lower, in fact, than our average income during the years 1936–39, which included the recession year 1938.

We began, earlier than any other corporation I know of, to think seriously about our place in the postwar world, and to develop specific and comprehensive programs for action. Indeed, I delivered an address on "Industry's Post-War Responsibilities" to the National Association of Manufacturers on December 4, 1941—three days *before* Pearl Harbor. As the war years went by, and it became possible to discern some of the outlines of the postwar world, we faced the necessity of planning for commercial production again. Specifically, we had to decide whether to figure on an expanding economy, or to pull in our horns for the "postwar depression," which many economists—and businessmen—took for granted. I am proud to say that we planned for expansion. Indeed, I think it is fair to state that our plans, which I announced in a speech to the N.A.M. in December 1943, were themselves a force for an expanding economy, a positive inducement to other businessmen to plan for growth. I quote from the speech in order to show some of our specific calculations:

Here is the General Motors approach: We start with the conviction that the prewar standards of national income passed with the prewar period itself. Our increased productive capacity as a nation, our broader distribution of know-how, our improved techniques, the acceleration of our technical knowledge resulting from the stimulation of the war—all justify a reasonable demand on the part of our people for an advanced order of things. Our enormous public debt and the constantly increasing costs of Government, legitimate and otherwise, demand a greater volume of production and a higher national income base. Otherwise, the burden of Government on enterprise and on the individual will seriously prejudice the possibility of an expanding economy.

Let us assume, as a prewar base, a national income of 65 to 70 billion dollars. Under the postwar circumstances, a new base of 100 billion of the same dollars should be a reasonable objective. We then determine the potential volume of each of our products or services, both old and new, on the basis of the expanded production opportunity, recognizing that each item of necessity has a different elasticity of demand. The result is a measure of the new operating base and determines the needed economic resources of production, such as manpower, organization, plant, and machinery. In terms of such a projection in General Motors, including the cost of reconversion, the advancement of present equipment to the latest standards of technology and retooling for postwar products, there will be involved an aggregate expenditure of approximately $500,-000,000. That is the contribution we are prepared to make to help preserve the free competitive enterprise system as the keystone of the American economy.

I might note that the national income forecasts in this passage, which were considered wildly optimistic when I made them, actually proved to be conservative. In 1946 our national income (measured in 1939 dollars) was around $125 billion—not $100 billion. Since then, the figure has increased to about $200 billion (in 1939 dollars).

Immediately after V-J Day we received, of course, an avalanche of contract terminations amounting to approximately $1.75 billion of war orders. The suddenness with which the war ended made an orderly transition to peacetime operations impossible, and ensured that we would be snowed under by paper work—the bulk of it connected with termination claims—for many months. We were also confronted, suddenly, with the vast job of physical reconstruction that had to be done on General Motors' plants throughout the country. I am informed that it required 9000 freight-car loads to haul away our military inventories, and another 8000 to dispose of government-owned machinery and equipment. Meanwhile, we were rushing to equip our plants for commercial production. Altogether, there was a mess but no confusion. The planning which had been done, and the co-operation of the armed services, cut down the period of plant clearance and reconversion so that our first automobile was produced and shipped about forty-five days after V-J Day.

In General Motors, reconversion after World War II did not mean simply getting plants back into the shape they had been in before the war. The postwar program was carefully planned for expansion and improvement. It included the organizing and balancing of existing production facilities, new machines and equipment, and some completely new plants. Much of it was aimed at improved working conditions for our employees—for example, providing new cafeterias and better medical facilities. The result was a production plant which was much more efficient in several different respects.

The Korean War confronted us with another complex planning problem, its peculiarity being that it involved partial mobilization. The military effort during this war, as I have said, was in no way comparable to our mobilization during World War II. The total volume involved in 1952, for example—some $1.4 billion of defense production—was less than 40 per cent of the volume of armaments we had produced in 1944. We knew, soon after the war broke out, that we would be expected again to take on about 10 per cent of the nation's armament manufacture. We were also being encouraged by the government to expand our facilities—to build new plants that could be converted to defense production if the armaments requirements should grow. We wanted to accommodate the government, but we certainly did not want to be "stuck" with a lot of excess capacity. On the other hand, we did not want to be short of capacity in the future. It gradually became clear, as the year 1950 wore on, that some serious planning about expansion was called for. On November 17, 1950, I addressed a memorandum to Mr. Bradley, then chairman of the Financial Policy Committee, in which I stated my own beliefs:

1. That the long term economic activity of the country will continue to increase in the future as it has in the past, stimulated by scientific knowledge and technological progress related thereto, and an expanding population. This will be reflected in expanding demands for General Motors products.

2. That the economic consequences of having too little capacity as measured by loss in competitive position, prestige and reduced profits, is entirely out of relation to the cost of carrying surplus capacity. Surplus capacity, within reason, is always temporary as judged by the past and, I believe, the future. For my purpose here I am defining "demand" as

not only normal demand but abnormal demand, such as results from arbitrary curtailment of production, providing such abnormalities are reasonably consequential and can be expected to continue over even a restricted period.

3. Notwithstanding our ambitious postwar program, we have lost position by not having sufficient capacity to meet our sales potentiality. Hence we have strengthened competition at our own cost . . .

4. It does not appear that our effective capacity as a percentage of that of the industry has moved up in relation to the gains made as a percentage of the business during the late prewar years.

I then went on to suggest that we make a serious effort to gauge the demand over the next five to ten years, and make plans to meet that demand. In building new facilities, I suggested that we "use corporation funds for such new plants needed for armament if that gives us better control over same from the long term position in relation to the master plan." Accelerated depreciation made the use of corporate funds all the more feasible, and relieved the government of the necessity of providing capital for the plants.

Our market forecasts suggested that expansion was indeed called for. In February and March 1951 we decided on a program, of which these were the main elements:

We would plan in the circumstances to retain about 80 per cent of our capacity for commercial production.

We would expand our capacity in the United States and Canada by about 24 per cent—from 14,500 cars and trucks per day to 18,000. (Figuring on a 250-day work year, which would include some overtime days, this would enable us to produce 4,500,000 cars and trucks a year.)

The expansion would not be uniform, however. Chevrolet would gain 21 per cent; Pontiac, 31 per cent; Oldsmobile, 25 per cent; Buick, 15 per cent; Cadillac, 35 per cent. These figures were, of course, modified in the ensuing years.

We would need some fifteen to twenty million additional square feet of plant (an increase of 25 per cent in the floor space used for car and truck production) for production of military products for the Korean War, costing about $300 million. We estimated that the machinery and equipment required to outfit these new plants for commercial production after the emergency would cost an additional $450 million.

In short, the new program was even more ambitious (by $250

million) than the $500 million expansion program we undertook
after World War II. We had no cause to regret this second great
expansion. It served its purpose by providing facilities for military
production during the Korean War, and for civilian production afterward. Indeed, our new facilities were severely strained in 1955, a
year of record demand, when we sold 4,638,000 cars and trucks of
United States and Canadian origin, and the entire industry was at
an all-time high.

The military products we turned out during the Korean War were
essentially advanced versions of the products we had made in
World War II—tanks, aircraft, trucks, guns, and so forth. Today not
only has modern defense equipment changed radically but the main
activity is in research and development rather than in production.
This has had a considerable bearing on the role of General Motors in
defense. We do research and development in our fields of competence, but we are largely a production organization, and production is not primarily what the defense establishment needs at this
time. This accounts for the fact that our defense business is only
3 per cent of our total sales.

A large part of our role in the new permanent defense industry
is played by two divisions: Allison and AC Spark Plug. Allison was
the first supplier of turbo-prop jet engines used in military aircraft
(in 1956). These engines, designated T-56, are currently used in
the Lockheed C-130, the Grumman E2A "Hawkeye," and the Lockheed P3A antisubmarine aircraft. More powerful engines of this
type are being developed. A lightweight Allison 250-horsepower
T-63 turbo-shaft engine, under development since 1958, was accepted in 1962 as a power plant for both military and commercial
light observation helicopters. Allison was also awarded a contract
in 1962 for the development, construction, and operation of a nuclear reactor for the army. At the present time it is supplying five
military-type transmissions for various army vehicles. These transmissions provide full power shift, steering, and braking functions
for diesel-powered battle tanks, medium recovery vehicles, and
armored amphibious personnel carriers and cargo carriers. Another
phase of Allison's defense business is the supplying of steel and
titanium rocket-motor cases for the Minuteman missile program.

AC-Milwaukee, which produced large quantities of bombing
navigational computer systems during the Korean War, extended
the range and capabilities of this system. The air force in 1957 as-

signed to AC Spark Plug complete systems responsibility for bombing navigational computers and for modification of the systems used in strategic air-force bombers. This division has also played the leading role in the corporation's missile work. An inertial guidance system, designated the "AChiever," was successfully flight tested in the air force's Thor long-range ballistic missile in 1957. We continued to make refinements on this system, and it was also successfully used in the Mace and Titan II missiles. In 1962, contracts for two important space guidance systems were awarded to AC-Milwaukee. The National Aeronautics and Space Administration (NASA) chose AC to assist in the design, development, and manufacture of navigation and guidance systems for the Apollo spacecraft, which is being built to carry three astronauts to the moon and back. The air force also selected AC to furnish the guidance system for its space-launch vehicle, Titan III.

Other General Motors divisions have recently undertaken projects for the nation's new defense program and space activities. GMC Truck & Coach is manufacturing transporter-erector units for the Minuteman missile program. Detroit Diesel Engine provides various diesel turbo-charged "V" engines to the government for use in tracklaying self-propelled artillery and retriever vehicles. Silver-zinc batteries are produced by Delco-Remy for the Minuteman program and Delco Radio is providing power supplies for use in various missile programs. In 1962 the Cadillac-Cleveland Ordnance Plant, which supplied tanks in the Korean War, began production on three new aluminum armored vehicles.

The corporation is looking forward to the production of even newer products which are now under development in the divisions and in the recently organized GM Defense Research Laboratories. General Motors will no doubt continue to play a prominent role in the national defense program. Should we be called upon, we stand ready to be of service to national defense to the maximum.

Chapter 21

PERSONNEL AND
LABOR RELATIONS

A<small>T</small> the time I write this, it is more than seventeen years since there has been an extended strike over national issues at General Motors. To those of us who recall the violent and crisis-ridden atmosphere of the mid-1930s, or the long ordeal of the great postwar strike of 1945–46, the record of the past seventeen years seems almost incredible. And we have achieved this record without surrendering any of the basic responsibilities of management. It is often argued that we got labor peace only by promoting a contract which stimulates inflation. This is a matter of too great complexity for discussion here, but let me say I do not believe it.

Before taking up our relations with labor organizations, I think it is appropriate to remind the reader that many of our personnel policies exist independently of collective bargaining. General Motors at the beginning of 1963 had, world-wide, 635,000 employees, of whom about 160,000 were salaried employees. Very few of the latter are represented by labor organizations. In addition, our approximately 350,000 union members receive a large number of benefits which are not mentioned in the contract and which, in some cases, were being provided by the corporation before modern industrial labor organizations came on the scene. Our plant recreation facilities, our payments for employees' suggestions, our arrangements for employee training, our provisions for employing handicapped workers—all of these fall outside the scope of the contract. As far back as the 1920s, General Motors was providing many benefits to its employees. Some of these were in the form of facilities —for example, our first-rate medical services, fine cafeterias, locker rooms, showers, and parking lots for our employees.

We had a group life-insurance program open to all employees as early as 1926. We had a savings and investment plan, set up by John J. Raskob, in 1919. In 1929 there were 185,000 employees in the plan, or 93 per cent of all our employees; their reserves in the plan came to $90 million. When the banks closed in 1933, we anticipated that our employees would withdraw their savings from the plan. Instead they were almost unanimous in insisting that we continue to hold the money—a vote of confidence in the stability of the corporation. The plan was suspended at the end of 1935 after enactment of the Social Security Act and the Securities Act of 1933.

General Motors today has its Savings-Stock Purchase Program for U.S. and Canadian salaried personnel. Under this program, employees may put up to 10 per cent of their base earnings into a special fund. For every two dollars put in by our salaried employees, the corporation puts in one dollar. Half the employee's savings are invested in government bonds, the other half in General Motors common stock. The corporation's contributions are invested entirely in General Motors common stock. All interest and dividends are reinvested for the participants, who constitute now over 85 per cent of our eligible salaried employees. The plan was offered to the hourly-rated employees in 1955 in contract negotiations, but was rejected in favor of the Supplementary Unemployment Benefit Plan, which will be discussed later.

The Savings-Stock Purchase Program is only one of the fringe benefits now available to salaried employees. The great majority receive cost-of-living allowances, as the hourly-rated employees do. And salaried men and women are benefited by a group life-insurance program, medical-expense coverage, health and accident insurance, a pension program, and provisions for separation pay. In short, they get a comprehensive program of benefits. Hourly-rated employees also receive benefits in these areas.

Our Personnel Staff is responsible for a great deal more than employee benefits, of course. Personnel is also entrusted with general supervision over recruiting, hiring, and training employees. Our foreman-training program, for example, is one of which we are especially proud. We have always taken great pains to keep foremen's morale at the highest level. In 1934 foremen were placed on a salary basis, and in 1941 we adopted the rule that their salaries had to be at least 25 per cent higher than the earnings of the highest-paid group of employees under their supervision. In addition, our foremen, who constitute our first line of supervision, have been getting overtime allowances since the early days of World War II —though the Federal Wage and Hour Law does not require the payment of overtime to supervisors. But perhaps the most important reason for the high morale of our foremen is the solid support we have given them on matters of discipline and work standards. They know that they are considered members of management.

As the foregoing facts indicate, our Personnel Staff has a great many responsibilities besides its well-publicized negotiations with the United Automobile Workers. Although personnel administration first became a regular responsibility at the corporation staff level in 1931, all our personnel programs were not centralized in one department until 1937. Since then, the Personnel Staff has served the corporation in two ways: as a specialized staff of experts on which the corporation can rely for advice and consultation; and as a group of executives entrusted with line responsibilities in union negotiations and in administering the provisions of the contract. The staff does not, by the way, ordinarily get into the settlement of employee grievances under our four-step grievance procedure; it does so only when grievance cases go to the fourth, or arbitration, step. In the years from 1948 through 1962, an average of 76,000 grievances a year were settled under this procedure. Some 60 per cent of these cases were settled at the first stage, in which the negotiations are handled for the most part by foremen and union committeemen. Another 30 per cent were settled at the second stage, in negotiations between the union's shop committee and a management committee generally comprised of members of the plant's own personnel staff. Another 10 per cent went to the third stage and were settled by a four-man appeal board, consisting characteristically of two men from the union's regional office and two representatives of local or divisional management. An average of only sixty-three cases a year—less than one tenth of 1 per cent of the total—went to the fourth stage for resolution by an impartial umpire.

The responsibilities of the Personnel Staff are, obviously, very grave ones, especially as they relate to our dealings with unions. For in these dealings there is always the possibility of great damage to the corporation—and of severe suffering to its employees. On the one hand, we must, wherever possible, avoid big strikes, and small ones too. On the other hand, we must not succumb to unreasonable economic demands or surrender the basic responsibilities of management. Avoiding both of these hazards is no easy task. And yet we have, in the past decade and a half, been reasonably successful at doing so.

In the early postwar period, our prospects for workable labor relations appeared to be remote. At the end of the 1945–46 strike, the United Automobile Workers was one of the two or three largest unions in the country, with a membership of almost a million. Many of its spokesmen were hostile to private enterprise. The UAW was besieged by factional conflicts, both internally and with respect to other unions. The principal result of these conflicts, as it appeared to us, was a tendency for every side to compete with the others in a show of "militance" against the corporation.

To make matters worse, it appeared that the UAW was able to enlist the support of the government in any great crisis. The government's attitude went back as far as the 1937 sit-down strikes, when we took the view that we would not negotiate with the union while its agents forcibly held possession of our properties. Sit-down strikes were plainly illegal—a judgment later confirmed by the Supreme Court. Yet President Franklin D. Roosevelt, Secretary of Labor Frances Perkins, and Governor Frank Murphy of Michigan exerted steady pressure upon the corporation, and upon me personally, to negotiate with the strikers who had seized our property, until finally we felt obliged to do so. Again in 1945–46, during the 119-day strike, President Truman formally backed up the union's controversial insistence that our "ability to pay" should affect the size of the wage increase. We successfully resisted this unsound proposition, but there is no doubt in my mind that the President's statement served to strengthen the union's public position and thus prolong the strike.

There was one other reason for concern about our labor prospects in the early postwar period, and that was the sharp inflation then under way. In 1946 price controls were taken off and in nine months consumer prices rose by 17 per cent. In 1947–48 they rose almost 10 per cent higher. The natural inclination of unions in an inflationary period is to bargain for wage increases high enough to allow for future price increases; and in anticipating these high prices, the wage gains tend to push them up still higher. The annual rounds of wage and price increases after the war were a perfect example of this inflationary spiral. Since the United Automobile Workers regarded itself, perhaps accurately, as a pace-setter for labor, General Motors faced the possibility that, when it granted demands, it would be a conspicuous target in each new round of inflationary demands.

Our apprehensions about our postwar labor relations were not diminished by the fact that we got through 1947 without a major strike. During that year's negotiations, in fact, something happened that pointed up the problems we faced. In mid-April, while we were still in negotiations, we began to hear reports that the UAW planned to pull all its members in the Detroit area off their jobs so that they could attend a union-sponsored demonstration against the Taft-Hartley bill, then being considered in Congress. The demonstration, which was to be held in downtown Detroit, was the union's own business, of course; but the work stoppages were very much our concern. We pointed out to the union's negotiators on three occasions that stopping work to attend the rally would be a clear violation of the Strikes and Stoppages Section of our contract, and that employees who walked out would be subject to discipline. (After the 1937 sit-down strikes, we had insisted that future contracts provide for penalties for work stoppages prohibited during the term of the contract.) In reply the union men blandly told us that the walkout had been authorized by the International Executive Board, but that our view of the case would be conveyed to the board.

At 2:00 P.M. on the 24th of April, 1947, the very day a new contract was signed, the walkout began. It was only partially successful, since 19,000 hourly-rated employees, in seven of the corporation's Detroit plants, did not go out. But 13,000 did, and in the course of the walkout they committed numerous acts of intimidation or near violence. It seemed to us that this was a reversion by the UAW to its earlier-day inclination to violate the contract at will. Accordingly, we responded firmly, as we had in the past. We discharged fifteen employees, and gave long-term disciplinary layoffs to twenty-five others, for extraordinary overt actions. These forty employees included four presidents of local unions, six chairmen of shop committees, and twenty-two shop and district committeemen. In addition, 401 employees were given short-term disciplinary layoffs.

The union had, of course, the right to appeal all these actions to the permanent umpire. However, it chose to negotiate with the corporation, and finally did concede that it had violated the agreement. A formal Memorandum of Understanding, signed on May 8, included an explicit statement by the union that all such work stoppages were violations. In return, the corporation reduced the fifteen discharges to long-term layoffs, and in other ways modified the original penalties.

During the year that followed, our labor relations were dramatically changed for the better. That year saw the defeat and discrediting of the Communist element in the United Automobile Workers and the beginning then of somewhat greater stability in the union's internal affairs.

The major instrument of change in our labor relations was the collective-bargaining agreement of 1948, the principal new features of which have been retained in subsequent agreements. Since these features have proved so important in the affairs of General Motors, I shall devote most of the remainder of this chapter to a discussion of them, and of their background.

The 1948 agreement brought two major innovations to our dealings with our hourly-rated employees. For one thing, it eliminated annual economic negotiations with the union and introduced the idea of longer-term contracts. The agreement ran for two years. It was followed, in 1950, by a five-year contract, and then by three successive three-year contracts. These longer intervals gave the corporation more assurance that it could meet its long-range production schedules; and they also meant an important saving to us in executive man-hours, for labor negotiations have invariably consumed a great deal of the time of the highest officials of the corporation. The longer-term contracts also relieved our employees of their annual concern over the prospects of a strike and enabled them to plan their own affairs with greater confidence.

The other innovation of the 1948 contract was the so-called General Motors wage formula. This formula had two features: an "escalator clause," which provided for wage allowances to employees based on changes in the cost of living; and an "annual improvement factor," which assured employees of a regular share in the benefits of increased efficiency resulting from advancing technology. The entire formula represented an effort to introduce an element of reason, and of predictability, into our wage program;

especially it aimed to end at least in part the contests of strength in which our wages had often been set in the past.

Our search for a rational wage program of this sort really began in the 1930s. In 1935, specifically, we became interested in the possibility of tying wages to changes in the cost of living. Initially, we thought in terms of the local cost-of-living indices prepared by the Bureau of Labor Statistics, rather than of the bureau's national index. In 1935 the bureau published semiannual reports on changes in living costs in thirty-two cities. In twelve of these cities, including Detroit, General Motors had plants. However, there were many other cities with General Motors plants which the bureau did not report on. This practical difficulty was one reason we did not pursue the subject at the time. Another reason was the relative stability of consumer prices in 1935, and, indeed, in the years through 1940. Price fluctuations were no real issue in our wage adjustments during those years.

But during 1941 the defense program stimulated a sharp increase in prices, and the problem of inflation confronted us—and our employees—in an inescapable fashion. On April 4, 1941, accordingly, I wrote to Virgil Jordan, the president of the National Industrial Conference Board, and asked him what he thought about the possibility of a wage formula tied to a cost-of-living index:

Do you think there would be any sense to an approach to establishing an economic formula for wage adjustments, if we base it upon the assumption that real wages are bound to increase in the future just as they have in the last twenty-five years, and that we recognize that fact in such a formula, by increasing the dollar wage rate as the cost of living increases, preferably on a community basis, in some ratio that might be worked out which would cover the objective, but in the event that the cost of living should decline, the decrease in the dollar wage rate would be at a lower percentage rate than the increase. This would insure, over the years, an increase in real wages to which I believe the worker is entitled and which industry is obligated to make possible through capitalization of increased technological efficiency.

This informal suggestion elicited a generally pessimistic reaction from Mr. Jordan. He replied that he was doubtful about our chances of getting unions to go along with an automatic wage formula; union leaders, he suggested, would prefer to play an active role in setting wages. Nevertheless, the exchange of letters served to stimulate our interest in the broad principle of tying wages to living costs.

Early in 1941 Charles E. Wilson, then president of General Motors, advanced our thinking on this subject further. He was confined to the hospital with a broken hip and gave a good deal of his time there to the study of a wage formula. He came out with two new points regarding wage adjustments. One was that, as a practical matter, wage adjustments based on changes in the cost of living must be tied to the national Consumer Price Index. Otherwise, the corporation would continually be in the position of giving increases to some of its employees and not to others—which would be logical enough as far as the economics of the case went, but which might create real psychological problems.

The other point put forward by Mr. Wilson concerned the means of affording our workers a share in rising productivity. It was his contention that the only feasible way to do this was to set a fixed increase which each worker would receive annually. This proposal was the origin of the "annual improvement factor" in the General Motors formula.

Though the basic elements of the wage formula were worked out by Mr. Wilson in 1941, there was no good opportunity to introduce the formula in collective bargaining until the 1948 negotiations. During the wartime years the government's wage-stabilization policy made it difficult to initiate any new proposals. In 1945 it was apparent that our employees would be interested only in a very large increase in basic wages, to enable them to "catch up" with the wartime rise in living costs. Furthermore, the union's insistence during the long strike of 1945–46 that wage increases be determined by our ability to pay and that we should in effect negotiate our selling prices, raised a crucial issue of principle which we felt had to be settled before any new wage program could be adopted. Again in 1947 we felt that our employees' principal need was a sizable increase in basic wages.

The 1948 negotiations began on March 12 and appeared, at the outset, to follow the pattern of the preceding years. The union demands were, if anything, more extreme than ever. They amounted, in fact, to a proposal to rewrite virtually the whole basic contract, developed painfully during the preceding decade. The demands also included a wage increase of twenty-five cents an hour, a pension program, a social security program, a guaranteed forty-hour work week, and many other economic items. We regarded these demands as extravagant beyond reason and feared that if the UAW persisted in them we would have another disastrous strike similar to the 1945–46 one. Indeed it seemed in the spring of 1948 as though the nation might be in for one of the most severe years of strikes it had ever faced. Most of the steel and electrical industry negotiations were deadlocked. On May 12 the UAW struck Chrysler, and at about that time began to conduct strike votes among their General Motors locals.

There was, however, one circumstance favoring us in the 1948 negotiations. This was that we had reached an agreement with the UAW that negotiations would be conducted in relative privacy. In previous years, our collective bargaining had come to resemble a public political forum in which the union fed a stream of provocative statements to the press, and we felt obliged to answer publicly. The privacy of the 1948 negotiations made their tone more realistic from the start.

Nevertheless, the negotiations went slowly and in May a strike seemed imminent. At this point we decided to introduce our wage formula into the bargaining. On May 21 we handed it to the UAW in written form. We had no indication in advance that the union would respond affirmatively to our contract proposal. However, the union accepted it in principle, and we began to work on the details. To speed up bargaining we suggested that General Motors and the union appoint four-man task forces to study the question.

The details of the new formula were worked out in three days of almost continuous bargaining. The contract was, as I have said, for two years; its novelty made the union unwilling to commit itself for a longer period. The annual improvement factor was set at three cents an hour for every worker covered by the contract. And the base date finally agreed upon for use in calculating the cost-of-living formula was 1940—the last year in which prices had been fairly stable.

There are several points about the General Motors formula that need to be understood. First, as to the annual improvement factor, which is often misinterpreted even by persons familiar with labor questions. Section 101(a) of the contract, which deals with the improvement factor, states "that a continuing improvement in the standard of living of employees depends upon technological progress, better tools, methods, processes and equipment, and a cooperative attitude on the part of all parties in such progress . . . to produce more with the same amount of human effort is a sound economic and social objective . . ." In other words, the real source of income is productivity. The union's acceptance of these sensible words was surely a milestone in labor relations.

But contrary to a widespread assumption, the improvement factor is not linked to a definitely known increase in productivity at General Motors. There is, to my knowledge, no satisfactory technique with which to measure productivity at General Motors, or, in fact, at any corporation which manufactures constantly changing products. And even if an industrial productivity measurement could somehow be provided, it would still not be desirable to relate it in direct proportion to wage increases. Such a policy applied to the economy as a whole would bring about intolerable discrepancies between the wages paid in industries where technological progress is rapidly increasing, and the wages paid where technological progress must be limited—as it is in the so-called service industries. It is my belief that the improvement factor should reflect the long-term productivity increase of the U.S. economy as a whole.

Over the years, it had been estimated, productivity in the United States had been rising about 2 per cent a year. How good that estimate was, I do not know. In any case we set the improvement factor in the General Motors formula at three cents an hour. This amounted to a 2 per cent annual increase in wage rates: three cents is 2 per cent of $1.49, which was then the average hourly rate at General Motors. In subsequent negotiations the improvement factor has been increased several times. Note that the corporation commits itself to deliver this increase over the period of the contract no matter what actually happens to the productivity of U.S. industry. Even if productivity should decline, for the country as a whole or for General Motors in particular, we would still be obliged to pay the annual improvement factor.

I have always felt that it was a source of confusion to label the improvement factor a "productivity increase." I prefer to think of it as a group merit raise of sorts, and I suspect that many General Motors employees see it in that light.

In the end, increased efficiency flows not so much from the increased effectiveness of the workers, but primarily from more efficient management and from the investment of additional capital in labor-saving devices. Some union spokesmen talk as though the entire benefits of increased productivity should go to labor. I do not believe that is sound. New machinery costs money and the additional investment must be justified by a return on that investment. An argument could be made that the consumer, and the economy as a whole, would benefit most if productivity increases were applied entirely to the lowering of prices. Ideally that might be a good thing. But since it is in the nature of people to work better with the incentive of an individual or group gain and to want to bargain over it, it is a good thing to have something to bargain over. And so I conclude that the benefits of productivity increases should be apportioned among the consumer (lower prices or better product), labor (higher wages), and the shareholders (return on investment).

The improvement factor as it was first applied in the General Motors formula had one curious effect. Under the 1948 and 1950 agreements, the improvement came to exactly the same rate per hour for all workers, floor sweepers and highly skilled tool- and die-makers alike. The decision to take the average worker and pay 2 per cent of his rate (that is, three cents an hour) to all our men was clearly a move in the direction of equalitarianism. The effect, of course, was that the improvement factor given the tool- and die-makers did not come to as much as 2 per cent a year, while the sweepers were getting an increase of perhaps 3 per cent. Thus from 1948 to 1955, the improvement factor had a tendency to narrow percentage wage differentials. This tendency was corrected in the 1955 contract, which put the improvement factor on a basis of 2.5 per cent—with a minimum of six cents—for all workers.

While the improvement factor was changed, the escalator formula remained substantially unchanged—even though it, too, has tended to equalize rates of pay over the years. Here again, there was no theoretical reason why the formula could not have provided, simply, for a 1 per cent increase in pay every time the cost of living rose by 1 per cent. Instead, the formula was set so that every worker would get the same amount of money added to his pay when living costs rose. The cost-of-living program was calculated in this manner: First, it was determined that consumer prices had gone up about 69 per cent since the 1940 base date. The hourly rate of the average General Motors worker had gone up only about 60 per cent in that interval. To make up the 9 per cent difference, eight cents an hour was added to the rate. But this increase obviously amounted to more than 9 per cent for low-paid workers, and less than that for higher-paid workers. In its provisions for future increases, the escalator clause had a similarly equalizing effect. We took the average hourly wage and the April 1948 Consumer Price Index—the latest available at that time—and determined to preserve the relationship between them. Dividing the average wage of $1.49 into the index figure of 169.3, we came up with a one-cent increase for each upward movement of 1.14 points in the price index; accordingly, this became the rule for all our workers. But note again that our highest-paid workers really needed more rapid increases to keep up with the cost of living, while a janitor making $1.20 an hour in 1948 would clearly be more than compensated for any inflation. In thinking about the cost-of-living part of the General Motors wage formula, it is important to remember that it is the average wage rate that is really tied to the price index, and that the escalator clause tends to pull all other wage rates toward the average. Whether this equalitarian effect is something good or bad in the long run, I am not prepared to say. I think it is interesting to observe that the many wage formulas adopted by other unions in imitation of our own program almost invariably tend to preserve this equalizing feature.

On several occasions we have granted skilled-trades employees special increases. These increases have offset the equalitarian effect of the formula as far as the skilled men are concerned. Altogether, special increases for tool- and die-men for the period 1950 through 1962 have amounted to thirty-one cents an hour.

In other ways, too, the original concepts underlying the wage formula have been deflected somewhat by the exigencies of collective bargaining. One recurrent problem has been the "floor" under wages in our cost-of-living agreements. As I had suggested in my original letter to Mr. Jordan, workers would want some limit on wage reductions, even in a period of severe deflation. In the 1948 agreement we specified that no matter how much the cost of living might fall, no more than five cents of the original eight-cent cost-of-living raise could be taken away. Again in 1953, 1958, and 1961, the "floor" was raised by an agreement between the union and the corporation. The logic of escalator clauses apparently cannot be extended to periods of severe deflation because workers are always reluctant to take wage cuts.

The 1953 negotiations, incidentally, present an interesting example of the kind of public pressures which have been steadily exerted on the General Motors wage formula, and which have made it difficult for the formula to operate as Mr. Wilson originally intended. In principle, there should not have been any 1953 negotiations, because in the five-year contract signed in 1950, the union "unqualifiedly waive[d] the right" to bargain on any issue covered in the contract. But toward the end of 1952, the UAW became dissatisfied with the cost-of-living provisions of the contract. The union feared, as many others did at the time, that the post-Korea inflation had about run its course. If the cost of living declined, its members would lose some, conceivably all, of the special allowance which they were then receiving under the escalator clause. To make matters worse, the Wage Stabilization Board had allowed other groups of workers, that is, in the steel, electrical, and other industries, to receive living-cost increases which were added to their base rates. In other words, a deflation would mean that UAW members would lose some take-home pay, while other union members would not. We agreed with the union that wages at General Motors should not lag behind those in comparable industries. And so we reopened the contract and incorporated nineteen cents of the cost-of-living allowance (which was then up to twenty-four cents) into the permanent base rate. This episode illustrates the difficulties of adhering strictly to the original concept of the wage formula.

Our wage formula has often been attacked as inflationary. I would agree with Mr. Wilson that the formula itself does no more than protect our employees against inflation. However, the formula is by no means our whole labor contract. Because we have granted many fringe benefits some critics maintain that the cost increases are in excess of productivity and that, therefore, the formula plus the fringe benefits may have inflationary implications.

There is another factor of importance that must be considered. In discussing the improvement factor, I have said that, in my opinion, it is more of an incentive or a bonus than it is an improvement factor per se. And from that point of view I think the fact that our workers benefit on a definite and prescribed basis, resulting in an increase in their standard of living, gives us a more sympathetic co-operation in the introduction of labor-saving devices and other improvements that flow from technological progress, which on the whole have a healthy influence on the efficiency of the corporation's operations.

It is undeniable—as of this writing—that the formula has served to bring relative peace and stability to our labor relations. We have had no extended strikes over negotiation of a national agreement since the formula went into effect in 1948.

The most widely publicized addition to the General Motors labor contract in the last few years has been the provision for supplementary unemployment benefits—a provision often, though not accurately, described as the guaranteed annual wage. As all the major automobile companies approached the 1955 labor negotiations, it was apparent that the union regarded this program as a great milestone in its history, and intended to win it at all costs. A large part of the idea behind this program—that is, the idea of an employer-financed supplement to state unemployment compensation—had already been worked out by the union, apparently in 1954 and 1955. However, the plan proposed by the Ford Motor Company and finally accepted, differed in many respects from the union's specific proposals—and was much more conservatively financed. We agreed to this program shortly after Ford did, although we disagreed with several aspects of the plan. Ultimately, the entire industry conceded the point.

Actually, we at General Motors had been considering alternative plans of this broad type for about two decades. In December 1934, before the state unemployment-insurance laws were on the books, some thoughts on a private insurance program for the corporation's own employees were outlined. Among the ideas suggested, we endorsed these:

General Motors subscribes to the principle of accumulating reserves to be paid to employes in periods of involuntary unemployment.

We also subscribe to the principle of joint contribution to such reserves by both employers and eligible employes.

We also believe in the justice of a probationary period before any employe becomes eligible.

I was impressed with the merit of these points and so, I think, were most of my colleagues. However, the sudden growth in federal and state unemployment insurance programs in the mid-1930s altered our perspective on the problem. With insurance against unemployment now available, we developed a program designed to allay the hardships caused by our cyclical production. It worked in general this way: Any employee with five years' seniority who was temporarily laid off—in a model change-over, for example—or who was earning less than twenty-four hours' pay in a week, could borrow from the company each week the difference between his earnings and twenty-four hours' pay. No interest was charged. In weeks when he had an income in excess of twenty-four hours' pay, he would repay the loan at the rate of one half of the excess over twenty-four hours' pay. In the case of employees with less than five years' but more than two years' seniority, the corporation made advances up to sixteen hours' pay with a maximum aggregate advance of seventy-two hours' pay. In other words, the earnings of our workers were being spread more evenly over the entire year. The program was discontinued when defense production made it unnecessary.

In addition to this program of interest-free loans, we began to consider whether we could somehow guarantee a substantial proportion of our workers some minimum number of working hours during a year. The Social Security Act of 1935 included one section which was intended to give employers an incentive to devise such plans. Under this section, employers who guaranteed their workers 1200 hours of work a year were exempted from paying the 3 per cent payroll tax. We seriously considered offering some such guarantee to our workers in 1938. However, Donaldson Brown, then vice chairman of the board, stated the case against it very persuasively. In a memorandum to me dated July 18, 1938, Mr. Brown argued that the guarantee could not be extended to very many workers—or that if it could, these workers could not be guaranteed very many hours. Further, he said:

The extension of a guaranteed annual number of hours of employment to a given segment of the employes inevitably will tend to freeze the average hours of employment at that level. A plan of the kind would be taken as implying the purpose—in event of declining business—to spread work to the end of averaging hours at the guaranteed level. Union pressure towards this result inevitably would be exerted.

All of us were dubious about the feasibility of work-sharing in such a large and complex organization as General Motors. Personally, I regarded work-sharing at low levels of hours over long periods as unsound, economically and socially. But in the early postwar period, I felt that the corporation would have to devise some kind of guarantee. On May 15, 1946, I expressed my view on supplementary unemployment compensation:

. . . if we could determine what the limitations are we might get ahead of the pressure that is going to be put on us, and determine in our own way and in a factual way, just how far it would be practical to go, which might result in a better relationship between our people and ourselves without the liability of paying for work that was not accomplished.

On balance, the plan which was finally written into the contract seems to me to represent less of an innovation than its proponents believe it to be. As many economists have pointed out, the plan is merely another extension of unemployment insurance, which has been in effect for more than twenty years, and which has always been financed by the employers. I suspect that the real benefit of the new plan is not simply the degree of protection it will give to workers in slack periods; after all, many workers will always be ineligible for coverage, and many other workers will receive only small payments. Rather, it is that the plan gives our workers a greater feeling of economic security; and perhaps in the long run that is merit enough.

Before 1933 General Motors had no dealings with labor unions, except for a few craft organizations in the construction field. For this and perhaps other reasons we were largely unprepared for the change in political climate and the growth of unionism that began in 1933. One is inclined to forget that unionization in large industries was not then the custom in the United States. The significance of large-scale unionization was not yet clear to us. We knew that some political radicals regarded unions as instruments for the attainment of power. But even orthodox "business unionism" seemed to us a potential threat to the prerogatives of management. As a businessman, I was unaccustomed to the whole idea. Our early experiences with the AF of L unions in the automobile industry were unhappy; the chief issue with these unions became organizational. They demanded that they represent all our workers, even those who did not want to be represented by them. Our initial encounter with the CIO was even more unhappy; for that organization attempted to enforce its demands for exclusive recognition by the most terrible acts of violence, and finally seized our properties in the sit-down strikes of 1937. I have no desire to revive the bitter controversies that arose over these early encounters with labor organizations. I mention them merely to suggest one of the reasons why our initial reaction to unionism was negative.

What made the prospect seem especially grim in those early years was the persistent union attempt to invade basic management prerogatives. Our rights to determine production schedules, to set work standards, and to discipline workers were all suddenly called into question. Add to this the recurrent tendency of the union to inject itself into pricing policy, and it is easy to understand why it seemed, to some corporate officials, as though the union might one day be virtually in control of our operations.

In the end, we were fairly successful in combating these invasions of management rights. There is no longer any real doubt that pricing is a management, not a union, function. So far as our operations are concerned, we have moved to codify certain practices, to discuss workers' grievances with union representatives, and to submit for arbitration the few grievances that remain unsettled. But on the whole, we have retained all the basic powers to manage.

The issue of unionism at General Motors is long since settled. We have achieved workable relations with all of the unions representing our employees.

Chapter 22

INCENTIVE COMPENSATION

T HE General Motors Bonus Plan has been since 1918 an integral part of our management philosophy and organization, and, I believe, an essential element in the progress of the corporation. Our management policy, as the 1942 annual report formally stated it, "has evolved from the belief that the most effective results and the maximum progress and stability of the business are achieved by placing its executives in the same relative position, so far as possible, that they would occupy if they were conducting a business on their own account. This provides opportunity for accomplishment through the exercise of individual initiative, and opportunity for economic progress commensurate with performance. In that way managerial talent is attracted to and retained by the Corporation."

The Bonus Plan and the policy of decentralization are related, since decentralization gives executives the opportunity for accomplishment, and the Bonus Plan makes it possible for each executive to earn a reward commensurate with his own performance, and so gives him an incentive to put forth his best effort at all times.

Although the General Motors Bonus Plan was first adopted on August 27, 1918, its fundamental principles have never changed—that the interests of the corporation and its stockholders are best served by making key employees partners in the corporation's prosperity, and that each individual should be rewarded in proportion to his contribution to the profit of his own division and of the corporation as a whole. We have made alterations, of course, from time to time; for example, in 1957 the incentive program was expanded to include a stock-option plan for a group of top executives. At the present time, bonuses may be awarded out of net earnings only if the corporation has earned more than 6 per cent on its net capital employed. The maximum annual credit to the bonus reserve is limited to 12 per cent of the net earnings after taxes and after the 6 per cent return, and in its discretion the Bonus and Salary Committee may determine to credit less than the maximum. For 1962, some 14,000 employees were awarded bonuses totaling $94,102,089 in General Motors stock and cash. In addition, contingent credits under the stock-option plan amounted to $7,337,239. These amounts, together with $3,550,085 applicable to the separate bonus plans of four overseas manufacturing subsidiaries, were distributed out of a credit to the reserve of $105 million for 1962, which was $38 million less than the maximum permitted under the plan.

But while bonus awards depend on profits, the bonus system is not a profit-sharing plan. It does not entitle any employee to any regular share in the earnings of the corporation or any of its divisions. The Bonus and Salary Committee may—and sometimes does—award less than the maximum sum available for bonus payments. More important, each man must earn the right to be considered for a bonus award each year by his own effort. Since his effort is judged each year, his bonus award may fluctuate widely from year to year—if, indeed, he receives one every year. The knowledge that his contribution to the corporation is weighed periodically, and a price put on it, acts as an incentive for each executive at all times.

The Bonus Plan has also had an important effect in creating an identity of interest between management and shareholders by creating an owner-management group: in most cases, bonus awards have been made partly or wholly in General Motors stock. As a result, General Motors has always had a top management group with a heavy stock interest in the corporation—heavy, that is, from the standpoint of the executives' total personal assets, if not from the standpoint of the corporation's total stock outstanding. Since the bulk of their own assets usually consists of General Motors stock, General Motors executives are more conscious of the identity between their interests and those of the shareholders than they would be if they were professional managers only.

But the Bonus Plan has done more than stimulate and reward individual effort per se; when the plan was first started, it made a tremendous contribution in encouraging executives to relate their own individual effort to the welfare of the whole corporation. Indeed, the Bonus Plan played almost as big a role as our system of co-ordination in making decentralization work effectively. O. E. Hunt observed in a letter to me:

Decentralization provided the opportunity; [the incentive compensation] . . . provided the stimulation; jointly they made the top level executives in the Corporation a cooperatively constructive group without destroying individual ambition and initiative.

Before we had the Bonus Plan in operation throughout the corporation, one of the obstacles to integrating the various decentralized divisions was the fact that key executives had little incentive to think in terms of the welfare of the whole corporation. On the contrary, the general managers were encouraged to think primarily of their own division's profits. Under the incentive system in operation before 1918, a small number of division managers had contracts providing them with a stated share in the profits of their own divisions, irrespective of how much the corporation as a whole earned. Inevitably, this system exaggerated the self-interest of each division at the expense of the interests of the corporation itself. It was even possible for a division manager to act contrary to the interests of the corporation in his effort to maximize his own division's profits.

The Bonus Plan established the concept of corporate profit in place of divisional profits, which only incidentally added up to the corporation's net income. Suitably, it provided for bonuses to be paid to employees "who have contributed to its [General Motors'] success in a special degree by their inventions, ability, industry, loyalty or exceptional service." At first total bonus awards were limited to 10 per cent of the net earnings after taxes and after a 6 per cent return. In 1918 more than 2000 employees received bonus awards, and in 1919 and 1920, more than 6000. In 1921, when the recession and inventory liquidation cut profits sharply, no bonus was awarded under the plan.

The first major modification of the Bonus Plan was made in 1922, when bonus awards were resumed. The minimum return on capital that had to be earned before any bonus provision could be made was raised from 6 to 7 per cent, after taxes. It stayed at that level until 1947, when the minimum return on capital was reduced to 5 per cent and the per cent of net earnings after taxes available for bonus above the minimum return was increased to 12 per cent. In 1962 the minimum return on capital was increased to 6 per cent.

The 1922 revisions also related the employee's level of responsibility to his eligibility for bonuses. Since the simplest measure of an employee's level of responsibility is his salary, eligibility for the bonus was set on that basis: for several years, beginning with 1922, the minimum salary for bonus eligibility was $5000 per year. As a result of this change we awarded a total of only 550 bonuses in 1922.

Managers Securities Company

Another important change was made in November 1923 with the establishment of the Managers Securities Company. Managers Securities Company was set up, essentially, in order to give our top executives an opportunity to increase their ownership interest in General Motors. We had in mind that this would provide added incentive. A block of stock, made available by the du Pont Company, was in effect purchased by the executives selected for participation in the plan at the then market price. Through their participation in the Managers Securities Plan, the executives made a partial payment for the stock in cash at the outset, and agreed to pay the balance by applying their participation in supplemental compensation for a number of years in the future. This meant that, if the business was successful, they would be in a position to become substantial owners of stock. Those who benefited by this plan are indebted to Pierre S. du Pont and John J. Raskob, who arranged that General Motors stock be made available for that purpose, and to Donaldson Brown, who developed a highly effective plan for creating a reality out of an opportunity. Here are the essentials of the plan worked out by Mr. Brown.

Managers Securities Company was organized with an authorized capital stock of $33.8 million divided as follows: $28.8 million of 7 per cent cumulative nonvoting convertible preferred stock; $4 million of Class A stock with a par value of $100; $1 million of Class B stock with a par value of $25.

On formation Managers Securities Company bought a block of General Motors Securities Company stock, which was the equivalent of 2,250,000 shares of General Motors common stock. General Motors Securities Company was a holding company for du Pont's ownership in General Motors stock. The purchase by Managers Securities Company represented a 30 per cent participation in General Motors Securities Company.

The reason du Pont was willing to sell at the market a 30 per cent interest in its entire holding of General Motors stock was twofold. First, du Pont believed firmly that it was thereby creating a partnership relationship between General Motors' management and itself. It was convinced that the resulting incentive to General Motors' executives would be reflected in increased dividends and would enhance the value of the stock, thereby compensating du Pont through the increased value of its remaining interest. Second, du Pont sold because the stock in question was an extra investment originally acquired under duress, so to speak, in connection with the financial adjustment of Mr. Durant's affairs. These circumstances led Pierre S. du Pont to request Mr. Brown to consider possible avenues through which du Pont's objectives might be effected.

Managers Securities Company paid General Motors Securities Company $15 per share for the 2,250,000 shares, or an aggregate purchase price of $33,750,000. This purchase was financed by paying for same with $28,800,000 par value 7 per cent convertible preferred stock and the balance in cash to the extent of $4,950,000. Managers Securities Company obtained the cash by selling its entire Class A and Class B stock to General Motors Corporation for the aggregate sum of $5 million. General Motors undertook to pay to Managers Securities Company an amount equal to 5 per cent of the net earnings after taxes of the corporation less 7 per cent on capital employed during each year. This payment was equivalent to one half the aggregate bonus fund for each year. The agreement was to last eight years, beginning with 1923 and ending with 1930.

General Motors further agreed that, should the contract payment to Managers Securities Company in any year come to less than $2 million, then General Motors would make up the difference in the form of an unsecured loan, to Managers Securities Company, bearing interest at 6 per cent. (Payments under this provision were in fact made in both 1923 and 1924.)

General Motors in turn resold Class A and Class B stock to about eighty of its top executives by an allotment based upon recommendations submitted by me to a special committee appointed by the board of directors of General Motors. Employees paid $100 cash for each share of Class A stock and $25 for each share of Class B stock, the same price that General Motors had paid Managers Securities.

In general, the number of shares allotted depended upon the executive's position with the corporation. I personally visited every executive who appeared to qualify under the plan, and discussed his situation with a view to determining whether he wished to join the plan and whether he could afford to pay cash for his allotment. I tried, in general terms, to limit the investment on the part of each executive to an amount no greater than his annual salary. Not all the shares of Managers Securities Company were originally allotted. A block was set aside for future allotments; first, to executives who might later qualify, and second, to supplement an executive's holdings in the event that his responsibilities increased.

General Motors held an irrevocable option to repurchase all or part of any executive's holdings should he resign, or should his position or performance in the corporation change. In order to maintain participation in the Managers Securities Company on a current basis, an annual review was required of the performance of each executive in the Managers Securities Plan to determine whether his participation was out of line compared with other executives, including those not in the plan. Where the discrepancies were significant I could recommend an additional allotment of unused Managers Securities Company stock or an award out of the half of the bonus that did not flow to Managers Securities Company.

Here is how the plan worked.

The annual payments by General Motors Corporation to Managers Securities Company, which were 5 per cent of the net earnings after taxes of General Motors less 7 per cent on the capital employed, were credited to Class A surplus for the benefit of the Class A stock. Dividends received on the General Motors stock owned by Managers Securities Company (through General Motors Securities Company) were credited to Class B surplus along with all other income of Managers Securities. Dividends on the outstanding 7 per cent preferred stock of Managers Securities were paid out of Class B surplus.

The Managers Securities Company was obligated each year to retire 7 per cent preferred stock in an amount equivalent to all its income after taxes and expenses and after deducting an amount equal to the dividends paid on the preferred stock. Managers Securities Company could also pay dividends on its Class A and Class B stock—not in excess, however, of 7 per cent per annum on such paid-in capital ($5 million) and the surplus earned thereon —provided that all cumulative dividends on the 7 per cent convertible preferred stock were paid.

As a result of the success attained by General Motors during the period after 1923, the Managers Securities Company plan was successful beyond the most optimistic expectation. As I have pointed out, this was a period of remarkable accomplishment for General Motors. Significantly, the over-all automobile market did not show much growth during the period—as a matter of fact, it remained at a level of around four million cars and trucks annually in the period 1923 through 1928. But General Motors sales more than doubled over this period and our share of the market increased from less than 20 per cent in 1923 to over 40 per cent in 1928. This, of course, resulted in a rapid increase in earnings and with it increased payments to the Managers Securities Company representing the supplemental compensation of the participants. The preferred stock was completely retired by April 1927 and so the total assets of the company were held exclusively, and without encumbrance, for the benefit of the Class A and Class B stock with their respective surplus accounts.

The expansion of the earnings of General Motors Corporation not only permitted the retirement of the 7 per cent preferred stock of Managers Securities, but also enhanced the market value of General Motors stock. This, together with the increased dividends on the General Motors stock, resulted in such a high value for Managers Securities Company stock that it could no longer be offered to executives who had been advanced to top management after the plan had been started. In consequence, the contemplated period of eight years was reduced to seven years, and ended with the year 1929 instead of 1930. The purpose of this was to facilitate the organization of General Motors Management Corporation—which was designed to carry on the general concept of the Managers Securities Company for another seven years, with a broadened executive participation commensurate with the increased size of the business.

I have already stated that the Managers Securities Company plan was successful beyond the most optimistic expectation. Perhaps that can best be demonstrated by stating the results in terms of each $1000 of stock purchased in Managers Securities Company Class A and Class B stock in December 1923. At that time such an investment represented in effect a partial payment on 450 shares of General Motors no par value common stock, with a then market value of $15 a share, and the executive had agreed to apply his future bonus participation to pay off the balance due. Over the next seven years, the applicable share of the contract payments made to the company by General Motors totaled $9800 on such an investment. These represented amounts which the executive would have received as bonus during the period and in effect constituted additional investments in the company, increasing each $1000 of original investment to a total of $10,800.

During the period from 1923 to 1930, the applicable 450-share equity had, through exchanges, stock dividends, and additional purchases by Managers Securities, increased to 902 shares. After General Motors made the last contract payment to Managers Securities on April 15, 1930, the resulting total investment represented an unencumbered claim on 902 shares of General Motors $10 par value common stock. Expressed another way, by that time the total of $10,800, represented by a $1000 original investment and the $9800 applicable share of supplemental compensation, had in effect purchased 902 shares of General Motors $10 par value common stock. As a result of the appreciation in the market value of General Motors common stock during the interim period, the 902 shares had a value of $52.375 per share, or a total market value of $47,232. Taking into account the redemption of a portion of the investment for $2050 in 1927 and 1928 and dividend income of $11,936 received over the period, the final value growing out of the total $10,800 invested was $61,218.

The Managers Securities Company Plan rewarded the General Motors Corporation and its shareholders as handsomely as it rewarded the participating executives. The success of the plan reflected the success of General Motors between 1923 and 1929, and I am confident that this success was due in part to the fact that Managers Securities Company created a top management team with a heavy personal stake in the success of the corporation as a whole. Managers Securities Company was certainly a great individual financial incentive. But as Walter S. Carpenter, Jr., of the du Pont Company has written me, it also supported the enterprise as a whole and led to greater co-operation. Mr. Carpenter said:

> The importance of Managers Securities Company was that it created in these many individuals . . . an urgent and continuing desire to make a success of the whole as distinguished from their previous parochial and separate interests . . .
> You know, perhaps as well as anyone, that the design of that so-called financial mechanism was such that the benefits of the earnings of the corporation as a whole were pyramided in a form to give a tremendous leverage upon the individual's participation in the results. That is now so old and has been used so much that we accept it now as more or less a matter of course. We must recognize that in that form and at that time it was quite new and in that way contributed enormously to the drive and determination . . . to make the corporation as a whole a success. This, of course, in turn facilitated the development of cooperation and correlation and interdependence, all of which later played such an important part in the success of that corporation.

At the close of each year I held a Managers Securities Company shareholders meeting, attended by all the participating executives, in order to review the results of the year just ended. This gave me a chance to emphasize the mutuality of interest between its executive shareholders and the General Motors shareholders. At these all-day meetings, Donaldson Brown recalls that "comprehensive statements were presented to display how those common interests were served by effective control of capital expenditures, of inventories and receivables, efficiencies in manufacture, sales and distribution, and in product-appeal to the consuming public."

General Motors Management Corporation

The concept of the Management Corporation was similar to that of the Managers Securities Company, though the technique was in some respects necessarily different. It, too, was set up to give our executives an opportunity to increase their ownership interest in General Motors and to provide added incentive. This was accomplished, as in the case of Managers Securities Company, by setting aside a block of General Motors common stock to be paid for by the participants by an initial, partial cash payment and by the application of their participation in supplemental compensation for a number of years in the future.

To effectuate the new plan, of course, another large block of General Motors stock was necessary. In anticipation of this need, General Motors Corporation had accumulated, over the three years previous to 1930, 1,375,000 shares of General Motors common stock. This was sold to the Management Corporation at the market price of $40 a share, at an aggregate cost of $55 million. Management Corporation financed this purchase by selling 50,000 shares of its own common stock for $5 million and by issuing $50 million of seven-year, 6 per cent serial bonds; both offerings were subscribed by General Motors Corporation. General Motors, in turn, sold the common stock of the Management Corporation for cash to some 250 executives—more than three times as many as participated in the original Managers Securities Company.

The early life span of the Management Corporation covered the years of the great depression, which affected adversely virtually every commercial arrangement. While General Motors, as I have indicated, maintained its share of the over-all automobile market, industry sales declined because of the economic conditions and our volume was reduced correspondingly. Under the circumstances, the performance of General Motors was remarkable—even in the lowest year of the depression, the corporation was able to operate profitably, although earnings after taxes fell below 7 per cent on capital employed and so no bonus fund accrued. Furthermore, as a result of the low level of earnings, the Management Corporation was unable to retire its debt or even to pay the interest on it. Needless to say, the market value of General Motors stock also fell drastically—it was down to about $8 per share at one point (which in terms of today's $1⅔ par value common stock would be the equivalent of a little over $1 per share). At these depressed levels, the market value of the General Motors common stock held by the Management Corporation was far less than its outstanding bonded indebtedness to General Motors.

General Motors was seriously embarrassed by these developments and executive morale was badly hurt, for the executives, as shareholders in Management Corporation, were liable for that corporation's debt to the extent of their accumulated normal annual bonus payments and their initial capital investments. I urged the Finance

Committee of General Motors, therefore, to make some adjustment so that executives would not see their entire bonus swallowed up each year in the Management Corporation's loss.

In urging the Finance Committee to take action, I was guided by concern for the well-being of the General Motors shareholders as much as that of the General Motors executives. One was intimately related to the other. I felt it crucial to the best interests of all concerned in General Motors to restore executive morale. The Finance Committee was reluctant to offer any relief at first, because it felt that the price of General Motors stock would recover. Nevertheless, in 1934 after much consideration, it adopted a revision of the original plan.

This revision contemplated certain adjustments in the capital structure of Management Corporation, as well as an adjustment of the past-due interest on the bonded indebtedness. The most significant change, however, was a provision that the indebtedness to General Motors at the expiration of the plan could be satisfied by delivery to it by the Management Corporation of the entire number of available shares of General Motors common stock at $40 per share; or, at its option, Management Corporation could deliver one half of the shares (again at $40), and make the concurrent payment of one half of the indebtedness in cash. This provided a more flexible basis for the handling of the debt.

As matters turned out, the Finance Committee's original judgment was correct. The price of General Motors stock recovered to $65.375 per share by the time the plan terminated on March 15, 1937. By using part of their equity in the Management Corporation's holdings of General Motors stock at $40 per share to pay off the debt, the executives, as Management Corporation shareholders, gave up a $5 million profit. This profit flowed to the benefit of General Motors Corporation.

While the Management Corporation did not prove to be as successful as Managers Securities, it did accomplish the objective of increased stock ownership and both General Motors and its executives benefited from its operation. Again, as an illustration, let me state the results in terms of each $1000 invested in the stock of the Management Corporation in 1930. Each $1000 represented in effect a partial payment on 275 shares of General Motors $10 par value common stock with a then market value of $40 per share, and the executive had agreed to apply his future bonus participation to pay off the balance due. Over the next seven years, the applicable share of contract payments made to the company by General Motors totaled $4988 on such an investment. Again, these represented amounts which the executive would have received as bonus during the period and in effect constituted additional investments in the company by the executive, increasing each $1000 of original investment to $5988.

On March 15, 1937, at the termination of the plan, the resulting total investment represented an unencumbered claim on 179 shares of General Motors $10 par value common stock with a cost of $40 per share. The reduction in the proportionate interest in General Motors common stock reflected the sale by the Management Corporation of 187,300 shares on the market and the delivery of 293,098 shares of General Motors common stock to reduce its indebtedness to General Motors. During the interim, the market value of General Motors common stock had appreciated from $40 per share to $65.375 per share, so that the 179 shares had a market value of $11,702 at March 15, 1937. Taking into account dividends of $893 received during the period, the final value of the $5988 investment was $12,595.

The Basic Bonus Plan

Participation in the General Motors Bonus Plan has shown an increase paralleling the growth of General Motors. In a period of over forty years the number of employees receiving a bonus award increased about twenty-five times—from 550 in 1922 to about 14,000 in 1962. In 1962 some 9 per cent of all salaried employees received a bonus award, compared with only 5 per cent in 1922.

During the middle and late 1920s the coverage of the Bonus Plan widened considerably, without any basic change in the rules for eligibility, simply because of the vast expansion of the corporation's management organization. By 1929 nearly 3000 salaried employees were receiving bonus awards—a fivefold increase in seven years.

The increased coverage since the 1920s has come in several big steps. In 1936 the incentive plan was extended to a large number of additional salaried employees, by reserving a portion of the annual bonus provision for employees earning between $2400 and $4200 a year. In the depression year 1931 the minimum salary for eligibility had been reduced from $5000 to $4200 a year to adjust for a salary cut. When the minimum salary for eligibility was then reduced to $2400 in 1936, this quadrupled the number of bonus participants from 2312 in 1935 to 9483 in 1936.

Except for 1938, which was a year of low earnings and hence of a relatively small bonus fund, the number of awards ranged around the 10,000 level until 1942. In the latter year the minimum salary was restored to $4200 and the number of bonus awards dropped to about 4000 a year.

During the first few postwar years, the Bonus and Salary Committee kept the number of recipients at about that same level, increasing the minimum salary as inflation raised the general pay level. In 1950, however, the Bonus and Salary Committee again widened the coverage of the Bonus Plan—from 4201 participants in 1949 to 10,352 in 1950—by lowering the minimum salary for eligibility from $7800 to $6000. "The action of the Committee in reducing the minimum salary rate for 1950 bonus consideration to $500 a month," as the annual report put it, "gives recognition to the fact that there are many employees in this classification who contribute importantly to the success of the business. It is expected that this broader base for bonus distribution will have a very stimulating effect on the General Motors organization."

Time has certainly vindicated that judgment. Although the minimum salary for eligibility has been raised steadily, to keep pace with the general increase in salaries, the number of employees receiving bonus awards has climbed fairly steadily, and now is about 14,000 a year.

In general, it has been the practice to deliver bonus awards in installments over a period of years. Since 1947, for example, awards up to $5000 have been paid in installments of $1000 each, while larger awards are paid in five equal annual installments. The plan also contains provisions under which an employee may lose his right to earn out his undelivered bonus installments if he leaves the employ of the corporation under certain circumstances. This basis of earning out recognizes that one of the purposes of the Bonus Plan is to furnish an incentive for executives to remain in the employ of the corporation.

One of the basic purposes of our incentive program is to make our executives partners in the business. Part of this concept has been that bonus awards should be made in General Motors stock.

Common stock is purchased in the market from month to month to meet each year's needs for bonus purposes. Originally, the entire bonus award was payable in stock, but with the development of high personal income taxes, it became evident to the Bonus and Salary Committee that delivering the entire award in stock was futile if the beneficiary had to sell a large part of that stock in order to pay the related income taxes. Therefore, in 1943 the corporation adopted a policy of making bonus awards partly in cash and partly in stock. Since 1950, the general objective has been to award in cash such portion of the bonus award as will enable the recipient to pay the tax on his total bonus and retain the stock portion of his bonus. The stock which is not delivered to the executive at the time of his award is retained by the corporation as treasury stock until the bonus installments are earned out. During the earning-out period the executive is paid cash amounts equal to the dividends which would be paid on the stock if it had already been earned out and delivered.

Notwithstanding the impact of high personal income taxes, the amount of stock held by the operating executives of the corporation is substantial. As of March 31, 1963, the aggregate stockholdings of some 350 of the corporation's top executives, plus stock to be earned out in their undelivered bonuses and contingent credits and stock held through the Savings-Stock Purchase Program, totaled more than 1,800,000 shares. If you assume a market value of $75 per share, which is in line with the recent trading range, it follows that the capital investment of the top executives in the business to which most of them are devoting their lives, amounts to more than $135 million at the present time. That, if I may say so, is a substantial proprietorship.

The Stock Option Plan

High personal income taxes have, for some time, reduced the portion of bonus awards that the principal executives have been able to retain as an investment in General Motors stock.

Since one of the major objectives of the Bonus Plan is to create and maintain an owner-management group, the shareholders supplemented the Bonus Plan in 1957 by approving a stock-option plan for key employees, which provided for the granting of options in each of the years 1958 through 1962. It was felt that this would provide an opportunity for increased stockholdings on the part of the participants and together with the Bonus Plan would furnish even more effective incentive than the Bonus Plan by itself. In 1962 the stockholders approved the extension of the plan without change through the year 1967. The stock-option plan is based upon what are known as the Restricted Stock Option Plan provisions of the Revenue Act of 1950. The Bonus and Salary Committee continues to determine individual bonus awards. It also determines those who shall receive stock options. However, the bonus awards to executives who receive stock options are, in the aggregate, only 75 per cent of the amount they would otherwise be awarded. The bonuses are paid in the usual installments, although entirely in cash. At the same time, these executives are conditionally credited with contingent credits, in the form of General Motors common stock, in an amount equal to one third of the reduced bonus awarded to them. Thus, their bonus awards plus the contingent credits which were conditionally credited to them are equivalent to the amounts they would have been awarded as bonus if they had not received stock options. Each of these executives is then granted an option to buy three times as many shares of stock as are in his contingent credit. The option price is the fair market value of the stock at the time the option is granted.

The plan as extended authorizes stock options in any or all of the years 1958 through 1967, up to a total of four million shares. No executive, however, may receive options for more than a total of 75,000 shares over the ten-year period. Options may be exercised only if the executive continues in the corporation's employ for eighteen months after the option is granted, and, except in the case of termination of employment, are good for a period of ten years from date of grant. If the executive exercises his option or any part of it, he loses any right to the related contingent credit, but any shares remaining in the contingent credit when the option expires are distributed to the executive over a five-year period. As long as the contingent credit is conditionally credited to the executive, he is paid cash amounts equal to the dividends which would be paid on the stock in the contingent credit if he had it in his own name.

One of the benefits flowing to an executive from the stock-option plan lies in the fact that, under current tax law, should he exercise the option or any part of it within the ten-year period, and should

e stock that he purchases under the option for a period
an six months, any profit, if he sells the stock, is taxed
ng-term capital gain. The stock-option plan does not en-
, change in the underlying principles or even the method
of administration of the General Motors Bonus Plan. It was adopted
simply to make the incentive and proprietor-ownership concepts
more effective.

The Administration of the Bonus Plan

The heart of the General Motors incentive program lies in the
procedure for determining how much, if anything, to award to each
eligible employee.

The Bonus and Salary Committee has full discretion over bonus
awards. It is composed of directors who are not eligible for bonus
consideration. This committee alone can determine the bonus to be
awarded to executives who are members of the board of directors.
In all other cases the Bonus and Salary Committee reviews and
approves, or disapproves, bonuses recommended jointly by the
chairman of the board and the president. In keeping with the policy of decentralization with co-ordinated control, the initiative in
recommending individual bonuses is delegated to the operating divisions and staff organizations. To start with, the committee is advised by the independent public accountants each year of the maximum amount that is available out of the year's earnings for bonus
purposes, which currently is 12 per cent of the net earnings after
taxes and after deducting 6 per cent on net capital. The committee
must then first decide whether this full amount or some lesser
amount shall be transferred to the bonus reserve. For example, in
five of the years during the sixteen-year period 1947 through 1962,
the amount transferred to the bonus reserve by the committee was
less than the full amount available. The total credited to the bonus
reserve over this period was $131 million less than the maximum.
In 1962 the amount credited was $38 million less than the allowable
maximum.

Furthermore, the amount of bonus actually awarded in any
year may be less than the sum transferred to the bonus reserve for
that year. Thus, during the first three postwar years, more than
$19 million of the amount credited to the reserve was not awarded,

but was carried forward, available for use in some subsequent year. However, in 1957 the Bonus and Salary Committee determined that the entire unawarded balance in the reserve at the end of 1956, which then approximated $20 million, should be restored to the income of the corporation. This amount was not included in net earnings subject to bonus.

After deciding how much to transfer to the bonus reserve and how much of that sum to award in aggregate bonus, the committee must determine the awards to each individual. This process requires several steps. The minimum salary for bonus eligibility is set by the committee each year after receiving a recommendation from the chairman of the board and the president. The plan also permits awards to be made in special cases to employees whose salaries are below the minimum, to permit recognition of outstanding merit at all levels.

In the allocation of the fund, eligible employees are divided into certain categories for administrative purposes, as follows:

(a) Directors of the corporation who are operating executives.

(b) General managers of the operating divisions and the heads of the various staff organizations.

(These two groups comprise the top administration area of the corporation's organization.)

(c) The balance of the organization, down to those whose salary is equal to the minimum set by the committee.

In considering the allocation of the fund to these various categories, the committee considers the amount available to be awarded as bonus and its relationship to the aggregate eligible salaries and the performance for that year.

The first step taken by the committee is to determine a tentative allotment to the directors of the corporation who as operating officers are eligible for bonus consideration. Each individual director is considered separately and his performance is reviewed by the members of the committee. In this connection, the committee may consult informally with the president and the chairman on the performance of the individual directors, exclusive of those two officers. With this accomplished, a determination is made of the aggregate allotment to all the directors as a percentage of the total bonus available.

The next step is to determine the allotment for the second category: general managers of divisions and heads of the staff organizations.

The committee considers what the tentative allotment should be to this entire group in relation to the aggregate bonus available. After the committee establishes the allotment for this category, the chairman and president make the individual recommendations and report them back to the Bonus and Salary Committee for approval or revision.

Having established allotments for the directors, and for the general managers of the operating divisions and the heads of the staff organizations, the chairman and president are advised of the balance which is available for the personnel of the operating divisions and the staff organizations. Then the chairman and the president, together with some of their principal associates, recommend a breakdown of the total sum available among those various groups.

Dealing first with the operating divisions, which are the profit-making instrumentalities of the corporation, the committee, after consulting with the chairman and the president, establishes the general basis of allocation to be followed. Allocations to divisions give consideration to aggregate salaries of eligible employees, relative return on invested capital, and an over-all judgment on divisional performance, taking into account any special circumstances that may justify special consideration. Following committee approval of the divisional allotments recommended by the chairman and the president, the general managers of the operating divisions are notified of the allotments for their divisions and it then becomes their responsibility to make the recommendations, according to their judgment, for individual bonus awards for employees within their divisions (excluding themselves, of course). In the case of staff organizations which are not profit-making activities per se, the allocations are made to each group based upon their eligible salaries and an evaluation of the staff performances.

Within the various divisions and staff organizations, there is no single formula for determining individual bonus recommendations. Each has its own technique. Each individual, however, is awarded a bonus on the basis of the most careful and searching analysis his superiors can make of his contribution to the corporation during the year. Normally, the point of origin of the recommendation for a given individual is his immediate supervisor. The supervisor's appraisal is reviewed through the succeeding levels of management, up to the general manager of the division or to the appropriate staff head. The general manager or staff head reviews all the recommended awards for those under his jurisdiction and transmits them to the group executive under whom he serves. The group executive in turn reviews and passes on the recommendations and then submits them to the chairman and the president. After all such recommendations have been reviewed by the latter executives, together with the executive vice presidents, they are transmitted to the Bonus and Salary Committee for final decision.

While each division follows its own procedures in recommending bonus awards, the review process reduces any inequities to the minimum. It is impossible, of course, for the Bonus and Salary Committee to familiarize itself with the detailed qualifications of some 14,000 beneficiaries. However, the committee receives detailed pertinent statistical summaries of all the individual bonus recommendations, designed to aid their evaluation of the recommended bonus distributions, along with complete listings of all bonus eligibles and the proposed individual participants and awards. Moreover, the committee evaluates the individual recommendations pertaining to approximately 750 principal executives, and compares awards for those in comparable positions throughout the corporation, in the various divisions as well as in the central office staffs. The committee carefully reviews the performance of each of these executives to assure that bonuses reflect variations in accomplishment and provide the most equitable distribution possible. In the nature of a by-product, the careful review of the progress and development of individual executives is very valuable from the standpoint of analyzing the strengths and weaknesses of the corporation's management personnel. This is particularly useful in planning ahead and preparing for inevitable organization changes.

The Value of the Bonus to General Motors

Is the Bonus Plan really worth all the executive time and effort taken up by its administration? And is it worth the money it costs? I believe so emphatically. I am convinced that the Bonus Plan has not cost the shareholders a single dollar, but has, on the contrary, greatly increased their return over the years. I believe that the Bonus Plan has been, and continues to be, a major factor in the remarkable success of the General Motors Corporation. When an enterprise is new and small and is operated by a few people who have invested their own savings, it is perfectly apparent to them that their own interests are interwoven with those of the enterprise. But as the enterprise grows and more and more men participate in its management, this connection becomes remote and needs periodic expression and emphasis, such as the Bonus Plan provides.

The Bonus Plan creates different kinds of incentives at different levels of the corporation. It creates a tremendous incentive among employees not yet eligible for bonus awards to become eligible. One of our top executives recalled a while back in a letter to me: "I well remember the thrill that came with the time when I was first awarded a bonus—the feeling of having made the team and the determination to continue to advance in the organization." I believe that same feeling has been shared by all who have had the opportunity to participate in the Bonus Plan. And for many of them, bonus awards today probably comprise the great bulk of their personal assets.

Since bonuses are awarded annually, the incentive continues as long as the man stays with the corporation. The stimulus in fact becomes increasingly effective as a man advances in the organization, for the bonus is generally larger in relation to salary at high-salary brackets than it is at low brackets. In other words, the bonus tends to increase in a kind of geometric (rather than arithmetic) progression as a man is promoted. And so there is a tremendous incentive for him not only to do the best possible work in the job he already has, but to do such an outstanding job that he will be promoted to a higher rank.

The incentives and rewards are not solely financial, however. Again, I quote from the letter mentioned above:

There is still another value which I am sure the Corporation derives from the administration of the Bonus Plan. It is the intangible incentive it provides as distinct from the tangible incentive of a monetary reward. The potential rewards of the Bonus Plan to ego satisfaction generate a tremendous driving force within the Corporation.

Each bonus award carries with it considerably more than the intrinsic value of its cash and common stock. To the recipient it is also an evaluation of his personal contribution to the success of the business. It is a means of conveying to the executive a form of recognition which he prizes independently of his monetary compensation.

This nonfinancial incentive is reinforced by a fairly general practice of having each recipient's supervisor deliver the bonus notification letter. This furnishes an opportunity for a review and discussion of the recipient's performance.

One important side-effect of the Bonus Plan is that it makes each participant acutely aware of his relation to his job and his superiors; he is obliged, as it were, to dwell on his own and the corporation's progress. A man derives satisfaction from knowing that his superiors have judged his value, and at the same time there is the spur of having his work reviewed annually.

This kind of atmosphere cannot be generated or maintained under a straight salary system, or a salary system supplemented by an automatic bonus or profit-sharing system, in which an employee is conscious of being judged only when he receives or fails to receive a raise. And penalties are more difficult under the usual arrangement, for salaries generally are inelastic on the down side. Under the General Motors Bonus Plan, however, a substantial reduction in a man's bonus that runs counter to the trend in the total amount of bonus awarded, constitutes a severe penalty—and one of which the individual concerned is very much aware. The total amount to be awarded is published in the annual report.

The Bonus Plan also provides much more flexibility on the up side than is possible under a salary system. It may be difficult to reward a man for superior performance by raising his salary, since the increase may upset the whole salary stratification. A salary increase, moreover, commits the company indefinitely, whereas the bonus makes it possible to tailor the reward to the period in which performance was unusual. And so the Bonus Plan makes it possible for the exceptional individual to break out of the over-all salary schedule without at the same time upsetting the schedule.

The Bonus Plan, moreover, tends to keep executives with the corporation. As explained earlier, bonuses are currently paid in five annual installments; an employee who leaves voluntarily may lose the right to earn out the undelivered balance of his bonuses—in some cases, a very substantial sum. The net result of this deterrent —plus the stimulus the plan provides—has been that over the years General Motors has lost relatively few executives it has wished to retain, especially in the upper levels.

In the last analysis, of course, it may not be possible to "prove" the success of the Bonus Plan, for we can only conjecture what might have happened if the plan hadn't existed. My friend and associate of many years, Walter S. Carpenter, Jr., has expressed my own sentiments in response to my request to him for an evaluation of the effectiveness of the Bonus Plan. He wrote:

If by the "effectiveness" of the bonus plan you infer some more or less factual, perhaps even mathematical, proof of the results achieved by the Bonus Plan, I will have to admit right at the start I am afraid I cannot be of much help. I say this because we have given this matter a great deal of thought over the years. We have considered it particularly at those times when we have revised the bonus plan in an effort to ascertain even in rough measure what percentage figures we should use in deriving the amount of the annual bonus fund. Again each year we have given this matter our thought when we have endeavored to formulate the percentage of the earnings to be set aside, of course all within the maximums provided for in the bonus plan itself. I have pretty well come to the conclusion that it is one of those things that we have to accept largely on the basis of our judgment of the results which we have observed during our experience with the plan over the long period of years. To this might be added our confidence in the general underlying philosophy on which the principles of the bonus plan have been based.

There are one or two factual circumstances from which I think we can derive some measure of support for our feeling that the bonus plan is an effective tool even though they cannot be closely measured.

I refer first to the fact that the du Pont Company and the General Motors Corporation, both of which I believe have been the most prominent exponents of the bonus plan, have been extraordinarily successful. Here, of course, the detractors can say there were many other reasons for this success and no doubt there were. It is, however, impressive that these two companies have been outstandingly successful . . .

And so it is, Alfred, that while we may not have isolated or mathematically demonstrable proof of the effectiveness of the bonus plan, we do have to support our assurance in its effectiveness the record of success of two great enterprises over a long period of years in which it played an important rol[e], we have evidence of its contribution toward the assembling and retention of an organization of outstanding men and we have in addition our confidence and faith in the basic principle on which it is founded.

To this I should like to add my own profound conviction that to abolish or seriously modify the Bonus Plan after forty-five years of successful operation might very well destroy the spirit and organization of the corporation's management.

Chapter 23

THE MANAGEMENT:
HOW IT WORKS

IT is not easy to say why one management is successful and another is not. The causes of success or failure are deep and complex, and chance plays a part. Experience has convinced me, however, that for those who are responsible for a business, two important factors are motivation and opportunity. The former is supplied in good part by incentive compensation, the latter by decentralization.

But the matter does not end there. It has been a thesis of this book that good management rests on a reconciliation of centralization and decentralization, or "decentralization with co-ordinated control."

Each of the conflicting elements brought together in this concept has its unique results in the operation of a business. From decentralization we get initiative, responsibility, development of personnel, decisions close to the facts, flexibility—in short, all the qualities necessary for an organization to adapt to new conditions. From co-ordination we get efficiencies and economies. It must be apparent that co-ordinated decentralization is not an easy concept to apply. There is no hard and fast rule for sorting out the various responsibilities and the best way to assign them. The balance which is struck between corporate and divisional responsibility varies according to what is being decided, the circumstances of the time, past experience, and the temperaments and skills of the executives involved.

The concept of co-ordinated decentralization evolved gradually at General Motors as we responded to tangible problems of management. As I have shown, at the time its development began, some four decades ago, it was clearly advisable to give each division a strong management which would be primarily responsible for the conduct of its business. But our experience in 1920–21 also demonstrated the need for a greater measure of control over the divisions than we had attained. Without adequate control from the central office, the divisions got out of hand, and failed to follow the policies set by corporation management, to the great detriment of the corporation. Meanwhile, the corporation management was in no position to set the best policies, since it was without appropriate and timely data from the divisions. A steady flow of operating data, for which procedures were later set up, finally made real co-ordination possible.

That still left us with the problem of finding the right combination of freedom for the divisions and control over them. The combination could not be set once and for all, of course. It varies with changing circumstances, and the responsibility for determining administrative organization is a continuing one. Thus, at one time, responsibility for the styling of the cars and other products was vested in the divisions. Since then it has been found desirable to place the responsibility for developing the general style characteristics of all our major products in the Styling Staff. This was suggested partly by the physical economies to be gained by co-ordinated styling. In addition, we learned from experience that work of higher quality could be obtained by utilizing, corporation-wide, the highly developed talents of the specialists. The adoption of any particular style is now a joint responsibility of the division concerned, the Styling Staff, and the central management.

Such continuing adjustments in the relative responsibility assumed by the division management and central management are permitted by the decentralized organization of General Motors whenever experience or changed circumstances present opportunities for improved or more economical performance. In my time as chief executive officer only a modest degree of supervision was actually exercised by general officers over division managers. I believe that basically the same is the case today, although changed circumstances and new and more complex problems have resulted in a somewhat closer degree of co-ordination than existed in my time.

In General Motors we do not follow the textbook definition of line and staff. Our distinction is between the central office (which includes staff) and the divisions. Broadly speaking, the staff officers —being primarily specialists—do not have line authority, yet in certain matters of established policy, they may communicate the application of such policy directly to a division.

The responsibility of the central management is to determine which decisions can be made more effectively and efficiently by the central office and which by the divisions. In order that such determinations be informed and knowledgeable, the central management depends heavily on the staff officers. Indeed, many of the important decisions of central management are first formulated in collaboration with the staff in the policy groups, and then adopted, after discussion, by the governing committees. Consequently, the staff is the real source of many decisions that are formally adopted by the committees. For example, the basic decision to participate in the manufacture of diesel locomotives was largely based on product research by the staff.

Some of the general staff activities, such as legal work, have no counterparts in the divisions. Other general staff activities correspond to activities in each of the divisions, among them engineering, manufacturing, and distribution activities. But there are some important distinctions between these staff and divisional activities: the general staffs are concerned with longer-range problems, and with problems of broader application, than their opposite numbers in the divisions. The corresponding divisional staffs are engaged largely in the application of policies and programs already developed. There have been exceptions to this, however, as when a project has been approved for development in a division. An example is the development of the Corvair, which is referred to in the next chapter.

The economies that flow from central-office activities are considerable and the cost comes on the average to less than 1 per cent of the corporation's net sales. Through the general staff the divisions get their services cheaper than if they provided them or bought them on the outside, and they get better services. The latter feature is, in my opinion, by far the more important. The staff contributions in the fields of styling, finance, technical research, advanced engineering, personnel and labor relations, legal affairs, manufacturing, and distribution are outstanding and certainly worth a large multiple of their cost.

Several kinds of economies are made possible by centralized staff operations. Among the most important are the economies that derive from the co-ordination of the divisions. These arise through the sharing of ideas and developments among general officers and divisional personnel. The divisions contribute ideas and techniques both to each other and to central management. Much of our managerial and engineering talent, and many of our general officers, have come out of the divisions. The development of high-compression engines and automatic transmissions, for example, was the work of both staff and divisions. Our progress in aviation engines and in diesel engines came out of the development work of both.

Under the decentralized operation of the divisions, problems of like kind are met in different ways by different division managers, subject to the advice of the central office of the corporation. Out of this process comes a winnowing of techniques and ideas, and a development of judgments and skills. The quality of General Motors' management as a whole derives in part from this shared experience with common goals and from divisional rivalry within the framework of these common goals.

There are also the economies of specialization possible under our decentralized system. It is an axiom of economics that costs are reduced and trade created by specialization and the division of labor. Applied to General Motors, this has meant that our internal supplying divisions which specialize in the production of components must be fully competitive in price, quality, and service; if they are not, the purchasing divisions are free to buy from outside sources. Even when we have decided to make an item rather than to buy it, and have established production of the item, it is by no means a closed decision that we will stay in that line of production. We try, wherever possible, to test our internal supplying divisions against external competitors and to make a continuing judgment on whether it is better to make or to buy.

The popular misconception that it always pays to make an item yourself rather than to buy it is based on the assumption of a cost saving. The argument runs that by making instead of buying, you can save the extra cost of your supplier's profit. But the fact is that if the supplier's profit is a normal, competitive one, you must expect to make it on your own investment, or else there is no net saving. General Motors does not engage in the production of raw materials, as do some of its competitors, and we purchase a large proportion of the items that go into our end products, because there is no reason to believe that by producing them we could obtain better products or service, or a lower price.

Of the total cost of sales of our products, purchases of parts, materials, and services from outside sources account for 55 to 60 per cent.

The role of the division managers is an important one in our continuing efforts to maintain both efficiency and adaptability. These managers make almost all of the divisional operating decisions, subject, however, to some important qualifications. Their decisions must be consistent with the corporation's general policies; the results of the division's operations must be reported to the central management; and the division officers must "sell" central management on any substantial changes in operating policies and be open to suggestions from the general officers.

The practice of selling major proposals is an important feature of General Motors' management. Any proposal must be sold to central management and if it affects other divisions it must be sold to them as well. Sound management also requires that the central office should in most cases sell its proposals to the divisions, which it does through the policy groups and group executives. The selling approach provides an important extra safeguard in General Motors against ill-considered decisions, over and above the safeguards normally implied in the responsibility of corporate officers to shareholders. It assures that any basic decision is made only after thorough consideration by all parties concerned.

Our decentralized organization and our tradition of selling ideas, rather than simply giving orders, impose the need upon all levels of management to make a good case for what they propose. The manager who would like to operate on a hunch will usually find it hard to sell his ideas to others on this basis. But, in general, whatever sacrifice might be entailed in ruling out a possibly brilliant hunch is compensated for by the better-than-average results which can be expected from a policy that can be strongly defended against well-informed and sympathetic criticism. In short, General Motors is not the appropriate organization for purely intuitive executives, but it provides a favorable environment for capable and rational men. In some organizations, in order to tap the potentialities of a genius, it is necessary to build around him and tailor the organization to his temperament. General Motors on the whole is not such an organization although Mr. Kettering was an obvious exception.

Our management policy decisions are arrived at by discussions in the governing committees and policy groups. These were not the creation of a single inspired moment, but the result of a long process of development in dealing with a fundamental problem of management, that of placing responsibility for policy in the hands of those best able both to make the decisions and to assume the responsibility. To a certain extent this involves a contradiction. On the one hand, those best able to assume responsibility must have broad business perspective oriented toward the interest of the shareholder. On the other hand, those best qualified to make specific decisions must be close to the actual operation of the business. We have attempted to resolve this contradiction principally by dividing the policy-making responsibilities within central management between the Finance Committee and the Executive Committee, as I have shown.

Another source of policy recommendation is the Administration Committee, which is charged with the responsibility of making recommendations to the president with respect to the manufacturing and selling activities of the corporation, and on any other matters affecting the business and affairs of the corporation that may be referred to it by the president or the Executive Committee. The president is the chairman of the committee and, at the present time, its membership includes the members of the Executive Committee, two group executives who are not members of the Executive Committee, the general managers of the car and truck divisions, the general manager of Fisher Body Division, and the general manager of the Overseas Operations Division.

Under this separation of responsibility, policy development and recommendation are mainly the duty of the groups in central management made up of the men closest to operations. They work very closely, of course, with men from the divisions, and divisional men are on some policy groups. The Executive Committee, which views the corporation as a whole and at the same time is closely familiar with operating problems, has a somewhat judicial function. It makes the fundamental decisions on the basis of the work of the policy groups and the Administration Committee, plus the committee members' close knowledge of operating conditions. The Finance Committee, which includes non-employee directors in its membership, exercises its responsibility and authority in the area of broader corporate policy.

Much of my life in General Motors was devoted to the development, organization, and periodic reorganization of these governing groups in central management. This was required because of the paramount importance, in an organization like General Motors, of providing the right framework for decisions. There is a natural tendency to erode that framework unless it is consciously maintained. Group decisions do not always come easily. There is a strong temptation for the leading officers to make decisions themselves without the sometimes onerous process of discussion, which involves selling your ideas to others. The group will not always make a better decision than any particular member would make; there is even the possibility of some averaging down. But in General Motors I think the record shows that we have averaged up. Essentially this means that, through our form of organization, we have been able to adapt to the great changes that have taken place in the automobile market in each of the decades since 1920.

Chapter 24

CHANGE AND PROGRESS

I T is clear from the events and ideas I have described that my generation had an opportunity unique in the history of American industry. When we started in business, the automobile was a new product, and the large-scale corporation was a new type of business organization. We knew that the product had a great potential, but I can hardly say that any of us, at the beginning, realized the extent to which the automobile would transform the United States and the world, reshape the entire economy, call new industries into being, and alter the pace and style of everyday life. It was our satisfaction to assist in the development of the industry which in this century made individual units of transportation available to almost everyone. It was my personal satisfaction to be associated in a business way, as a supplier or a competitor, with a large number of the able citizens who created and contributed to the development of this industry. The names of a few of them, by their association with cars and companies, stand for a new American legend. For me, because of my age and past associations, it is natural to think as well as speak in terms of Mr. Ford, Mr. Buick, Mr. Chevrolet, Mr. Olds, Mr. Chrysler, Mr. Nash, Mr. Willys, and so on. Involved with thousands of others in the destiny of this industry, they conducted the prosaic operations of running a business without being aware of the revolution they were making.

Most successful enterprises in American industry have tended to grow. General Motors obviously is a successful enterprise. It is successful because it is efficient, and it has grown accordingly. It is not surprising that the large corporation should have become a feature of an economy with as much vitality as ours. Yet it has its critics, of course. To rational critics, let me say this. General Motors has become what it is because of its people and the way they work together, and because of the opportunity afforded those people to participate in an enterprise which combined their activities efficiently. The field was open to all; technical knowledge flows from a common storehouse of scientific progress; the techniques of production are an open book, and the related instruments of production are available to all. The market is world-wide, and there are no favorites except those chosen by the customers.

I should like to point out that today's large successful enterprises have not always been large. This book has shown that when we started on this great adventure in the early 1900s the whole automotive industry was searching for ways and means to find itself. In those early days we along with the industry lacked the techniques that today are taken for granted. Things just seemed to happen—to us, and to the industry. The number of sales by dealers was unknown. The number of cars held by dealers was unknown. Trends in consumer demand were unknown. There was no awareness of the importance of the used-car market. There were no statistics on the different cars' market penetration; no one kept track of registrations. Production schedules, therefore, were set with no real relationship to final demand. Our products had no planned relation to one another or to the market. The concept of a line of products to meet the full challenge of the market place had not been thought of. The annual model change as we know it today was still far in the future. The quality of the products was sometimes good, sometimes bad.

We had to start from that beginning. It was our task to find out what forms of organization were suitable to our company. This meant, above all, an organization that could adapt to great changes in the market. Any rigidity by an automobile manufacturer, no matter how large or how well established, is severely penalized in the market—as we have seen was the case with Mr. Ford in the 1920s, when he stayed too long with his old and once dominantly successful concept of the business. We had a different concept of the business, which we put into competition with his. It could have happened that he was right, but for that to have occurred, one would have to postulate the continuation of the kind of national economy that supported his concept of the automobile. As it happened, our concept was more in accord with the economy, the progress of the automobile art, and the changing interests and tastes of consumers. But after our first success, we too might have failed. There have been and always will be many opportunities to fail in the automobile industry. The circumstances of the ever-changing market and ever-changing product are capable of breaking any business organization if that organization is unprepared for change —indeed, in my opinion, if it has not provided procedures for anticipating change.

In General Motors these procedures are provided by the central management, which is in a position to appraise the broad long-term trends of the market. This is well illustrated by the changes in our product over the years. The gradual evolution of our product line during the 1920s started with a passive adaptation to the problems of the market and proceeded to the policy which we defined simply as "a car for every purse and purpose." As the industry has grown and evolved, we have adhered to this policy and have demonstrated an ability to meet competition and the shifts of customer demand. I want, in this connection, to sketch the evolution of our products.

Four million cars and trucks were sold in 1923, and the market remained more or less at this level throughout the 1920s. During this time our product was improved continuously in many ways, the most important being the development of the closed body. The sale of higher-priced cars rose with national prosperity. In the early thirties, during the depression, the demand reversed itself and became concentrated in the low-price area. In 1933 and 1934 almost three quarters of the cars sold in the United States were in the low-price group. We adjusted to that demand. With the recovery of the economy, consumers again sought a higher proportion of higher-priced lines, and in the years 1939–41, immediately before the U.S. entry into the war, the low-price group was accounting for only 57 per cent of the over-all market, or about the same proportion as in the year 1929. We responded accordingly.

With the resumption of production after World War II, it was necessary because of shortages, particularly of steel, for the industry to operate under material controls. These allocations favored the smaller manufacturers (Kaiser-Frazer, Nash, Hudson, Studebaker, and Packard) whose product representation at that time was concentrated in the medium-price ranges, with the result that the proportion of the market accounted for by their cars increased sharply. Competition, in this period, was largely confined to production—that is, whatever a manufacturer could make, customers were waiting to purchase. By 1948, when registrations of new cars approached the prewar peaks established in 1929 and 1941, the medium-price group was accounting for 45.6 per cent of the over-all market, and nearly equaled the share (46.6 per cent) accounted for by the low-price group.

In the years after 1948, normal competitive influences began to reassert themselves in some areas of the market and the sales of the smaller manufacturers in the medium-price group declined. On the surface, it appeared that customer demand was returning to the prewar pattern; by 1954 the traditional low-price group seemingly again accounted for about 60 per cent of all sales. Actually, however, a significant change was taking place in the industry's product offerings in the low-price group. The producers in this group along with others were offering more and more optional equipment to attract the increased consumer purchasing power of the fifties. The character of the market at that time was well expressed in *Fortune* in September 1953 ("A New Kind of Car Market"), as follows: "In the postwar sellers market, it [the car industry] has found itself selling more car per car—more accessories, luxuries, improvements and innovations. Now it has to plan it that way . . . The widening spread between unit demand and purchasing power will create a powerful drive to sell still more car per unit." With the "new look" the 1955 cars grew larger and more powerful and many accessories became standard equipment. The whole automobile market became further variegated with the increasing popularity of such relatively expensive models as hardtops, convertibles, and station wagons. Sales were strong in what had been known as the medium-price area and Ford, for example, in efforts to broaden its representation there, expanded its Mercury line and in 1957 brought out an entirely new car, the Edsel. But cars in the former low-price group meanwhile were being upgraded both in size and quality; Ford, Chevrolet, and Plymouth all added to the top grade of their respective lines new, more expensive series of cars which were, in effect, part of the medium-price group in everything but name.[1] In

---

[1] Ultimately this fact was recognized, and the price groupings reported by the statistical organizations covering the industry were modified so that such models are now included in the medium-price ranges.

principle this was simply a recognition by the industry of the consumer's new purse and a catering to his new desires.

It is interesting to note that, in the middle fifties, so-called "stripped" models, that is, the cars in the low-price group with a minimum of equipment, did not attract many customers. In view of this fact, the upsurge of demand for the so-called compact or economy car, which gathered momentum in the years after 1957, at first sight may seem confusing. On looking closer, however, it is evident that this demand was essentially a further expression of the customer's desire for greater variety. Throughout its history, the industry has been faced with the problem of trying to anticipate changes in customer preference. Even though it takes years to develop a new product, it is our job to be ready with it when there is an effective demand. Mr. Donner, chairman and chief executive officer of General Motors, recently put it this way:

. . . To meet the challenge of the market place, we must recognize changes in customer needs and desires far enough ahead to have the right products in the right places at the right time and in the right quantity.

We must balance trends in preference against the many compromises that are necessary to make a final product that is both reliable and good looking, that performs well and that sells at a competitive price in the necessary volume. We must design, not just the cars we would like to build, but more importantly, the cars that our customers want to buy.

The dramatic events in the market of the late 1950s and early 1960s are a good example of how rapidly consumer tastes can change—and also an example of the industry's ability to respond to such changes. In 1955, when car sales reached a new high, 98 per cent of the industry's volume was accounted for by standard-size domestic cars. The balance of 2 per cent, representing fewer than 150,000 cars, included some forty-five foreign and smaller domestic lines. By 1957 foreign imports and the domestic smaller cars had increased to 5 per cent of the total. In 1957 it still appeared far from certain that the demand for smaller cars would continue to grow, but the possibility had been recognized by General Motors for some time, and the designs for such cars had already been initiated. As early as 1952, Chevrolet had, with the approval of central management, set up a research and development group charged with the task of developing such a car, which would be ready if and when demand rose sufficiently to justify volume production. To some extent, this activity was a projection of work done prior to 1947, when the development of a small car had been actively considered by General Motors.

The design of the Corvair was made final in late 1957, and the car was introduced in the fall of 1959. Other manufacturers introduced new small cars at about the same time. Later, we added other lines, including the Buick Special, the Oldsmobile F-85, and the Pontiac Tempest, all introduced in 1960, the Chevy II, introduced in 1961, and the Chevelle in 1963. While the smaller cars were designed to appeal to the economy-minded customer who wanted lower initial cost and lower costs of operation, it soon became apparent, somewhat contradictorily, that the customer had not lost his taste for the comfort, convenience, and styling of the regular-size cars; he was ordering his smaller car with better interior appointments, convenient and useful accessories, and equipment such as automatic transmissions, power steering, and power brakes, which he had previously specified on the regular-size car. The Corvair Monza, featuring automatic transmission, bucket seats, special upholstery, and deluxe trim, was brought out in 1960, and almost from its introduction accounted for well over half the Corvair sales. Moreover, it soon became evident that the customers wanted the smaller cars in the same range of models and body styles that were available in the regular cars—that is, they wanted hardtops, convertibles, and station wagons as well as two- and four-door sedans. The addition of these smaller cars to the wide range of standard-size cars has provided the customer with an unprecedented variety of models from which to choose.

Certainly the late 1950s and early 1960s saw the most dramatic change in the car market since the 1920s, when the closed body rose to dominance, the Model T came to an end, and the upgrading of cars began. The events of the past few years in the car market, I believe, have validated the General Motors product policy that we formulated in 1921. John Gordon, president of General Motors, recently observed that our slogan of "a car for every purse and purpose" is as appropriate as ever; indeed, we have never offered our customers greater variety and choice than we do today. In the 1963 model year the industry offered 429 models of domestically produced cars, compared with 272 in 1955; General Motors alone had 138 models in 1963, compared with 85 in 1955. Of this, Mr.

Gordon said: "Taking into account all of the colors available and all of the optional equipment and accessories we now offer—power assists, air conditioning, tilt steering wheels, autronic eyes and so on—we could, in theory at least, go through a whole year's production without making any two cars exactly alike. Our objective is not only a car for every purse and purpose but, you might say, a car for every purse, purpose and person."

The trend toward the smaller car was clearly visible after 1957, and by 1959 foreign imports were accounting for 10 per cent of industry sales in the United States, while domestically produced smaller cars accounted for an additional 10 per cent. The foreign imports declined in relative importance after 1959, and in 1963 were accounting for about 5 per cent of the total market. However, sales of the domestically produced smaller cars continued to increase, and after 1960 accounted for about one third of the entire market. Meanwhile, part of the formerly low-price group has become established in the medium group.

In the face of these trends, some of the domestic manufacturers reduced their offerings in what were traditionally called the medium-price ranges. The Edsel, introduced late in 1957, was discontinued in 1959; the De Soto, which had a long history at Chrysler, was discontinued in 1960; and the Mercury, certain Dodge models, and American Motors' Ambassador were reduced in size and appointments. In General Motors, we elected to maintain our regular-size cars in the medium-price group at about the same weight, size, and number of models, while at the same time adding smaller cars to these lines.

The automobile constitutes 90 per cent of our business, but each operation or potential operation is considered as a separate problem. We have no inflexible policy on products that we might manufacture, but motors are at the center of the business. Our product decisions must, of necessity, be in part empirical, and actual experience with some products may suggest that they are not well suited to our managerial skills. In such cases we withdraw from the activity.

For example, in 1921 we found it best to withdraw from the agricultural tractor business, because we did not believe that we could make a special contribution in that field. Since then we have built up and subsequently disposed of interests in companies which manufactured airplanes, household radios, glass, and chemicals.

We entered the aviation-engine and diesel-engine fields to put our know-how in engineering and mass production to work and create new values. We developed a new concept of the diesel—the two-cycle engine—put it into a locomotive, and revolutionized the American railroads. We poured many millions of dollars into this unproven product at a time when many of the customers for it were in serious financial condition or bankrupt and the majority of them appeared to be totally uninterested in innovation; and we thereby helped the railroads back to solvency—a fact that is acknowledged by railroad management today.

In none of our product markets did we achieve a prominent place by buying out a company. In general we entered each of our related activities at a very early stage and then labored to develop the market for our product, whether automobiles, household refrigerators, diesel locomotives, or aircraft engines. We have not bought our way into operations, we have built them up.

In describing the General Motors organization I hope I have not left an impression that I think it is a finished product. No company ever stops changing. Change will come for better or worse. I also hope I have not left an impression that the organization runs itself automatically. An organization does not make decisions; its function is to provide a framework, based upon established criteria, within which decisions can be fashioned in an orderly manner. Individuals make the decisions and take the responsibility for them. The men who have made General Motors' decisions in the years since I retired from active management have had a remarkable record of success in tackling some very complex problems. In no instance was the answer explicitly provided by the automatic operation of the organization. The task of management is not to apply a formula but to decide issues on a case-by-case basis. No fixed, inflexible rule can ever be substituted for the exercise of sound business judgment in the decision-making process.

The end product of what I have described in this book is efficiency, using that concept in its broadest sense. I hold that General Motors' efficiency and growth are interrelated in our highly competitive economy. And I hold that if companies are attacked simply because they are big then an attack on efficiency must be a corollary of that attack. If we penalize efficiency, how can we as a nation compete in the economy of the world at large?

So far as I am concerned, my work is done. Long ago, in 1946, at seventy-one, I reduced my commitments when I retired as chief executive officer of the corporation, though I continued as chairman of the board. In 1956 I became honorary chairman. Since then my active participation has been limited to service on the Finance Committee, on the Bonus and Salary Committee, and on the board of directors. In the board, time is taking its toll. Great changes have been under way, affecting its composition. The du Ponts, who accounted for about 25 per cent of the corporation's shares in the past, and who served the corporation so well, have already passed out of the board. Many of the old generation of members have died. The remaining older members from management, who have been and continue to be large individual shareholders, among them Messrs. Mott, Pratt, Bradley, Hunt, McLaughlin, Fisher, and myself, cannot be expected to serve many more years on the board and its committees. The responsibilities we have discharged for so long, in intimate association as operating executives, have been or soon must be assumed by others. Each new generation must meet changes—in the automotive market, in the general administration of the enterprise, and in the involvement of the corporation in a changing world. For the present management, the work is only beginning. Some of their problems are similar to those I met in my time; some are problems I never dreamed of. The work of creating goes on.

GENERAL MOTORS CORPORATION
UNIT SALES OF CARS AND TRUCKS
BY DIVISIONS

GENERAL MOTORS CORPORATION
UNIT SALES OF TOTAL CARS AND TRUCKS—BY DIVISIONS

CALENDAR YEAR	MANUFACTURED IN U.S. PLANTS								Manufactured in Canadian Plants	Total U.S. and Canada	MANUFACTURED IN OVERSEAS PLANTS				TOTAL CORPORATION
	Buick (Marq.)	Cadillac (LaSalle)	Chevrolet	Oldsmobile (Viking)	Pontiac (Oakland)	GMC Truck(c)	Misc. (d)	Total U.S.			Brazil	Holden	Opel	Vauxhall	
1909 (a)	14,140	6,484		1,690	948	372	1,047	24,681		24,681					24,681
1909 (b)	4,437	2,156		336	157	102	442	7,630		7,630					7,630
1910	20,758	10,039		1,425	4,049	656	2,373	39,300		39,300					39,300
1911	18,844	10,071		1,271	3,386	293	1,887	35,752		35,752					35,752
1912	26,796	12,708		1,155	5,838	372	2,827	49,696		49,696					49,696
1913	29,722	17,284		888	7,030	601	1,745	57,270		57,270					57,270
1914	42,803	7,818		2,254	6,105	708	1,896	61,584		61,584					61,584
1915	60,662	20,404		7,696	11,952	1,408	266	102,388		102,388					102,388
1916	90,925	16,323		10,263	25,675	2,999		146,185		146,185					146,185
1917	122,262	19,759		22,042	33,171	5,885		203,119		203,119					203,119
1918	81,413	12,329	52,689	18,871	27,757	8,999	1,956	204,014	1,312	205,326					205,326
1919	115,401	19,851	117,840	41,127	52,124	7,730	13,334	367,407	24,331	391,738					391,738
1920	112,208	19,790	134,117	33,949	34,839	5,137	30,627	370,667	22,408	393,075					393,075
1921	80,122	11,130	68,080	18,978	11,852	2,760	6,493	199,415	15,384	214,799					214,799
1922	123,048	22,021	223,840	21,505	19,636	5,277	4,355	419,682	37,081	456,763					456,763
1923	200,759	22,009	454,386	34,721	35,847	6,968	120	754,810	43,745	798,555					798,555
1924	156,627	17,748	293,849	44,309	35,792	5,508		553,833	33,508	587,341					587,341
1925	196,863	22,542	481,267	42,701	44,642	2,865		790,880	45,022	835,902					835,902
1926	267,991	27,340	692,417	57,862	133,604			1,179,214	55,636	1,234,850				1,513	1,236,363
1927	254,350	34,811	940,277	54,888	188,168			1,472,494	90,254	1,562,748				1,606	1,564,354
1928	218,779	41,172	1,118,993	86,235	244,584			1,709,763	101,043	1,810,806				2,587	1,813,393
1929	190,662	36,698	1,259,434	101,579	211,054			1,799,427	99,840	1,899,267				1,387	1,900,654
1930	121,816	22,559	825,287	49,886	86,225			1,105,773	52,520	1,158,293			26,312	8,930	1,193,535
1931	91,485	15,012	756,790	48,000	86,307			997,594	35,924	1,033,518			26,355	14,836	1,074,709
1932	45,356	9,153	383,892	21,933	46,594			506,928	18,799	525,727			20,914	16,329	562,970
1933	42,191	6,736	607,973	36,357	85,772			779,029	23,075	802,104			39,295	27,636	869,035
1934	78,327	11,468	835,812	80,911	79,803			1,086,321	42,005	1,128,326			71,665	40,456	1,240,447
1935	106,590	22,675	1,020,055	182,483	172,895			1,504,698	59,554	1,564,252			102,765	48,671	1,715,688
1936	179,279	28,741	1,228,816	186,324	180,115			1,803,275	63,314	1,866,589			120,397	50,704	2,037,690
1937	225,936	44,724	1,132,631	211,715	231,615			1,846,621	81,212	1,927,833			128,370	59,746	2,115,949
1938	175,369	28,297	655,771	94,225	99,211			1,052,873	56,028	1,108,901			139,631	60,111	1,308,643
1939	230,088	38,390	891,572	158,005	169,320			1,487,375	55,170	1,542,345			122,856	61,454	1,726,855

Year													
1940	2,080,566	55,353	—	—	2,025,213	75,071	1,950,142	—	—	249,380	213,907	1,135,826	40,206	310,823
1941	2,300,028	43,010	—	—	2,257,018	107,214	2,149,804	—	—	283,885	231,788	1,256,108	60,037	317,986
1942	348,806	47,316	—	—	301,490	83,686	217,804	—	—	16,409	14,262	166,043	2,865	18,225
1943 (d)	194,144	41,598	—	—	152,546	61,437	91,109	665	30,187	—	—	60,257	—	—
1944 (d)	317,032	38,493	—	—	278,539	54,312	224,227	66	152,530	5,301	3,183	71,631	—	2,337
1945	308,044	32,471	—	—	275,573	45,644	229,929	—	115,279	129,700	112,680	102,896	933	153,733
1946	1,229,034	53,586	—	—	1,175,448	51,997	1,123,451	—	36,393	221,747	192,684	662,952	27,993	—
1947	1,992,371	61,453	—	—	1,930,918	85,033	1,845,885	—	65,895	—	—	1,037,109	59,652	—
1948	2,220,993	74,576	—	112	2,146,305	94,563	2,051,742	—	97,306	254,684	193,853	1,166,340	65,714	273,845
1949	2,896,348	84,168	40,058	7,725	2,764,397	91,503	2,672,894	—	86,677	335,820	282,734	1,487,642	82,043	397,978
1950	3,992,298	87,454	72,568	20,113	3,812,163	158,805	3,653,358	—	112,557	469,465	397,884	2,009,611	109,515	554,326
1951	3,197,134	77,877	77,594	25,177	3,016,486	186,996	2,829,490	—	129,644	347,057	286,452	1,555,856	104,601	405,880
1952	2,629,200	79,813	83,282	31,945	2,434,160	199,763	2,234,397	—	123,258	275,145	224,684	1,200,589	95,420	315,301
1953	3,760,479	110,141	110,164	44,175	3,495,999	219,413	3,276,586	—	113,026	414,413	323,361	1,839,230	104,999	481,557
1954	3,799,628	130,951	164,117	54,796	3,449,764	153,808	3,295,956	—	83,823	372,055	431,462	1,749,578	122,144	536,894
1955	5,030,994	142,149	186,999	63,800	4,638,046	161,374	4,476,672	—	106,793	580,464	642,156	2,213,888	153,134	780,237
1956	4,090,863	123,643	205,605	68,893	3,692,722	184,981	3,507,741	—	93,787	334,628	433,061	1,970,610	140,340	535,315
1957	3,885,366	143,573	228,736	94,557	3,418,500	181,322	3,237,178	—	72,890	341,875	390,305	1,871,902	152,660	407,546
1958	3,310,493	174,124	312,873	110,626	2,712,870	186,625	2,526,245	—	66,096	220,767	310,909	1,543,992	126,087	258,394
1959	3,850,914	244,655	334,444	115,308	3,140,233	180,216	2,960,017	16,274	77,371	389,616	366,879	1,754,784	138,610	232,757
1960	4,660,996	245,981	366,817	140,336	3,889,734	208,357	3,681,377	18,128	102,567	447,868	400,379	2,267,759	158,719	304,085
1961	4,036,629	186,388	377,258	112,680	3,346,719	196,407	3,150,312	13,584	76,333	362,147	322,366	1,949,111	147,957	292,398
1962	5,238,601	215,974	378,878	133,325	4,491,447	268,624	4,222,823	18,977	88,712	545,884	458,045	2,555,081	159,014	416,087

(a) — Fiscal year ending September 30, 1909.

(b) — Three months ending December 31, 1909.

(c) — GMC Truck is not included with Corporation figures from July 1, 1925 through September 30, 1943 when it was part of Yellow Truck & Coach Manufacturing Co.

(d) — Misc. — For period 1909 through 1923 includes Cartercar, Elmore, Marquette, Randolph, Scripps-Booth and Welch passenger cars; and Samson trucks and tractors. For 1943 and 1944 represents sales of passenger cars produced in the U.S. prior to cessation of car production on February 10, 1942 due to war requirements. Chevrolet figures shown for 1943 and 1944 represent truck sales only.

GENERAL MOTORS STAFF CHARTS
DISCUSSED IN TEXT

FINANCIAL STAFF

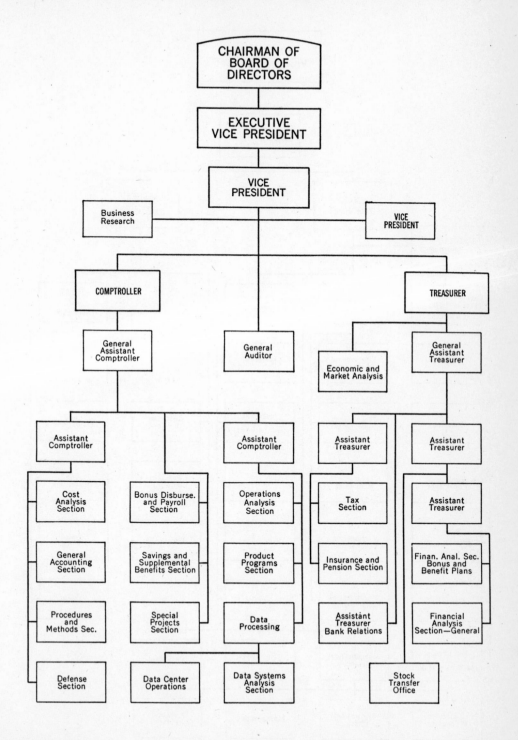

MAY, 1963

RESEARCH LABORATORIES

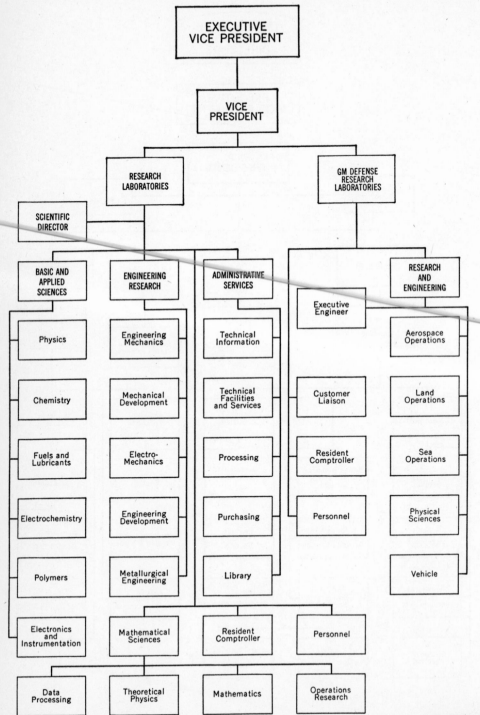

EXECUTIVE VICE PRESIDENT

VICE PRESIDENT

RESEARCH LABORATORIES

GM DEFENSE RESEARCH LABORATORIES

SCIENTIFIC DIRECTOR

BASIC AND APPLIED SCIENCES
- Physics
- Chemistry
- Fuels and Lubricants
- Electrochemistry
- Polymers
- Electronics and Instrumentation

ENGINEERING RESEARCH
- Engineering Mechanics
- Mechanical Development
- Electro-Mechanics
- Engineering Development
- Metallurgical Engineering
- Mathematical Sciences

ADMINISTRATIVE SERVICES
- Technical Information
- Technical Facilities and Services
- Processing
- Purchasing
- Library
- Resident Comptroller

Executive Engineer
- Customer Liaison
- Resident Comptroller
- Personnel

Personnel

RESEARCH AND ENGINEERING
- Aerospace Operations
- Land Operations
- Sea Operations
- Physical Sciences
- Vehicle

- Data Processing
- Theoretical Physics
- Mathematics
- Operations Research

JULY, 1963

ENGINEERING STAFF

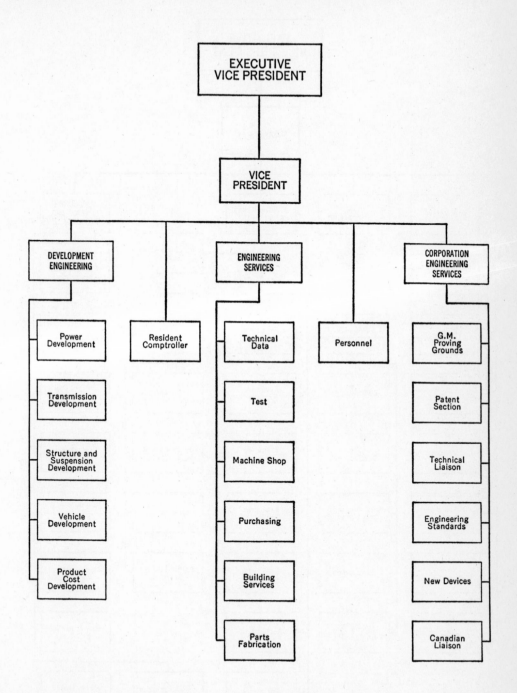

EXECUTIVE VICE PRESIDENT

VICE PRESIDENT

DEVELOPMENT ENGINEERING
- Power Development
- Transmission Development
- Structure and Suspension Development
- Vehicle Development
- Product Cost Development

Resident Comptroller

ENGINEERING SERVICES
- Technical Data
- Test
- Machine Shop
- Purchasing
- Building Services
- Parts Fabrication

Personnel

CORPORATION ENGINEERING SERVICES
- G.M. Proving Grounds
- Patent Section
- Technical Liaison
- Engineering Standards
- New Devices
- Canadian Liaison

JUNE, 1963

MANUFACTURING STAFF

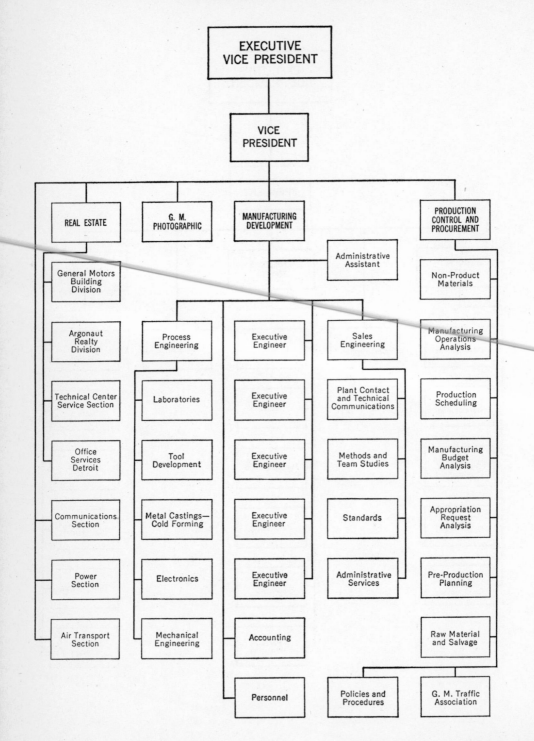

EXECUTIVE VICE PRESIDENT

VICE PRESIDENT

REAL ESTATE
- General Motors Building Division
- Argonaut Realty Division
- Technical Center Service Section
- Office Services Detroit
- Communications Section
- Power Section
- Air Transport Section

G. M. PHOTOGRAPHIC
- Process Engineering
- Laboratories
- Tool Development
- Metal Castings—Cold Forming
- Electronics
- Mechanical Engineering

MANUFACTURING DEVELOPMENT
- Administrative Assistant
- Executive Engineer
- Executive Engineer
- Executive Engineer
- Executive Engineer
- Executive Engineer
- Accounting
- Personnel

- Sales Engineering
- Plant Contact and Technical Communications
- Methods and Team Studies
- Standards
- Administrative Services
- Policies and Procedures

PRODUCTION CONTROL AND PROCUREMENT
- Non-Product Materials
- Manufacturing Operations Analysis
- Production Scheduling
- Manufacturing Budget Analysis
- Appropriation Request Analysis
- Pre-Production Planning
- Raw Material and Salvage
- G. M. Traffic Association

MAY, 1963

STYLING STAFF

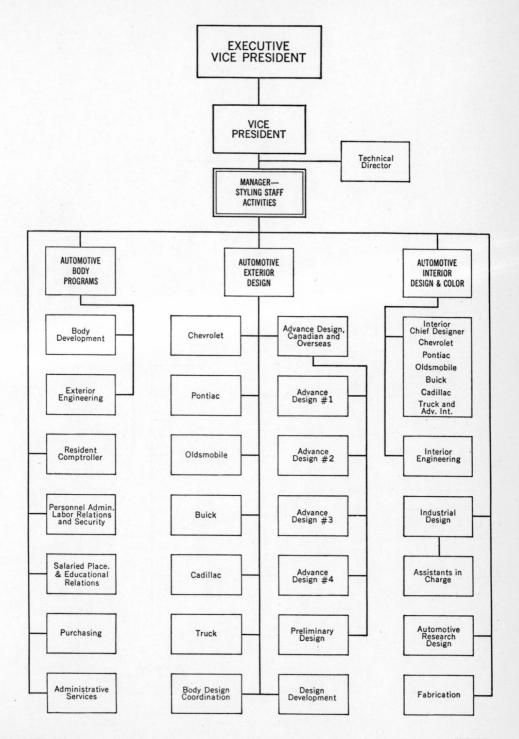

EXECUTIVE VICE PRESIDENT

VICE PRESIDENT

Technical Director

MANAGER— STYLING STAFF ACTIVITIES

AUTOMOTIVE BODY PROGRAMS

AUTOMOTIVE EXTERIOR DESIGN

AUTOMOTIVE INTERIOR DESIGN & COLOR

Body Development

Chevrolet

Advance Design, Canadian and Overseas

Interior Chief Designer
Chevrolet
Pontiac
Oldsmobile
Buick
Cadillac
Truck and Adv. Int.

Exterior Engineering

Pontiac

Advance Design #1

Resident Comptroller

Oldsmobile

Advance Design #2

Interior Engineering

Personnel Admin. Labor Relations and Security

Buick

Advance Design #3

Industrial Design

Salaried Place. & Educational Relations

Cadillac

Advance Design #4

Assistants in Charge

Purchasing

Truck

Preliminary Design

Automotive Research Design

Administrative Services

Body Design Coordination

Design Development

Fabrication

STYLING STAFF

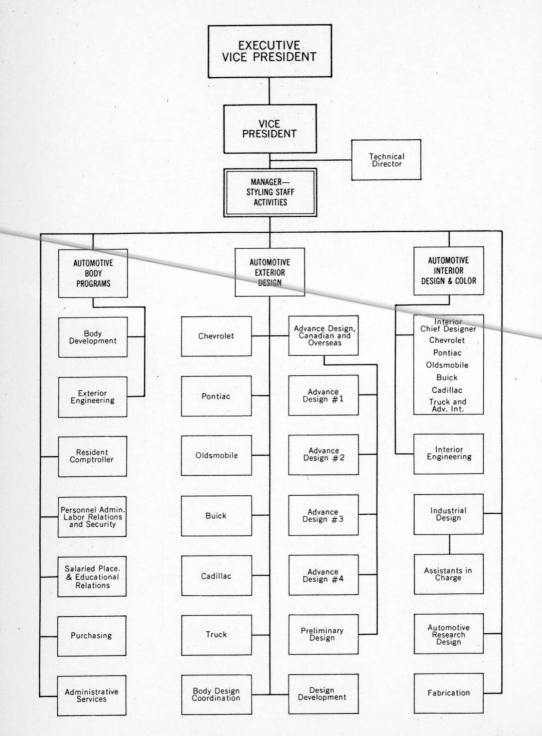

```
                    EXECUTIVE
                  VICE PRESIDENT


                       VICE
                     PRESIDENT ──────────── Technical
                                              Director
                      MANAGER—
                    STYLING STAFF
                     ACTIVITIES


   AUTOMOTIVE          AUTOMOTIVE          AUTOMOTIVE
     BODY              EXTERIOR            INTERIOR
   PROGRAMS             DESIGN           DESIGN & COLOR


     Body                                Interior
  Development        Chevrolet    Advance Design,   Chief Designer
                                  Canadian and        Chevrolet
                                    Overseas          Pontiac
    Exterior                                          Oldsmobile
   Engineering        Pontiac       Advance           Buick
                                    Design #1         Cadillac
                                                    Truck and
    Resident                                         Adv. Int.
   Comptroller       Oldsmobile     Advance
                                    Design #2        Interior
                                                    Engineering
 Personnel Admin.
 Labor Relations      Buick         Advance         Industrial
  and Security                      Design #3         Design

 Salaried Place.
 & Educational       Cadillac       Advance        Assistants in
   Relations                        Design #4          Charge

                                                    Automotive
    Purchasing        Truck       Preliminary        Research
                                    Design            Design

 Administrative    Body Design      Design
   Services        Coordination   Development       Fabrication
```

PERSONNEL STAFF

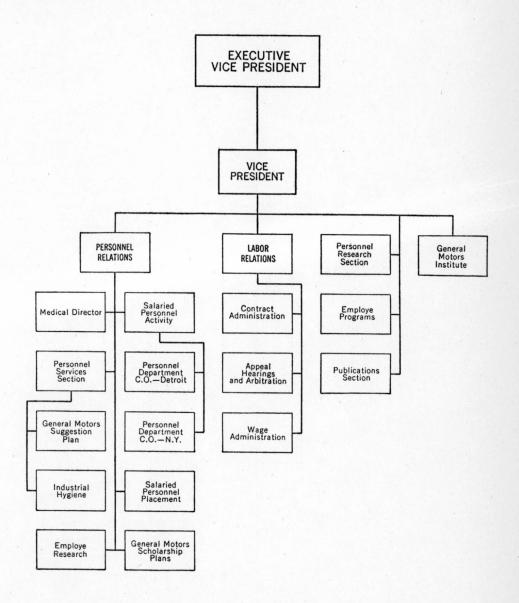

EXECUTIVE
VICE PRESIDENT

VICE
PRESIDENT

PERSONNEL
RELATIONS

LABOR
RELATIONS

Personnel
Research
Section

General
Motors
Institute

Medical Director

Salaried
Personnel
Activity

Contract
Administration

Employe
Programs

Personnel
Services
Section

Personnel
Department
C.O.—Detroit

Appeal
Hearings
and Arbitration

Publications
Section

General Motors
Suggestion
Plan

Personnel
Department
C.O.—N.Y.

Wage
Administration

Industrial
Hygiene

Salaried
Personnel
Placement

Employe
Research

General Motors
Scholarship
Plans

Index